Ste

D0051939

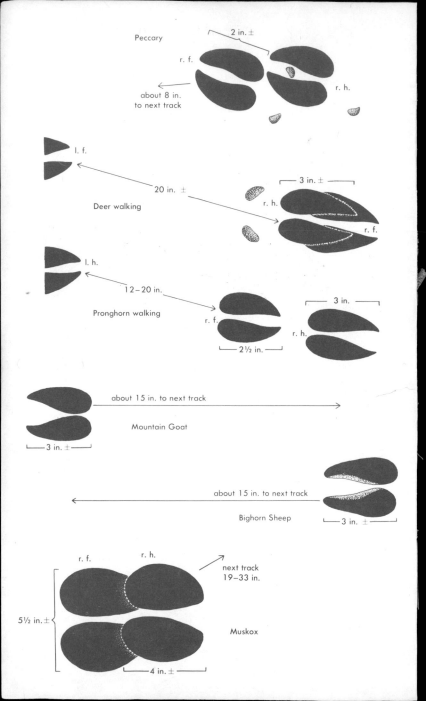

Peccary

2 in. ±

r. f.

r. h.

about 8 in.
to next track

l. f.

20 in. ±

Deer walking

3 in. ±

r. h.

r. f.

l. h.

12 – 20 in.

Pronghorn walking

r. f.

2½ in.

3 in.

r. h.

about 15 in. to next track

Mountain Goat

3 in. ±

about 15 in. to next track

Bighorn Sheep

3 in. ±

r. f.

r. h.

next track
19–33 in.

5½ in. ±

Muskox

4 in. ±

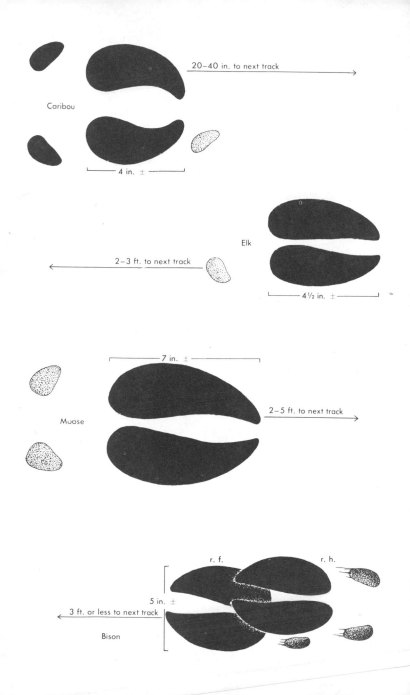

Caribou

20–40 in. to next track

4 in. ±

Elk

2–3 ft. to next track

4½ in. ±

7 in. ±

Moose

2–5 ft. to next track

r. f.

r. h.

5 in. ±

3 ft. or less to next track

Bison

A Field Guide
to the Mammals

THE PETERSON FIELD GUIDE SERIES
EDITED BY ROGER TORY PETERSON

THE PETERSON FIELD GUIDE SERIES

A FIELD GUIDE
to THE MAMMALS

Field marks of all
North American species
found north of Mexico

Text and Maps by
WILLIAM HENRY BURT

Illustrations by
RICHARD PHILIP GROSSENHEIDER

THIRD EDITION

Sponsored by the National Audubon Society
and National Wildlife Federation

HOUGHTON MIFFLIN COMPANY BOSTON
1976

Library of Congress Cataloging in Publication Data

Burt, William Henry, 1903–
  A field guide to the mammals.

  (The Peterson field guide series; 5)
  Bibliography: p.
  Includes index.
  1. Mammals—North America—Identification.
I. Grossenheider, Richard Philip. II. Title.
QL715.B8 1976 599'.09'73 75-26885
ISBN 0-395-24082-4
ISBN 0-395-24084-0 pbk.

Printed in the United States of America

c   10   9   8   7   6   5   4   3   2   1

Editor's Note

OUR VIEWS OF MAMMALS are often so brief that it is even more important than it is with birds to know exactly what to look for—to know their "field marks." A large percentage of mammals are nocturnal; we find their tracks in the mud by the riverbank, and in the snow, but except for the squirrels and a few others, we get scarcely more than an occasional glimpse of these shy creatures.

William H. Burt and Richard P. Grossenheider combined their talents to produce this *Field Guide,* one which Ernest Thompson Seton would have enthusiastically endorsed, because it was he who pointed out that each animal has its particular badge, or identification tag, by which it may be known at a glance. This idea was first developed fully in *A Field Guide to the Birds,* in which all eastern birds were reduced to simple patterns. An added innovation was the use of arrows pointing to distinctive field marks. The success of the book and its companion volume, *A Field Guide to Western Birds,* was immediate, far exceeding the expectations of the author and the publisher. It was inevitable that students would urge us to extend the system to other fields of natural history; thus the Field Guide Series was launched.

A Field Guide to the Mammals is the second book on which Dr. Burt and Mr. Grossenheider have collaborated. Their earlier work was the well-known volume *The Mammals of Michigan.* Dr. Burt, through years of teaching at the University of Michigan, his custodianship of the mammal collection at the Museum of Zoology in Ann Arbor, and through a term as editor of the *Journal of Mammalogy,* is ideally equipped to inform us in the clearest, most direct terms about North American mammals. Familiar with mammals both in the wild and in the hand, he knows where to draw the line between field marks and taxonomic characters. A few small mammals, it will be seen, simply cannot be identified with certainty except in the hand, by means of dentition and skull characters. Dr. Burt has avoided the problem of subspecies, since that too is more properly within the realm of the specialist and the specimen tray. Moreover, had he treated them at this stage in our taxonomic knowledge the book would probably become obsolete in a short time.

Richard Grossenheider's drawings are so sensitive in handling that one must study them carefully to appreciate fully their artistry. He loved the small mammals in particular, and no one has ever portrayed them with greater understanding. The exquisite textural quality of his drawings reminds one of an earlier master,

Albrecht Durer. Unfortunately, Richard Grossenheider did not live to see this revised edition completed, for he died tragically in a motor accident.

George Sutton, the distinguished wildlife artist, in eulogizing Grossenheider's work writes: "Those who study these drawings will, I am confident, concur that they possess that rarest of qualities—the life-spark. This subtle quality in a picture invariably puzzles me. I have studied living birds and mammals for years, and believe I know *why* they look alive. But the aliveness of a picture is amazing and wondrous nonetheless. There must have been something of the small mammal in Dick Grossenheider himself—something very sensitive to sounds, something keenly aware of passing shadows, something ever on the alert for signs and warnings—how else could his drawings have the *autobiographical* authenticity they possess?"

In the second edition (1964), the *Field Guide to the Mammals* came of age. Having undergone the scrutiny of tens of thousands of students, the maps reflected the increased knowledge of mammal distribution on the North American continent. The species accounts were strengthened and expanded with sections on habitat, habits, reproduction, and economic status. Although these inclusions added many pages to the book it still fitted the pocket easily and became far more satisfying to readers who wished to know a bit more about each species than just its recognition marks.

In this third edition (1976), 380 species are described (378 in the second edition). Many have been further expanded with new information. Because of the recent spate of interest in whales and porpoises and their conservation, the descriptions of these marine mammals have been greatly amplified and four new line drawings of skulls by Robert F. Wilson have been added. The Atlantic white-sided dolphin on the jacket was painted by Charles Ripper from transparencies provided by the staff of the New England Aquarium.

The plates by Grossenheider, although the same as in the earlier editions, have been reproduced by a different process. Following the trend of the times, it was deemed advisable to add metric conversions of all measurements.

When you start out on a camping trip take this book with you. Do not leave it on your library shelf; it is a field guide intended to be used.

ROGER TORY PETERSON

Preface

In the Second Edition of *A Field Guide to the Mammals* there were maps showing the geographic distribution of 291 species of land mammals. The same number appears in this, the Third Edition. However, additional information makes it necessary to alter the maps for 56 species in order to bring them up to date. As in the Second Edition, range maps are not included for species restricted to islands, for those mainland species known from a single locality, for those restricted to an area such as a single mountaintop, or for marine species. Instead, a statement is made in the text under the heading **Range.**

The treatment of subspecies has again been omitted purposely. It is still my opinion that the average user will be satisfied to know which species he is seeing. If he is concerned about the subspecies, he should turn to the more technical literature, some of which is listed under "References," or seek the opinion of the specialist in mammalogy.

An important change from previous editions will be found in the position of the plates. They are grouped together at the center of the book for easy and rapid perusal.

The section on cetaceans has been rewritten for the most part, and the names updated. The relationships of the whales are still poorly understood; series of specimens are not available for study. I have followed Dale W. Rice and Victor B. Scheffer (U.S. Fish and Wildlife Service. Special Scientific Report, 1968, Fisheries No. 579) for current names.

For those who wish to keep a record of the kinds of mammals they have seen and identified, there is a Checklist (p. xxi) of all species treated in the text.

I wish again to thank my many colleagues, especially the graduate students, for help and constructive advice. Also, many readers of the previous editions have given me valuable information on the occurrence of mammals in parts of the country unfamiliar to me. To those individuals, my most sincere thanks.

To those on the staff of Houghton Mifflin Company whose expertise and patience make for a most cordial publisher-author relationship, my sincere gratitude. The continued interest of Paul Brooks, the book production skills of Morton Baker and Katharine Bernard, and, above all, the unsurpassed editorial competence of Helen Phillips for the previous edition and James F. Thompson for the present edition, all go to make an author's dream materialize. As always, the counsel of Roger Tory Peterson is invaluable.

1975   William Henry Burt

Contents

Illustrations

How to Use This Book

MOST MAMMALS, unlike birds, are nocturnal and secretive in their habits. They are therefore much more difficult to see and identify in the field. An exception is the squirrel family. Tree squirrels, ground squirrels, chipmunks, marmots, and prairie dogs are active by day and present themselves in favorable situations for the field naturalist. Also in this category are many of the big game mammals, deer, Elk, Moose, caribou, sheep, goats, Bison, Pronghorns, and Muskox, as well as the marine mammals, whales, dolphins, seals, and sea lions. Cats, foxes, Coyotes, rabbits, and hares, too, although most active at night, are often seen by day. Most of the small mammals—bats, moles, shrews, mice, and rats—sleep during the day and come out only as darkness falls. Although one occasionally sees these small mammals in daytime, particularly in early morning or just before darkness, they are difficult to identify except at very close range. Even then, some are puzzling and cannot be determined by external characters alone. If characterizations sometimes seem vague it is because those species being discussed do not possess outstanding field marks. I consider it better to treat obscure species in this way than to give characters nobody can see.

Identification: To use this *Field Guide* effectively for identifying mammals, I suggest the following procedure. First, by thumbing through the plates of illustrations, determine the kind or large group to which the mammal belongs. Arrows point to the outstanding recognition marks mentioned on the legend page opposite the plate. Often these and the indication of the mammal's general geographic area given on the legend pages (see p. xv for explanation) will suffice for proper identification. If not, then turn to the maps showing the ranges of the species in this group. A rapid perusal of the maps will show you the kinds to be found in your area. You need be concerned *only* with these. If but one species occurs there you need look no further. If you have two or more kinds to select from, turn to the text where one of the species is treated. Read the characters given and also those given under **Similar Species.** Be concerned *only with those found in your area;* this should give you the answer in most instances.

Here is an example, follow it and you will know how to use the book. You are in Rocky Mountain National Park, Colorado. You see a small mammal at one of the turnouts; it is brownish and has stripes on its sides. While looking through the illustrations you come to Plate 11 showing squirrel-like mammals, all with stripes on them. The animal you saw has stripes on the sides of the body but none on the sides of its face. Further, the color of the head may be coppery. If it fits this description you need look no further: it is a Golden-mantled Squirrel. Then another slightly larger squirrel-like mammal appears, reddish olive with a rather indistinct black stripe along the lower side of the body separating the olive back from the white belly. The animal is definitely squirrel-like (Plates 11–12). Now turn to the maps where the ranges of the squirrels are shown. You discover that in the Rocky Mountain National Park there are two species of tree squirrels, the Tassel-eared Squirrel and the Red Squirrel. Other species of squirrel need not concern you. Since both species are illustrated on Plates 11 and 12, you should be able to determine the species from the illustrations alone. If identification is not certain, turn to the Red Squirrel (p. 120) and read the account under **Identification.** Also read the account of the Tassel-eared Squirrel under **Similar species.** This should convince you that you are seeing a Red Squirrel, although the color fits better with that of the Chickaree because of geographic variation in color.

Mammal skulls are often picked up in the field or taken from owl pellets. Many of these can be identified, at least as to the large group to which they belong, by comparing them with the pictures (Plates 25–32 and p. 265). In many instances they may be identified to the species just by counting the teeth and referring to the list of "Dental Formulae."

The measurement "head and body" refers to the outstretched animal from tip of nose to base of tail. The tail measurement does not include the hairs at the tip, but only the tail vertebrae. Measurements are given in feet and inches, weight in pounds and ounces. Metric equivalents are given in parentheses (See **Metric measurements,** p. xvi). In the short list of characters under **Identification** the most important ones are in *italics*.

Similar species: Under this subheading the most similar species is given first and the least similar listed last. Only those species occurring in the same area are listed.

Habitat: Where a mammal is seen can be an important clue to its identification, particularly with mammals confined to limited sets of conditions; tree squirrels, for example, are restricted to wooded areas and prairie dogs to open grasslands. The information on habitat is included to indicate the types of places where each species is most likely to be found.

Habits: This part indicates the time, day or night, when the mammal is most active. When known, information is also given on food, nests, populations, longevity, breeding season, and other habits considered to be of interest.

Young: The number of young in a litter and the number of litters a year, as well as gestation period and other details, are given when known.

Economic status: Sometimes this is given under the introductory family or general description, if it applies to all within that group. In other instances it is under the last subheading of the species entry.

Range: Distribution of marine mammals, mammals confined to islands, and some mainland species with restricted ranges or known from a single locality are not shown on maps. Instead, a statement under the subheading **Range** will indicate where they occur. When it appears in the text the range is given from north to south and from east to west if an extensive area, rather than a local, limited area, is involved.

Number of species: There are 380 species accounts in the text. This is probably a minimum; 42 additional doubtful species are included under **Identification.** In some cases, two or more so-called species have been grouped under a single entry heading because it is difficult or impossible to give distinctive characters that the nonspecialist would be able to use. Further research may show some of these to be subspecies, not species.

Geographic coverage: This book includes all species of wild mammals that occur on the North American continent and adjacent islands north of Mexico. It includes those species of marine mammals occurring in the waters of mainland United States and Canada.

Distribution maps: Except for the bats and marine species, migrations of mammals are slight or nonexistent—most mammals stay put. This is an aid to identification by elimination. The maps are arranged so that each is near its respective species account. The shaded parts of the maps represent the approximate areas within which the different species may be expected. This does not mean that the species will be found over the entire area, but possibly wherever suitable conditions exist within it. The outer boundaries represent approximate limits of distribution. Present, not past, distributions are indicated; many game species have been introduced into areas beyond their original ranges. Occasionally they become established but many disappear. Some of these are shown on the maps, and others (if known to the author) are indicated in the text.

Area designations on legend pages: The general section of the North American continent where the species occurs is indicated by N and S for north and south of the 40th parallel, E and W for east and west of the 100th meridian. Some species overlap these arbitrary boundaries, but the major part of the range will be found in the sector indicated. In a few instances where the range is confined to the central plains the term Central has been used, sometimes with N, S, E, or W modifications; also Arctic and

Subarctic are used for a few species confined to the Far North. See map on p. 129 for the area breakdowns.

Metric measurements: Because the United States is gradually adopting the metric system Système International (SI), metric equivalents are now being provided in the *Field Guides*. These appear in parentheses immediately after the U.S. measurements in the text and in the endpaper drawings of mammal tracks, but have been omitted, because of space limitations, from other mammal track drawings. In addition, a conversion table and rule that will be helpful to users of this guide are presented below, and a larger inch/centimeter rule appears on the fore edge of the back cover.

Our policy is to keep these metric conversions simple, remembering that most of the original measurements are necessarily approximate. The rules given here for conversion and rounding off have been followed to effect a reasonable balance between accuracy, approximation, and consistency:

1. When conversion is from a U.S. unit to a larger metric unit (e.g., pounds to kilograms) or when the U.S. measurement is less than 1, any resulting fraction is given as a decimal and rounded off to the nearest tenth.

2. When the metric unit is smaller than the U.S. unit (as with inches to centimeters), the conversion is rounded off to the nearest whole number.

3. In most cases, even when the U.S. measurement is a round figure (habitat altitudes given in thousands of feet, for example), these rules are followed to avoid apparent inconsistencies in the metric equivalents. One exception is the conversion from tons to kilograms, where the latter have been rounded off to the nearest thousand.

Common names: There is no official list of common names for mammals. Usage has determined most of the names, and many of these do not indicate relationships. The Mountain Beaver (*Aplodontia rufa*) is not even closely related to the Beaver (*Castor canadensis*); yet in certain areas the name persists instead of the proper one, Aplodontia. Common names also change from one locality to another; this is especially true for wide-ranging species. The name Mountain Lion for *Felis concolor* is appropriate for the western mountain country, but in Florida, where there are no mountains, the name is quite inappropriate. In this instance, as in several others, alternate names are provided in parentheses.

The spelling of a few of the common names needs explanation. A system worked out by the American Fisheries Society for uniform spelling of common names for fishes seemed to me to be a good one. It is used in part in this Third Edition, as it was in the previous editions. My own slight departure is that if an unpaired structure is involved in the name (tail, nose, etc.), com-

UNITED STATES AND METRIC (SI) EQUIVALENTS

United States	*Metric*
WEIGHT	
1 ounce (oz.)	28.35 grams (g)
5 oz.	141.75 g
10 oz.	283.5 g
1 pound (lb.)	454 g
1 lb.	0.454 kilogram (kg)
$2\frac{1}{5}$ lb.	1 kg
LINEAR MEASURE	
1 inch (in.)	25.4 millimeters (mm)
1 foot (ft.)	30.48 centimeters (cm)
1 yard (yd.)	91.44 cm
$39\frac{3}{8}$ in.	1 meter (m)
100 ft.	30.48 m
1 mile (mi.)	1.6 kilometers (km)
$\frac{3}{5}$ mi.	1 km
AREA	
1 acre	0.4 hectare (ha)
$2\frac{1}{2}$ acres	1 ha
1 square mile (sq. mi.)	259 ha
LIQUID MEASURE	
$1\frac{1}{20}$ quarts (qt.)	1 liter (l)

TEMPERATURE

To convert degrees Fahrenheit to degrees Celsius (centigrade), subtract 32° and multiply by $\frac{5}{9}$; to convert degrees Celsius to degrees Fahrenheit, multiply by $\frac{9}{5}$ and add 32°.

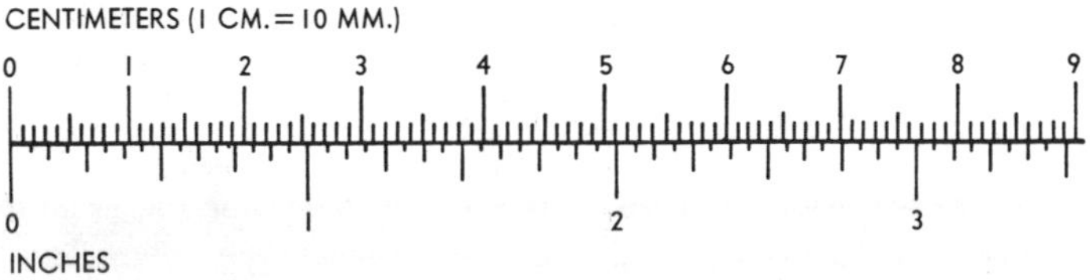

CENTIMETERS (1 CM. = 10 MM.)

Comparison of inch and centimeter scales.

pounded words are written as one word without a hyphen (long-tail, longnose, etc.), but if paired structures are involved they are hyphenated (white-footed, big-eared, etc.). This is a deviation from the rule followed by the American Fisheries Society, which hyphenates only where orthographically essential, where a special meaning is involved, or where it is necessary to avoid misunderstanding. Finally, I have attempted, not always with success, to use euphonious names.

Scientific names: Each mammal, whether or not it has a vernacular name, is known by a scientific name. The scientific name is universal and if properly proposed it should stand for all time, unchanged, and should apply to one kind of mammal only. If more than one scientific name has been proposed for the same species, the name first proposed is the applicable one. This is the "law of priority." Theoretically this system should lead to stability in nomenclature, but it has not done so. We have a minority group whom I should like to designate "the grave diggers," a group who delve into old and obscure publications in hopes of finding an early name for some species that has been known by its present name for many years. If they succeed, they then apply the law of priority and a name change is in order. I object to this and tend to be conservative where changes that I consider unnecessary are proposed. I shall continue, regardless of priority, to use names that have been established in the scientific literature and have not been challenged for 50 years or more.

An explanation is in order for my use of the generic name *Citellus* instead of *Spermophilus* for the ground squirrels. The name *Citellus* was proposed by Oken and was used for nearly 50 years in all major and many minor publications throughout the world. Then in 1949 one individual decided that Oken's names had not been properly proposed and were therefore not available. The next available name was *Spermophilus*—the law of priority. Many mammalogists did not question the decision and immediately started using the name *Spermophilus* instead of the familiar *Citellus*. In the meantime it was decided by another individual that the Arctic Ground Squirrel (Parka Squirrel), known as *Citellus parryi,* was of the same species on the Asiatic side of the Bering Strait as the one in Alaska, and the name *Spermophilus undulatus* was applied to this squirrel. At the present writing (1975) the result of further research indicates that the squirrels in Alaska are not *undulatus* but *parryi*. Now we are almost back where we started, and the only thing that has been added is confusion for those not familiar with the vagaries of mammalogists. This is why I tend to be conservative in the use of scientific names, and why I still use the name *Citellus* for the ground squirrels. The name is familiar to nonmammalogists such as parasitologists, physiologists, ecologists, ethologists, and others. To them, *Spermophilus* represents a different mammal from the

Citellus with which they have an acquaintance. This is not according to the rules, but sometimes rules are to be broken—in this case common sense should prevail.

Classification: The primary purpose of any classification is to arrange things in an orderly manner. In the classification of mammals we also try to arrange them in a way that will indicate relationships and at the same time tell us something of their evolutionary history. This, of course, is impossible with our present knowledge, but we think we can approach the solution in a few groups where there have been adequate studies in comparative anatomy, paleontology, and, in a very few kinds, physiology and genetics.

In the revised edition the arrangement of the orders and families is the same as it was in the Second Edition. In theory, the most primitive (or oldest) group (marsupials) is listed first and the least primitive (youngest) group last. But some groups are equally primitive or equally advanced in comparison with others, so their place in the classification becomes somewhat arbitrary. If we did know the true relationships, it would be physically impossible to arrange them in linear fashion to show those relationships—we would need a third dimension to do it properly. I have retained the order used in the Second Edition. I believe it is quite as satisfactory as some of the rearrangements by recent authors.

Checklist

KEEP YOUR LIFE LIST up to date by checking the mammals you have seen.

.... OPOSSUM
.... MASKED SHREW
.... MOUNT LYELL SHREW
.... MALHEUR SHREW
.... SMOKY SHREW
.... ARCTIC SHREW
.... UNALASKA SHREW
.... PRIBILOF SHREW
.... MERRIAM SHREW
.... SOUTHEASTERN SHREW
.... LONGTAIL SHREW
.... GASPÉ SHREW
.... TROWBRIDGE SHREW
.... VAGRANT SHREW
.... DUSKY SHREW
.... PACIFIC SHREW
.... ORNATE SHREW
.... ASHLAND SHREW
.... SANTA CATALINA SHREW
.... SUISUN SHREW
.... INYO SHREW
.... DWARF SHREW
.... NORTHERN WATER SHREW
.... PACIFIC WATER SHREW
.... PYGMY SHREW
.... GRAY SHREW
.... LEAST SHREW
.... SHORTTAIL SHREW
.... SHREW-MOLE
.... STARNOSE MOLE
.... EASTERN MOLE
.... HAIRYTAIL MOLE
.... TOWNSEND MOLE
.... PACIFIC MOLE
.... CALIFORNIA MOLE

.... LEAFCHIN BAT
.... LEAFNOSE BAT
.... HOGNOSE BAT
.... LONGNOSE BAT
.... HAIRY-LEGGED VAMPIRE BAT
.... LITTLE BROWN MYOTIS
.... YUMA MYOTIS
.... MISSISSIPPI MYOTIS
.... GRAY MYOTIS
.... CAVE MYOTIS
.... ARIZONA MYOTIS
.... KEEN MYOTIS
.... LONG-EARED MYOTIS
.... FRINGED MYOTIS
.... INDIANA MYOTIS
.... LONG-LEGGED MYOTIS
.... CALIFORNIA MYOTIS
.... SMALL-FOOTED MYOTIS
.... SILVER-HAIRED BAT
.... WESTERN PIPISTREL
.... EASTERN PIPISTREL
.... BIG BROWN BAT
.... RED BAT
.... SEMINOLE BAT
.... HOARY BAT
.... EASTERN YELLOW BAT
.... WESTERN YELLOW BAT
.... EVENING BAT
.... SPOTTED BAT
.... WESTERN BIG-EARED BAT
.... EASTERN BIG-EARED BAT
.... MEXICAN BIG-EARED BAT
.... PALLID BAT
.... MEXICAN FREETAIL BAT
.... POCKETED FREETAIL BAT

.... BIG FREETAIL BAT
.... WESTERN MASTIFF BAT
.... UNDERWOOD MASTIFF
        BAT
.... EASTERN MASTIFF BAT
.... BLACK BEAR
.... GRIZZLY BEAR
.... ALASKAN BROWN BEAR
.... POLAR BEAR
.... RACCOON
.... COATI
.... RINGTAIL
.... MARTEN
.... FISHER
.... SHORTTAIL WEASEL
.... LEAST WEASEL
.... LONGTAIL WEASEL
.... BLACK-FOOTED FERRET
.... MINK
.... RIVER OTTER
.... SEA OTTER
.... WOLVERINE
.... BADGER
.... SPOTTED SKUNK
.... STRIPED SKUNK
.... HOODED SKUNK
.... HOGNOSE SKUNK
.... COYOTE
.... GRAY WOLF
.... RED WOLF
.... RED FOX
.... SWIFT FOX
.... KIT FOX
.... ARCTIC FOX
.... GRAY FOX
.... JAGUAR
.... MOUNTAIN LION
.... OCELOT
.... MARGAY CAT
.... JAGUARUNDI CAT
.... LYNX
.... BOBCAT
.... NORTHERN SEA LION

.... CALIFORNIA SEA LION
.... GUADALUPE FUR SEAL
.... ALASKA FUR SEAL
.... WALRUS
.... HARBOR SEAL
.... RINGED SEAL
.... RIBBON SEAL
.... HARP SEAL
.... GRAY SEAL
.... BEARDED SEAL
.... CARIBBEAN MONK SEAL
.... HOODED SEAL
.... ELEPHANT SEAL
.... APLODONTIA
.... WOODCHUCK
.... YELLOWBELLY MARMOT
.... HOARY MARMOT
.... OLYMPIC MARMOT
.... VANCOUVER MARMOT
... BLACKTAIL PRAIRIE DOG
... WHITETAIL PRAIRIE DOG
.... CALIFORNIA GR. SQUIRREL
.... ROCK SQUIRREL
.... TOWNSEND GROUND SQUIRREL
.... WASHINGTON GR. SQUIRREL
.... IDAHO GROUND SQUIRREL
.... RICHARDSON GR. SQUIRREL
.... UINTA GROUND SQUIRREL
.... BELDING GROUND SQUIRREL
.... COLUMBIAN GROUND SQUIRREL
.... ARCTIC GROUND SQUIRREL
.... THIRTEEN-LINED GR. SQUIRREL
.... MEXICAN GROUND SQUIRREL
.... SPOTTED GROUND SQUIRREL
.... MOHAVE GROUND SQUIRREL
.... ROUNDTAIL GROUND SQUIRREL
.... FRANKLIN GROUND SQUIRREL
.... GOLDEN-MANTLED SQUIRREL
.... YUMA ANTELOPE SQUIRREL
.... WHITETAIL ANTELOPE SQ.
.... SAN JOAQUIN ANTELOPE SQ.
.... EASTERN CHIPMUNK
.... ALPINE CHIPMUNK

.... LEAST CHIPMUNK
.... TOWNSEND CHIPMUNK
.... CLIFF CHIPMUNK
.... SONOMA CHIPMUNK
.... YELLOW PINE CHIPMUNK
.... MERRIAM CHIPMUNK
.... GRAYNECK CHIPMUNK
.... LONG-EARED CHIPMUNK
.... REDTAIL CHIPMUNK
.... COLORADO CHIPMUNK
.... UINTA CHIPMUNK
.... PANAMINT CHIPMUNK
.... LODGEPOLE CHIPMUNK
.... CHARLESTON MT. CHIPMUNK
.... WESTERN GRAY SQUIRREL
.... TASSEL-EARED SQUIRREL
.... EASTERN GRAY SQUIRREL
.... ARIZONA GRAY SQUIRREL
.... EASTERN FOX SQUIRREL
.... APACHE FOX SQUIRREL
.... RED SQUIRREL
.... CHICKAREE
.... SOUTHERN FLYING SQUIRREL
.... NORTHERN FLYING SQUIRREL
.... VALLEY POCKET GOPHER
.... BAILEY POCKET GOPHER
.... PYGMY POCKET GOPHER
.... NORTHERN POCKET GOPHER
.... SIERRA POCKET GOPHER
.... MAZAMA POCKET GOPHER
.... TOWNSEND POCKET GOPHER
.... GIANT POCKET GOPHER
.... PLAINS POCKET GOPHER
.... SO. TEXAS POCKET GOPHER
.... SOUTHEASTERN POCKET GO.
.... MEXICAN POCKET GOPHER
.... MEXICAN POCKET MOUSE
.... WYOMING POCKET MOUSE
.... PLAINS POCKET MOUSE
.... MERRIAM POCKET MOUSE
.... SILKY POCKET MOUSE
.... APACHE POCKET MOUSE
.... LITTLE POCKET MOUSE

.... ARIZONA POCKET MOUSE
.... SAN JOAQUIN POCKET
    MOUSE
.... GREAT BASIN POCKET
    MOUSE
.... WHITE-EARED POCKET
    MOUSE
.... WALKER PASS POCKET
    MOUSE
.... DESERT POCKET MOUSE
.... ROCK POCKET MOUSE
.... NELSON POCKET MOUSE
.... SAN DIEGO POCKET
    MOUSE
.... CALIFORNIA POCKET
    MOUSE
.... SPINY POCKET MOUSE
.... LONGTAIL POCKET MOUSE
.... BAILEY POCKET MOUSE
.... HISPID POCKET MOUSE
.... DARK KANGAROO MOUSE
.... PALE KANGAROO MOUSE
.... BANNERTAIL KANGAROO
    RAT
.... HEERMANN KANGAROO
    RAT
.... PANAMINT KANGAROO RAT
.... STEPHENS KANGAROO RAT
.... GIANT KANGAROO RAT
.... ORD KANGAROO RAT
.... PACIFIC KANGAROO RAT
.... SANTA CRUZ KANGAROO
    RAT
.... BIG-EARED KANGAROO
    RAT
.... GREAT BASIN KANGAROO
    RAT
.... DESERT KANGAROO RAT
.... TEXAS KANGAROO RAT
.... MERRIAM KANGAROO RAT
.... FRESNO KANGAROO RAT
.... BEAVER
.... EASTERN HARVEST MOUSE

.... NEW ENGLAND COTTONTAIL
.... DESERT COTTONTAIL
.... BRUSH RABBIT
.... MARSH RABBIT
.... SWAMP RABBIT
.... PYGMY RABBIT
.... PECCARY
.... WILD BOAR
.... ELK
.... MULE DEER
.... WHITETAIL DEER
.... MOOSE
.... WOODLAND CARIBOU
.... BARREN GROUND CARIBOU
.... GREENLAND CARIBOU
.... PRONGHORN
.... BISON
.... MOUNTAIN GOAT
.... MUSKOX
.... BIGHORN SHEEP
.... WHITE SHEEP
.... ARMADILLO
.... MANATEE
.... BAIRD BEAKED WHALE
.... SOWERBY BEAKED WHALE
.... ATLANTIC BEAKED WHALE
.... GERVAIS BEAKED WHALE
.... TRUE BEAKED WHALE
.... PACIFIC BEAKED WHALE
.... JAPANESE BEAKED WHALE
.... ARCHBEAK WHALE
.... GOOSEBEAK WHALE
.... BOTTLENOSE WHALE
.... SPERM WHALE
.... PYGMY SPERM WHALE

.... DWARF SPERM WHALE
.... WHITE WHALE
.... NARWHAL
.... SPOTTED DOLPHIN
.... STRIPED DOLPHIN
.... LONGBEAK DOLPHIN
.... ROUGH-TOOTHED DOLPHIN
.... COMMON DOLPHIN
.... ATLANTIC BOTTLENOSE DOL-
     PHIN
.... PACIFIC BOTTLENOSE DOL-
     PHIN
.... RIGHT WHALE DOLPHIN
.... ATLANTIC WHITE-SIDED DOL-
     PHIN
.... PACIFIC WHITE-SIDED DOL-
     PHIN
.... WHITEBEAK DOLPHIN
.... KILLER WHALE
.... PYGMY KILLER WHALE
.... GRAMPUS
.... FALSE KILLER
.... COMMON BLACKFISH
.... SHORT-FINNED BLACKFISH
.... HARBOR PORPOISE
.... DALL PORPOISE
.... GRAY WHALE
.... FINBACK WHALE
.... RORQUAL
.... PIKED WHALE
.... BLUE WHALE
.... BRYLE'S WHALE
.... HUMPBACK WHALE
.... RIGHT WHALE
.... BOWHEAD WHALE

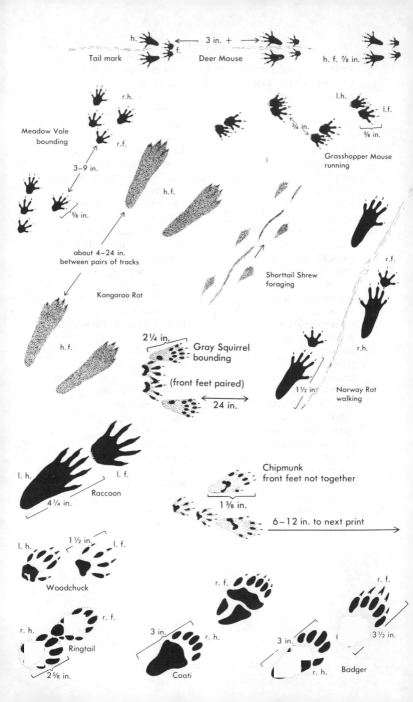

Tail mark · h. · f. ← 3 in. + → Deer Mouse · h. f. ⅞ in.

Meadow Vole bounding · r.h. · r.f.
3–9 in. · ⅝ in.
about 4–24 in. between pairs of tracks
Kangaroo Rat · h. f.

Grasshopper Mouse running · l.h. · l.f. · ¾ in. · ⅝ in.

Shorttail Shrew foraging

Norway Rat walking · r.f. · r.h. · 1½ in.

Gray Squirrel bounding · 2¼ in. · (front feet paired) · 24 in.

Raccoon · l. h. · l. f. · 4¼ in.

Chipmunk front feet not together · 1⅝ in. · 6–12 in. to next print

Woodchuck · l. h. · l. f. · 1½ in.

Ringtail · r. h. · r. f. · 2⅝ in.

Coati · 3 in. · r. f. · r. h.

Badger · r. f. · r. h. · 3 in. · 3½ in.

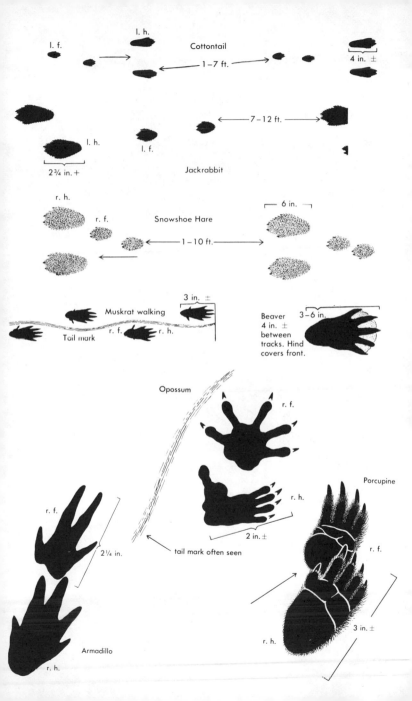

l. f.   l. h.   Cottontail   4 in. ±

← 1–7 ft. →

l. h.   l. f.   ← 7–12 ft. →

2¾ in. +   Jackrabbit

r. h.   r. f.   Snowshoe Hare   6 in.

← 1–10 ft. →

3 in. ±

Muskrat walking

Tail mark   r. f.   r. h.

Beaver 4 in. ± between tracks. Hind covers front.   3–6 in.

Opossum   r. f.

r. f.   r. h.   Porcupine

r. h.

2¼ in.

tail mark often seen   2 in. ±

r. f.

Armadillo   r. h.   3 in. ±

A Field Guide
to the Mammals

Pouched Mammals: Marsupialia

YOUNG are born premature in most kinds and complete their development in fur-lined pouch (marsupium) on belly of female.

Opossums: Didelphiidae

THE ONLY marsupials in N. America. Five toes on each foot; inside toe on hind foot opposable (an aid in climbing) and without claw; prehensile tail scaly and similar to a rat's. Among the most primitive of living mammals. As fossils, date back to Upper Cretaceous time.

OPOSSUM *Didelphis marsupialis* **Pl. 19**
   Identification: Head and body 15–20 in. (38–51 cm); tail 9–20 in. (23–51 cm); wt. 9–13 lb. (4–5.9 kg). Often seen in beam of auto headlights or dead along highways. About the size of a House Cat, but body heavier, legs shorter, nose pointed, *face white,* paper-thin *ears black,* often tipped with whitish; *tail* ratlike, round, prehensile, and black for basal $\frac{1}{3}$ to $\frac{1}{2}$, white on end. Ears and tail may be partially missing in North, owing to freezing. Usually whitish gray in North, gray to nearly black in South. Eyeshine dull orange. Skull (Plate 31) has 50 teeth. Up to 17 mammae in pouch.
   Formerly known as Virginia Opossum (*D. virginiana*); now considered same species as the one in Mexico.
   Similar species: Nutria (p. 200) has a sparsely haired tail the same color throughout, webs between toes of hind foot, and blunt (not pointed) face suggestive of a large Muskrat.
   Habitat: Farming areas preferred, also found in woodlands and along streams.
   Habits: Usually active only at night. Eats fruits, vegetables, nuts, meat, eggs, insects, carrion. Seeks shelter in old dens, beneath outbuildings, in hollow trees or logs, culverts, brushpiles. May feign death ("play possum") when cornered. Usual home range 15–40 acres (6–16 ha), but may wander widely, especially in fall. Has extended its range northward and become more numerous in recent years. May live 7 years or more.
   Young: Up to 14 per litter; gestation period about 13 days; 1

1

or 2 litters per year. Tiny at birth, weigh $\frac{1}{15}$ oz. (2 g) each; entire litter may be put in a teaspoon. Remain in pouch about 2 months; later may travel on mother's back with tails grasping hers.

Economic status: Sometimes hunted for sport, especially in the South. Edible, but meat oily. Occasionally raids poultry yards, but also destroys many mice and insects. Fur salable, but of little value.   Map below

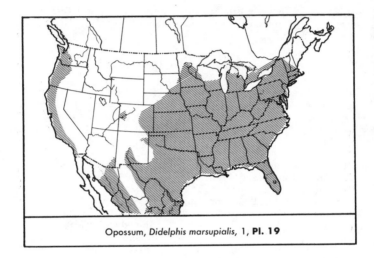

Opossum, *Didelphis marsupialis*, 1, **Pl. 19**

Insect-eaters: Insectivora

NORTH AMERICAN representatives of this group, nearly worldwide in distribution, are relatively small (largest, length about 9 in.; 23 cm), with long pointed noses and tiny beadlike eyes; 5 toes on each foot.

Shrews: Soricidae

THESE bundles of energy are *mouse size; beadlike eyes not covered* with skin; ears concealed or nearly concealed by soft fur; always *5 toes* on each foot (most mice have 4 toes on front foot); teeth usually pigmented in part with chestnut. Many shrews are difficult to identify; if recognition questionable, they should be sent to a museum. Found over most of N. America. Usually prefer moist situations, but some are found in sagebrush regions of arid West. Date back to Lower Oligocene as fossils.

Economic status: Either neutral or beneficial; eat many insects and do no harm.

MASKED SHREW *Sorex cinereus* **Pl. 1**
   Identification: Head and body 2 – 2½ in. (51 – 64 mm); tail 1¼ – 2 in. (31 – 51 mm); wt. $\frac{1}{10}$ – $\frac{1}{5}$ oz. (3 – 6 g). Body grayish brown, tail bicolored; underparts paler than upperparts. In the North and along Rocky and Appalachian Mts., particularly in *moist habitat,* usually the commonest shrew. Skull (Plate 25) has 32 teeth. There are 6 mammae.
   Similar species: (1) Pygmy Shrew is slightly smaller and can be distinguished for certain only by the unicuspids (single-cusped teeth in upper jaw), 3 instead of 5 on each side. (2) Smoky Shrew is larger and has dark underparts. (3) Merriam Shrew is pale grayish with whitish underparts. (4) Arctic, (5) Longtail, (6) Vagrant, (7) Dusky, and (8) Trowbridge Shrews are all larger. In the (9) Gaspé and (10) Dwarf Shrews the tail is not distinctly bicolored. (11) Southeastern Shrew is about same size, but ranges overlap only slightly. (12) Least Shrew has shorter tail.
   Habitat: Moist situations in forests, open country, brushland.
   Habits: Active day or night; when not sleeping, searching for food. Eats more than own weight each day; a captive ate more than 3 times own weight; food mostly insects, but includes many other small animals. Nest of dry leaves or grasses, in stumps or under logs or piles of brush. Concentrations of these shrews have been observed several times. Recorded heartbeats, more than 1200 per min.; respirations equally high. Breeding season probably March – Oct.; some females may reach sexual maturity at ages 4 – 5 months.
   Young: 2 – 10; probably more than 1 litter a year. Embryos reported for Jan., April, May, and Sept.   Map p. 4

MOUNT LYELL SHREW *Sorex lyelli*
   Identification: Head and body 2¼ in. (57 mm); tail 1½ – 1¾ in. (38 – 41 mm). Found only in a small section of the high Sierra Nevada, *6900 ft.* (2103 m) *altitude and above.* Skull has 32 teeth.   Map p. 7

MALHEUR SHREW *Sorex preblei*
   Identification: Head and body 2 – 2¼ in. (51 – 57 mm); tail 1½ in. (38 mm). One of the *smallest* western shrews. Skull has 32 teeth.

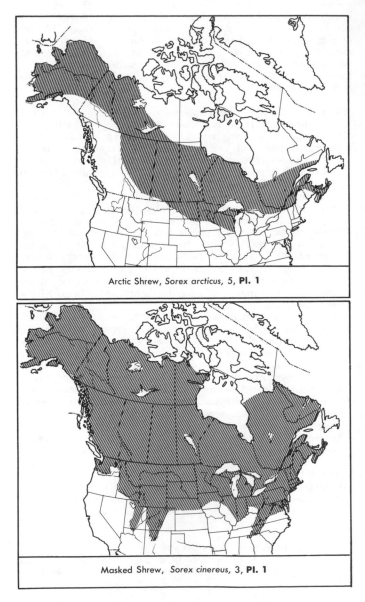

Arctic Shrew, *Sorex arcticus*, 5, **Pl. 1**

Masked Shrew, *Sorex cinereus*, 3, **Pl. 1**

Similar species: (1) Merriam and (2) Vagrant Shrews are larger.
Habitat: As far as known, marshes and near streams.

Map p. 7

SMOKY SHREW *Sorex fumeus*

Identification: Head and body 2½-3 in. (64-76 mm); tail 1¾-2 in. (44-51 mm); wt. ⅕-⅓ oz. (6-9 g). A *dull brown* shrew; *uniformly colored* except for *bicolored* tail (yellowish below, brown above) and *pale feet.* Common within its range. Skull has 32 teeth. There are 6 mammae.
Similar species: (1) Longtail Shrew has longer tail. (2) Masked Shrew is smaller, with underparts paler than upperparts. (3) Pygmy and (4) Gaspé Shrews are smaller. (5) Arctic Shrew has shorter tail, body not uniform color. (6) Southeastern Shrew is smaller.
Habitat: Birch and hemlock forests with deep layer of leaf mold on ground preferred.
Habits: Makes own burrows or uses those of other small mammals through damp leaf mold. Food, insects and other small animals. Nest of dry vegetation in stumps, logs, and among rocks. May be abundant locally at times, suggests colonial habits; suspected that few live more than a year in the wild.
Young: Born April-June; possibly 2nd litter in July, Aug., or occasionally as late as Oct.; 2-7; gestation period probably 3 weeks or less (not known). Naked, blind. Map p. 7

ARCTIC SHREW *Sorex arcticus* Pl. 1

Identification: Head and body 2¾-3 in. (70-76 mm); tail 1¼-1⅔ in. (31-42 mm); wt. ¼-⅓ oz. (7-9 g). The most *brilliantly* colored and most attractive of the shrews. The back, sides, and belly all contrast. In winter *tricolored,* with back nearly black; in summer *dull brown.* Skull has 32 teeth. There are 6 mammae.
On St. Lawrence I. known as *S. jacksoni.*
Similar species: (1) Smoky Shrew has longer tail and uniform body color. (2) Dusky and (3) Gaspé Shrews are not tricolored but light brown. (4) Masked and (5) Pygmy Shrews are smaller, grayish brown.
Habitat: Tamarack and spruce swamps.
Habits: Food, chiefly insects and other invertebrates; not well known.
Young: Record of 1 female with 6 embryos. Map opposite

UNALASKA SHREW *Sorex hydrodromus*
Range: Confined to *Unalaska I.* in Aleutians.

PRIBILOF SHREW *Sorex pribilofensis*
Range: Confined to *St. Paul I.* in Pribilofs.

MERRIAM SHREW *Sorex merriami*   **Pl. 1**
   Identification: Head and body 2¼-2½ in. (57-64 mm); tail 1¼-1⅝ in. (32-41 mm). Upperparts *pale gray; underparts and feet whitish;* tail bicolored. Skull has 32 teeth.
   Similar species: (1) Dwarf Shrew has indistinctly bicolored tail. (2) Malheur Shrew is smaller. (3) Gray Shrew paler with shorter tail. (4) Masked Shrew slightly larger, grayish brown. (5) Dusky Shrew larger, brownish. (6) Vagrant Shrew larger and has dark feet. (7) Inyo Shrew darker, inhabits high mts.
   Habitat: Arid areas; sagebrush or bunchgrass.   Map opposite

SOUTHEASTERN SHREW *Sorex longirostris*
   Identification: Head and body 2-2½ in. (51-64 mm); tail 1-1½ in. (25-38 mm); wt. ⅛-⅕ oz. (3-6 g). This *dark brown* shrew with paler underparts is the only longtail shrew found over most of its range in the Atlantic Plain and Piedmont region. Skull has 32 teeth. There are 6 mammae.
   Similar species: (1) Masked Shrew is about the same, but ranges overlap only slightly. (2) Other shrews have longer tail.
   Habitat: Open fields and woodlots; moist areas preferred. Not confined to one kind of habitat.
   Habits: Probably eats insects, worms, and other small animals. Nest of dry grass or leaves in shallow depression.
   Young: Born April; usually 4; probably 1 litter a year.
                                                         Map opposite

LONGTAIL SHREW *Sorex dispar*
   Identification: Head and body 2¾ in. (70 mm); tail 2⅕-2½ in. (56-64 mm); wt. ⅕± oz. (5-6 g). In summer, *dark grayish* with slightly paler underparts and almost *uniformly colored tail;* in winter, slate color throughout; restricted range. Skull has 32 teeth. There are 6 mammae.
   Similar species: (1) Masked and (2) Pygmy Shrews are smaller. (3) Smoky and (4) Southeastern Shrews have shorter tail.
   Habitat: Cool, moist, rocky situations in deciduous or mixed deciduous-coniferous forests.
   Habits: Food includes centipedes, spiders, insects, and possibly other small invertebrates. Sometimes found in concentrations.
   Young: Born May; 5 reported; probably 1 litter a year.
                                                         Map opposite

GASPÉ SHREW *Sorex gaspensis*
   Identification: Head and body 2-2⅕ in. (51-56 mm); tail 1⅝-2⅛ in. (41-54 mm). Similar to Longtail Shrew, but slightly smaller. Skull has 32 teeth. There are 6 mammae.
   Similar species: (1) Masked, (2) Pygmy, and (3) Smoky Shrews have bicolored tail. (4) Arctic Shrew has tricolored body.

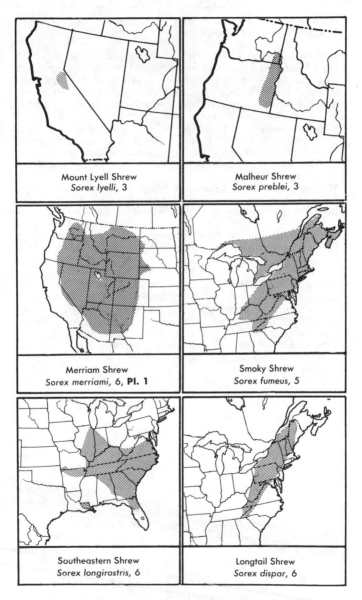

Mount Lyell Shrew
Sorex lyelli, 3

Malheur Shrew
Sorex preblei, 3

Merriam Shrew
Sorex merriami, 6, **Pl. 1**

Smoky Shrew
Sorex fumeus, 5

Southeastern Shrew
Sorex longirostris, 6

Longtail Shrew
Sorex dispar, 6

Habitat: Along streams in coniferous forests.
Range: Confined to Gaspé Pen.

TROWBRIDGE SHREW *Sorex trowbridgei*
Identification: Head and body $2\frac{1}{2}$-$2\frac{4}{5}$ in. (64-71 mm); tail 2-$2\frac{1}{2}$ in. (51-64 mm); wt. $\frac{1}{5}$-$\frac{1}{3}$ oz. (6-9 g). A fairly large shrew with nearly uniform dark *mouse-gray to brownish* body and a distinctly *bicolored tail, nearly white below.* Skull has 32 teeth. There are 6 mammae.
Similar species: (1) Pacific Shrew is larger; tail not bicolored. (2) Vagrant Shrew has shorter tail. (3) Ornate Shrew and (4) Masked Shrew are smaller. (5) Dusky Shrew is dull brown with whitish underparts. (6) Shrew-Mole (p. 16) is larger and has broad front feet.
Habitat: Coniferous forests and other wooded areas.
Habits: Food consists of insects, isopods, probably other small invertebrates, and Douglas fir seeds. Few live as long as 18 months.
Young: Born March-May, occasionally July; 3-6; number of litters a year not known, probably 1. Brown until 1st molt in Sept.   Map p. 11

VAGRANT SHREW *Sorex vagrans*
Identification: Head and body $2\frac{1}{3}$-$2\frac{4}{5}$ in. (59-71 mm); tail $1\frac{1}{2}$-$1\frac{4}{5}$ in. (38-46 mm); wt. $\frac{1}{4}\pm$ oz. ($7\pm$ g). *Reddish brown* in summer, nearly *black* in winter; feet dark; common in our western mts. Skull has 32 teeth. There are 6 mammae.

Some authors consider the following 2 species, *S. obscurus* and *S. pacificus,* as subspecies of *vagrans.*
Similar species: (1) Dusky Shrew is dull brown. (2) Pacific and (3) Trowbridge Shrews are larger. (4) Masked and (5) Pygmy Shrews smaller, grayish brown. (6) Dwarf Shrew is smaller, pale brown. (7) Merriam Shrew is smaller, pale gray. (8) Malheur Shrew smaller.
Habitat: Marshes, bogs, wet meadows; also along streams in forests.
Habits: Active day and night. Known to eat insects, sowbugs, centipedes, spiders, earthworms, slugs, and some vegetable matter. Captives have eaten $1\frac{1}{3}$ times own weight each day. Nest of dry grass or leaves in stumps or logs. Molts twice a year. Few live more than 16 months. Breeds as early as late Jan. and at least through May, then again in Oct. or Nov.
Young: 2-9; gestation period about 20 days; probably more than 1 litter a year. Eyes open in about 1 week; weaned at about 20 days.   Map p. 11

DUSKY SHREW *Sorex obscurus*
Identification: Head and body $2\frac{1}{2}$-3 in. (64-76 mm); tail $1\frac{3}{5}$-$2\frac{1}{2}$ in. (41-64 mm). Upperparts *dull brown,* underparts

whitish; tail *bicolored.* Skull has 32 teeth. There are 6 mammae.

This shrew is difficult to distinguish from some others occurring in the same areas. In case of doubt, specimens should be sent to a museum. Some authors consider this and *S. vagrans* as same species.

Similar species: (1) Vagrant Shrew is reddish brown or blackish. (2) Arctic Shrew is tricolored. (3) Trowbridge Shrew has dark underparts. (4) Pacific Shrew is larger. (5) Masked, (6) Dwarf, and (7) Pygmy Shrews are smaller. (8) Merriam Shrew is smaller, pale gray, and found on desert.

Habitat: Marshes, coniferous forests, heather, dry hillsides, rain-forest thickets.

Habits: Active day and night. Nests in stumps, logs, beneath debris.

Young: Recorded for July; 4–7. Map below

PACIFIC SHREW *Sorex pacificus*

Identification: Head and body $3\frac{1}{3}$ in. (84 mm); tail $2-2\frac{3}{4}$ in. (51–70 mm). This *large brown* western shrew is exceeded in size

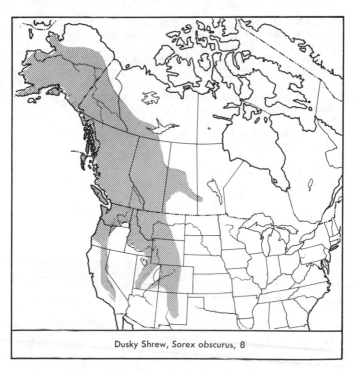

Dusky Shrew, *Sorex obscurus,* 8

only by the Pacific Water Shrew. It is generally medium brown, including tail, feet, and underparts. Skull has 32 teeth.

Some authors consider this a subspecies of *S. vagrans*.

Similar species: (1) Vagrant, (2) Dusky, and (3) Trowbridge Shrews are smaller, with bicolored tail. (4) Pacific Water Shrew is larger, blackish; stiff hairs on sides of hind feet.

Habitat: Redwood and spruce forests, marshes, swamps.

Map opposite

ORNATE SHREW *Sorex ornatus*

Identification: Head and body $2\frac{1}{3}$ - $2\frac{1}{2}$ in. (59 - 64 mm); tail $1\frac{1}{2}$ - $1\frac{4}{5}$ in. (38 - 46 mm). This small *grayish-brown* shrew, *pale beneath*, is the only shrew found over much of its range. Skull has 32 teeth.

It may be the same as the Ashland Shrew.

Similar species: (1) Trowbridge Shrew is larger; dark underparts. (2) Gray Shrew is pale ash-gray and found on the desert.

Habitat: Near streams and in wet meadows.

Habits: Active both day and night.   Map opposite

ASHLAND SHREW *Sorex trigonirostris*

Identification: Head and body $2\frac{1}{2}$ in. (64 mm); tail $1\frac{1}{3}$ in. (34 mm). A small *grayish-brown* shrew.

May be the same as the Ornate Shrew.

Range: Known only from Ashland, Oregon.

SANTA CATALINA SHREW *Sorex willetti*

Identification: Head and body $2\frac{3}{5}$ in. (66 mm); tail $1\frac{5}{8}$ in. (41 mm).

Range: Known only from *Santa Catalina I.,* California. No other shrew is known from the island.

SUISUN SHREW *Sorex sinuosus*

Identification: Head and body $2\frac{1}{5}$ - $2\frac{1}{2}$ in. (56 - 64 mm); tail $1\frac{1}{2}$ in. (38 mm). *Nearly* black.

Range: Known only from *Grizzly I.,* near Suisun, Solano Co., California.

INYO SHREW *Sorex tenellus*

Identification: Head and body $2\frac{2}{5}$ in. (61 mm); tail $1\frac{3}{8}$ - $1\frac{5}{8}$ in. (35 - 41 mm). *Grayish brown;* known only from a few *high mt. peaks* in California and Nevada. Skull has 32 teeth.

Similar species: Merriam Shrew has nearly white underparts and is found on low deserts.

Habitat: Near water; rock ledges and old logs in bottoms of canyons.

Habits: Active day and night.   Map opposite

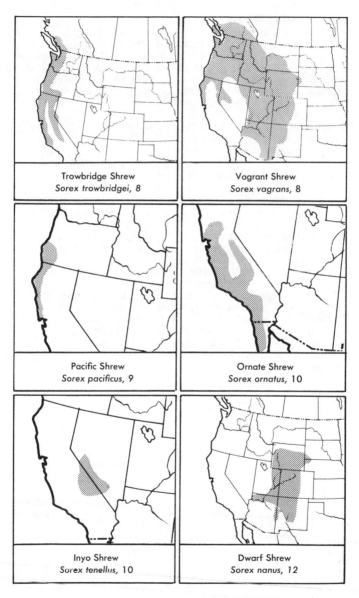

Trowbridge Shrew
Sorex trowbridgei, 8

Vagrant Shrew
Sorex vagrans, 8

Pacific Shrew
Sorex pacificus, 9

Ornate Shrew
Sorex ornatus, 10

Inyo Shrew
Sorex tenellus, 10

Dwarf Shrew
Sorex nanus, 12

DWARF SHREW   *Sorex nanus*
Identification: Head and body 2½ in. (64 mm); tail 1¾ in. (44 mm). A *small* shrew. Body *pale grayish brown,* tail indistinctly bicolored. Known from a few scattered locations within its general range. Skull has 32 teeth.
Similar species: (1) Merriam and (2) Masked Shrews have distinctly bicolored tail. (3) Dusky and (4) Vagrant Shrews are larger.   Map p. 11

NORTHERN WATER SHREW   *Sorex palustris*   **Pl. 1**
Identification: Head and body 3⅕–3½ in. (81–89 mm); tail 2½–3 in. (64–76 mm); wt. ⅓–½+ oz. (9–14 g). A *large blackish-gray* shrew; in some areas underparts are silver, in others slightly paler than back. *Stiff hairs along sides of hind feet* will distinguish it from all but the Pacific Water Shrew. Skull has 32 teeth. There are 6 mammae.
The population from Pt. Gustavus, Glacier Bay, Alaska, is considered a distinct species (*S. alaskanus*) by some authors.
Similar species: (1) Pacific Water Shrew is larger and brownish. (2) The Shrew-Mole (p. 16) has a naked nose and broad front feet.
Habitat: Along cold, small streams with cover on banks, and in bogs; confined to mts. in South.
Habits: Adapted for swimming, readily takes to water, where it feeds on small aquatic organisms; sometimes caught in fish traps. Nest of dried sticks and leaves, diam. about 4 in. (102 mm), found in beaver lodge in New Hampshire.
Young: Born late Feb. through June; 4–8; more than 1 litter a year. A few females may breed when slightly more than 3 months old.   Map opposite

PACIFIC WATER SHREW   *Sorex bendirei*
Identification: Head and body 3½–3⅘ in. (89–97 mm); tail 2½–3⅕ in. (64–81 mm). A *large, dark brown* shrew; hind foot has *stiff, bristle-like hairs along sides* (adaptations for swimming). Skull has 32 teeth.
Similar species: Only other shrew with stiff hairs on hind feet is the (1) Northern Water Shrew which is smaller, blackish, and occurs higher in mts. (2) Shrew-Mole (p. 16) has a naked nose and broad front feet.
Habitat: Wet wooded areas; near sluggish streams, beach debris; humid Pacific Coast.   Map p. 14

PYGMY SHREW   *Microsorex hoyi*
Identification: Head and body 2–2½ in. (51–64 mm); tail 1–1⅖ in. (25–36 mm); wt. ⅒–⅐ oz. (3–4 g). By weight, probably the *smallest living mammal;* weighs about the same as a dime. Eyes, tiny black beads; nose, pointed, long. Skull (Plate 25) has 32 teeth.

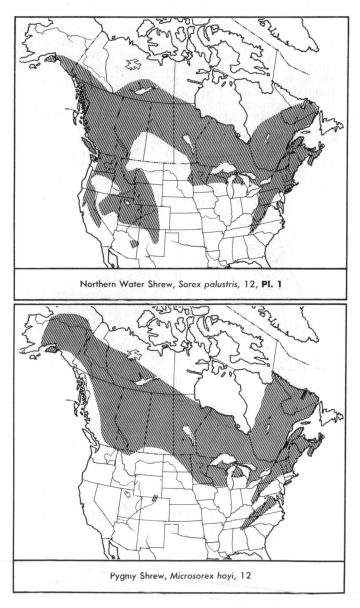

Northern Water Shrew, *Sorex palustris*, 12, **Pl. 1**

Pygmy Shrew, *Microsorex hoyi*, 12

Similar species: (1) Masked Shrew has longer tail; cannot be distinguished for certain without examining teeth; has 5 instead of 3 upper unicuspids (single-cusped teeth) on each side of upper jaw. (2) Arctic Shrew is larger, more brightly colored. (3) Smoky, (4) Dusky, (5) Longtail, (6) Gaspé, and (7) Vagrant Shrews all are larger.
Habitat: Wooded and open areas, wet or dry.
Habits: Active day and night. In captivity has eaten insects and flesh of other shrews and mice.   Map p. 13

GRAY SHREW (Desert Shrew)   *Notiosorex crawfordi*
Identification: Head and body 2–2⅗ in. (51–66 mm); tail 1+ in. (25+ mm). A *pale ashy* shrew; has been found on few occasions. Skull has 28 teeth. There are 6 mammae.
Similar species: (1) Merriam Shrew is slightly larger, darker, and has a longer tail. (2) Other shrews occur in moist situations in mts.

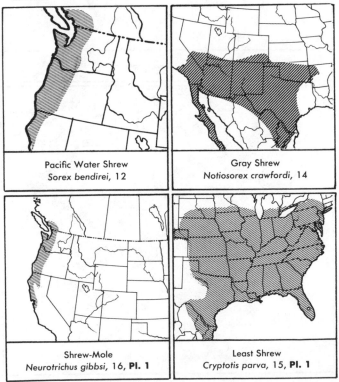

Pacific Water Shrew
Sorex bendirei, 12

Gray Shrew
Notiosorex crawfordi, 14

Shrew-Mole
Neurotrichus gibbsi, 16, **Pl. 1**

Least Shrew
Cryptotis parva, 15, **Pl. 1**

Habitat: Dry alluvial fans or chaparral slopes; sagebrush and other low desert shrubs; arid conditions.

Habits; Nest of fine vegetation, sometimes with hair, beneath *Agave* plants, boards, or debris.

Young: Aug.; 1 female contained 5 embryos.   Map opposite

LEAST SHREW *Cryptotis parva*   **Pl. 1**
Identification: Head and body 2⅕–2½ in. (56–64 mm); tail ½–¾ in. (12–19 mm); wt. ⅐–¼ oz. (4–7 g). Small, *cinnamon* color; *short tail.* May be distinguished from all other shrews by color and extremely short tail. Skull (Plate 25) has 30 teeth.
Similar species: (1) Shorttail Shrew is larger, lead color. (2) Other shrews have longer tail.
Habitat: Open grass-covered areas, which may have scattered brush; also marshes.
Habits: Active day and night. Often uses same runways as voles. Eats insects and other small animals, may eat more than own weight in food each day. Nests under debris, if available, or beneath surface of ground, sometimes in beehives; as many as 31 have been found in 1 nest in winter. Breeds March–Nov. in North, also Feb. in South.
Young: 3–6; gestation period 21–23 days; more than 1 litter a year. Naked; eyes and ears closed; weaned at about 21 days; appearance of adults at 1 month.   Map opposite

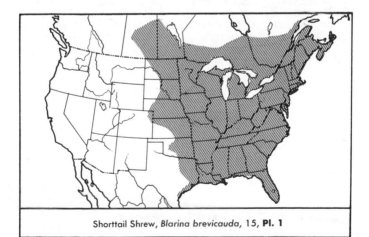

Shorttail Shrew, *Blarina brevicauda,* 15, **Pl. 1**

SHORTTAIL SHREW *Blarina brevicauda*   **Pl. 1**
Identification: Head and body 3–4 in. (76–102 mm); tail ¾–1⅕ in. (19–30 mm); wt. ⅖–⅘ oz. (11–22 g). *Lead color,* short tail, *no external ears;* eyes so small they are *barely appar-*

ent. Skull (Plate 25) has 32 teeth. There are 6 mammae.
   Those from the Dismal Swamp, Virginia, considered distinct
species (*B. telmalestes*) by some authors.
Similar species: (1) The Least Shrew is smaller and of cinnamon color. (2) Other shrews have longer tail.
Habitat: Forests, grasslands, marshes, brushy areas; not restricted.
Habits: Active day and night throughout year. Makes own
tunnels in ground or snow; also uses those of other animals.
Feeds on insects, worms, snails, other invertebrates, and possibly
young mice; saliva poisonous. Nest of dry leaves, grass, hair
(diam. 6–8 in; 152–203 mm), beneath logs, stumps, rocks, or
debris. Home range ½–1 acre (0.2–0.4 ha). Populations as high
as 25 per acre (62 per ha), usually fewer. Longevity 1–2 years.
Breeds March–May and Aug.–Sept.
Young: 5–8; gestation period 21+ days; 2–3 litters a year.
Naked, pink, about size of honeybee when born; eyes and ears
closed.   Map p. 15

Moles: Talpidae

MOLES live most of their lives *beneath* the surface of the ground.
Their presence may be detected by the *low ridges* pushed up as
they move just under the surface; also by the *mounds,* each con-
sisting of from ½ to 2 gallons (2–8 l) of earth, which they push
up from below. No indication of entrance to burrow as in a pocket
gopher mound. Front feet *broad,* palms usually face outward.
Eyes of *pinhead size* or smaller, some covered with a thin skin;
no external ears; fur soft and thick. Do not occur in Rocky Mt.
or Great Basin areas. Length, from tip of nose to tip of tail, 4–9 in.
(102–229 mm). As fossils, date back to Upper Eocene. Local
control of moles, when needed, is best achieved by use of special
traps obtainable at most hardware stores and mail-order houses.
To locate an active subsurface runway, press down ridges of earth
in several places and next day observe which ones have been
raised. For control on large areas, poisoned raw peanuts or poisoned earthworms placed in active tunnels are most effective.
These *should not* be used by the inexperienced person, however.

SHREW-MOLE   *Neurotrichus gibbsi*   **Pl. 1**
   Identification: Head and body 2½–3 in. (64–76 mm); tail
1–1½ in. (25–38 mm); wt. ⅖ oz. (11 g). Body and tail black.
Front feet *longer than broad;* nose naked; nostrils open *to the
sides;* eyes *small but apparent;* tail *haired.* Smallest of
N. American moles. Skull (Plate 25) has 36 teeth.
   Similar species: (1) Water shrews (p. 12) do not have con-

spicuously broad front feet; nose not naked. (2) Trowbridge Shrew (p. 8) is smaller and front feet not unusually broad.

Habitat: Moist areas in shady ravines and along streams where ground is free of turf; from sea level to 8000 ft. (2440 m).

Habits: Active day and night. Moves slowly and cautiously over surface unless frightened, then rapidly to shelter. Searches for food in tunnels beneath layer of leaves and other decaying vegetation; eats mostly small invertebrates; may eat up to $1\frac{1}{2}$ times own weight in a day. Nests in rotting stumps or logs. Breeds throughout year, except possibly Dec. and Jan.

Young: 1–4; more than 1 litter a year.

Economic status: Probably wholly beneficial; destroys insects, cultivates soil.   Map p. 14

STARNOSE MOLE *Condylura cristata*   **Pl. 1**
Identification: Head and body $4\frac{1}{2}$–5 in. (114–127 mm); tail 3–$3\frac{1}{2}$ in. (76–89 mm); wt. $1\frac{1}{5}$–$2\frac{4}{5}$ oz. (34–78 g). Dark brown or black. This is the only kind of mammal that has nose surrounded by *fingerlike, fleshy projections* (22 tentacles), giving appearance of a star. Eyes small but apparent; front feet as long as broad. Tail *hairy,* constricted near body. Skull (Plate 25) has 44 teeth. There are 8 mammae.

Similar species: (1) Eastern and (2) Hairytail Moles have naked nose without fingerlike projections.

Habitat: Low, wet ground near lakes or streams preferred.

Habits: Active day and night. Pushes up mounds of black dirt 12 in. (30 cm) or more in diam. Often appears aboveground or in water; good swimmer. Tunnels not usually visible as ridges on surface of ground; may use same tunnels as Eastern Mole. Eats worms and insects, many aquatic. Detects food with sensitive tentacles on snout, but sense of smell poor. Underground spherical nest of grass and leaves. Often gregarious; populations of 10 or more to an acre (25 to a ha) are common.

Young: Born April–June; 3–7; 1 litter a year. Independent at 3 weeks, mature at 10 months.

Economic status: Neutral. Occasionally does damage to greens on lawns or golf courses; destroys many insects; aerates soil. Fur of some value.   Map p. 18

EASTERN MOLE *Scalopus aquaticus*   **Pl. 1**
Identification: Head and body $4\frac{1}{2}$–$6\frac{1}{2}$ in. (114–165 mm); tail 1–$1\frac{1}{2}$ in. (25–38 mm); wt. $2\frac{2}{5}$–5 oz. (67–140 g). Front feet *broader than long,* palms turn outward; snout pointed, end *naked,* nostrils open *upward; tail naked;* no external ears; tiny eyes covered with thin skin. Fur with a silvery sheen; slate color in North, brown to golden in South and West. Skull (Plate 25) has 36 teeth. There are 6 mammae.

Similar species: (1) Hairytail Mole has haired, not naked tail.

(2) Starnose Mole has end of nose surrounded with 22 fingerlike projections.

Habitat: This mole prefers moist sandy loam; lawns, golf courses, gardens, fields, meadows; avoids extremely dry soil.

Habits: Active day and night in burrows, all seasons. Feeds on worms, insects, and some vegetable matter, chiefly in ridge-covered burrows just below the surface which it makes by pushing through the soil with its piglike snout and spadelike forefeet. Grass-lined nest in burrow 18 to 24 in. (46–61 cm) below surface.

Young: Born March in South, May in North; 4–5; gestation period probably about 6 weeks; 1 litter a year. Naked at birth; independent at 1 month; do not breed until 1 year old.

Economic status: Damages lawns and gardens, but destroys many insects and aerates uncultivated soil.   Map below

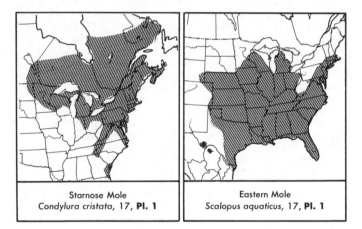

Starnose Mole
Condylura cristata, 17, **Pl. 1**

Eastern Mole
Scalopus aquaticus, 17, **Pl. 1**

HAIRYTAIL MOLE *Parascalops breweri*   **Pl. 1**

Identification: Head and body 4½–5½ in. (114–140 mm); tail 1–1½ in. (25–38 mm); wt. 1½–2⅓ oz. (42–65 g). Fur slate color, with sheen. Smallest of eastern moles. Front feet as broad as long; nose pointed; eyes not apparent; *tail distinctly haired.* Skull (Plate 25) has 44 teeth. There are 8 mammae.

Similar species: (1) Eastern Mole is larger and has a naked tail. (2) Starnose Mole has 22 fingerlike projections around nose.

Habitat: Sandy loam with good vegetative cover preferred, not heavy wet soils.

Habits: Active day and night. Feeds chiefly on insects and earthworms; may consume 3 times own weight in 24 hrs. Burrows near surface as well as deep down (about 18 in.; 46 cm). Nests in deep tunnels; tunnels may be used for 8 years or more by successive generations. Home range about $\frac{1}{5}$ acre (0.1 ha); populations to 11 per acre (27 per ha), usually fewer. Longevity 4–5 years.

Young: Born early May; usually 4; gestation period probably 4 weeks; 1, possibly 2 litters a year. Naked; remain in nest about 1 month; sexually mature at 10 months.

Economic status: Beneficial except when in lawns, gardens, and golf greens; destroys many insects.   Map p. 20

TOWNSEND MOLE   *Scapanus townsendi*   **Pl. 1**
Identification: Head and body 6–7 in. (152–178 mm); tail 2± in. (51± mm); wt. 4–6 oz. (112–168 g). Blackish brown to black. Front feet *broader than long;* nose naked; nostrils open *upward;* tail slightly haired. Skull (Plate 25) has 44 teeth. There are 8 mammae.
Similar species: Pacific Mole is smaller and paler.
Habitat: Moist areas (meadows and floodplains) where soil is easily worked, especially in fields, gardens, and coniferous forests.
Habits: Not well known; more active at night than during day. Eats earthworms, sowbugs, insects, tubers, and some root crops. Has surface as well as deep tunnels. Males are in breeding condition in Feb.
Young: Born March–April; 2–6; 1 litter a year. By May nearly as large as adults.
Economic status: Does damage to some root crops and tubers. In wild areas, beneficial.   Map p. 20

PACIFIC MOLE   *Scapanus orarius*
Identification: Head and body 5–5$\frac{1}{4}$ in. (127–133 mm); tail 1$\frac{1}{3}$ in. (34 mm); wt. 2± oz. (56± g). Front feet *broader than long,* nose naked; nostrils open above; tail slightly haired; color, blackish brown to black. Skull has 44 teeth. There are 8 mammae.
Similar species: (1) California Mole is difficult to distinguish when alive; where the two occur together, specimens should be sent to a museum for identification. (2) Townsend Mole is larger and darker.
Habitat: Well-drained soils, meadows, deciduous forests.
Habits: Active day and night; rarely comes above surface. Eats insects and other small invertebrates. Males are in breeding condition in late Jan.
Young: Born March–April; usually 4; 1 litter a year.
Economic status: Mostly beneficial; does some harm to gardens and other cultivated areas.   Map p. 20

CALIFORNIA MOLE   *Scapanus latimanus*
Identification: Head and body 5–6 in. (127–152 mm); tail

1 ½ in. (38 mm); wt. 2± oz. (56± g). Front feet *broader than long;* nose naked; nostrils open upward; blackish brown to black; tail slightly haired. Skull has 44 teeth. There are 8 mammae.

Similar species: The Pacific Mole is difficult to distinguish; where the two occur together, specimens should be sent to a museum for positive identification.

Habitat: Porous soils in valleys, meadows in mts.

Habits: Rarely comes aboveground. Feeds on insects, earthworms, and other small invertebrates; in captivity will eat 63–107 percent of own weight in earthworms each day; also requires water.

Young: Born March–April; 2–5; 1 litter a year.

Economic status: Beneficial in much of area; may do damage to lawns or gardens.   Map below

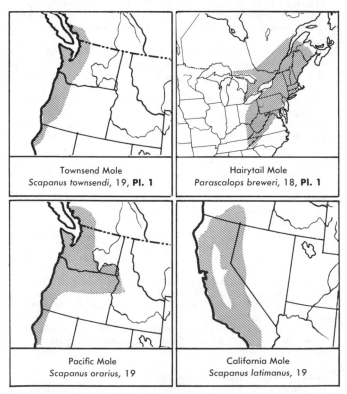

Townsend Mole
Scapanus townsendi, 19, **Pl. 1**

Hairytail Mole
Parascalops breweri, 18, **Pl. 1**

Pacific Mole
Scapanus orarius, 19

California Mole
Scapanus latimanus, 19

Bats: Chiroptera

THESE are the only *truly flying* mammals. The hand is formed into a wing with a double membrane of skin covering (and stretching between) the hand and finger bones, and extending to the forearm, side of body, and hind leg. Thumb is free and terminates in a claw. Most bats also have an *interfemoral membrane* connecting the legs (including the tail). The only measurement given in the following descriptions is that of forearm (from elbow to wrist). This indicates relative size of the animal fairly accurately. The *calcar,* a cartilaginous support for the free edge of the interfemoral membrane, is anchored to the inside of the foot and extends out along the edge of the membrane. If keeled, there will be a definite extension of the free edge of the membrane beyond the calcar. If the calcar lies along the free edge, it is not keeled. The *tragus* is a leaflike structure in the ear.

Habits: All bats within the area covered are nocturnal; nearly all eat insects, which they usually capture on the wing. Their small beady eyes are probably of little use in their night flights. To substitute for poor vision, they have evolved a sonar system for locating solid objects. As they fly they emit a series of supersonic sounds that bounce back from other objects and are picked up by the bats. This is called *echolocation;* it enables them to fly in absolute darkness. Some bats (solitary) pass the day hanging among the foliage of trees, others hang in hollow trees or attics of buildings, and still others (colonial) seek shelter in natural caves or abandoned mine tunnels. All hang with heads down when at rest. Some migrate and others go into hibernation for the winter.

Young: Usually 1 or 2, but a few bats may give birth to as many as 4 at a time. Young bats may cling to their mother for some time after birth, but when they become a burden to her flight they are left at the roosting site while she feeds.

Economic status: All insect-eating bats are probably beneficial; at least they do no obvious harm. Occasionally they take up residence in the attic or walls of a house and may cause the occupants some discomfort. If screening is placed over all possible entrances they may be eliminated. A few instances of rabid bats have been reported, especially in the vampire bats, but these are so rare that there is little reason for alarm. However, it is not advisable to handle them with bare hands because of the chance of encountering a rabid individual. The guano deposits in some caves have been mined for fertilizer; many tons were taken from the Carlsbad Caverns, New Mexico.

Leafnose Bats: Phyllostomidae

MEMBERS of this family, except those of the genus *Mormoops,* have a *leaflike, triangular flap* of thick skin *projecting upward from tip of the nose.* The only bats described here that possess these structures. Not known as fossils.

LEAFCHIN BAT   *Mormoops megalophylla*
  Identification: Forearm $2-2\frac{1}{5}$ in. (51–56 mm). A brownish bat with prominent *leaflike folds of skin* across chin, reaching from ear to ear, the central one, in front of lower lip, covered with small *wartlike prominences;* end of tail appears on *upperside of interfemoral membrane;* face short, forehead high. We have no other bat in the U.S. with the above characters. Skull (Plate 25) has 34 teeth.
  Habitat: Usually tunnels or caves; it may roost in buildings.
  Habits: Colonial; probably feeds on insects.
  Young: Born June or July in this area; 1 young.

Map opposite

LEAFNOSE BAT   *Macrotus californicus*   **Pl. 3**
  Identification: Forearm 2 in. (51 mm). This *large-eared, grayish* bat has a distinct *leaflike flap* of thick skin *projecting upward from tip of nose;* tail extends to edge of complete interfemoral membrane. Skull (Plate 25) has 34 teeth.
   Sometimes known as *M. waterhousi.*
  Similar species: (1) Hognose Bat has a long, slender rostrum and small ears; it is dark brown and the interfemoral membrane is about $\frac{1}{2}$ in. (13 mm) wide in the middle. (2) Longnose Bat has a long rostrum, no tail.
  Habitat: Usually caves or old mine tunnels during day, sometimes buildings during night.
  Habits: Flies late; returns to roost when stomach is full. When alighting, gives a half-roll and attaches directly with the feet. Sexes usually apart except during mating season.
  Young: Born May–July; 1.   Map opposite

HOGNOSE BAT   *Choeronycteris mexicana*   **Pl. 3**
  Identification: Forearm $1\frac{3}{4}$ in. (44 mm); wt. $\frac{3}{4}$ oz. (21 g). This bat has a *long, slender nose* with *triangular flap* of skin projecting upward from tip; ears small, barely projecting above head; color light brown; tail extends *less than halfway to edge* of interfemoral membrane, which is reduced. Skull (Plate 25) has 30 teeth.
  Similar species: (1) Longnose Bat has no tail. (2) Leafnose

Bat has large ears; tail extends to edge of interfemoral membrane.

Habitat: By day, natural caves, old mine tunnels, and buildings.

Habits: During the day prefers area of deep shadow or twilight, not extreme darkness of tunnels. Wary and takes flight when approached. Feeds, in part at least, on pollen and nectar.

Young: Born June or July in this area; 1.   Map below

LONGNOSE BAT   *Leptonycteris nivalis*

Identification: Forearm $2\frac{1}{5}$ in. (56 mm); wt. $\frac{3}{4}$ oz. (21 g). This rather large, brownish bat has an extremely *long slender nose* with a *leaflike projection* of thick skin on its end. Ears extend well above top of head. Interfemoral membrane narrow; there is *no tail*. Skull (Plate 25) has 30 teeth.

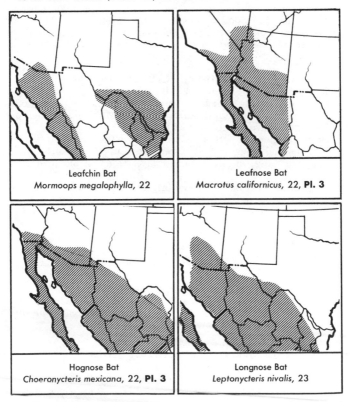

Leafchin Bat
Mormoops megalophylla, 22

Leafnose Bat
Macrotus californicus, 22, **Pl. 3**

Hognose Bat
Choeronycteris mexicana, 22, **Pl. 3**

Longnose Bat
Leptonycteris nivalis, 23

Some authors consider *L. sanborni* a distinct species.
Similar species: (1) Hognose and (2) Leafnose Bats have conspicuous tail.
Habitat: This bat hangs in caves, old mine tunnels, and buildings by day.
Habits: Feeds chiefly on pollen and nectar; also some insects. Females may congregate in nurseries where young and adults intermingle during midsummer.
Young: Born April, May, or June in this area; 1–2.

Map p. 23

Vampire Bats: Desmodontidae

MEMBERS of this family have specialized, razor-sharp upper incisors that enable them to cut the skin of a larger mammal and start the flow of blood; the bat then laps up the blood. The other teeth are nonfunctional. One species enters the United States; for the most part vampire bats are tropical or subtropical in distribution.

HAIRY-LEGGED VAMPIRE BAT   *Diphylla ecaudata*
  Identification: Forearm 2⅕ in. (56 mm). Ears small and rounded, separate. Nostrils surrounded by leaflike dermal outgrowths; nose short and blunt. No tail. Middle upper incisors large and sharp. Skull has 22 teeth.
  Similar species: Other leafnose bats either have a tail or a long pointed nose; none has specialized upper incisors.
  Habits: Hangs in caves during day. Feeds on blood of large mammals.
  Economic status: Detrimental to livestock; also transmits rabies. Barely enters U.S.
  Range: In U.S. reported from near Comstock, Val Verde Co., Texas.

Plainnose Bats: Vespertilionidae

BATS in this family have *simple, unmodified muzzles.* They all have *complete* interfemoral membranes, and in all the *tail* reaches to the *back edge* of the membrane *but not noticeably beyond.* As fossils, date back to Lower Oligocene.

Myotis Group of Bats

THESE BATS form the largest and most widely distributed group. They are all relatively *small,* some shade of *brown,* and have simple snouts. The *tragus* (a leaflike projection arising from the base of the inside of the external ear) is long and pointed. The membranes are always complete, and the tail reaches to the edge of the interfemoral membrane. This membrane is sometimes scantily haired, especially at the base, but *never thickly covered with hair.* Skull has 38 teeth. There are 2 pectoral mammae.

Many of the species are difficult to identify, even in a museum. When reading the following descriptions this should be borne in mind. In case of doubt, specimens should be sent to an authority for identification.

Similar species: (1) Big Brown Bat is larger and has a blunt tragus. (2) Evening Bat and (3) Pipistrels have blunt tragus.

LITTLE BROWN MYOTIS *Myotis lucifugus*   Pl. 2
Identification: Forearm $1\frac{1}{2}$ in. (38 mm); wt. $\frac{1}{4}$-$\frac{1}{3}$ oz. (7-9 g). The ear is moderate in size, when laid forward reaches to the nostril. Hairs on back have *long glossy tips;* glossy sheen is fairly characteristic. Skull (Plate 25) has 38 teeth.
Similar species: (1) Indiana Myotis has a definite keel on calcar. (2) Mississippi Myotis is larger and a duller color. (3) Gray and (4) Cave Myotis are larger. (5) Keen and (6) Long-eared Myotis have large ears (when laid forward, reach beyond nose). (7) Long-legged Myotis is larger, fur not glossy. (8) Yuma Myotis is smaller. (9) Fringed Myotis has conspicuous fringe of hairs along edge of interfemoral membrane. (10) California and (11) Small-footed Myotis are smaller.
Habitat: Caves, mine tunnels, hollow trees, or buildings serve as roosting places.
Habits: Leaves daytime retreat at dusk, returns to roosting site just before dawn. Colonial. Feeds on insects on the wing near water or forests; flight erratic. In the North, most migrate South in the fall and go into hibernation in a cave or other suitable retreat. Although they become torpid, they do not go into a deep sleep. Have been known to return home in 3 weeks after release at distance of 270 mi. (432 km). One banded bat known to have lived more than 20 years. They may breed during late fall and winter, but embryonic development does not begin until Feb. in the North.
Young: Born May – July; usually 1, occasionally 2; gestation period about 80 days. Naked; eyes open in 2 or 3 days. May or may not be carried by the mother; normally left hanging in roost. When about a month old, take to wing and become self-supporting.   Map p. 26

YUMA MYOTIS *Myotis yumanensis*
Identification: Forearm $1\frac{1}{3}$-$1\frac{1}{2}$ in. (34–38 mm); wt. $\frac{1}{5}$-$\frac{1}{4}$ oz. (6 – 7 g). Color *dull brownish* with hairs dark at bases; interfemoral membrane *haired nearly to knee.* One of the commonest of the western myotis.

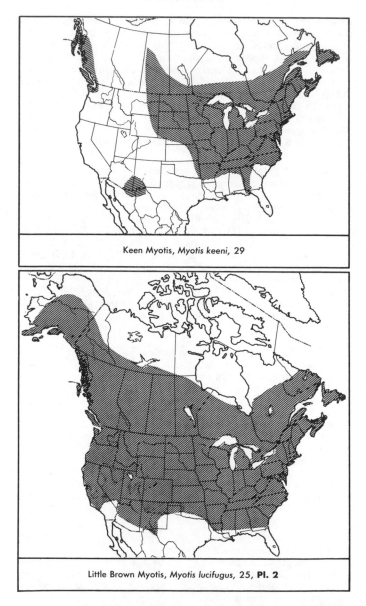

Keen Myotis, *Myotis keeni*, 29

Little Brown Myotis, *Myotis lucifugus*, 25, **Pl. 2**

Similar species: (1) The Cave Myotis is larger. (2) Arizona Myotis has ochraceous, glossy fur. (3) Little Brown and (4) Long-legged Myotis are larger, with glossy hair. (5) Keen and (6) Long-eared Myotis have large ears (when laid forward extend beyond nose). (7) Fringed Myotis has conspicuous fringe of hairs along edge of tail membrane. (8) California and (9) Small-footed Myotis are smaller.
Habitat: Caves, tunnels, or buildings; arid areas.
Habits: Late fliers, usually fly close to ground. Colonial. Hang in closely grouped clumps.
Young: Born May or June; 1. Clings to mother for a few days.
Map p. 32

MISSISSIPPI MYOTIS *Myotis austroriparius*
Identification: Forearm $1\frac{1}{2}-1\frac{3}{5}$ in. (38–41 mm). Hair woolly, *dull yellowish brown,* dark at base.
Similar species: (1) Little Brown Myotis is smaller, with glossy fur. (2) Indiana Myotis is smaller. (3) Gray Myotis is larger; hairs not dark at bases. (4) Keen Myotis has large ears.
Habitat: Mostly caves, but also mine tunnels, hollow trees, buildings, culverts, and beneath bridges.
Habits: Appears from roosting site when nearly dark; flies low over water and fields to feed. Colonial. Hangs in large clusters; density of cluster about 150 bats for each sq. ft. (1600 per sq. m); up to 90,000 in a cave. Hibernates in caves in North, intermittently active all winter in Florida. Requires body of water and expanse of ceiling at least 6 ft. (183 cm) above. Has returned 45 mi. (72 km) to home cave. Females and some males enter maternity caves in South in mid-March.
Young: Born May in South, June in North; normally 2, occasionally 1. Able to fly and feed themselves at 5 or 6 weeks; sexually mature at 1 year. Females do not carry young when feeding. Map p. 28

GRAY MYOTIS *Myotis grisescens*
Identification: Forearm $1\frac{3}{5}-1\frac{4}{5}$ in. (41–46 mm); wt. $\frac{1}{4}-\frac{1}{3}$ oz. (7–9 g). A *dull grayish-brown* bat with hairs about the same color to the bases.
Similar species: (1) Mississippi, (2) Small-footed, and (3) Indiana Myotis are smaller. (4) Little Brown Myotis is smaller; fur glossy and dark at bases.
Habitat: Caves for roosting and bearing young.
Habits: Colonial. Hangs in compact clusters from ceilings of caves. May migrate from one cave to another. Sexes segregate when young are born.
Young: Born May in South, June in North; 1. Naked; clings to mother for less than a week, then remains in cave.
Map p. 28

CAVE MYOTIS *Myotis velifer*
  Identification: Forearm $1\frac{3}{5}$-$1\frac{4}{5}$ in. (41-46 mm). Color *dull brown;* ears moderate in size; wing membrane arises *from base of toes.* Common in *caves* of Southwest.
  Similar species: (1) Little Brown, (2) Arizona, (3) Yuma, (4) Long-legged, (5) California, and (6) Small-footed Myotis are smaller. (7) Long-eared Myotis is smaller but has larger ears. (8) Fringed Myotis has fringe of hairs along edge of tail membrane.
  Habitat: Typically, caves and mine tunnels, also buildings.
  Habits: Colonial. Seeks crevices or vertical walls, moves from place to place.
  Young: Born June or July; 1.   Map below

ARIZONA MYOTIS *Myotis occultus*
  Identification: Forearm $1\frac{2}{5}$-$1\frac{3}{5}$ in. (36-41 mm). This is a

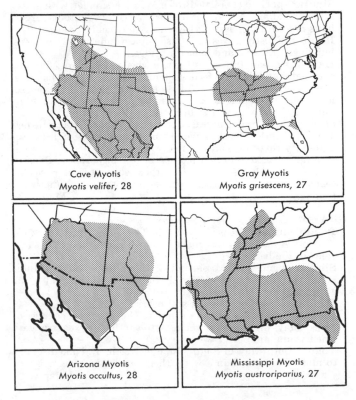

Cave Myotis
Myotis velifer, 28

Gray Myotis
Myotis grisescens, 27

Arizona Myotis
Myotis occultus, 28

Mississippi Myotis
Myotis austroriparius, 27

relatively rare bat with a limited distribution in the Southwest. Color strongly *ochraceous;* hairs of back with burnished tips and a *glossy sheen.*

Some authors consider this the same as the Little Brown Myotis (*M. lucifugus*).

Similar species: (1) Long-legged Myotis has underside of wing furred to elbow. (2) Yuma Myotis is brownish. (3) Cave Myotis is larger. (4) Long-eared Myotis has large ears. (5) Fringed Myotis has fringe of hairs at edge of tail membrane. (6) California and (7) Small-footed Myotis are smaller.

Habitat: Buildings, mine tunnels, beneath bridges.

Habits: Colonial. Migratory. Feeds among trees. Sexes may segregate when young are born.

Young: Born late May or early June; 1.   Map opposite

KEEN MYOTIS   *Myotis keeni*

Identification: Forearm $1\frac{2}{5}$–$1\frac{3}{5}$ in. (36–41 mm); wt. $\frac{1}{4}$–$\frac{1}{3}$ oz. (7–9 g). This northern member of the myotis group may be distinguished from all other myotis within its range, except the Long-eared Myotis, by the size of its ears. When laid forward, ears *extend about* $\frac{1}{16}$ in. (1.5 mm) *beyond the nose.* Fur is *dark brown.*

Similar species: (1) Long-eared Myotis has larger ears, extending $\frac{1}{5}$ in. (5 mm) beyond nose when laid forward. (2) Fringed Myotis has fringe of hairs on edge of tail membrane. (3) All other myotis have smaller ears.

Habitat: Mine tunnels, caves, buildings, hollow trees, storm sewers, forested areas.

Habits: Probably occurs in small scattered colonies; may spend winter in hibernation in North. Known to live $18\frac{1}{2}$ years in wild.

Young: Born late June or July; 1.   Map p. 26

LONG-EARED MYOTIS   *Myotis evotis*   **Pl. 2**

Identification: Forearm $1\frac{2}{5}$–$1\frac{3}{5}$ in. (36–41 mm). May be distinguished from all other species of myotis by its *large black ears* (when laid forward they extend about $\frac{1}{5}$ in. (5 mm); beyond the nose). General coloration is a *pale brown.* Those from southern N. Mexico considered a distinct species (*M. auriculus*) by some.

Similar species: (1) Keen Myotis has slightly smaller ears and is dark brown. (2) The Little Brown, (3) Arizona, and (4) Yuma Myotis have smaller ears. (5) Cave Myotis is larger, with smaller ears. (6) Long-legged, (7) California, and (8) Small-footed Myotis are smaller. (9) The Fringed Myotis has distinct fringe of hairs on edge of interfemoral membrane; smaller ears.

Habitat: Thinly forested areas, around buildings or trees; occasionally caves.

Habits: Usually flies late, but at high altitudes may fly in early evening before temperature drops. Not known to occur in large colonies.

Young: Born late June or July; 1. Map below

FRINGED MYOTIS *Myotis thysanodes*

Identification: Forearm $1\frac{3}{5}$ – $1\frac{4}{5}$ in. (41 – 46 mm). Buffy brown in color; this bat may be distinguished from all other myotis by presence of a conspicuous *fringe of stiff hairs* along free edge of the *interfemoral (tail) membrane*. It also has relatively large ears.

Similar species: The following species of myotis may be found within the range of the Fringed Myotis; all but the Cave Myotis are smaller, and none has the distinct fringe of hairs on edge of tail membrane: (1) Little Brown, (2) Yuma, (3) Cave, (4) Arizona, (5) Keen, (6) Long-eared, (7) Long-legged, (8) California, and (9) Small-footed Myotis.

Habitat: Caves, attics of old buildings.

Habits: Colonial. When in caves, hangs in clumps in deep twilight zone. Sexes separate during summer.

Young: Born June or July; 1. Map below

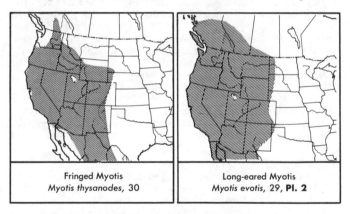

Fringed Myotis	Long-eared Myotis
Myotis thysanodes, 30	*Myotis evotis*, 29, **Pl. 2**

INDIANA MYOTIS *Myotis sodalis*

Identification: Forearm $1\frac{2}{5}$ – $1\frac{3}{5}$ in. (36 – 41 mm); wt. $\frac{1}{4}$ – $\frac{1}{3}$ oz. (7 – 9 g). Calcar with definite *keel*. Very difficult to distinguish from the Little Brown Myotis, especially in the field.

Similar species: (1) Little Brown Myotis has no definite keel on calcar. (2) Mississippi Myotis is larger. (3) Gray Myotis is larger and hairs are not dark at bases. (4) Keen Myotis has larger ear. (5) Small-footed Myotis is smaller.

Habitat: Caves in winter, man-made structures and possibly hollow trees in summer.

Habits: Colonial in winter, may scatter in summer. Hangs in compact clusters. Sexes segregate for part of year.
Young: Born probably in June; immature bats taken in July.
Map below

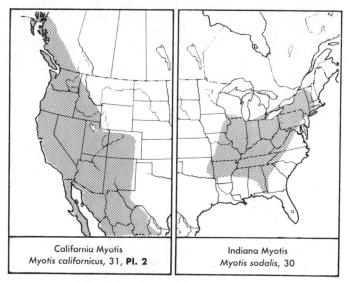

California Myotis
Myotis californicus, 31, **Pl. 2**

Indiana Myotis
Myotis sodalis, 30

LONG-LEGGED MYOTIS *Myotis volans*
Identification: Forearm 1½–1⅗ in. (38–41 mm). Distinguished from other species of myotis by the *short rounded ears, small foot,* well-developed *keel on calcar,* and fur on underside of the membranes as far out as the elbow and knee.
Similar species: (1) The Cave Myotis is larger. (2) Little Brown, (3) Small-footed, (4) California, and (5) Yuma Myotis are smaller. (6) In the Arizona Myotis the underside of wing is not furred to elbow. (7) Keen and (8) Long-eared Myotis have larger ear. (9) Fringed Myotis is larger and has a fringe on edge of tail membrane.
Habitat: Buildings; small pockets and crevices in rock ledges.
Habits: Colonial. Less erratic flight than most myotis.
Young: Born June; 1.   Map p. 32

CALIFORNIA MYOTIS *Myotis californicus*   **Pl. 2**
Identification: Forearm 1 ⅕–1⅖ in. (31–36 mm). One of the small species of myotis. Color varies from light buff (in desert) to rich brown (along Northwest Coast). Color of hair bases *much darker than that of tips.*

Similar species: Sometimes difficult to distinguish from (1) Yuma Myotis (usually larger, with larger foot) or (2) Small-footed Myotis (*distinct black mask across face*). (3) Little Brown, (4) Cave, (5) Arizona, (6) Keen, (7) Long-eared, (8) Fringed, and (9) Long-legged Myotis are larger.
Habitat: Mine tunnels, hollow trees, loose rocks, buildings, bridges; it is chiefly a crevice dweller.
Habits: Leaves roost shortly after sunset to forage near trees, rarely more than 15 ft. (4.6 m) aboveground; hangs up several times during night. Occurs in small colonies or singly. Moves from place to place, except females in nursery colonies. Hibernating temperature near that of surroundings. Sexes separate for most of year.
Young: Born May or June; 1. Naked.   Map p. 31

SMALL-FOOTED MYOTIS *Myotis subulatus*   **Pl. 2**
Identification: Forearm $1\frac{1}{5}$ – $1\frac{2}{5}$ in. (31 – 36 mm); wt. $\frac{1}{5}$ – $\frac{1}{3}$ oz. (6 – 9 g). This is the *smallest* myotis in the eastern area and, except for the California Myotis, in the western area also. *Long silky fur* is *yellowish;* there is a distinct *black mask* across face. Ears are black.
   It is also known as *M. leibii.*

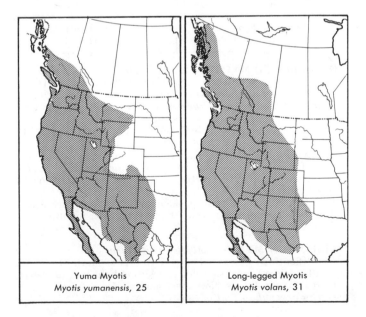

Yuma Myotis
Myotis yumanensis, 25

Long-legged Myotis
Myotis volans, 31

Similar species: (1) California Myotis (sometimes difficult to distinguish) has brown mask and dark brown ears. (2) Yuma Myotis is larger, no black mask. (3) Little Brown, (4) Cave, (5) Arizona, (6) Keen, (7) Long-eared, (8) Fringed, (9) Indiana, (10) Gray, and (11) Long-legged Myotis are larger.

Habitat: Caves, mine tunnels, crevices in rocks, buildings; in or near forested areas.

Habits: Appears fairly early in evening. Colonial or solitary. Hangs with wings partially spread; may move to different cave in winter. Feeds low among trees or over brush.

Young: Born May–July; 1.   Map p. 34

Other Plainnose Bats

INCLUDED here are all of the genera in the family Vespertilionidae except *Myotis*. A rather diverse group; all have simple unmodified noses and complete interfemoral membranes; tail reaches to edge of membrane, but not beyond.

SILVER-HAIRED BAT *Lasionycteris noctivagans* **Pl. 3**
Identification: Forearm 1 $\frac{2}{3}$ in. (42 mm); wt. $\frac{1}{5}$ - $\frac{2}{5}$ oz. (6–11 g). A *blackish-brown* bat with hairs on middle of back *tipped with white;* tail membrane furred above on basal half. Distinguished from all other bats by color. Skull (Plate 25) has 36 teeth. There are 2 mammae.

Similar species: (1) Hoary Bat is larger and has a buffy throat. (2) Red Bat is brick- or rusty-red. (3) Seminole Bat is mahogany-brown.

Habitat: Forested areas; buildings or occasionally caves.

Habits: Solitary. Flies high and fairly straight. Feeds among trees. Probably migrates south in winter.

Young: Born June or July; usually 2, sometimes 1. Naked, blind. May cling to mother in flight for several days.

Map p. 34

WESTERN PIPISTREL *Pipistrellus hesperus* **Pl. 2**
Identification: Forearm 1–1 $\frac{1}{5}$ in. (25–30 mm); wt. $\frac{1}{6}$ - $\frac{1}{5}$ oz. (5–6 g). Tragus *blunt,* with tip bent forward; color *ashy gray or yellowish gray. Smallest* of the bats here considered. Small size and pale coloration distinguish it from other bats. Skull has 34 teeth. There are 2 mammae.

Similar species: (1) All myotis are larger; pointed tragus. (2) Other bats are larger.

Habitat: Caves, under loose rocks, crevices in cliffs, buildings; arid conditions, but near watercourses.

Habits: Flies early in evening, sometimes before sundown; flight erratic. Feeds on insects.

Young: Born June or July; usually 2, occasionally 1. Cling to
mother for several days.   Map opposite

EASTERN PIPISTREL *Pipistrellus subflavus*   Pl. 2
Identification: Forearm 1⅕± in. (30± mm); wt. ⅛–⅕ oz.
(3.5–6 g). Tragus *blunt* and straight; color *yellowish brown* to

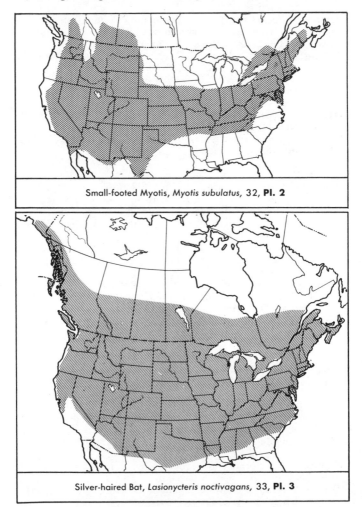

Small-footed Myotis, *Myotis subulatus*, 32, **Pl. 2**

Silver-haired Bat, *Lasionycteris noctivagans*, 33, **Pl. 3**

drab brown. One of the *smallest* eastern bats. Small size and blunt tragus distinguish this from other bats. Skull (Plate 25) has 34 teeth. There are 2 mammae.

Similar species: (1) All myotis have pointed tragus. (2) Other bats are larger.

Habitat: Caves, mine tunnels, crevices in rocks, buildings, wooded areas, near water.

Habits: Appears in early evening. Flight slow and erratic. Hangs singly or in small clusters. Feeds on small insects; probably rests several times during night. Some hibernate in North; some may migrate and return to same roost following year. Has returned 80 mi. (128 km) to original roost. Known to live 7 years in wild.

Young: Born May in South, June or July in North; normally 2, occasionally 1. Carried by mother on feeding flights for about 1 week, then left hanging at roost; fly at 4 weeks. Map below

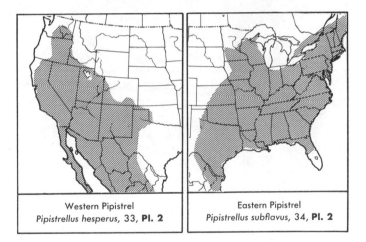

Western Pipistrel
Pipistrellus hesperus, 33, **Pl. 2**

Eastern Pipistrel
Pipistrellus subflavus, 34, **Pl. 2**

BIG BROWN BAT *Eptesicus fuscus*   **Pl. 2**
   Identification: Forearm 1⅘–2 in. (46–51 mm); wt. ⅖–⅗ oz. (11–17 g). Pale brown (on desert) to dark brown, membranes black, *tragus blunt.* One of the commonest and most widely distributed of our bats. Large size and color distinguish this from all others. Skull (Plate 25) has 32 teeth. There are 2 mammae.

Similar species: (1) Evening Bat is smaller. (2) All myotis are smaller, with pointed tragus.

Habitat: Caves, tunnels, crevices, hollow trees, buildings, wooded areas.

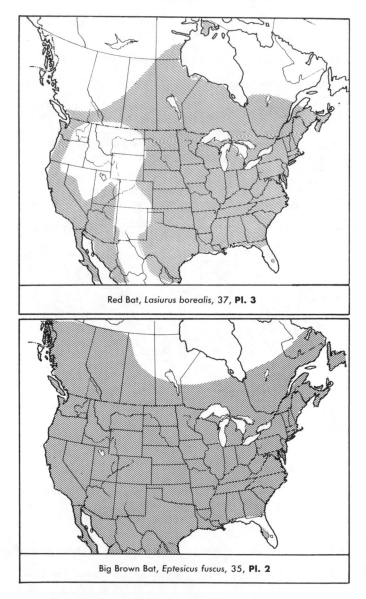

Red Bat, *Lasiurus borealis*, 37, **Pl. 3**

Big Brown Bat, *Eptesicus fuscus*, 35, **Pl. 2**

Habits: Roosts singly or in small clusters. Feeds on insects, chiefly beetles. Some migrate, others winter over in North. Common in buildings in winter.

Young: Born May or June; usually 2, occasionally 1.

Map opposite

RED BAT *Lasiurus borealis* **Pl. 3**
Identification: Forearm 1 ½ – 1 ⅔ in. (38 – 42 mm); wt. ¼ – ½ oz. (7 – 14 g). This is a *brick-red* to *rusty-red* bat with hairs *tipped with white;* tail membrane fully furred above. Females distinctly paler than males. Skull (Plate 25) has 32 teeth. There are 4 mammae.
Similar species: (1) Seminole Bat is mahogany-brown. (2) The yellow bats do not have tail membrane heavily furred to edge. (3) Hoary Bat is larger. (4) Silver-haired Bat is blackish brown.
Habitat: Wooded areas; it normally roosts in trees, occasionally enters caves.
Habits: Leaves roost at deep dusk. Solitary. Flight rather steady and rapid. Has regular feeding areas; usually feeds in pairs, working same route of about 100 yd. (91 m) over and over. Migrates south in autumn; has been seen far out to sea.
Young: Born June; 2 – 4. Cling to mother until too heavy to support in flight. Map opposite

SEMINOLE BAT *Lasiurus seminolus* **Pl. 3**
Identification: Forearm 1 ½ – 1 ⅔ in. (38 – 42 mm); wt. ¼ – ½ oz. (7 – 14 g). Rich *mahogany-brown* with hairs *tipped with white.* Similar in other respects to Red Bat.
Similar species: (1) Red Bat is brick-red or rusty red. (2) Eastern Yellow Bat has heavily furred tail membrane for only basal 3rd; yellowish brown. (3) Hoary Bat is larger. (4) Silver-haired Bat is blackish brown.
Habitat: Wooded areas; trees for roost.
Habits: Solitary. Similar to those of Red Bat.
Young: Born June; 2 – 4. Cling to mother for several days.

Map p. 40

HOARY BAT *Lasiurus cinereus* **Pl. 3**
Identification: Forearm 2 + in. (51 + mm); wt. 1 ± oz. (28 ± g). Yellowish brown to mahogany-brown, the hairs tipped with white over most of body; *throat buffy;* tail membrane heavily furred on top to edges; ears rounded. Size and color distinguish it. Skull (Plate 25) has 32 teeth. There are 4 mammae.
Similar species: (1) Silver-haired, (2) Red, and (3) Seminole Bats are all smaller. (4) In the yellow bats the hairs are not frosted.
Habitat: Wooded areas.

Habits: Flies late, high. Solitary. Hangs in trees. Occasionally in caves. Migrates south in autumn.
Young: Born June; 2. Carried by mother on feeding excursions for several days; able to fly at 4 weeks.   Map below

EASTERN YELLOW BAT *Lasiurus intermedius*   **Pl. 3**
Identification: Forearm 2 – 2 ⅕ in. (51 – 56 mm). A large, pale, *yellowish-brown* bat with tail membrane heavily *furred only on basal 3rd.* Skull (Plate 25) has 30 teeth. There are 4 mammae.
   Formerly known as *Dasypterus.*
Similar species: (1) Hoary, (2) Red, and (3) Seminole Bats all have tail membrane heavily furred to edge.
Habitat: Wooded areas.
Habits: Probably solitary for the most part; may occur in small colonies.   Map p. 40

WESTERN YELLOW BAT *Lasiurus ega*
Identification: Forearm 1 ⅘ in. (46 mm). This pale, *yellowish brown* bat barely enters s. California. Tail membrane heavily *furred only on its basal 3rd.* Skull has 30 teeth.

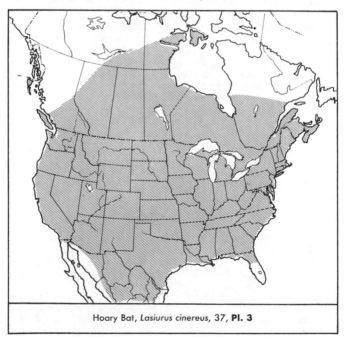

Hoary Bat, *Lasiurus cinereus*, 37, **Pl. 3**

Similar species: (1) Hoary and (2) Red Bats have tail membrane completely furred.
Habitat: Wooded areas.
Habits: Probably similar to those of Eastern Yellow Bat.

Map p. 40

EVENING BAT   *Nycticeius humeralis*
Identification: Forearm $1\frac{2}{5}$–$1\frac{1}{2}$ in. (36–38 mm); wt. $\frac{1}{4}$–$\frac{1}{3}$ oz. (7–9 g). Dark brown; black membranes; *blunt tragus*. Combination of size, color, and blunt tragus distinguishes this from all other species in its range. Skull (Plate 25) has 30 teeth. There are 2 mammae.
Similar species: (1) Big Brown Bat is larger. (2) All myotis have pointed tragus.
Habitat: Buildings and hollow trees.
Habits: Usually colonial, sometimes solitary. Flight fairly steady and straight. Sexes segregate when young are born. Common in South, rare in North.
Young: Born May or June; usually 2, occasionally 1.

Map p. 40

SPOTTED BAT   *Euderma maculata*   Pl. 3
Identification: Forearm 2 in. (51 mm). This rare and spectacular bat has *huge ears, is dark sepia,* with a *white spot* on *rump* and another on *each shoulder.* Only bat with such contrasting colors. Skull has 34 teeth.
Habitat: Arid country. It occasionally enters buildings and caves.   Map p. 40

WESTERN BIG-EARED BAT   *Plecotus townsendi*
Identification: Forearm $1\frac{3}{5}$–$1\frac{4}{5}$ in. (41–46 mm); wt. $\frac{1}{3}$–$\frac{2}{5}$ oz. (9–11 g). Extremely *large ears,* over 1 in. (25 mm) high, *joined across forehead.* On nose, in front of eyes, are 2 prominent lumps. General color clove-brown; bases of ventral hairs gray or brown, tips brown or buffy; tail membrane naked. Skull (Plate 25) has 36 teeth. There are 2 mammae.
  Formerly known as *Corynorhinus rafinesquei.*
Similar species: (1) In the Eastern Big-eared Bat the bases of the ventral hairs are black with white tips. (2) Mexican Big-eared Bat has a small lobe at inner base of ear. (3) In the Pallid Bat the ears are separate; no prominent lumps on nose.
Habitat: Caves, mine tunnels, and buildings for roosts.
Habits: Colonial in nurseries and hibernation; may be solitary part of the year. Hangs in tight clusters. Moves from cave to cave, even in winter; when removed, has returned 28 mi. (45 km) to roost in 2 days. When resting, ears folded back over neck or coiled like ram's horn. Body temperature approaches that of surroundings. Mates Oct.–Feb.; ovulation Feb.–April. Sexes segregate in summer.

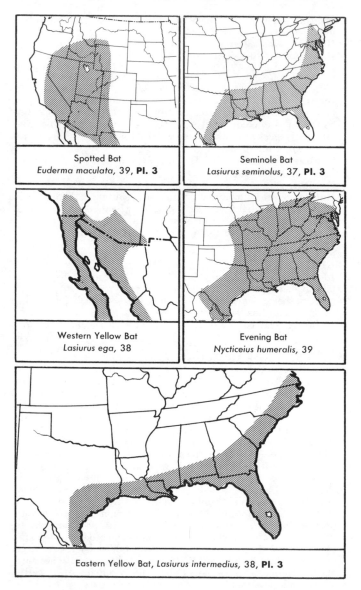

Spotted Bat
Euderma maculata, 39, **Pl. 3**

Seminole Bat
Lasiurus seminolus, 37, **Pl. 3**

Western Yellow Bat
Lasiurus ega, 38

Evening Bat
Nycticeius humeralis, 39

Eastern Yellow Bat, *Lasiurus intermedius,* 38, **Pl. 3**

Young: Born April – July; normally 1; gestation period 56 – 100 days. Naked; eyes open at 8 – 10 days; flies at 3 weeks; not normally carried by mother.   Map below

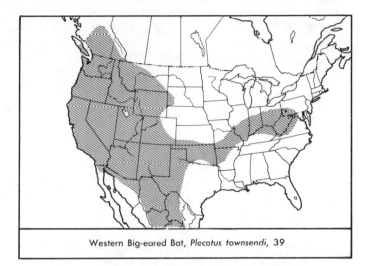

Western Big-eared Bat, *Plecotus townsendi*, 39

EASTERN BIG-EARED BAT *Plecotus rafinesquei*   **Pl.2**
 Identification: Forearm $1\frac{3}{5}$ – $1\frac{4}{5}$ in. (41 – 46 mm); wt. $\frac{1}{3}$ – $\frac{2}{5}$ oz. (9 – 12 g). Within its range, this bat may be distinguished from all others except the Western Big-eared Bat by the *tremendous ears* (over 1 in.; 25 mm, high) *joined in the middle,* and 2 prominent lumps on top of nose. Color pale *brown;* ventral hairs black at bases with white tips. Skull has 36 teeth. There are 2 mammae.
 Formerly known as *Corynorhinus macrotis.*
 Similar species: In the Western Big-eared Bat the bases of ventral hairs are gray or brown, tips brown or buff.
 Habitat: Caves, mine tunnels, buildings.
 Habits: Colonial. Some hibernate, especially in North.
 Young: Born May or June; 1.   Map p. 42

MEXICAN BIG-EARED BAT *Plecotus phyllotis*
 Identification: Forearm $1\frac{4}{5}$ in. (46 mm); wt. $\frac{1}{3}$ – $\frac{1}{2}$ oz. (9 – 14 g). Large ears with lappets or *small lobes* on inner edge near base; *ears joined* by membrane across forehead. Skull has 36 teeth.
 Also known as *Idionycteris* and *Corynorhinus.*

Similar species: (1) Western Big-eared and (2) Pallid Bats have no lappets at inner edge of ears.
Habitat: Caves in pine-oak forests.
Habits: Late flier. Flies rapidly; folds ears back over shoulders or coils them in ram's horn fashion when resting.
Young: Born probably June or July.   Map below

PALLID BAT *Antrozous pallidus*   **Pl. 2**
Identification: Forearm 2–2⅖ in. (51–61 mm); wt. 1–1⅓ oz. (28–37 g). This *large-eared* (over 1 in.; 25 mm high) *pallid* bat has a simple muzzle; ears *not joined*. Color yellowish drab (palest in desert, darkest along North Pacific Coast). Skull (Plate 25) has 28 teeth. There are 2 mammae.
Similar species: (1) Western Big-eared and (2) Mexican Big-eared Bats have the ears joined.
Habitat: Caves, mine tunnels, crevices in rocks, buildings, trees for roosts.

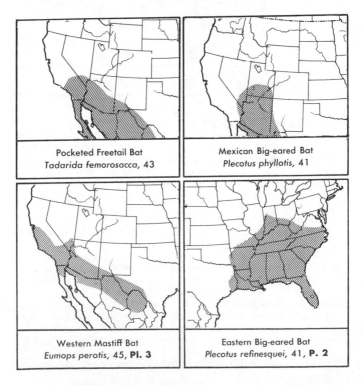

Pocketed Freetail Bat
Tadarida femorosacca, 43

Mexican Big-eared Bat
Plecotus phyllotis, 41

Western Mastiff Bat
Eumops perotis, 45, **Pl. 3**

Eastern Big-eared Bat
Plecotus refinesquei, 41, **P. 2**

Habits: Late flier. Colonial. Night roost, for feeding, different from day roost. Feeds low, near ground; often lands to pick up beetles, Jerusalem crickets, other large insects; 10-12 wingbeats per second. Hibernates in winter. Sexes segregate in summer.

Young: Born April-June; normally 2, occasionally 1 or 3. Naked: eyes closed. Fly at 6 or 7 weeks.   Map p. 44

Freetail Bats: Molossidae

MEMBERS of this family have the tail extending *well beyond edge of tail membrane*. All have short, dense, *dark brown* fur; they give off a *musty odor*. Primarily cave bats, but also found in buildings. Colonial in habits. The Carlsbad Caverns house one of the largest colonies (of Mexican Freetail Bat) in this country. Freetail bats are known from the Lower Oligocene as fossils.

MEXICAN FREETAIL BAT *Tadarida brasiliensis* **Pl. 3**
(Guano Bat)
    Identification: Forearm 1⅗-1⅘ in. (41-46 mm). This is the common freetail bat of s. U.S. Short *velvety fur* is usually *chocolate-brown*. Smallest of the freetails within its range. Ears separate. Skull (Plate 25) has 32 teeth.
        Formerly known as *T. mexicana*.
    Similar species: (1) The Pocketed Freetail and (2) Big Freetail Bats have ears connected at the base. (3) Eastern, (4) Underwood, and (5) Western Mastiff Bats are larger.
    Habitat: Caves and buildings for roosts.
    Habits: Usually in large colonies; some, as those in the Carlsbad Caverns, New Mexico, and Nye Cave, near Bandera, Texas, comprise thousands of individuals. Flies high and fast. Emerges from roosting site at dusk and flies to feeding grounds, sometimes several miles distant. Feeds mostly on moths, but takes other insects also. Migrates south for winter; known to have migrated 800 mi. (1280 km). Has lived 4 years, 5 months in captivity.
    Young: Born late June; usually 1. Weaned in July or Aug.
                    Map p. 44

POCKETED FREETAIL BAT *Tadarida femorosacca*
    Identification: Forearm 1⅘-2 in. (46-51 mm). Ears connected at base. Skull has 30 teeth. This rare bat barely ranges into the U.S. in the Southwest.
    Similar species: (1) In the Mexican Freetail Bat the ears are separate. (2) The Big Freetail, (3) Underwood Mastiff, and (4) Western Mastiff Bats are larger.

Habitat: Caves and crevices in rocks for roosts.
Habits: Little known; may be similar to those of other freetail
bats.   Map p. 42

BIG FREETAIL BAT   *Tadarida molossa*
Identification: Forearm $2\frac{1}{3}$–$2\frac{1}{2}$ in. (59–64 mm). Ears con-
nected at base. Skull has 30 teeth.
Similar species: (1) In the Mexican Freetail Bat the ears are
separate. (2) Pocketed Freetail Bat is smaller. (3) Underwood
and (4) Western Mastiff Bats are larger.
Habitat: Caves, crevices in cliffs, and buildings for roosts.
Habits: Leaves roost when nearly dark. Colonial.
Young: Born late May or early June; 1.   Map below

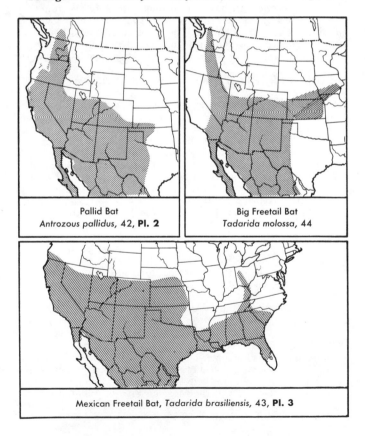

Pallid Bat
Antrozous pallidus, 42, **Pl. 2**

Big Freetail Bat
Tadarida molossa, 44

Mexican Freetail Bat, *Tadarida brasiliensis*, 43, **Pl. 3**

WESTERN MASTIFF BAT   *Eumops perotis*   **Pl. 3**
Identification: Forearm $2\frac{7}{8} - 3\frac{1}{8}$ in. (73 – 79 mm). This is the *largest* of the bats described here. Chocolate-brown. The *free tail,* extending well beyond the membrane, and *large size* serve to distinguish it. Skull (Plate 25) has 30 teeth.
Similar species: (1) Underwood Mastiff Bat and (2) freetail bats are smaller.
Habitat: This bat roosts on or in buildings, crevices in cliffs, in trees, and in tunnels.
Habits: Emerges at late dusk. Normally colonial, but may roost singly. Feeds on various insects, mostly hymenopterous kinds.
Young: Born May – July; usually 1, occasionally 2.

Map p. 42

UNDERWOOD MASTIFF BAT   *Eumops underwoodi*
Identification: Forearm $2\frac{3}{5} - 2\frac{4}{5}$ in. (66 – 71 mm); wt. $1\frac{2}{5} - 2\frac{1}{3}$ oz. (40 – 68 g). Similar to Western Mastiff Bat but slightly smaller. Skull has 30 teeth.
Similar species: (1) Western Mastiff Bat is larger. (2) Freetail bats are smaller.
Habitat: Roosting sites not known.
Habits: Flies late, in fairly straight course; makes high-pitched peeps while flying.
Young: Born July; 1.
Range: In U.S. known only from Pima Co., Arizona.

EASTERN MASTIFF BAT   *Eumops glaucinus*
Identification: Forearm $2\frac{1}{3} - 2\frac{2}{5}$ in. (59 – 61 mm). Similar to Western Mastiff Bat (above) but smaller. Skull has 30 teeth.
Similar species: The Mexican Freetail Bat is smaller.
Range: In U.S. known only from vicinity of Miami, Florida.

Flesh-eaters: Carnivora

THIS ORDER includes those mammals that are primarily *meat-eaters.* Many of them also eat berries, nuts, and fruits, but usually their main diet is flesh. They vary in size from the small Least Weasel (wt. about $\frac{1}{10}$ lb.; 45 g) to the Alaskan Brown Bear (which may weigh more than 1500 lb.; 675 kg). All have *5 toes on front foot;* some have the inner toe high on foot, so that only 4 toes touch the ground. Can have 4 or 5 toes on hind foot. Large *canine teeth* are present in all.

Bears: Ursidae

IN THIS family we have the *largest* living carnivores. They walk
on the entire foot, as does man, have 5 toes on front and back
feet, and have *short tails* that are almost concealed in their long
fur. Ears are relatively small and rounded. Date from Middle
Miocene as fossils.

BLACK BEAR (Cinnamon Bear)   *Ursus americanus*   **Pl. 4**
  Identification: Head and body 5–6 ft. (152–183 cm); height at
  shoulders 2–3 ft. (61–91 cm); wt. 200–475+ lb. (90–214+ kg).
  Color varies from *black* (in East) to *cinnamon* or black (in West)
  to *nearly white* (on Gribble I., B.C.). The "Blue" or "Glacier"
  Bear from near Yakutat Bay, Alaska, is probably a color phase
  of the Black Bear. Face in profile, straight or Roman, always
  brown. There is usually a small patch of *white* on breast.
  Commonest and most widely distributed of the bears; also the
  smallest. Skull (Plate 31) has 42 teeth. There are 6 mammae.
  Similar species: (1) Grizzly and (2) Alaskan Brown Bears are
  larger; have a hump above shoulders and a dish-faced profile.
  Habitat: In East, primarily forests and swamps; in West, chiefly
  mountainous areas.
  Habits: Primarily nocturnal, but occasionally abroad at mid-
  day. Usually solitary, except female with cubs. Eats berries,
  nuts, tubers, insects and their larvae, small mammals, eggs,
  honey, carrion, garbage. Dens beneath down tree, in hollow log
  or tree, beneath roots, or wherever there is shelter. Semihiber-
  nates in winter in North. Males may range 15 mi. (24 km) or
  more, females less. Speed more than 30 mph (48 kmph) for short
  distances. Sight poor, hearing moderate, sense of smell good.
  Voice varies from a loud growl when fighting to a *woof-woof*
  to warn cubs of danger and a whimper to call cubs. May live
  30 years or more.
  Young: Born in winter den, Jan. or Feb.; normally 2, occasionally 1 or 3, reported maximum of 6; gestation period 7–7½
  months; 1 litter every other year; wt. 7–12 oz. (198–340 g).
  Eyes open at 25–30 days; weaned in Aug. but may stay with
  mother for 1 year; first mate at 3½ years.
  Economic status: An important game animal; occasionally
  attacks young domestic animals and does damage to apiaries
  and fruit trees where man's activities border on wilderness
  areas. May be seen in most of the parks within its range, particularly in West.   Map p. 49

GRIZZLY BEAR   *Ursus horribilis*   **Pl. 4**
  Identification: Head and body 6–7 ft. (180–213 cm); height at

shoulders 3–3½ ft. (91–107 cm); wt. 325–850 lb. (146–382 kg).
Color ranges from pale *yellowish* to dark brown, *nearly black;*
usually white tips on hairs, especially on the back, giving it the
frosted or *grizzly* effect. Dish-faced in profile. Claws on front
feet long (about 4 in.; 102 mm) and curved. A *noticeable hump*
is present above shoulders. Skull has 42 teeth. There are 6
mammae.

Some authors recognize as many as 74 "species" of Grizzly
Bears, while others recognize as few as only 1 (*Ursus arctos*)
for North America, Asia, and Europe. Obviously, 74 is too
many, and to try to treat them separately would lead only to
confusion. These are all treated as Grizzly Bears here, but this
does not imply that all belong to the same species *horribilis.*
Most of them probably do. *U. inopinatus,* the Yellow Bear,
from Rendezvous Lake, Mackenzie, Canada, may be distinct.
Similar species: (1) The Alaskan Brown Bear is larger. (2)
Black Bear is smaller; profile of face not dished; no distinct
hump in shoulder region.
Habitat: High mts. of West and onto tundra in the Far North;
wilderness areas.
Habits: Prefers twilight hours, but may be abroad any time
of day or night. Mostly solitary or in small family groups. Eats
meat, fruit, grass, grubs, or any edible material; digs small
rodents from dens, gorges on salmon during runs. May dig own
den on slope. Hibernates in North and in high mts. in winter.
Home range may be 50 mi. (80 km), but usually less than half
that. Uses trails over and over, stepping in same footprints.
Lives 25 years or more in captivity. Breeds first when 3 years
old, then in alternate years or at 3-year intervals. Mates May–
July.
Young: Born Jan.; usually 2, sometimes 3, rarely 4; gestation
period about 6 months; wt. 10–24 oz. (280–780 g). Nearly
naked; eyes open at about 10 days.
Economic status: A magnificent game animal that should be
preserved; now restricted to wilderness areas, particularly our
national parks, Glacier, Yellowstone, Banff, Jasper, and Mt.
McKinley.   Map p. 48

ALASKAN BROWN BEAR *Ursus middendorffi*   **Pl. 4**
(Kodiak Bear, Big Brown Bear)
Identification: Head and body about 8 ft. (244 cm); height at
shoulders 4–4½ ft. (122–137 cm); wt. to 1500 lb. (675 kg).
Largest of the bears. Dish-faced in profile. A *noticeable hump*
is present above shoulders. Claws relatively smaller than Grizzly's, but size is the best character separating the two. Color
ranges from *yellowish to dark brown,* often with white-tipped
hairs. Skull (Plate 31) has 42 teeth.

According to some authors there are 9 species of Alaskan
Brown Bears; others would place them in the species *arctos* with

the Grizzly Bear. All are included under one general heading
here. Those from the islands off Alaska are: *arctos* from St.
Lawrence I. (1 reported); *sitkensis,* Baranof and Chicagof Is.;
shirasi, Admiralty I.; *nuchek,* Hinchinbrook I. and mainland;
middendorffi, Kodiak I.; and *sheldoni,* Montague I. Mainland
forms are: *gyas, dalli,* and *kenaiensis.*

Similar species: (1) The Grizzly Bear is smaller. (2) Black
Bear is smaller, not dish-faced.

Habitat: Alaskan coast and adjacent islands; forests and open
country, but near the sea.

Habits: Active day and night; usually solitary. Emerges in
April, when it feeds primarily on seaweed and carrion; in spring
and early summer grazes on grasses, forbs, and sedges; turns
to fish during salmon run, then to berries in fall; eats mice
whenever available, also stranded whales; omnivorous in diet,
but eats more plant than animal food. Dens up in late autumn,
but may appear in midwinter. Unprovoked attacks on man
rare; dangerous if wounded or if cubs or food threatened. Lives
20 years or more in captivity. Mates in July. In captivity has
crossed with Polar Bear.

Young: Born Jan.; 1–4; usually 2, probably every 3rd year;
wt. about 1½ lb. (680 g). Naked; eyes open at about 6 weeks;
remain with mother for year or more.

Economic status: One of the most prized of the big game

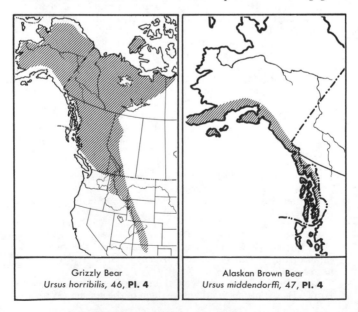

Grizzly Bear
Ursus horribilis, 46, **Pl. 4**

Alaskan Brown Bear
Ursus middendorffi, 47, **Pl. 4**

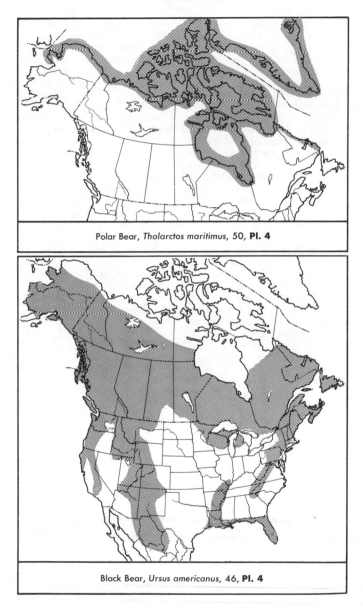

Polar Bear, *Thalarctos maritimus*, 50, **Pl. 4**

Black Bear, *Ursus americanus*, 46, **Pl. 4**

mammals. Eats some salmon on their way up streams, but many that it consumes have already spawned. We should be able to spend a few salmon for this largest of all carnivores; it would be tragic if it were to disappear from the Alaskan wilderness. Map p. 48

POLAR BEAR *Thalarctos maritimus* Pl. 4
Identification: Head and body 6½–7½ ft. (198–203 cm); height at shoulders 3–4 ft. (91–122 cm); wt. 600–1100 lb. (270–495 kg) or more. By its large size and *white* or pale *yellowish-white* fur it may be distinguished from all other bears within its range. Eyeshine pale silvery blue. Skull has 42 teeth.
Polar Bears on the eastern coast of Greenland and along coast of Labrador are usually listed as distinct species (*T. eogroenlandicus* and *T. labradorensis*). Some authors place the Polar Bear in the genus *Ursus*.
Habitat: Ice floes and barren rocky shores and islands.
Habits: Solitary, except during mating season in midsummer or when mother is with cubs. A strong swimmer, keeps head and neck out of water; readily takes to water when endangered, and will float if killed there. Feeds mostly on seals, but feasts on stranded whales or other dead animals on shore; also eats birds and their eggs as well as vegetation if available. Dens in deep snowbank in winter; emerges in late March. Apparently has good sense of smell and sight. Lives 30 years or more in captivity. Breeds in alternate years. In captivity has crossed with Alaskan Brown Bear.
Young: Born in winter den; normally 2, sometimes 1; gestation period probably 7–8 months. Stay with mother at least until next winter.
Economic status: In Canada, an important food animal for Eskimos and their dogs; protected from trophy hunters. Liver toxic because of concentration of vitamin A, but remainder edible. Hide used for bedding, formerly for clothing.
Map p. 49

Raccoons and Coatis: Procyonidae

MEMBERS of this family are of medium size, about that of a small dog. They have 5 toes on each foot with nonretractile claws, and walk on entire foot. Tail has distinct *yellowish-white rings* or very indistinct rings. Date from Lower Miocene as fossils.

RACCOON (Coon, Ringtail) *Procyon lotor* Pl. 9
Identification: Head and body 18–28 in. (46–71 cm); tail 8–12 in. (20–30 cm); wt. 12–35 lb. (5.4–15.8 kg). Often seen

dead along highway. Body pepper-and-salt mixture. May be recognized by *black mask* over eyes and alternating *rings* of yellowish white and black on tail. Skull (Plate 29) has 40 teeth. There are 6 mammae.

Similar species: (1) Ringtail has a slender body and the tail is as long or longer than head and body. (2) In the Coati the tail is as long as head and body and is indistinctly ringed.

Habitat: Along streams and lake borders near wooded areas or rock cliffs.

Habits: Chiefly nocturnal, but occasionally abroad during day. Feeds mostly along streams and lakes; omnivorous; eats fruits, nuts, grains, insects, frogs, crayfish, bird eggs — anything available; may dunk food in water before eating. Dens up in hollow trees (usually), hollow logs, rock crevices, or ground burrows during cold spells in North, but does not hibernate. Home range up to 2 mi. (3.2 km) across, normally less than 1 mi. (1.6 km); young known to disperse up to 165 mi. (264 km) from birth place, mostly less than 30 mi. (50 km). Recorded population of 1 per acre (0.4 ha) (highest) to 1 per 15 acres (6 ha) (considered high). Captives live to 14 years. Voice variable. A low twittering sound from the mother assures young, but growls and snarls denote anger. Some females mate 1st year; mate Feb.–March in North, earlier in South.

Young: Born April or May; 2–7, average 4; gestation period

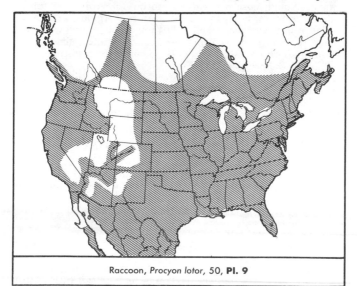

Raccoon, *Procyon lotor*, 50, **Pl. 9**

63 days; 1 litter a year; wt. 2½ oz. (85 g). Eyes open in about 3 weeks. Abroad with mother at 2 months; leave mother in fall. **Economic status:** May damage roasting-ear corn and raid poultry yards; for many, value of pelts and pleasure of seeing them in the wild outweighs harm done; meat edible.

Map p. 51

COATI   *Nasua narica*   **Pl. 9**
   Identification: Head and body 20–25 in. (51–63 cm); tail 20–25 in. (51–63 cm); wt. 15–25 lb. (6.8–11.3 kg). This *long-snouted* grizzled-brown invader from the tropics barely enters s. U.S. The *long tail,* which is often carried erect, is indistinctly ringed. There are *white spots above and below each eye.* Has 5 toes on each foot, and walks on entire foot. *Nose whitish.* Eyeshine blue-green to gold. Skull (Plate 29) has 40 teeth. There are 6 mammae.
   Similar species: (1) In the Raccoon and (2) Ringtail the tail is distinctly ringed.
   Habitat: Open forests in U.S.
   Habits: More active by day than at night. Usually runs in bands of up to a dozen, but old males may be solitary. An excellent climber; uses tail to balance on branches, also as brake by wrapping it around small branches or vines when descending headfirst; when on ground, tail held nearly vertical. Omnivorous; a tough nose pad aids in rooting for grubs and tubers; also eats fruits, nuts, bird eggs, lizards, scorpions, and tarantulas; rolls poisonous and other arthropods on ground with front paws to remove scales, wings, etc., before eating them.
   Young: Born probably July in this area; 4–6; gestation period about 2½ months.
   Economic status: Has little effect on man's activities; an interesting animal that is rare in U.S.   Map opposite

Ringtails: Bassariscidae

SOME authors consider the Ringtails a subfamily of the Procyonidae. They have long slender bodies, tail as long as head and body, short legs, large ears and eyes, semiretractile claws, and distinct black and white bands on the bushy tail. Date from Upper Miocene as fossils.

RINGTAIL   *Bassariscus astutus*   **Pl. 9**
(Ringtail Cat, Miner's Cat)
   Identification: Head and body 14–16 in. (36–41 cm); tail 15 in. (38 cm); wt. 2–2½ lb. (900–1130 g). The *long tail* with whitish

and blackish-brown rings will identify the Ringtail. Body pale yellowish gray. Has thick fur between pads on feet. Eyeshine red to yellowish green. The only species of this family occurring north of the Mexican border. Skull (Plate 30) has 40 teeth. There are 6 mammae.

Similar species: (1) Raccoon has a shorter tail and a black mask. (2) Coati has a tail indistinctly ringed.

Habitat: Chaparral, rocky ridges and cliffs; near water.

Habits: Nocturnal. May be partially colonial, usually 2 (a pair) together. Feeds chiefly on small mammals, insects, birds, and fruits; also eats lizards and various invertebrates. Dens in caves or crevices along cliffs, in hollow trees, under rock piles, or in unused buildings. Populations of 5–10 per sq. mi. (259 ha) considered high. Has lived 8 years in captivity. When agitated, makes a coughing bark similar to that of a fox; also whimpers.

Young: Born May or June; 3–4; 1 litter a year. Covered with white fuzz; eyes open in 4–5 weeks. Go abroad at 2 months; leave mother in Aug. or Sept.

Economic status: Fur occasionally of some value; a good mouser; probably wholly beneficial.   Map below

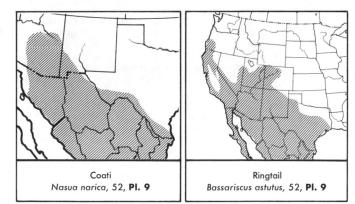

Coati
Nasua narica, 52, **Pl. 9**

Ringtail
Bassariscus astutus, 52, **Pl. 9**

Weasels, Skunks, etc.:
Mustelidae

MEMBERS of this family are varied in size and color. Usually they have long slender bodies and short legs, short, rounded ears, and anal scent glands. In many species, males are distinctly larger than females. Date from Lower Oligocene as fossils.

MARTEN *Martes americana* **Pl. 5**
Identification: Head and body: males, 16–17 in. (41–43 cm); females, 14–15 in. (35–38 cm). Tail: males, 8–9 in. (20–23 cm); females, 7–8 in. (18–20 cm). Wt.: males, $1\frac{2}{3}$–$2\frac{3}{4}$ lb. (754–1248 g); females, $1\frac{1}{2}$–$1\frac{7}{8}$ lb. (681–851 g). This graceful furbearer has soft, dense, *yellowish-brown* fur shading to *dark brown* on bushy tail and on legs. Has a *pale buff patch* on throat and breast, and belly is paler than back. Skull (Plate 29) has 38 teeth. There are 8 mammae.
Similar species: (1) Mink has white patch on chin. (2) Fisher is larger, dark brown; grizzled on head and back. (3) Red Fox has a white tip on tail.
Habitat: Fir, spruce, and hemlock forests preferred in West; cedar swamps in East.
Habits: Chiefly nocturnal. Spends much time in trees, but also forages and moves on ground. Eats chiefly red squirrels and other small mammals, but varies diet with insects, birds, fruits, and nuts. Dens in hollow tree or log. Normal home range 1 sq. mi. (259 ha) for male, $\frac{1}{4}$ sq. mi. (65 ha) for female; may range as far as 15 mi. (24 km). Population of 2 per sq. mi. (259 ha) probably high. Has lived 17 years in captivity. Mates in late July or early Aug.
Young: Born April; 2–4; gestation period $8\frac{1}{2}$–9 months; wt. 1 oz. (28 g). Covered with fine yellowish hair; eyes open at 5–6 weeks; weaned at 6–7 weeks. May breed 1st year.
Economic status: Valuable as a furbearer; lives in areas remote from civilization, so does not interfere with man's activities.
Map opposite

FISHER (Pekan) *Martes pennanti* **Pl. 5**
Identification: Head and body 20–25 in. (51–63 cm); tail 13–15 in. (33–38 cm). Wt.: males, 6–12 lb. (2.7–5.4 kg); females, 3–7 lb. (1.4–3.2 kg). This magnificent furbearer is *dark brown to nearly black, with white-tipped hairs* over most of its body, giving it a *frosted* appearance. Long, slim body and bushy tail. Skull has 38 teeth. There are 4 mammae.
Similar species: (1) Marten is smaller and has a buffy patch on throat and breast. (2) Wolverine has yellowish stripes on sides and rump. (3) Red Fox has a white tip on tail.
Habitat: Extensive mixed hardwood forests, cutover wilderness areas.
Habits: Active day and night. At home both on ground and in trees. Feeds primarily on small mammals, birds, carrion, fruits, and fern tips; one of few predators that feed on Porcupines. Dens in hollow tree or in ground. Home range about 10 sq. mi. (2590 ha) males range farther than females. Has lived more than 9 years in captivity. Mates soon after young are born.

Young: Born late March or early April; 1-4; gestation period 11-12 months.
Economic status: A valuable furbearer; also beneficial to forests by destroying Porcupines.   Map below

SHORTTAIL WEASEL (Ermine) *Mustela erminea*   Pl. 6
Identification: Head and body: males, 6-9 in. (15-23 cm);

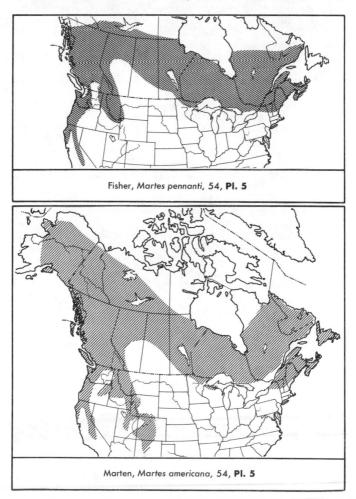

Fisher, *Martes pennanti,* 54, **Pl. 5**

Marten, *Martes americana,* 54, **Pl. 5**

females, 5 - 7 $\frac{1}{2}$ in. (13 - 19 cm). Tail: males, 2 $\frac{1}{4}$ - 4 in. (58 - 102 mm; females, 2 - 3 in. (51 - 76 mm). Wt.: males, 2 $\frac{1}{2}$ - 6 oz. (71 - 170 g); females, 1 - 3 oz. (28 - 85 g). Largest in East and North, smallest in West. Males are distinctly larger than females. *Dark brown* with *white underparts and feet* in summer; *white in winter,* except along Pacific Coast, where it is light brown; always has *black tip on tail.* In summer, has a *white line down hind leg,* connecting the white of underparts with that of toes. Skull has 34 teeth. There are 8 - 10 mammae.

Similar species: (1) Longtail Weasel is larger, both sexes; tail longer; no white line on hind leg. (2) Least Weasel has no black tip on tail. (3) Mink is of uniform color and is larger.

Habitat: Brushy or wooded areas, usually not far from water.

Habits: Chiefly nocturnal, but also hunts during day. Climbs trees, but more at home on ground. Food mostly small mammals (mice) and a few birds, but other animals also consumed; kills by piercing skull with canine teeth. Dens in ground burrows, under stumps, rock piles, or old buildings; nest usually contains fur of mice. Home range probably 30 - 40 acres (12 - 16 ha); may move 3 mi. (5 km) or more; has returned 2 mi. (3 km) to homesite. Population high of 20 per sq. mi. (259 ha) in good habitat. Voice a shrill shriek when agitated or seizing prey.

Young: Born April - May; 4 - 8; gestation period 8 $\frac{1}{2}$ - 10 months; 1 litter a year. Definite mane on neck; eyes open at 30 - 45 days.

Economic status: Beneficial; an expert mouser. Winter pelts (ermine) of some value when fur prices are high; rarely destroys poultry. Map opposite

LEAST WEASEL *Mustela rixosa* **Pl. 6**

Identification: Head and body: males, 6 - 6 $\frac{1}{2}$ in. (150 - 165 mm); females, 5 $\frac{1}{2}$ - 6 in. (140 - 152 mm). Tail: males, 1 $\frac{1}{5}$ - 1 $\frac{1}{2}$ in. (30 - 38 mm); females, 1 - 1 $\frac{1}{5}$ in. (25 - 30 mm). Wt.: males, 1 $\frac{2}{5}$ - 2 $\frac{1}{4}$ oz. (39 - 63 g); females, 1 $\frac{1}{3}$ - 1 $\frac{2}{5}$ oz. (38 - 39 g). The *smallest* living carnivore. Brown above, whitish below in summer; white all over in winter except in South, where it may be partially white. Sometimes a few black hairs, but *no black tip,* at end of short tail. Rare throughout most of its range. Skull has 34 teeth. There are 8 mammae.

Some authors consider this the same as the Old World species, *M. nivalis.*

Similar species: (1) Both Shorttail and (2) Longtail Weasels have black tip on tail.

Habitat: Meadows, fields, brushy areas, and open woods.

Habits: Most active at night. Feeds almost entirely on mice; often caches several near nest. Kills by biting through base of skull; death of prey nearly instantaneous. May take over re-

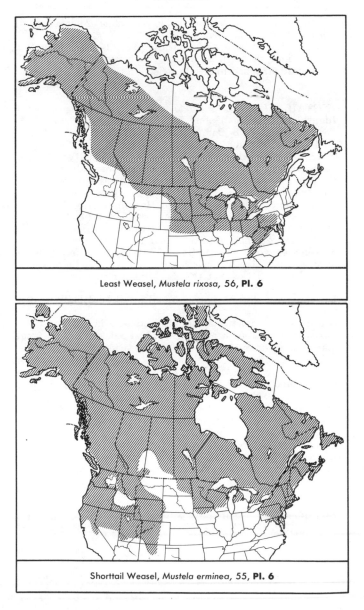

Least Weasel, *Mustela rixosa*, 56, **Pl. 6**

Shorttail Weasel, *Mustela erminea*, 55, **Pl. 6**

vamped mouse nest. Normal home range about 2 acres (0.8 ha).
Voice a shrill shriek when agitated.
Young: May be born any month of year; 3–10, usually 4–5;
may be more than 1 litter a year.
Economic status: Entirely beneficial; a very effective mouser.

Map p. 57

LONGTAIL WEASEL   *Mustela frenata*   **Pl. 6**
Identification: Head and body; males, 9–10½ in. (228–
266 mm); females, 8–9 in. (203–228 mm). Tail: males, 4–6 in.
(102–152 mm); females, 3–5 in. (76–127 mm). Wt.: males,
7–12 oz. (198–340 g); females, 3–7 oz. (85–198 g). Distinguished by its long slender body, long neck (head slightly larger
than neck), *yellowish-white underparts,* black tip on tail, and
no whitish line down inside of hind leg. In winter, in North,
white except for black tip on tail. In some parts of its range
(Southwest) has a white bridle across face, and head is usually
of a darker brown than body. Most widely distributed weasel.
Skull (Plate 29) has 34 teeth. There are 8 mammae.
Similar species: (1) In Shorttail Weasel, respective sexes
smaller; white line down inside of hind leg. (2) Least weasel
is smaller; no black tip on tail. (3) Mink is nearly uniform dark
brown.
Habitat: Not restricted; it is found in all land habitats near
water.
Habits: Chiefly nocturnal, but also active by day. Climbs trees,
but spends most of time on ground. Feeds mostly on small
mammals up to rabbit size; also takes a few birds and other
animals; kills by piercing skull with canines. Usually nests in
old burrows of other animals, sometimes under wood or rock
piles. Home range normally 30–40 acres (12–16 ha). Population of 15–20 per sq. mi. (259 ha) is probably high. Voice a
high-pitched shriek. Mates in July or Aug.
Young: Born late April or early May; 4–8; gestation period
205–337 days. Eyes open at 35 days; males mate at 1 year,
females at 3–4 months.
Economic status: Beneficial; kills many small rodents and
seldom kills poultry. Fur (ermine) of some value.

Map opposite

BLACK-FOOTED FERRET   *Mustela nigripes*   **Pl. 6**
Identification: Head and body 15–18 in. (38–46 cm); tail
5–6 in. (13–15 cm); wt. (2 males) 2⅛, 2⅜ lb. (964, 1078 g). This
large weasel-like mammal may be recognized by its *yellowish-
brown to buffy* body, *black forehead,* black-tipped tail, and
black feet. Skull has 34 teeth.
Similar species: Kit Fox has bushy tail and its feet are not
black.

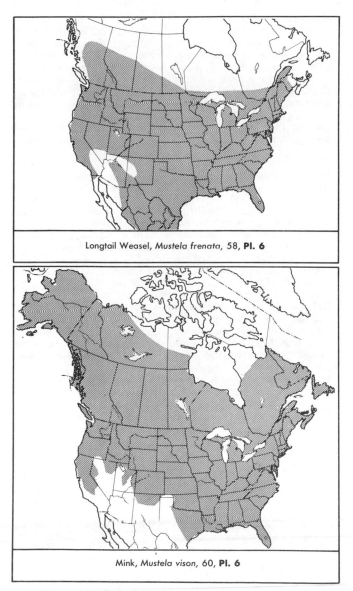

Longtail Weasel, *Mustela frenata*, 58, **Pl. 6**

Mink, *Mustela vison*, 60, **Pl. 6**

Habitat: Prairies.

Habits: Usually found in prairie dog towns, but may occur elsewhere. Feeds on prairie dogs and any other animal that it can overpower. The decrease, owing to poison campaigns, in number and extent of prairie dog towns has undoubtedly brought about a decrease in numbers of Black-footed Ferrets. There is hope that the Black-footed Ferret, although an endangered species, can adapt to other areas and thereby survive the decline of its prey.

Young: Born June; 2–5 observed with mother; reach adult stage in Aug.   Map opposite

MINK *Mustela vison*   **Pl. 6**
Identification: Head and body: males, 13–17 in. (33–43 cm); females, 12–14 in. (30–36 cm). Tail: males, 7–9 in. (18–23 cm); females, 5–8 in. (13–20 cm). Wt.: males, 1½–3 lb. (681–1362 g); females, 1¼–2⅖ lb. (567–1089 g). The Mink is usually *rich dark brown* with a *white chin patch,* and sometimes with scattered small white spots on its belly. Tail is slightly bushy. Eyeshine yellowish green. Skull (Plate 29) has 34 teeth. There are 8 mammae.

Similar species: (1) Weasels have white or yellowish underparts. (2) Marten has buffy patch on throat and breast. (3) River Otter is larger.

Habitat: Along streams and lakes.

Habits: Chiefly nocturnal; solitary except for family groups. An excellent swimmer. Feeds primarily on small mammals, birds, eggs, frogs, crayfish, and fish. Dens along stream or lake banks. Males may range several miles along a stream. Mates Jan.–March.

Young: Born April or May; usually 2–6, occasionally as many as 10; gestation period 39–76 days, normally about 42. Eyes open at 25 days. May breed 1st year.

Economic status: One of the most valuable fur animals; occasionally raids a poultry yard.   Map p. 59

RIVER OTTER *Lutra canadensis*   **Pl. 5**
Identification: Head and body 26–30 in. (66–76 cm); tail 12–17 in. (30–43 cm); wt. 10–25 lb. (4.5–11.2 kg). A large weasel-like mammal, *rich brown above,* with a *silvery sheen below,* and with small ears and *broad snout;* feet *webbed,* tail thick at base, tapering toward tip. Eyeshine pale amber. Skull (Plate 29) has 36 teeth. There are 4 mammae. Some authors would place the River Otter in the genus *Lontra.*

Similar species: (1) Beaver (p. 151) has a flat, scaly tail. (2) Mink is smaller; its feet are not webbed. (3) The Sea Otter has a grayish head.

Habitat: Along streams and lake borders.

Habits: Aquatic, but may travel several miles over land to reach another stream or lake. A sociable animal, usually 2 or more travel together. Eats fish, frogs, crayfish, and other aquatic invertebrates. Dens in banks, with entrance below water, or other suitable places. Home range 15 mi. (24 km) or more. Has lived $14\frac{1}{2}$ years in captivity.

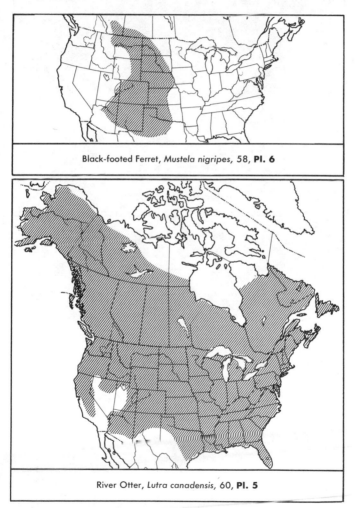

Black-footed Ferret, *Mustela nigripes*, 58, **Pl. 6**

River Otter, *Lutra canadensis*, 60, **Pl. 5**

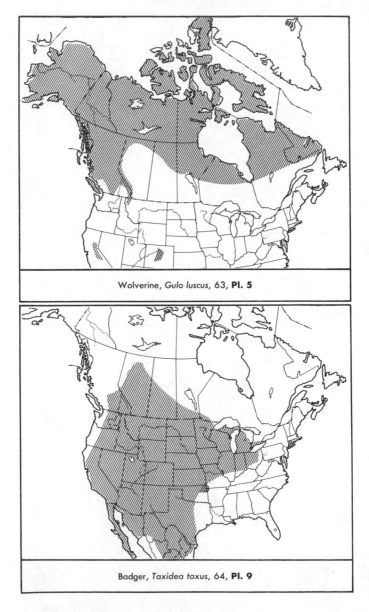

Wolverine, *Gulo luscus*, 63, **Pl. 5**

Badger, *Taxidea taxus*, 64, **Pl. 9**

Young: Born April or May; 1–5, usually 2; gestation period 9½–10 months. Covered with dark brown fur; blind.
Economic status: Fur valuable. Eats some trout, but mostly rough fish.   Map p. 61

SEA OTTER *Enhydra lutris*   **Pl. 5**
Identification: Head and body 30–36 in. (76–91 cm); tail 11–13 in. (28–33 cm); wt. 30–85 lb. (13.5–38.2 kg). *Brownish black, glossy,* with white-tipped hairs, giving it a frosted effect; head and neck grayish or yellowish; feet completely *webbed and flipperlike.* Skull has 32 teeth.
Similar species: (1) Seals and (2) sea lions have shorter tails, well-developed flippers, and shorter fur. (3) River Otter has a dark brown head.
Habitat: Kelp beds and rocky shores.
Habits: Spends most of time resting and feeding among kelp beds. Hauls out onto shore during severe storms. Gregarious. Floats, feeds, and swims on back when not hurried. Brings abalones, sea urchins, and other marine animals to surface and uses chest for table; may bring rock from bottom to break sea urchin on.
Young: Born probably June; 1; body furred, eyes open; wt. about 3 lb. (1.3 kg). Brown, head and shoulders paler than remainder of body.
Economic status: The Sea Otter is fully protected. Fur formerly extremely valuable and ruthlessly sought after. Once thought to be extinct, it is now increasing in numbers. Abalone fishermen begrudge the few abalones eaten by this interesting mammal.
Range: From Aleutian Is. to California. Most likely to be seen off Amchitka I., Alaska, and Pt. Lobos, California.

WOLVERINE (Glutton) *Gulo luscus*   **Pl. 5**
Identification: Head and body 29–32 in. (74–81 cm); tail 7–9 in. (18–23 cm); wt. 35–60 lb. (16–27 kg). In general appearance, except for the bushy tail, the Wolverine looks like a small bear. *Dark brown, paler on the head,* and with *2 broad yellowish stripes* that start at shoulders and join on rump. Feet are large for its size. Skull (Plate 29) has 38 teeth.
  Considered by some to belong to Old World species (*Gulo gulo*).
Similar species: Fisher is without yellowish stripes.
Habitat: High mts. of West, near timberline, and onto tundra in the North; a wilderness mammal.
Habits: Active day or night. Solitary. Feeds on anything available in the form of meat, also larvae, eggs, berries; has reputation for robbing traps and destroying food caches of trap-

pers; travels many miles in search of food. Dens in any sheltered place. Has lived more than 15 years in captivity. Probably territorial. Mates April – Aug.

Young: Born Feb. – April; 2 – 3; probably 1 litter every 2 – 3 years. Yellowish white, blind.

Economic status: Apparently does damage to traplines; fur used primarily for trimming parkas. One of the few remnants of true wilderness, and should be preserved.   Map p. 62

BADGER   *Taxidea taxus*   **Pl. 9**
Identification: Head and body 18 – 22 in. (46 – 56 cm); tail 4 – 6 in. (10 – 15 cm); wt. 13 – 25 lb. (5.8 – 11.2 kg). Sometimes seen along highway in early morning. This heavy-bodied, short-legged, *yellowish-gray* mammal has a *median white stripe* from nose over the top of its head, *white* cheeks, and a *black spot* in front of each ear. Feet *black,* front claws extremely long. Belly and short tail yellowish. No other N. American mammal has above characters. Skull (Plate 29) has 34 teeth. There are 8 mammae.
Habitat: Open grasslands and deserts.
Habits: Mostly nocturnal, but often abroad during day, especially early morning. A great digger; digs out small rodents, its chief food; dens in burrows of own making. Has lived 12 years in captivity.
Young: Born Feb. – May, depending on altitude and latitude; 2 – 5.
Economic status: Destroys many rodents; fur of little value; open burrows may be hazardous to livestock.   Map p. 62

SPOTTED SKUNK   *Spilogale putorius*   **p. 68**
(Civet, Hydrophobia Cat)
Identification: Head and body 9 – 13 ½ in. (23 – 34 cm); tail 4 ½ – 9 in. (11.5 – 23 cm). Wt.: males, 1 – 2 ⅕ lb. (454 – 999 g); females, ⅘ – 1 ¼ lb. (363 – 567 g). Smallest in West, largest in Midwest and East. This handsome little carnivore is *black,* with a *white spot* on the forehead, *1 under each ear,* and with *4 broken white stripes* along *neck, back, and sides.* Tail has a white tip. Relative proportions of white and black vary considerably, but there is no other mammal with a similar color pattern. Eyeshine pale amber. Skull (Plate 29) has 34 teeth. There are 8 mammae.
Habitat: Brushy or sparsely wooded areas, along streams, among boulders; prairies.
Habits: Nocturnal. Will climb trees to escape danger, but normally stays on ground. Stands on front feet and discharges scent directly over its head; does this only in defense. Feeds on mice, birds, eggs, insects, carrion, and some vegetable matter. Nests in burrows, beneath buildings or rock piles. Several may den together in winter. Home range 160 acres (64 ha) or less,

males may wander farther. Populations to 13 or more per sq. mi. (259 ha).
Young: Born May or June; 4–7; gestation period, 120+ days. Weaned at 50 days.
Economic status: Beneficial as destroyer of rats and mice, especially around farm buildings; sometimes kills poultry. Fur of some value. Rabies occasionally detected in these skunks.

Map p. 66

STRIPED SKUNK *Mephitis mephitis*   **p. 68**
Identification: Head and body 13–18 in. (33–46 cm); tail 7–10 in. (18–25 cm); wt. 6–14 lb. (2.7–6.3 kg). Often seen dead along highway. Probably the best-known mammal in this *Field Guide*. About size of a House Cat, it may be recognized by its *black body, narrow white stripe* up middle of forehead, and *broad white area* on nape, which usually divides into a V at about the shoulders. The resulting 2 white lines may continue back to base of bushy tail, which may or may not have a white tip. Much variation in length and width of side stripes. Scent glands well developed. Often the presence of a skunk is first detected by *odor*. Eyeshine deep amber. Skull (Plate 29) has 34 teeth. There are 10–14 mammae.
Similar species: (1) Hooded Skunk has a longer tail; white V on back rarely present. (2) In the Hognose Skunk the white back stripe is not divided.
Habitat: Semi-open country; mixed woods, brushland, and open prairie preferred; normally within 2 mi. (3 km) of water.
Habits: Chiefly nocturnal; starts hunting shortly after sundown and retires at about sunrise. Omnivorous; feeds on mice, eggs, insects, grubs, berries, and carrion. Dens in ground burrows, beneath abandoned buildings, boulders, or wood or rock piles. Several females may den together in winter; males tend to be solitary. Does not hibernate; often appears abroad on warm nights in middle of winter in North; active all winter in South. Population of 1 skunk to 10 acres (4 ha) in good areas is high. Mates Feb.–March.
Young: Born early May; up to 10, usually 5 or 6; gestation period 63 days. Blind. Accompany mother late June or July; follow in single file.
Economic status: One of our most valuable fur animals; single pelt not very valuable, but tremendous numbers are taken. Rarely eats poultry; destroys many small rodents and insects. Makes fair pet if descented, but sometimes carries rabies.

Map p. 66

HOODED SKUNK *Mephitis macroura*   **p. 68**
Identification: Head and body 12–16 in. (30–40 cm); tail 14–15 in. (35–38 cm). This skunk barely enters s. U.S. There are 2 general color patterns, with intermediate variants, in this

species. In one, entire back is chiefly *white,* including tail; in the other, back is nearly all-*black* and there are 2 white side stripes — the belly being *black.* Hair on neck usually spreads

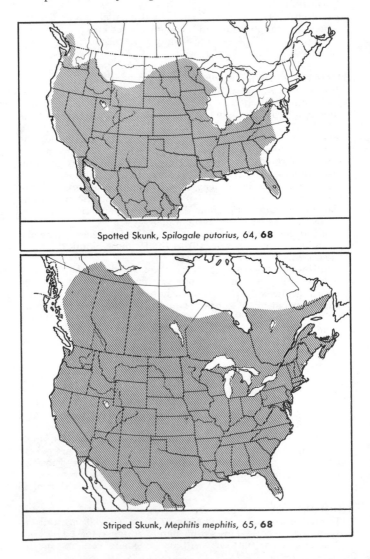

Spotted Skunk, *Spilogale putorius,* 64, **68**

Striped Skunk, *Mephitis mephitis,* 65, **68**

out into a *ruff*. Tail *as long as head and body*. Skull has 34 teeth.

Similar species: (1) Striped Skunk has white V on back, tail shorter. (2) Hognose Skunk has long, bare snout; entire back and tail white, with no black hairs; tail shorter.

Habitat: Along streams, rocky ledges.

Habits: Probably similar to those of Striped Skunk.

Young: Born May–June; 5 embryos reported from 1 female.

Economic status: Probably beneficial; fur of little value; destroys insects and small rodents.   Map below

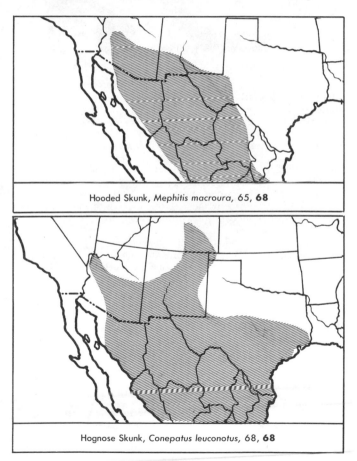

Hooded Skunk, *Mephitis macroura*, 65, **68**

Hognose Skunk, *Conepatus leuconotus*, 68, **68**

Striped Skunk

Spotted Skunk

Hognose Skunk

Hooded Skunk

HOGNOSE SKUNK   *Conepatus leuconotus*   **p. 68**
(Rooter Skunk)

  Identification: Head and body 14–19 in. (35–48 cm); tail
  7–12 in. (18–30 cm); wt. 2–6 lb. (0.9–2.7 kg). This 2-toned
  skunk is well named. It has a long *piglike snout* that is *naked*
  for about 1 in. (25 mm) *on top. Entire back and tail are white*
  and lower sides and belly are black. Fur is short and coarse.
  Skull (Plate 29) has 32 teeth. There are 6 mammae.
    Some authors recognize another species, *C. mesoleucus.*
  Similar species: (1) Striped Skunk has white blaze on forehead. (2) Hooded Skunk, if white on back, usually mixed with
  black; tail longer.
  Habitat: Partly wooded, brushy, rocky areas.
  Habits: Primarily nocturnal, but also active by day. Usually
  solitary. Feeds on insects, mollusks, and other invertebrates;
  also small mammals, reptiles, and vegetation; roots for much
  of its food. Dens in crevices in rock cliffs. Mates in Feb.
  Young: Born April–May; 2–4; gestation period about 2
  months.
  Economic status: Fur of little value; does no appreciable
  damage; destroys small rodents and insects.   Map p. 67

Dogs, Wolves, and Foxes: Canidae

MEMBERS of this family are all *doglike* in general appearance.
They have 5 toes on each front foot (inside toe is high) and 4
on each back foot (some domestic dogs have a 5th toe). All have
a scent gland at base of tail, on top; its position revealed by
black-tipped hairs without underfur. Rabies occurs sporadically

in all members of the family. Known as fossils back to Upper
Eocene.

COYOTE (Brush Wolf)   *Canis latrans*   **Pl. 7**
  Identification: Head and body 32–37 in. (81–94 cm); tail 11–
  16 in. (28–40 cm); wt. 20–50 lb. (9–22 kg). The Coyote looks
  like a medium-sized dog; it is *gray* or *reddish gray, with rusty
  legs, feet,* and *ears;* throat and belly whitish. Nose is more
  pointed and tail is bushier than normal in dogs; tail *held down*
  between hind legs *when running.* Pupil of eye round; nose pad
  less than 1 in. (25 mm) wide. In evening a series of high-pitched
  yaps may be heard, especially on desert. Eyeshine greenish
  gold. Skull (Plate 30) has 42 teeth. There are 8 mammae.
  Similar species: (1) The Red Wolf is usually larger; darker
  color. (2) The Gray Wolf is larger; holds tail high when running;

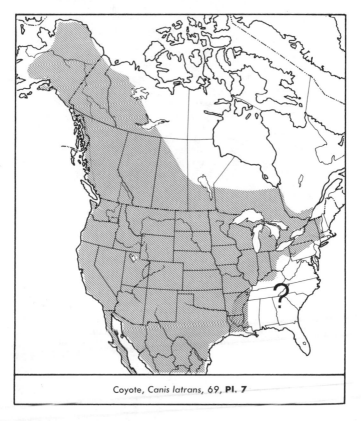

Coyote, Canis latrans, 69, **Pl. 7**

nose pad 1 in. (25 mm) or more wide. (3) Foxes are smaller;
hold tails out straight when running.
Habitat: Prairies, open woodlands, brushy or boulder-strewn
areas.
Habits: Chiefly nocturnal, but may be abroad at any time. A
true scavenger, Coyote will eat almost anything animal or vegetable; food predominantly small rodents and rabbits; sometimes
hunts in pairs; will cache uneaten food; hunting route normally
about 10 mi. (16 km), may move up to 100 mi. (160 km); kills
large animals by attacking at throat. Normally dens in ground,
but often uses other shelter, usually not more than 6 mi. (10 km)
from water. Has lived more than 18 years in captivity; can run
more than 40 mph (64 kmph) for short distances. Mates Jan.–
Feb.; will cross with domestic dog; females breed at 1 year.
Young: Born April–May; 5–10; gestation period 60–63 days.
Eyes open at 9–14 days. Pups brown all over.
Economic status: Since this country was settled there has
always been a bounty somewhere on the Coyote. The bounty
has not reduced its numbers. Much of damage to livestock
attributed to Coyote is probably done by wild dogs. Coyotes
kill many rodents and rabbits, and in this way do a real service
to the rancher. But they may also occasionally kill sheep and
calves. May they never cease to yap on moonlight nights in
the desert! Can be seen, or heard, in most western parks.

Map p. 69

GRAY WOLF (Timber Wolf)   *Canis lupus*   **Pl. 7**
Identification: Head and body 43–48 in. (109–122 cm); tail
12–19 in. (30–48 cm); height at shoulders 26–28 in. (66–71 cm);
wt. 70–120 lb. (31.5–54 kg). Largest of our wild dogs and found
only in wilder parts of its range. Color varies from *nearly white*
(in Arctic) *to nearly black;* usually gray. When running, *tail
is carried high;* ears more rounded and relatively smaller than
those of Coyote; also, more doglike in appearance. Nose pad
more than 1 in. (25 mm) wide. Eyeshine greenish orange. Skull
has 42 teeth. There are 10 mammae.
Similar species: Coyote is smaller; carries tail low when running; nose pad less than 1 in. (25 mm).
Habitat: Wilderness forests and tundra.
Habits: Most active at night, but may be abroad during day;
hunts in packs of up to 12 or more during nonbreeding season.
Both parents bring food to pups. Feeds on anything available,
primarily birds and mammals; deer and caribou constitute most
of big game prey. Hunting area may be 60 mi. (96 km) or more
in diam.; leaves scent posts along trails; often travels single file
in snow. Population estimates range from 1 wolf for 40 sq. mi.
(10,360 ha) to 1 for 100 or more sq. mi. (25,900 ha). Voice a deep
howl; whimpers, whines, and growls normally not heard by

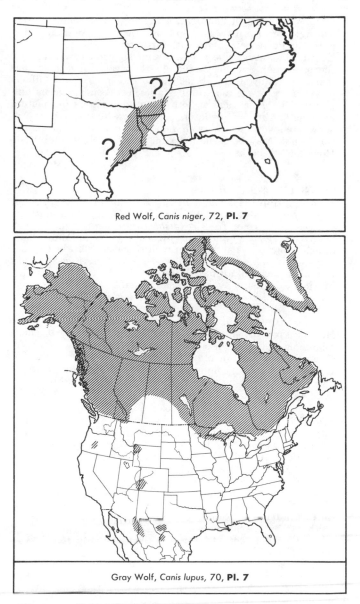

Red Wolf, *Canis niger*, 72, **Pl. 7**

Gray Wolf, *Canis lupus*, 70, **Pl. 7**

man. May breed in 2nd year; mates for season, Jan.–March.
Young: Born April–May; 3–14, usually 6–7; gestation period
9 weeks. Pups sooty black with dirty gray on head.
Economic status: The wolf kills some big game (deer, caribou,
sheep, Moose), but mostly the old, the weak, the diseased are
taken. Actually, this is beneficial to the species; for millions
of years there was a natural relation between predators and
prey, to the advantage of both. Now man enters the picture
and thinks that all predators should be exterminated. Local
control may be necessary in some instances, but extermina-
tion — no! May be seen, or heard, in Mt. McKinley and Isle
Royale Natl. Parks and Algonquin Provincial Park.

Map p. 71

RED WOLF   *Canis niger*   **Pl. 7**
Identification: Head and body 32–40 in. (81–123 cm); tail
13–17 in. (33–43 cm); wt. 40–70 lb. (18–31.5 kg). This southern
wolf varies in color from *reddish gray to nearly black,* with
tawny muzzle, ears, and outer parts of legs. Small individuals
in light-color phase are difficult to distinguish from the Coyote.
Runs with *tail held high,* not down between legs. Eyeshine gold
to bluish green. Skull has 42 teeth.
Similar species: Coyote is usually smaller and reddish gray;
runs with tail between legs; nose pad less than 1 in. (25 mm)
wide.
Habitat: Brushy and forested areas, river bottoms.
Habits: Probably similar to Coyote's. Feeds primarily on small
mammals and birds, also crabs along Gulf Coast.
Young: Born April or May; 4–7 pups.
Economic status: Undoubtedly kills some domestic animals
and game species, but also destroys rodents and rabbits that
compete with grazing livestock.   Map p. 71

RED FOX   *Vulpes fulva*   **Pl. 7**
Identification: Head and body 22–25 in. (56–63 cm); tail 14–
16 in. (35–41 cm); wt. 10–15 lb. (4.5–6.7 kg). Appearance of
small dog; normally *reddish yellow,* darkest on back; belly
white; *bushy tail* mixed with black hairs and *tipped with white;*
legs and feet *black.* There are many color variations: cross, with
dark area (cross) over shoulders and down middle of back; black
phase (silver), black with white-tipped body hairs and white tip
on tail; intermediates between these. Skull (Plate 30) has 42
teeth. There are 8 mammae.
    Some authors consider this and the Old World Red Fox as
one species (*V. vulpes*).
Similar species: (1) There is no white tip on the tail of the
Coyote, (2) Swift Fox, (3) Kit Fox, (4) Gray Fox, (5) Marten
(p. 54), or (6) Fisher (p. 54). (7) Arctic Fox is all-white or
without white tip on tail.

Habitat: Mixture of forest and open country preferred.
Habits: Most active at night, early morning, and late evening; often active during day. Food consists of available animals ranging in size from insects to hares; berries and other fruits round out diet; often caches rabbits, mice, or other animals near trails, especially when there is a cover of snow. Male brings food to vixen for a few days after pups are born; later both bring food to young in den; usually have one or more spare dens so pups may be moved on short notice if home den is disturbed; dens normally on slopes in porous soil. Home range, 1 to 2 sq. mi. (259–518 ha), but often travels greater distances, especially in winter. Known to have moved 126 mi. (202 km) from birth den. Male and female probably mate for the year.
Young: Born March or April, depending on latitude; 4–9; gestation period about 51 days; 1 litter a year. Dark brown with white tip on tail; eyes closed. Pups remain in den for about a month, then come to entrance to play and feed; leave parents in fall and shift for themselves.
Economic status: In much of its range the Red Fox has a bounty on its head. Whether it is beneficial or harmful depends on circumstances. If it kills a few pheasants, grouse, or rabbits, the hunter will consider it harmful, but if it kills hundreds of mice and rats the farmer might consider it beneficial. Many sportsmen enjoy hunting the fox when other seasons are closed. Actually foxes do more good than harm, as shown by many food studies. All bounties should be removed. May be seen in most parks within its range.   Map p. 74

SWIFT FOX   *Vulpes velox*   **Pl. 7**
Identification: Head and body 15–20 in. (38–51 cm); tail 9–12 in. (23–30 cm); wt. 4–6 lb. (1.8–2.7 kg). This small, large-eared, pale *buffy-yellow* fox with a blackish spot on each side of its snout and a *black tip* on its *bushy tail* is now rare over much of its range. Skull has 42 teeth.
Similar species: (1) Red Fox has a white tip on tail. (2) Gray Fox has a black streak along top of tail. (3) Coyote is larger.
Habitat: Open desert and plains.
Habits: Feeds mostly on small mammals, also insects; dens in ground burrows. Less wary than other foxes; easily trapped.
Young: Born Feb.–April; 4–7 pups.
Economic status: Probably wholly beneficial; has suffered from poison campaigns for other predators; should be protected.
                                                      Map p. 74

KIT FOX   *Vulpes macrotis*
Identification: Head and body 15–20 in. (38–51 cm); tail 9–12 in. (23–30 cm); wt. 3–6 lb. (1.4–2.7 kg). A small, slender fox with exceptionally *large ears;* body pale gray washed with rusty; belly whitish; *black tip* on tail. Skull has 42 teeth.

This may be a subspecies of *V. velox*.
Similar species: (1) Red Fox is larger and has a white tip on tail. (2) Gray Fox is larger and has a black streak along top of tail. (3) Coyote is larger. (4) Black-footed Ferret (p. 58) has black feet, tail not bushy.

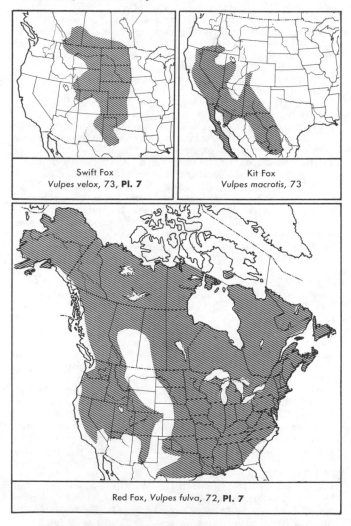

Swift Fox
Vulpes velox, 73, **Pl. 7**

Kit Fox
Vulpes macrotis, 73

Red Fox, *Vulpes fulva,* 72, **Pl. 7**

Habitat: Open, level, sandy ground preferred; low desert vegetation, junipers.
Habits: Remains in burrow during day and forages at night; feeds on small desert rodents.
Young: Born Feb.–April; 4–7 pups.
Economic status: Beneficial; destroys many rodents; now rare because of poison campaigns. Map opposite

ARCTIC FOX *Alopex lagopus* **Pl. 7**
Identification: Head and body 20± in. (51± cm); tail 11± in. (28± cm); wt. 7–15 lb. (3.2–6.7 kg). This far-northern fox has *short, rounded ears* and heavily furred feet, as becomes an arctic mammal. There are 2 color phases, *blue* and *white*. Both phases are similar in summer: dull *brownish* to slate with yellowish white on belly, sides of neck, and flanks. In winter, white phase is *white* throughout; the blue phase is *slate-blue,* sometimes with brownish on head and feet. No white tip on tail. On Pribilof Is. they are all-blue. Skull has 42 teeth.
Similar species: (1) The Red Fox is reddish yellow with a white tip on tail. (2) The Coyote is larger.
Habitat: Tundra of Far North, mostly near shores.
Habits: Scavenger in the true sense; follows Polar Bear in winter and eats scraps from his table; dead marine mammals, fish, or other animals on shore are eaten; also eats lemmings, hares, birds, and eggs, as well as berries in season. Dens on well-drained slopes. Home range limited until pups are able to take care of themselves; wanders widely throughout winter. Populations fluctuate, highs and lows follow those of lemmings by about 1 year. Has lived 14 years in captivity. Not as shy as most other foxes. Voice a sharp bark, heard especially during breeding season.
Young: Born April–June; 1–14 (usually 5–6); gestation period 51–54 days. Pups dark brown, blind.
Economic status: The economy of the Eskimo is closely tied to Arctic Fox abundance; this little fox had a large share in building the Hudson's Bay Company; definitely valuable to the Far North country; ranches established on some islands. Flesh edible. Map p. 76

GRAY FOX *Urocyon cinereoargenteus* **Pl. 7**
Identification: Head and body 21–29 in. (53–74 cm); tail 11–16 in. (28–41 cm); wt. 7–13 lb. (3.2–5.8 kg). Distinguished by the *pepper-and-salt* coat with buffy underfur, long *bushy tail* with a *median black stripe* down its total length (and *tipped with black*), and the rusty-yellowish sides of neck, backs of ears, legs, and feet. Skull (Plate 30) has 42 teeth. There are 6 mammae.
The Gray Foxes on the Santa Barbara Is., California (*U.*

littoralis), and along the Pacific Coast (*U. californicus*) have been considered separate species by some authors. One occurrence at Lake Athabaska, not shown on map.

Similar species: (1) Red Fox has white tip on tail. (2) Swift and (3) Kit Foxes have black on tail only at tip. (4) Coyote is larger.

Habitat: Chaparral, open forests, rimrock country.

Habits: Chiefly nocturnal, secretive. Will climb trees to escape enemies. Omnivorous; eats chiefly small mammals, but adds insects, fruits, acorns, birds, and eggs. Dens in hollow logs, beneath boulders, or sometimes in ground burrows. Has moved over 50 mi. (80 km) from place of release. Has lived 10 years in captivity. Speed of 28 mph (45 kmph) for short distances. Mates in Feb. or March.

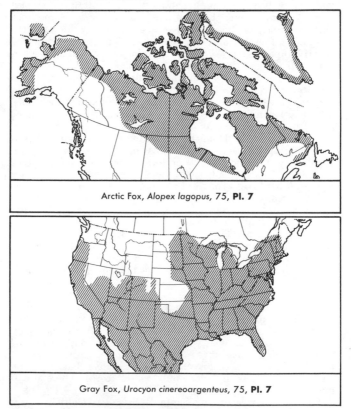

Arctic Fox, Alopex lagopus, 75, **Pl. 7**

Gray Fox, Urocyon cinereoargenteus, 75, **Pl. 7**

Young: Born April – May; 3 – 7; gestation period 51± days. Pups dark brown, blind.
Economic status: Fur of some value. A wonderful mouser; rarely invades poultry yards; probably wholly beneficial. May be seen in most of the western parks.   Map opposite

Cats: Felidae

THIS FAMILY, to which the House Cat belongs, is familiar to most people. Except for color and size, cats all look about alike. They have *short faces,* relatively small rounded ears, and *retractile claws.* There are 5 toes on each front foot, 4 on each back foot. Known as fossils first in Lower Pliocene.

JAGUAR   *Felis onca*   **Pl. 8**
Identification: Head and body 44 – 58 in. (112 – 147 cm); tail 21 – 26 in. (53 – 66 cm); height at shoulder 27 – 30 in. (69 – 76 cm); wt. 150 – 225 lb. (68 – 101 kg). This large tawny cat is uniformly spotted with black. *Spots* on sides and back *form rosettes,* a ring of black with a small black spot in the center; belly white with black spots. Eyeshine golden. Skull has 30 teeth. Rare in s. U.S.
Similar species: (1) Ocelot and (2) Margay Cat are small; spots do not form rosettes. (3) Mountain Lion is of uniform color.
Habitat: Low mts., chaparral, open forests.
Habits: Not well known. Feeds on Peccaries and other mammals, also turtles and fish; preys on livestock when available. Breeds in Jan.
Young: Born April – May; 2 – 4; gestation period 99 – 105 days.
Economic status: Of little importance in U. S. because of its rareness; does destroy domestic stock.   Map p. 79

MOUNTAIN LION   *Felis concolor*   **Pl. 8**
(Cougar, Puma, Panther)
Identification: Head and body 42 – 54 in. (107 – 137 cm); tail 30 – 36 in. (76 – 91 cm); height at shoulders 26 – 31 in. (66 – 79 cm); wt. 80 – 200 lb. (36 – 90 kg). This large, *tawny to grayish* cat, with *dark brown on tip of long tail* and on backs of ears and sides of nose, is fast disappearing from the scene. Eyeshine greenish gold. Skull (Plate 30) has 30 teeth. There are 8 mammae (6 functional).
Similar species: (1) Jaguarundi Cat is smaller. (2) Jaguar is spotted.
Habitat: Rugged mts., forests, swamps.

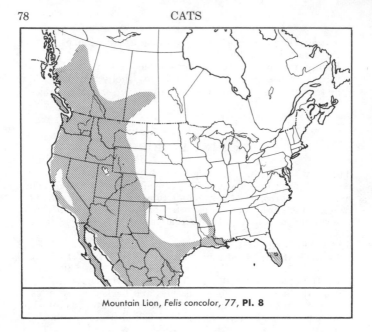

Mountain Lion, *Felis concolor*, 77, **Pl. 8**

Habits: Chiefly nocturnal, but may be abroad during day. Secretive, seldom seen. Most at home on ground, but climbs trees, especially to evade dogs. Feeds largely on deer, but also takes hares, rodents, and occasionally domestic animals; caches uneaten portions of kills; won't eat tainted meat. Dens in any concealed, sheltered spot. Roams widely except when cubs are small; may move 75–100 mi. (120–160 km) from place of birth. Has lived 18 years in captivity. Voice like ordinary tomcat, but much magnified. Breeds first at 2 or 3 years, then every 2 or 3 years; mates for season.

Young: May be born any month of year; 1–6, usually 2; gestation period 88–97 days. Cubs spotted; eyes open at about 10 days.

Economic status: Now inhabits mostly wilderness areas; kills some domestic animals, but mainly deer; a few Mountain Lions are good for the deer herd, but few sportsmen see it this way.

Map above

OCELOT *Felis pardalis*　　　　　　　　　　　　　**Pl. 8**
Identification: Head and body 27–35 in. (69–89 cm); tail 13–15 in. (33–38 cm); wt. 20–40 lb. (9–18 kg). This small, *spotted* cat with a long tail does not have the rosettes of the Jaguar. Some of the *dark markings* are *elongate,* more nearly stripes

than spots. Eyeshine golden. Skull has 30 teeth. There are 4 mammae.

Similar species: (1) Margay Cat is smaller. (2) Jaguar is larger, with rosettes. (3) Jaguarundi Cat has no spots.

Habitat: Thick thorn scrub, rocky areas.

Habits: Probably similar to those of other cats; little known; said to kill some domestic stock.

Young: Born in autumn; normally 2.

Economic status: Skins valuable as trophies; offers sport to the hunter; does little damage because of rareness.

Map below

MARGAY CAT *Felis wiedi*

Identification: Head and body 20–23 in. (51–58 cm); tail 14–16 in. (36–41 cm); wt. 5–7 lb. (2.2–3.2 kg). This *small, spotted* cat rarely gets into s. U.S. A miniature of the Ocelot, it is

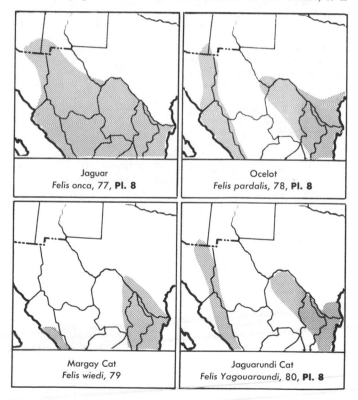

Jaguar
Felis onca, 77, **Pl. 8**

Ocelot
Felis pardalis, 78, **Pl. 8**

Margay Cat
Felis wiedi, 79

Jaguarundi Cat
Felis Yagouaroundi, 80, **Pl. 8**

distinguished chiefly by size. Ground color is buffy. There are 4 broken dark brown stripes on neck and 1 on back; brown spots on sides irregular in shape; some have dark buffy centers, giving a rosette-like appearance. Belly white, with dark brown spots. Skull has 30 teeth.

Similar species (1) Ocelot is larger, coloration similar. (2) Jaguar is larger, with rosettes. (3) Jaguarundi Cat has no spots.

Habitat: Forested areas.

Economic status: Rare in U.S.; does not affect the economy.

Map p. 79

JAGUARUNDI CAT *Felis yagouaroundi*   **Pl. 8**

Identification: Head and body 20–30 in. (51–76 cm); tail 13–24 in. (33–61 cm); wt. 15–18 lb. (6.7–8.1 kg). This long-bodied, short-legged, uniformly colored (either *reddish* or *bluish-gray*) cat is about twice the size of an ordinary House Cat. Tail is nearly as long as head and body. Skull has 30 teeth.

Extremely rare just north of the Mexican border. Formerly known as *F. eyra.*

Similar species: (1) Ocelot and (2) Margay Cat are spotted. (3) Mountain Lion is larger.

Habitat: Brushy areas, thorn thickets.

Habits: Chiefly nocturnal, but hunts also by day. Feeds mostly on small birds and mammals.

Young: 2–3; probably 2 litters a year. Not spotted.

Economic status: Too rare to be of importance; may furnish some sport to the hunter.   Map p. 79

LYNX (Canada Lynx) *Lynx canadensis*   **Pl. 8**

Identification: Head and body 32–36 in. (81–91 cm); tail 4 in. (102 mm); wt. 15–30 lb. (6.7–13.5 kg). This *bobtailed* cat of the north country is distinguished by the short tail, with a *completely black tip,* and *tufted ears.* Skull has 28 teeth. There are 4 mammae.

Similar species: In the Bobcat the tip of the tail is black only on top.

Habitat: Forested areas, swamps.

Habits: Primarily nocturnal and solitary. Extremely large feet enable it to travel easily over deep snow. Feeds for the most part on Snowshoe Hares; diet supplemented with rodents and birds. Dens in hollow log, beneath roots, other sheltered places. Ranges widely, up to 50 mi. (80 km) or more. Breeding range about 5 mi. (8 km). Populations fluctuate, with peak every 9–10 years. Lives 15–18 years in captivity. Mates Jan.–Feb.

Young: Born March–April; 1–4, usually 2; gestation period about 62 days.

Economic status: A valuable fur mammal; also benefits new forests by eliminating Snowshoe Hares.   Map opposite

BOBCAT (Bay Lynx)   *Lynx rufus*   **Pl. 8**
  Identification: Head and body 25–30 in. (63–76 cm); tail 5 in.
(127 mm); wt. 15–35 lb. (6.7–15.7 kg). This cat has a short tail
black only on top at the tip. Ear tufts are short and inconspicuous. Skull (Plate 30) has 28 teeth. There are 6 mammae.

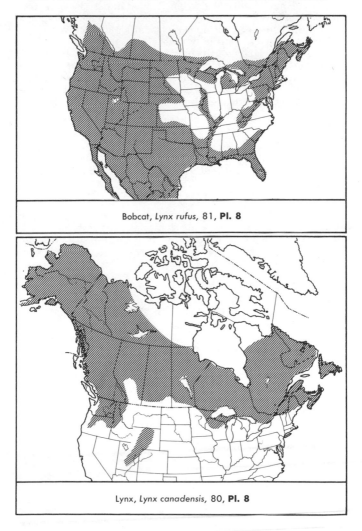

Bobcat, *Lynx rufus*, 81, **Pl. 8**

Lynx, *Lynx canadensis*, 80, **Pl. 8**

Similar species: (1) Lynx has tip of tail black all way around. (2) Other cats have long tail.
Habitat: Rimrock and chaparral areas in West, swamps and forests in East.
Habits: Mostly nocturnal and solitary. Feeds on small mammals and birds; will eat carrion if not tainted. Dens in rock crevices, hollow logs, beneath downfalls. May wander 25 – 50 mi. (40 – 80 km), usually within 2 mi. (3 km) radius. Lives 15 – 25 years in captivity. Normally mates in spring.
Young: Born any month, mostly in spring; 2–4, usually 2; gestation period 50 – 60 days; wt. 4 – 8 oz. (112 – 224 g). Eyes open at 10 – 11 days; leave mother in autumn or following year.
Economic status: Fur of some value; probably beneficial, although some sportsmen think otherwise.   Map p. 81

Sea Lions and Seals: Pinnipedia

MOSTLY MARINE mammals with front and hind limbs developed into *flippers.* They haul out onto land or ice to rest and to give birth to young. Usually seen only *along shores,* although they may go far out to sea when in migration.

Sea Lions and Fur Seals: Otariidae

MEMBERS of this family have external ears (eared seals); hind foot (flipper) can be turned forward so they can "walk" on land. Males are distinctly larger than females (as much as 4½ times). Skull has 34–38 teeth (variable). There are 4 mammae. Known as fossils from Lower Miocene.
Similar Species: Sea Otter is smaller and has a longer tail; usually in kelp bed.
Habitat: Haul out onto rocky beaches and offshore rocks.
Young: Born on land, June – July; normally 1. Pup does not enter water for 2 weeks or more.

NORTHERN SEA LION   *Eumetopias jubatus*   **p. 86**
(Steller Sea Lion)
    Identification: Head and body: males to 10½ ft. (3.2 m); females to 7 ft. (2.1 m). Wt.: males to 2000 lb. (900 kg); females to 600 lb. (270 kg). (Skull, p. 265). *Large yellowish-brown* to

brown sea lions; *low forehead.* Usually fairly *quiet* when not molested.

Similar species: (1) California Sea Lion is smaller and darker; has high forehead; usually barking. (2) Alaska Fur Seal is much smaller; reddish below, face brown. (3) Harbor Seal is smaller, spotted. (4) Elephant Seal is much larger; male has proboscis.

Habits: Gregarious; chiefly marine, but sometimes goes up rivers; able to dive to 480 ft. (144 m). Feeds mostly on fish and squids. Polygamous, harems of 10–15 cows. Breeds soon after pups are born. Gestation period about 1 year.

Economic status: Robs fishermen of some fish; Eskimos use hides to cover boats.

Range: Pacific Coast, south to Santa Rosa I., California. May be seen off coast at San Francisco.

CALIFORNIA SEA LION *Zalophus californianus* **p. 86**

Identification: Head and body: males to 8 ft. (2.4 m); females to 6 ft. (1.8 m). Wt.: males to 600 lb. (270 kg); females to 200 lb. (90 kg). This is a *small brown* (blackish when wet) sea lion with a *high forehead.* Has small, pointed ears and large eyes. *Continual honking bark* is also characteristic. This is the circus "seal."

Similar species: (1) Northern Sea Lion is larger and paler, with low forehead; seldom barks unless molested. (2) Guadalupe Fur Seal has low forehead, pointed nose, and is silvery on neck and head. (3) Elephant Seal is much larger, has no external ears; usually quiet. (4) Harbor Seal is spotted.

Habits: Gregarious; marine, occasionally seen on rocky beaches. Can swim 10 mph (16 kmph) when after food. Principal food, fish and squid. Has lived 23 years in captivity. Polygamous; females breed at 3 years, males at 5. Breeds shortly after pups are born.

Economic status: Does some damage to fishnets; eats fish. Valuable as a trained show animal.

Range: Pacific Coast; from B.C. south to California and coast of Mexico.

GUADALUPE FUR SEAL *Arctocephalus philippi*

Identification: Head and body; males to $5\frac{1}{2}$ ft. (1.7 m); females to $4\frac{1}{2}$ ft. (1.3 m). Wt.: males to 300± lb. (135± kg). This rare fur seal has a *pointed nose;* it is dark brown, with a *silvery grizzling of head and neck.* Sides of snout are rusty.

Formerly known as *A. townsendi.*

Similar species: (1) California Sea Lion is larger and has a high forehead. (2) Elephant Seal is much larger; male has proboscis. (3) Harbor Seal is spotted.

Habits: Marine; now on offshore islands; formerly thought to be extinct; estimated population, mostly off Mexican coast, 200–500.

Range: Pacific Coast, from San Nicolas I., California, south-ward.

ALASKA FUR SEAL   *Callorhinus ursinus*   **p. 86**
 Identification: Head and body: males to 6 ft. (1.8 m); females
 to 4 ½ ft. (1.4 m). Wt.: males to 600 lb. (270 kg); females to
 135 lb. (61 kg). Males *blackish above, reddish on belly,* and gray
 on shoulders and front of neck; face *brownish.* Females gray
 above, reddish below.
 Similar species: (1) Northern Sea Lion is larger; not reddish
 below. (2) Harbor Seal is spotted.
 Habits: Gregarious; spends 6–8 months of each year at sea.
 Top swimming speed 17 mph (27 kmph); can dive to 180 ft.
 (54 m). Feeds on 30 or more kinds of marine animals, mostly
 fish and squid; males can fast for over 2 months. Polygamous;
 harems of 40 or more. Females breed at 3 yr. Breeds soon after
 pups are born, on land. Gestation period 11–12 months.
 Economic status: The Alaskan herd is now managed, and
 about 60,000 of the 3– and 4–year bachelors and 30,000 females
 are harvested each year, pelts for fur and meat for oil and meal.
 The original purchase price of Alaska ($7,200,000) has been
 returned severalfold to the U.S. Treasury through fur seal opera-tions.
 Range: Pacific Coast, south to California. Seen principally on
 the *Pribilof Is.* and at other localities in the Bering Sea. In
 winter, may be seen as far south as San Diego, California.

Walrus: Odobenidae

HIND FEET (flippers) can be turned forward; no external ears; both
sexes have large tusks projecting downward from upper jaw; males
larger than females; nearly nude; 18–24 teeth; 4 mammae.
Known as fossils from Upper Miocene.

WALRUS   *Odobenus rosmarus*   **p. 86**
 Identification: Head and body: males to 12 ft. (3.6 m); females
 to 9 ft. (2.7 m). Wt.: males to 2700 lb. (1215 kg); females to
 1800 lb. (810 kg). A huge seal with 2 *large, white tusks;* bay
 color when dry, black when wet. No other marine mammal has
 these characters.
 Habitat: Ice floes and islands in Arctic.
 Habits: Usually found in groups. Bottom-feeder in fairly
 shallow water — 300 ft. (90 m) or less; grubs mollusks and other
 marine life from bottom with tusks; rarely swallows any shell;
 occasionally eats seals. When killed, will sink. Females first
 breed at 5 or 6 years, then every 2 or 3 years.

Young: Born April–June; 1; gestation period 11–12 months. Wt. to 130 lb. (60 kg); length 48 in. (122 cm). Calf remains with mother 2 years.

Economic status: One of the most important marine mammals for the Eskimo economy; hide used for lines, boats, etc., meat for dogs as well as Eskimos; meat may contain *Trichinella,* and should be cooked. Ivory carvings bring additional income to the Eskimo.

Range: Arctic waters, south into Hudson Bay and northeastern coast of Ungava Pen., and Bering Sea, Alaska.

Hair Seals: Phocidae

HIND FLIPPERS cannot be turned forward; must wriggle to move on land; no great disparity in sizes of two sexes; ears indicated by openings in skin, no pinnae. Known as fossils from Middle Miocene.

HARBOR SEAL (Common Seal)   *Phoca vitulina*   **p. 86**
Identification: Head and body to 5 ft. (1.5 m); wt. to 255 lb. (115 kg). A small seal; iron-gray with brown spots, brown with gray spots, or uniform silver-gray or brownish black. Skull has 34–36 teeth (variable). There are 2 mammae.

Similar species: (1) Sea lions and (2) fur seals have no spots, have external ears, and can rotate hind flippers forward. (3) Elephant Seal is larger; no spots. (4) Ringed Seal has both spots and streaks along back.

Habitat: Coastal waters, mouths of rivers, and inland lakes; spends much time on shore.

Habits: Often seen at mouths of rivers and in shallow harbors. Has limited seasonal movements. Can remain 20 min. underwater. Feeds on fish, shellfish, and squids. Females first breed at 2 years.

Young: Born on land, early summer; 1, rarely 2; gestation period more than 9 months. Pup bluish gray above, whitish below when born; first whitish pelage usually shed before birth, except possibly in Far North.

Economic status: Eats some commercial fish and damages some fishnets; is utilized as food in Far North; skin of slight value.

Range: Arctic; south into Hudson Bay and Seal Lakes (freshwater) on Ungava Pen.; also south along Atlantic Coast to Carolinas as well as south along Pacific.

RINGED SEAL   *Pusa hispida*
Identification: Head and body to 4½ ft. (1.4 m); wt. to 200 lb.

SEA LIONS AND SEALS

Harp Seal
6 ft. (1.8 m)

Ribbon Seal
5 ft. (1.5 m)

Harbor Seal 5 ft. (1.5 m)

Alaska Fur
Seal 4–6 ft.
(1.2–1.8 m)

Hooded Seal
7–11 ft.
(2.1–3.3 m)

California
Sea Lion
5½–8 ft.
(1.7–2.4 m)

Northern Sea Lion
8–10½ ft.
(2.4–3.2 m)

Bearded Seal
8–10 ft.
(2.4–3 m)

Walrus
10–12 ft. (3–3.6 m)

Elephant Seal
15–20 ft.
(4.5–6 m)

(90 kg). This small, dull *yellowish* to *brownish* seal has *dark spots* and *streaks* that are usually continuous *along the back.* There are pale buffy rings on the sides. Belly is yellowish, sometimes spotted. Skull has 34–36 teeth. There are 2 mammae.

Formerly known as *Phoca.*

Similar species: Harbor Seal has no streaks.

Habitat: Cold waters, usually near ice, not far from shore.

Habits: Not gregarious, but occasionally found in small groups. Either finds open water or keeps hole open in ice in winter. Can remain underwater 20 min.; normally hauls out onto ice to rest and sleep. Feeds mostly on marine invertebrates. Females breed in 5th year.

Young: Born on ice; 1; gestation period about 9 months. Woolly, white pup sheds to darker coat in 2 weeks.

Economic status: Both skin and meat are important in the economy of the Eskimo. Known to carry *Trichinella;* meat should be cooked.

Range: Arctic Ocean, south to Labrador, Hudson Bay, and Bristol Bay, Alaska; also found in freshwater lake (Nettilling) on Baffin I.

RIBBON SEAL   *Histriophoca fasciata*   **p. 86**

Identification: Head and body to 5 ft. (1.5 m). Wt.: males to 200 lb. (90 kg); females to 170 lb. (76 kg). This small, brown seal has *bands of yellowish white* around *neck,* around *front flipper,* and around *rump.* Females less brightly colored than males. The only seal with such markings. Skull has 34–36 teeth. There are 2 mammae.

Formerly known as *Phoca.*

Habitat: Ice packs of Arctic.

Habits: Occurs singly or in small groups; a rare, little known seal. Feeds on fish and squid.

Young: Born on ice in spring; 1. Pup covered with white fur; eyes open. Gestation period about 280 days.

Economic status: Of little importance because of rarity.

Range: Arctic-Pacific, south to Alaska Pen.

HARP SEAL   *Pagophilus groenlandicus*   **p. 86**
(Saddleback Seal)

Identification: Head and body to 6 ft. (1.8 m); wt. to 400 lb. (180 kg). This northern seal is grayish or yellowish, with a *dark brown or black face* and a dark, irregular band that crosses the shoulders and extends back along sides, sometimes over rump. Smaller spots may be present on flippers and neck. Females less distinctly marked or without dark markings; young *yellowish white.* No other seal has these markings. Skull has 34–36 teeth. There are 2 mammae.

Formerly known as *Phoca groenlandica.*
Habitat: Deep seas with drifting pack ice.
Habits: Makes long migrations; can dive 600 ft. (180 m). Feeds
on macroplankton and fish. Lives 30 years or more. Females
breed in 5th year.
Young: Born on pack ice; 1 (occasionally 2). Pup covered with
white fur; eyes open.
Economic status: More than 200,000 seals are harvested annually in w. North Atlantic. Skins of pups are used for clothing,
skins of adults for leather. Oil is extracted from the carcasses.
Range: Arctic-Atlantic; west to mouth of Mackenzie River,
south to Hudson Bay and Gulf of St. Lawrence; rarely south
to Virginia.

GRAY SEAL. *Halichoerus grypus*
   Identification: Head and body; males to 10 ft. (3 m); females
   to 7½ ft. (2.3 m). Wt.: males to 640 lb. (288 kg); females to
   550 lb. (248 kg). A *large* black or grayish seal with a Roman
   nose; *size* and *plain color* characterize it. Skull has 34–36
   teeth. There are 2 mammae.
   Habitat: Rocky shores, temperate waters, strong currents.
   Habits: Dives to 480 ft. (144 m); can remain underwater 20 min.
   Feeds on fish and cuttlefish; a fairly rare seal. Lives 40 years
   or more. Polygamous; harems of about 10.
   Young: Born on land in early winter; 1. Pup covered with white
   fur; eyes open.
   Economic status: Of little importance because of small num-
   bers.
   Range: Labrador, south to St. Lawrence River, rarely to New
   Jersey.

BEARDED SEAL   *Erignathus barbatus*   **p. 86**
(Square Flipper)
   Identification: Head and body: males to 10 ft. (3 m); females
   to 8 ft. (2.4 m). Wt.: males to 875 lb. (373 kg). This seal is
   uniformly dark *grayish to yellowish.* Has a prominent *tuft* of
   long flattened *bristles* on *each side of muzzle,* characteristic of
   this seal and no other. The *3rd digit* of the fore flipper is *longer
   than* the *other digits.* Skull has 34–36 teeth. There are 4
   mammae.
   Habitat: Shallow waters (90–150 ft.; 27–45 m) at edge of ice;
   mouths of creeks, small bays.
   Habits: Solitary except during breeding season, when up to 50
   may be seen on ice; occasionally goes up rivers some distance.
   Swims with head out of water; entire body breaks surface as
   it loops to dive. Feeds on bottom.
   Young: Born on ice; April and May; 1. Pup covered with dark
   fur; eyes open. Gestation period 11 months.

Economic status: A fairly important seal in the economy of the Eskimo. Its thick hide makes good boot bottoms and harpoon lines. Meat should be cooked because of possible *Trichinella* infection.

Range: Arctic waters, south to Bering Sea, Hudson Bay, and Ungava Bay.

CARIBBEAN MONK SEAL *Monachus tropicalis*

Identification: Head and body to 10 ft. (3 m); first and fifth toes of hind flipper longest; uniformly brown, slightly paler below; no spots. Skull has 32-34 teeth. There are 4 mammae. Only seal in Caribbean.

Habitat: Tropical waters.

Habits: Supposedly monogamous; rather sluggish.

Young: Pups black; eyes open.

Range: From s. Texas and Key West south.

HOODED SEAL (Bladdernose) *Cystophora cristata* **p. 86**

Identification: Head and body to 11 ft. (3.3 m); wt. to 900 lb. (405 kg). A *dark gray to slaty-black* seal with *paler sides,* which are *spotted with whitish.* Male has an inflatable bag on top of head. When male is angry this is "blown up" and makes the animal appear more formidable. Skull has 26-34 teeth. No other seal within its range has these characters.

Habitat: Deep waters with thick ice.

Habits: Nomadic. Occurs in small numbers except during breeding and molting times. Feeds on fish and squid. Monogamous.

Young: Born on ice, late Feb.; 1. Pup white or covered with dark fur (white embryonic coat may be shed before birth); eyes open.

Economic status: Numbers have been reduced to where they are of minor importance.

Range: Arctic-Atlantic waters, south to St. Lawrence River; accidentally as far south as Florida.

ELEPHANT SEAL *Mirounga angustirostris* **p. 86**

Identification: Head and body: males to 20 ft. (6 m); females to 11 ft. (3.3 m). Wt.: males to 8000 lb. (3600 kg); females to 2000 lb. (900 kg). These large seals are pale *brown to grayish,* lighter on belly; nearly nude. Old males have large, overhanging, *proboscis-like snouts.* Largest of the seals in their range. Skull has 26-34 teeth.

Similar species: (1) Sea lions and (2) fur seals are much smaller; have external ears; can rotate hind flippers forward. (3) Harbor Seal is smaller and usually spotted.

Habitat: Warm waters, sandy beaches.

Habits: Gregarious; lie close together on sandy beaches and

sleep by day. Feed on small sharks, squid, rays during night; can fast 3 months. Polygamous.
Young: Born on land; 1. Pup covered with dusky brown fur, eyes open. Gestation period, about 350 days.
Economic status: Now fully protected; once nearly extinct.
Range: From B.C. south along Pacific Coast.

Gnawing Mammals: Rodentia

THE ORDER of rodents is made up of small to medium-sized mammals. All are characterized by having only *2 incisors* (gnawing teeth) *above* and *2 below*. There is a distinct *space* between these teeth and the grinding (or cheek) teeth. Most, but not all, have 4 toes on each front foot, 5 on each hind foot. Earliest rodents known as fossils from Late Paleocene.
Similar kinds: Rabbits and Hares. These have a small pair of incisors immediately behind the large upper incisors, not apparent from the outside. They also have short, cottony tails.

Aplodontia: Aplodontiidae

THIS FAMILY of rodents, now restricted to a small strip along the western coast of N. America, contains but 1 species, presumed to be the most primitive living rodent. It has 5 toes on each foot, but the thumb is much reduced and without a claw. Skull (Plate 28) has 22 teeth. There are 6 mammae. Known as fossils from Upper Eocene.

APLODONTIA (Mountain Beaver)   *Aplodontia rufa*   **Pl. 19**
   Identification: Head and body 12–17 in. (30–43 cm); tail 1–1⅕ in. (25–30 mm) wt. 2–3 lb. (900–1350 g). This dark brown rodent, the size of a small House Cat but chunkier, has small rounded ears and small eyes. By size, color, and apparent absence of a tail, it may be distinguished from all other mammals in the area. It looks like a tailless Muskrat.
   Habitat: Forests and dense thickets, usually moist situations.
   Habits: More active at night than during day. Makes extensive tunnels, runways, and burrows beneath dense streamside vegetation; burrows are 6–10 in. (15–25 cm) in diam. Rarely climbs trees. Feeds on herbaceous plants and shrubs of many kinds;

builds hay piles along runways in late summer and early autumn. Home range not known, but probably less than 400 yd.
(360 m). Females first breed at 2 years.
Young: Born March–April; usually 2–3; gestation period
28–30 days; 1 litter a year. Young slate-brown.
Economic status: In the wild areas the Aplodontia is of little
importance, but it can be a nuisance in reforestation projects;
also, it may raid truck gardens and cause general damage by
its persistent burrowing. Meat is strong and the hide is worth-
less. It is an interesting element in the biological world, probably its only asset.   Map below

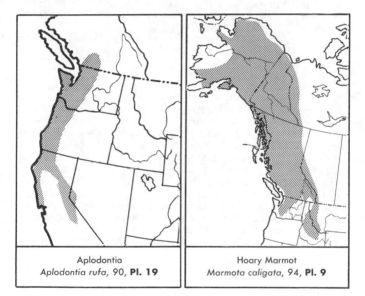

Aplodontia
Aplodontia rufa, 90, **Pl. 19**

Hoary Marmot
Marmota caligata, 94, **Pl. 9**

Squirrels: Sciuridae

THIS family includes a wide variety of mammals. Marmots,
woodchucks, prairie dogs, ground squirrels, chipmunks, and tree
squirrels all belong here. They have 4 toes on front foot, 5 on
back. Tail is always covered with hair, is sometimes bushy. All
are *active during the daytime* except the flying squirrels, which
come out only at night. Marmots, ground squirrels, prairie dogs,
and chipmunks all nest in burrows in the ground or beneath rocks
or logs. Tree squirrels and flying squirrels nest in trees. Most of

the ground-living species have a habit of sitting up "picket pin" fashion on their haunches. This enables them to see over low vegetation and avert danger. Ground squirrels and chipmunks have internal cheek pouches; most of them store food. Known as fossils from as far back as Miocene.

WOODCHUCK (Groundhog, Marmot) *Marmota monax* **Pl. 9**
Identification: Head and body 16–20 in. (40–51 cm); tail 4–7 in. (10–18 cm); wt. 5–10 lb. (2.2–4.5 kg). This heavy-bodied, short-legged, *yellowish-brown to brown* animal is best known in the eastern part of its range. Belly paler than the back; hairs on body have a slightly *frosted* appearance; feet *dark brown or black;* no white except around nose. Skull (Plate 28) has 22 teeth. There are 8 mammae.
Similar species: (1) Hoary Marmot has black and white on head and shoulders. (2) Arctic Ground Squirrel (p. 100) is smaller; feet not black.
Habitat: Open woods, brushy and rocky ravines.
Habits: Diurnal for most part; may wander at night in early spring. Feeds on tender, succulent plants. Dens in extensive burrow with 2 or more openings; may be 4–5 ft. (120–150 cm) deep and 25–30 ft. (8–9.5 m) long; known to have excavated dirt at 1 opening, others dug from below, concealed. Hibernates Oct.–Feb. Home range, 40–160 acres (16.2–65 ha). Voice a shrill whistle. Lives 4–5 years. Mates in March or April; breeds at 1 year.
Young: Born April–May; 2–6; gestation period 31–32 days; 1 litter a year. Naked; blind.
Economic status: In an agricultural area the Woodchuck can do considerable damage to crops; in other areas it is probably beneficial, since its burrows are refuges and homes for many other mammals such as game and furbearers. Map opposite

YELLOWBELLY MARMOT *Marmota flaviventris* **Pl. 9**
(Rockchuck)
Identification: Head and body 14–19 in. (35–48 cm); tail 4½–9 in. (11–23 cm); wt. 5–10 lb. (2.2–4.5 kg). This is a heavy-bodied, *yellowish-brown* marmot with *yellow belly,* and usually with *white between the eyes.* Sides of neck have conspicuous buffy patches. Feet are light buff to dark brown, *never black.* Skull has 22 teeth. There are 10 mammae.
Similar species: Hoary Marmot has conspicuous white and black head and shoulders.
Habitat: Rocky situations, talus slopes, valleys and foothills; up to 12,000 ft. (3658 m) elevation.
Habits: Chiefly diurnal. Feeds on grasses and forbs, relishes alfalfa. Den usually near large boulder, which is used as lookout post. Goes into estivation in late June, hibernation in Aug.;

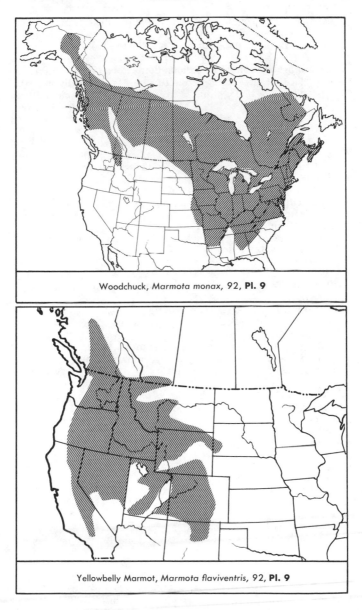

Woodchuck, *Marmota monax*, 92, **Pl. 9**

Yellowbelly Marmot, *Marmota flaviventris*, 92, **Pl. 9**

emerges in late Feb. or March. High-pitched chirp at short intervals warns of danger.
Young: Born March – April; 3 – 6. Emerge from den at about 30 days.
Economic status: Does serious damage to crops, notably alfalfa, locally; away from agricultural areas, especially in parks, has definite aesthetic value. Furnishes sport for some hunters. It hosts the tick for Rocky Mountain spotted fever.

Map p. 93

HOARY MARMOT (Whistler) *Marmota caligata* **Pl. 9**
Identification: Head and body 18 – 21 in. (46 – 53 cm); tail 7 – 10 in. (18 – 25 cm); wt. 8 – 20 lb. (3.6 – 9 kg). These *high-mt.* dwellers may be known by their *shrill whistle* or by the *black and white head and shoulders* and general grayish body washed with yellowish. Feet are *black* and belly is soiled whitish. Seen most commonly around *rockslides.* Skull has 22 teeth. There are 10 mammae.
Similar species: (1) Woodchuck has no black or white on head or shoulders. (2) Yellowbelly Marmot does not have black feet. (3) Arctic Ground Squirrel (p. 100) is smaller; feet tawny, not black.
Habitat: Talus slopes, alpine meadows, high in mts. near timberline.
Habits: Diurnal. Feeds on various herbaceous plants. Goes into hibernation in Sept. and emerges in late spring. Issues clear shrill whistle from lookout post.
Young: Born late spring or early summer; 4 – 5.
Economic status: Does no damage; furnishes pleasure for the alpine hiker interested in nature.   Map p. 91

OLYMPIC MARMOT *Marmota olympus*
Identification: Head and body 18 – 21 in. (46 – 53 cm); tail 7 – 10 in. (18 – 25 cm). Found only on *upper slopes* of *Olympic Mts.,* this brownish-drab marmot, with white intermixed, and with brown feet, is the only one in the area. Similar to Hoary Marmot in habitat and habits; may belong to same species.
Range: Olympic Pen.

VANCOUVER MARMOT *Marmota vancouverensis*
Identification: Head and body 16 – 18 in. (41 – 46 cm); tail 8 – 12 in. (20 – 30 cm). A dark brown marmot, not likely to be confused with any other kind of mammal on Vancouver I. Similar to Hoary Marmot in habitat and habits; may belong to same species.
Range: Vancouver I.

BLACKTAIL PRAIRIE DOG *Cynomys ludovicianus* **Pl. 10**
Identification: Head and body 11 – 13 in. (28 – 33 cm); tail

3–4 in. (76–102 mm); wt. 2–3 lb. (900–1350 g). The presence of the Blacktail Prairie Dog is usually revealed by a group of bare mounds 25–75 ft. (7.6–23 m) apart and each mound 1–2 ft. (30–60 cm) high. If, sitting erect on top of one of these mounds, there is a *yellowish* animal slightly smaller than a cat, it is probably a Blacktail. On closer inspection, it will be found to have the *terminal* ⅓ of its short tail *black*. Ears are small and belly is pale buff or whitish. Skull has 22 teeth. There are 8 mammae.

Similar species: (1) Whitetail Prairie Dog has tip of tail white. (2) Rock Squirrel is smaller, with longer tail.

Habitat: Dry upland prairies.

Habits: Diurnal; gregarious; lives in "towns." Within the town, small groups display territorial behavior toward adjacent groups. At least one is on alert while others feed; danger signal is a 2-syllable bark, issued at about 40 per min. Feeds mostly on forbs and grasses, but may eat grasshoppers and other insects. Digs own deep burrows; may be dormant for short periods of cold weather, but not true hibernators. Populations vary from 5 to 35 per acre (12–87 per ha). Has lived 8½ years in captivity. Mating begins last week in Jan. and continues 2–3 weeks; breeds first at 2 years.

Young: Born March–April; 3–5, rarely 8; gestation period 28–32 days. Naked; eyes open at 5 weeks. Come aboveground at 6 weeks.

Economic status: Competes with grazing stock for food; once numerous on prairies, now reduced to few towns through poisoning operations. Colonies are being preserved in Wind Cave Natl. Park, Devils Tower Natl. Monument, and near Lubbock, Texas.

Map p. 96

WHITETAIL PRAIRIE DOG *Cynomys gunnisoni* **Pl. 10**
Identification: Head and body 11–12 in. (28–30 cm); tail 1¼–2½ in. (32–64 mm); wt. 1½–2½ lb. (675–1125 g). Usually found in *high country,* this small prairie dog is similar in general to the Blacktail Prairie Dog. Tail is white-tipped. Skull (Plate 28) has 22 teeth. There are 10 mammae.

Two other species (*C. leucurus* and *C. parvidens*) are recorded in the literature. Subsequent study may show them to belong to this species. All are included on the one map.

Similar species: (1) Blacktail Prairie Dog has black tip on tail; low country. (2) Rock Squirrel is smaller with longer tail.

Habitat: Mt. valleys, 5000–12,000 ft. (1524–3658 m); open or slightly brushy country, scattered junipers and pines.

Habits: Similar to those of the Blacktail Prairie Dog but less likely to be colonial. Estivates in July, and young of the year hibernate with adults from Oct. or Nov. to March in the North and in high mt. valleys. Mates in March or April; young born early May.   Map p. 96

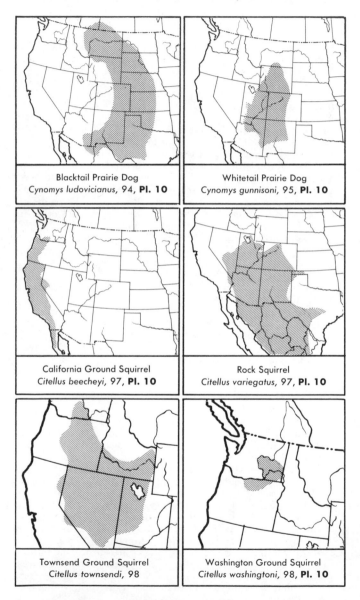

Blacktail Prairie Dog
Cynomys ludovicianus, 94, **Pl. 10**

Whitetail Prairie Dog
Cynomys gunnisoni, 95, **Pl. 10**

California Ground Squirrel
Citellus beecheyi, 97, **Pl. 10**

Rock Squirrel
Citellus variegatus, 97, **Pl. 10**

Townsend Ground Squirrel
Citellus townsendi, 98

Washington Ground Squirrel
Citellus washingtoni, 98, **Pl. 10**

CALIFORNIA GROUND SQUIRREL   Pl. 10
Citellus beecheyi
Identification: Head and body 9–11 in. (23–28 cm); tail
5–9 in. (13–23 cm); wt. 1–2⅕ lb. (454–999 g). Head brownish;
body brown, flecked with buffy white or buff; sides of *neck and
shoulders whitish;* a conspicuous dark triangle on back between
shoulders; belly buff; tail somewhat bushy. Skull has 22 teeth.
There are 11–14 (usually 12) mammae. Found also on Santa
Catalina I.
Similar species: (1) Other ground squirrels are all smaller,
with shorter, less bushy tails. (2) Western Gray Squirrel (p. 116)
has white belly; no buff; tail very bushy.
Habitat: Pastures, grainfields, slopes with scattered trees; rocky
ridges. It avoids thick chaparral and dense woods.
Habits: Diurnal; colonial. Eats green vegetation, seeds, acorns,
mushrooms, fruits, berries, birds, eggs, and insects; stores food
in dens. Burrows 5–200 ft. (1.5–61 m) long, on gentle slopes,
may have many openings; used for several years; runways from
hole to hole. Nest of dried vegetation. Most adults estivate in
July or Aug.; young and adults hibernate in Oct. or Nov.;
always a few aboveground; emerge in Jan. Home range normally less than 150 yd. (136 m) across. A loud chirp warns
others of danger. Breeding population of 2–3 per acre (5–7.5
per ha) is fairly high. Lives 5 years or more in wild.
Young: Born throughout spring, summer, and fall; usually
March–April; 4–15 (av. 7); gestation period 25–30 days. Remain underground 6 weeks.
Economic status: Does considerable damage to crops and
pastureland; has been host to the plague. Considered detrimental where man's interests are concerned.   Map opposite

ROCK SQUIRREL *Citellus variegatus*   Pl. 10
Identification: Head and body 10–11 in. (25–28 cm); tail
7–10 in. (18–25 cm); wt. 1½–1⅘ lb. (681–817 g). Largest of the
ground-living squirrels within its range; may be seen foraging
in the open or *sitting on top of a boulder* on the watch for
danger. Usual color is *grayish* (sometimes nearly black) mixed
with cinnamon or brown, sometimes with head and back blackish; tail nearly as long as head and body and somewhat bushy;
a slightly *mottled* effect over body. Skull has 22 teeth. There
are 10 mammae.
Similar species: (1) Other ground squirrels are smaller and
have shorter tail. (2) Prairie dogs have short tail; found only
on open prairies.
Habitat: Rocky canyons and boulder-strewn slopes.
Habits: Diurnal; not colonial. Climbs nearly as well as tree
squirrels. Feeds on seeds, fruits, nuts, eggs; meat; stores food
in den. Den usually beneath a boulder. Hibernates for short

periods, if at all. A clear whistle warns of danger. Has lived
10 years in captivity. Mates March–July.
Young: Born April–Aug.; 5–7; gestation period not known,
probably 30± days.
Economic status: Harmful in agricultural areas; in foothills,
probably neutral; young are edible.   Map p. 96

TOWNSEND GROUND SQUIRREL *Citellus townsendi*
Identification: Head and body 5½–7 in. (14–18 cm); tail
1⅓–2⅓ in. (34–60 mm); wt. 6–9 oz. (168–252 g). Tail *short,*
tawny beneath; body *smoke-gray* washed with *pinkish buff;*
belly and flanks whitish. Skull has 22 teeth. There are 10
mammae.
Similar species: (1) The Washington Ground Squirrel is
dappled. (2) Belding Ground Squirrel is larger; tail reddish
beneath. (3) Uinta Ground Squirrel is brownish down middle
of back; black in tail. (4) The Columbian Ground Squirrel is
larger; feet and legs are reddish. (5) Whitetail Antelope Squirrel
has stripes on sides; underpart of tail white.
Habitat: Dry soil: sagebrush and grassland.
Habits: Colonial. Feeds on green vegetation and seeds. Burrow
usually has rim of dirt 4–6 in. (101–152 mm) high around opening. Becomes dormant May–July; emerges Jan.–Feb. Voice a
faint peep; stands "picket pin" fashion at burrow entrance.
Young: Born March; usually 5–10, rarely 15.
Economic status: Damages green crops if nearby. Map p. 96

WASHINGTON GROUND SQUIRREL   Pl. 10
Citellus washingtoni
Identification: Head and body 6–7 in. (152–178 mm); tail
1⅓–2½ in. (34–64 mm); wt. 6–10 oz. (168–280 g). A small
dappled ground squirrel; body *smoky-gray flecked with whitish
spots;* short tail with *blackish tip.* Skull has 22 teeth. There
are 10 mammae.
Similar species: (1) Townsend and (2) Belding Ground Squir-
rels have no spots. (3) Columbian Ground Squirrel is larger;
feet and legs dark reddish.
Habitat: Sagebrush, grasslands, sandy flats, and rocky hillsides.
Habits: Similar to those of the Townsend Ground Squirrel.
Young: Born March; 5–11. Aboveground in April.
Economic status: Damages green crops if nearby. Map p. 96

IDAHO GROUND SQUIRREL *Citellus brunneus*
Identification: Head and body 6½–7¾ in. (165–197 mm); tail
2–2½ in. (51–64 mm). Ears relatively *large;* back distinctly
washed with cinnamon or light brown and sprinkled with *small
grayish-white spots;* tail rusty brown beneath; chin white. Skull
has 22 teeth.

Similar species: Columbian Ground Squirrel is larger; feet and legs reddish.
Habitat: Dry, rocky ridges, grass and low herbs.
Habits: Burrows beneath logs and rocks; may estivate in July or Aug.
Range: Known only from Weiser and Payette Valleys, w. Idaho.

RICHARDSON GROUND SQUIRREL *Citellus richardsoni*
(Picket Pin, Wyoming Ground Squirrel)
    Identification: Head and body $7\frac{3}{4}$–$9\frac{1}{2}$ in. (197–241 mm); tail 2–$4\frac{1}{2}$ in. (51–114 mm); wt. 11–18 oz. (308–504 g). This plains ground squirrel is drab *smoke-gray* washed with *cinnamon-buff*, sometimes dappled on back; belly pale buff or whitish; underside of tail clay color, buff, or light brown; tail *bordered with white or buff*. Skull has 22 teeth. There are 10 mammae.
    Similar species: (1) In the Belding Ground Squirrel the median area of the back is usually brownish; tail is reddish below. (2) Uinta Ground Squirrel has a black tail mixed with buffy white above and below. (3) Columbian Ground Squirrel is larger, with reddish legs and feet. (4) Spotted Ground Squirrel has distinct spots. (5) Thirteen-lined Ground Squirrel has stripes on body. (6) Franklin Ground Squirrel is larger and has a longer tail.
    Habitat: Sagebrush, grassland; usually near green vegetation (water); up to 11,000 ft. (3353 m) elevation.
    Habits: Feeds on green vegetation; fond of meat. Burrows may have several openings. Adults estivate in July, emerge late Jan. or Feb.
    Young: Born May; 2–10.
    Economic status: May damage green crops, but possibly destroys many insects.   Map p. 101

UINTA GROUND SQUIRREL *Citellus armatus*
    Identification: Head and body $8\frac{3}{4}$–9 in. (222–229 mm); tail $2\frac{1}{2}$–$3\frac{1}{4}$ in. (64–83 mm); wt. 10–15 oz. (284–425 g). Middle of back brownish; tail *black mixed with buffy white* above and below; belly hairs tipped with pale buff. Skull has 22 teeth. There are 10 mammae.
    Similar species: (1) Townsend Ground Squirrel, tail is not blackish. (2) In the Richardson Ground Squirrel the tail is clay color beneath. (3) Belding Ground Squirrel has a brownish streak down back. (4) Thirteen-lined Ground Squirrel has stripes.
    Habitat: Meadows, edges of fields, near green vegetation; up to 8000 ft. (2438 m) elevation.
    Habits: Colonial. Feeds primarily on green vegetation; hibernates in winter.
    Young: Born April; 4–6 recorded; 1 litter a year.

Economic status: Of little importance because of limited range; harms green crops in its area.   Map opposite

BELDING GROUND SQUIRREL   *Citellus beldingi*
Identification: Head and body 8–9 in. (203–229 mm); tail 2⅕–3 in. (56–76 mm); wt. 8–12 oz. (227–340 g). A medium-sized ground squirrel with upperparts *grayish,* usually washed with buff, and usually with a definite *broad brownish streak down back,* constrasting with sides. Tail reddish beneath, tipped with black and bordered with buff or white. Skull has 22 teeth. There are 10 mammae.
Similar species: (1) Townsend Ground Squirrel is smaller and the tail is tawny beneath. (2) In the Richardson Ground Squirrel the tail is pale buff or clay color beneath. (3) Washington Ground Squirrel is dappled above. (4) Uinta Ground Squirrel has no brown streak down back.
Habitat: Meadows, edges of fields, near green vegetation.
Habits: Similar to those of Uinta Ground Squirrel.
                                                        Map opposite

COLUMBIAN GROUND SQUIRREL   Pl. 10
Citellus columbianus
Identification: Head and body 10–12 in. (254–305 mm); tail 3–5 in. (76–127 mm); wt. ¾–1⅘ lb. (340–812 g). This rather large, *bushy-tailed* ground squirrel may be distinguished from all others within its range by the *dark reddish feet* and *legs* and the *mottled gray upperparts.* Skull has 22 teeth. There are 10 mammae.
Similar species: (1) Townsend, (2) Washington, (3) Idaho, and (4) Richardson Ground Squirrels are all smaller; none has deep reddish feet and legs.
Habitat: Meadows, edges of open forests, cultivated fields.
Habits: Colonial. Feeds on green vegetation spring and early summer; stores some seeds in late summer. Dormant from July–Aug. to Feb.–March; males emerge 2 weeks earlier than females. Voice a high-pitched chirp or whistle.
Young: Born late March or early April; 2–7; gestation period about 24 days.
Economic status: Harmful near green crops; neutral in other areas.   Map opposite

ARCTIC GROUND SQUIRREL   *Citellus parryi*   Pl. 10
(Parka Squirrel)
Identification: Head and body 8½–13¾ in. (216–349 mm); tail 3–6 in. (76–152 mm); wt. 1–2½ lb. (454–1135 g). In the *Far North* lives this *large* ground squirrel. It is also found on a number of the islands off Alaska. Upperparts tawny to reddish brown or dusky, abundantly flecked with white; sides gray; top

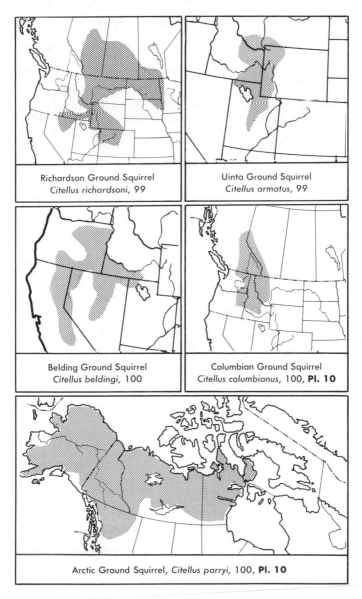

Richardson Ground Squirrel
Citellus richardsoni, 99

Uinta Ground Squirrel
Citellus armatus, 99

Belding Ground Squirrel
Citellus beldingi, 100

Columbian Ground Squirrel
Citellus columbianus, 100, **Pl. 10**

Arctic Ground Squirrel, *Citellus parryi*, 100, **Pl. 10**

of head reddish; feet and legs tawny; tail with some black. Only
ground squirrel in its range. Skull has 22 teeth.
    Formerly known as *C. undulatus* and *Spermophilus undula-
tus.*
Similar species: (1) Hoary Marmot and (2) Woodchuck are
larger and have black feet.
Habitat: Tundra and brushy meadows.
Habits: Eats variety of plants; also relishes meat. Hibernates
for about 7 months, Oct.-May; may appear through snow for
short periods. Highly vocal.
Young: Born June-July; 4-8; gestation period 25 days. Grow
rapidly.
Economic status: Utilized by Eskimo for food and clothing;
beneficial.   Map p. 101

THIRTEEN-LINED GROUND SQUIRREL   Pl. 10
Citellus tridecemlineatus
(Gopher)
    Identification: Head and body $4\frac{1}{2}$-$6\frac{1}{2}$ in. (114-165 mm); tail
$2\frac{1}{2}$-$5\frac{1}{4}$ in. (64-133 mm); wt. 5-9 oz. (140-252 g). This is the
most widely ranging of the ground squirrels. Base color varies
from light to dark brown. On sides and back are *13 whitish
stripes,* some broken into rows of spots, others more or less
continuous. Belly whitish. No other ground squirrel within its
range has definite stripes on body. Skull (Plate 27) has 22 teeth.
There are 10 mammae.
Similar species: (1) Spotted Ground Squirrel has spots but
not stripes. (2) Chipmunks (pp. 108-116) have stripes on sides
of face. (3) Richardson, (4) Uinta, and (5) Franklin Ground
Squirrels have no stripes.
Habitat: Shortgrass prairies, golf courses.
Habits: Solitary. Feeds on seeds, insects, and occasionally
meat. Opening to burrow usually concealed, may be more than
1 opening; dirt thrown out at one opening only. Hibernates
about 6 months of year, Oct.-March; prefers warm days. Home
range 2-3 acres (0.8-1.2 ha). Populations of 4-8 per acre
(10-20 per ha) probably high. Expanding general range north
and east, following clearing of land for agriculture. Mates in
April.
Young: Born May; usually 7-10, rarely 14; gestation period
28 days; possibly 2nd litter in late summer.
Economic status: May damage some crops, but does much
good by eating weed seeds and harmful insects; probably does
more good than harm.   Map p. 104

MEXICAN GROUND SQUIRREL   *Citellus mexicanus*
    Identification: Head and body $6\frac{3}{4}$-$7\frac{1}{2}$ in. (171-190 mm); tail
$4\frac{1}{2}$-5 in. (114-127 mm); wt. 7-12 oz. (198-340 g). This is a

medium-sized ground squirrel with a *long, slightly bushy tail,* the hairs of which are tipped with buff. Back and sides snuff-brown, with about *9 rows of light buff spots.* Skull has 22 teeth. There are 8-10 mammae.

Similar species: (1) Spotted Ground Squirrel has indistinct spots, but not in rows. (2) Rock Squirrel is larger; no spots in rows.

Habitat: Grassland, brush, mesquite, creosote bush, and cactus; it prefers sandy or gravelly soil.

Habits: Probably similar to those of Thirteen-lined Ground Squirrel. Feeds on green vegetation, seeds, insects, and meat. May be seen along highway eating dead animals. Makes most burrows without mound of earth; several refuge burrows to each den. Some hibernate, others may be active all winter. Home range about 100 yd. (91 m) across. Mates in April.

Young: Born May; 4-10. Map p. 104

SPOTTED GROUND SQUIRREL *Citellus spilosoma* **Pl. 10**
Identification: Head and body 5-6 in. (127-152 mm); tail $2\frac{1}{4}$-$3\frac{1}{2}$ in. (57-89 mm); wt. 3-4$\frac{1}{2}$ oz. (85-127 g). A small grayish-brown or reddish-brown squirrel with indistinct *squarish spots of white or buff* on back; tail pencil-like, *not bushy;* belly whitish. Skull has 22 teeth. There are 10 mammae.

Similar species: (1) Mexican Ground Squirrel has distinct spots in rows. (2) Thirteen-lined Ground Squirrel has stripes on body. (3) Richardson Ground Squirrel has no distinct spots.

Habitat: Open forests, scattered brush, grassy parks; sandy soil preferred.

Habits: Active throughout year. Shy and secretive; runs low to ground. Feeds on green vegetation, seeds, and insects. Burrows usually beneath bushes or rocks. Some may hibernate.

Young: 5-7; probably 2 litters a year. Map p. 106

MOHAVE GROUND SQUIRREL *Citellus mohavensis*
Identification: Head and body 6-6$\frac{1}{2}$ in. (152-165 mm); tail 2-3$\frac{1}{2}$ in. (51-89 mm). This little squirrel, found only in the *Mohave Desert,* is *cinnamon-gray* with a *short tail* that is *dusky above and white beneath.* There are *no stripes* on its sides. When running, holds tail over its back and exposes the white undersurface. Skull has 22 teeth. There are 10 mammae.

Similar species: The Whitetail Antelope Squirrel has white stripes on its body.

Habitat: Low desert with scattered brush; sandy or gravelly soil.

Habits: Most active on clear warm days. Solitary for most part. Feeds on tender green vegetation in spring. Openings to burrows (2 or more) without dirt mounds; several burrows used by each individual. Voice a shrill whistle, not very loud.

Young: March 29, 6 embryos reported; April 12, female suckling.   Map p. 106

ROUNDTAIL GROUND SQUIRREL   *Citellus tereticaudus*
Identification: Head and body 5¾–6½ in. (146–165 mm); tail 2½–4 in. (64–102 mm); wt. 5–6½ oz. (142–184 g). Upperparts *pinkish cinnamon* with a *grayish cast;* tail pencil-like, not bushy; belly slightly paler than back. There are *no contrasting markings.* Skull has 22 teeth. There are 8–10 mammae.
Similar species: Antelope squirrels have stripes on sides.
Habitat: Low desert, mesquite, creosote bush, cactus.
Habits: Most active mornings and evenings; seeks shade or retires to burrow in heat of day; may be seen resting in shade

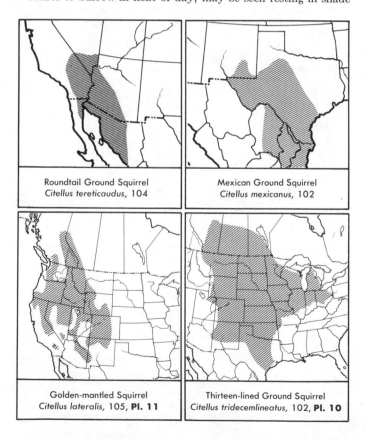

Roundtail Ground Squirrel
Citellus tereticaudus, 104

Mexican Ground Squirrel
Citellus mexicanus, 102

Golden-mantled Squirrel
Citellus lateralis, 105, **Pl. 11**

Thirteen-lined Ground Squirrel
Citellus tridecemlineatus, 102, **Pl. 10**

of plant or post. Aboveground throughout year. Feeds on seeds and probably insects.

Young: Born April (possibly other months); 6–12 embryos reported.   Map opposite

FRANKLIN GROUND SQUIRREL   *Citellus franklini*   **Pl. 10**
(Gray Gopher)

Identification: Head and body 9–10 in. (229–254 mm); tail 5–6 in. (127–152 mm); wt. 10–25 oz. (284–709 g). A *large, gray* squirrel with a tawny overwash on the back and rump. Belly nearly as dark as back; tail fairly long. Much larger and darker than any other ground squirrel in its range. Skull has 22 teeth. There are 10–12 mammae.

Similar species: (1) Richardson Ground Squirrel is smaller and has a short tail. (2) Thirteen-lined Ground Squirrel has spots or stripes.

Habitat: Fairly tall grass or herbs, borders of fields, open woods, edges of marshes.

Habits: Colonial, secretive. Climbs trees, but usually seen on ground. Prefers sunshine, little activity on cloudy days. Eats green vegetation, seeds, insects, meat, bird eggs. Conceals burrow in tall grass or weeds, some dirt at entrance. Hibernates in late Sept. and emerges in April or May; males appear first. Young often seen at edge of highway. Populations of 4–5 per acre (10–12 per ha) are high.

Young: Born May–June; 4–11; gestation period 28 days.

Economic status: Destroys some grain and eggs of ground-nesting birds, but also destroys many insects; may be harmful in one place, beneficial in another.   Map p. 106

GOLDEN-MANTLED SQUIRREL   *Citellus lateralis*   **Pl. 11**
(Copperhead)

Identification: Head and body 6–8 in. (152–203 mm); tail 2½–4¾ in. (64–120 mm); wt. 6–9¾ oz. (170–276 g). A chipmunk-like ground squirrel; *head coppery; a white stripe bordered with black* on each side of body; no stripes on sides of face; tail relatively short and fully haired, not bushy. Skull has 22 teeth. There are 8–10 mammae.

C. saturatus is included here; it may be a distinct species; found in the Cascades of B.C. and Washington.

Similar species: (1) Chipmunks have stripes on side of face. (2) In the Red Squirrel (p. 120) and (3) Chickaree (p. 121) there is no contrast between color of head and body; no white stripe on side.

Habitat: Mountainous areas, chaparral, open pine, fir, and spruce forests; to above timberline.

Habits: Feeds on seeds, fruits, insects, eggs, meat; stores food. Burrows usually near bushes, trees, rocks, or logs. Hibernates

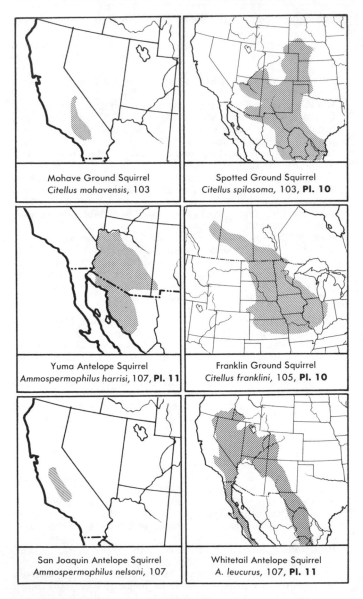

Mohave Ground Squirrel
Citellus mohavensis, 103

Spotted Ground Squirrel
Citellus spilosoma, 103, **Pl. 10**

Yuma Antelope Squirrel
Ammospermophilus harrisi, 107, **Pl. 11**

Franklin Ground Squirrel
Citellus franklini, 105, **Pl. 10**

San Joaquin Antelope Squirrel
Ammospermophilus nelsoni, 107

Whitetail Antelope Squirrel
A. leucurus, 107, **Pl. 11**

Oct. – Nov., emerges March – May; sometimes comes up through snow in winter. Home range less than 200 yd. (183 m) across. Populations of 2 – 5 per acre (5 – 12 per ha). Female may protect area near den. These squirrels become quite tame at camping areas.

Young: Born early spring; 2 – 8.

Economic status: Found principally in nonagricultural areas; affords pleasure to many campers and park visitors. Commonly seen in most western parks. Map p. 104

YUMA ANTELOPE SQUIRREL Pl. 11
Ammospermophilus harrisi

Identification: Head and body 6 – 6 $\frac{1}{4}$ in. (152 – 159 mm); tail 3 – 3 $\frac{3}{4}$ in. (76 – 95 mm); wt. 4 – 5 $\frac{3}{10}$ oz. (113 – 150 g). Body *pinkish cinnamon* to *mouse gray;* a narrow *white line* on each side of body. Tail gray above and below. Skull has 22 teeth. There are 10 mammae.

Similar species: (1) Chipmunks have stripes on sides of face; in mts. (2) Ground squirrels have no stripes on sides.

Habitat: Low arid desert with sparse vegetation.

Habits: Probably similar to those of the Whitetail Antelope Squirrel. Map opposite

WHITETAIL ANTELOPE SQUIRREL Pl. 11
Ammospermophilus leucurus

Identification: Head and body 5 $\frac{1}{2}$ – 6 $\frac{1}{2}$ in. (140 – 165 mm); tail 2 – 3 in. (51 – 76 mm); wt. 3 – 5 $\frac{1}{2}$ oz. (85 – 156 g). Body pale pinkish gray, a *white line on each side of body; undersurface of tail white.* Runs with tail curled over its back, exposing the white undersurface. No other ground squirrel within its range has its color pattern. Skull has 22 teeth. There are 10 mammae.

Those in sw. Texas and central s. New Mexico are considered a distinct species (*A. interpres*) by some authors.

Similar species: (1) Chipmunks have no white undertail. (2) Ground squirrels have no stripes on sides.

Habitat: Low desert and foothills, sparse vegetation, scattered junipers.

Habits: Active throughout year, even when snow on ground. Solitary for most part. Eats seeds, insects, meat; stores food; does not require drinking water. Some may hibernate. Often seen along highway.

Young: 6 – 10; possibly 2 litters a year.

Economic status: On irrigated land may do some damage to crops; also digs into banks of ditches. Map opposite

SAN JOAQUIN ANTELOPE SQUIRREL
Ammospermophilus nelsoni

Identification: Head and body 6 – 6 $\frac{1}{2}$ in. (152 – 165 mm); tail

2 ½ – 3 in. (64 – 76 mm); wt. 3 – 5 ½ oz. (85 – 156 g). In the *San Joaquin Valley,* California, this pinkish-buff squirrel, with a *creamy-white line on each side* of back and a creamy-white underside of tail, is the only ground squirrel with stripes. Curls tail over back when running, exposing white undersurface. Skull has 22 teeth.
Habitat: Dry, sparsely vegetated areas.
Habits: Similar to those of Whitetail Antelope Squirrel.

Map p. 106

EASTERN CHIPMUNK *Tamias striatus* **Pl. 11**
Identification: Head and body 5 – 6 in. (127 – 152 mm); tail 3 – 4 in. (76 – 102 mm); wt. 2 $\frac{3}{10}$ – 4 ½ oz. (65 – 127 g). Squirrel-like; runs with bushy *tail straight up; facial stripes* distinguish it from all other mammals over most of its range; *side and back stripes end at reddish rump.* Often seen in trees, but mostly on ground. Its rather sharp *chuck-chuck-chuck* may be heard before the animal is seen. Skull (Plate 27) has 20 teeth.
Similar species: (1) Least Chipmunk is smaller; side and back stripes continue to base of tail. (2) Thirteen-lined Ground Squirrel is yellowish; no stripes on face.
Habitat: Deciduous forests, brushy areas.
Habits: Solitary except for mother and young. Feeds on seeds, bulbs, fruits, nuts, insects, meat, eggs; stores food underground. Hibernates, but may come aboveground in middle of winter. Home range usually less than 100 yd. (91 m) across. Populations of 2 – 4 per acre (5 – 10 per ha). Lives 3 years or more in wild, 8 years in captivity. Readily comes to feeding table. Displays territorial behavior. Mates in April and again July – Aug.
Young: 1st litter May; 2 – 8; 2nd litter Aug. – Sept.; gestation period 31 days. Appear aboveground when ⅔ grown. Breed 1st year.
Economic status: May destroy some garden fruit and bulbs; also digs many burrows; an attractive animal around camping areas. Map opposite

ALPINE CHIPMUNK *Eutamias alpinus*
Identification: Head and body 4 ¼ – 4 ½ in. (108 – 114 mm); tail 2 ¾ – 3 ½ in. (70 – 89 mm); wt. 1 – 1 ¾ oz. (28 – 50 g). A small chipmunk. Head and body grayish, dark side stripes on face and body tawny. Skull has 22 teeth.
Similar species: (1) Yellow Pine and (2) Lodgepole Chipmunks are larger; the dark stripes are blackish or dark brown, and/or there are clear white patches behind ears.
Habitat: Cliffs and talus slopes from timberline to 8000 ft. (2438 m) elevation.
Range: High Sierra Nevada from Mt. Conness, Tuolumne Co., California, south to Olancha Peak, Inyo-Tulare Cos., California.

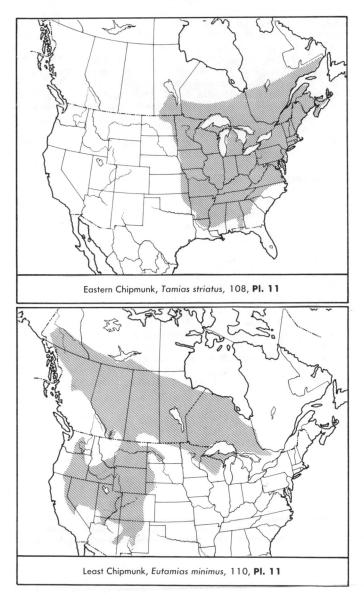

Eastern Chipmunk, *Tamias striatus*, 108, **Pl. 11**

Least Chipmunk, *Eutamias minimus*, 110, **Pl. 11**

LEAST CHIPMUNK *Eutamias minimus* **Pl. 11**

Identification: Head and body $3\frac{2}{3}$-$4\frac{1}{2}$ in. (93-114 mm); tail 3-$4\frac{1}{2}$ in. (76-114 mm); wt. 1-2 oz. (28-57 g). This is the most widely ranging, geographically and altitudinally, of the chipmunks. As a group, they are also the *smallest* and most variable. Color ranges from a washed-out *yellowish gray* with pale tawny dark stripes (Badlands, S. Dakota) to a *rich grayish tawny* with black dark stripes (Wisconsin and Michigan). Stripes continue to *base of tail*. When running, carry tail *straight up*. Skull has 22 teeth. There are 8 mammae.

Similar species: (1) Grayneck Chipmunk is larger; neck and shoulders gray. (2) Yellow Pine Chipmunk has ears blackish in front, whitish behind. (3) Panamint Chipmunk has a gray rump that contrasts with color of back and sides. (4) Townsend Chipmunk is larger; stripes indistinct. (5) Uinta, (6) Lodgepole, and (7) Colorado Chipmunks have ears blackish in front, white behind. (8) Cliff Chipmunk has indistinct side stripes. (9) Redtail Chipmunk has a gray rump; the tail is dark reddish below. (10) In Eastern Chipmunk the body stripes terminate at the reddish rump.

Habitat: Low sagebrush deserts, high-mt. coniferous forests, northern mixed-hardwood forests; varies with locality.

Habits: Active gathering and storing food during spring, summer, and fall. Climbs trees readily. Feeds on variety of vegetation, seeds, nuts, fruits; also insects and meat, readily adapts to camps, especially if food is forthcoming. Nests beneath stumps, logs, rocks; makes own burrow; hibernates.

Young: 2-6; possibly 2 litters a year.

Economic status: Affords pleasure to campers and tourists in many of our parks. May be seen at the turnouts in Badlands Natl. Monument, S. Dakota, and at most camping areas within its range. Map p. 109

TOWNSEND CHIPMUNK *Eutamias townsendi* **Pl. 11**

Identification: Head and body $5\frac{1}{3}$-$6\frac{1}{2}$ in. (135-165 mm); tail $3\frac{4}{5}$-6 in. (96-152 mm); wt. $2\frac{1}{2}$-$4\frac{1}{3}$ oz. (71-123 g). This large, *dark brown* chipmunk, found on the humid Pacific Coast, has indistinct dull yellowish or grayish light stripes along its sides and back. Dark body stripes blackish; stripe below ear brownish. Backs of ears dusky in front, gray behind. Skull has 22 teeth. There are 8 mammae.

Similar species: (1) Long-eared Chipmunk has a large white patch behind each ear and a black line below the ear. (2) Sonoma Chipmunk has backs of ears 1 color. (3) Least, (4) Yellow Pine, (5) Lodgepole, and (6) Uinta Chipmunks are smaller; the distinct stripes contrast with body colors.

Habitat: Coniferous forests and ajacent chaparral.

Habits: Climbs trees. Feeds mostly on forest floor and in

nearby chaparral; food habits probably similar to those of other chipmunks. Hibernates for short periods. Mates in April. May be seen at Mt. Rainier and Olympic Natl. Parks.
Young: Born May; 3-6.   Map p. 112

CLIFF CHIPMUNK *Eutamias dorsalis*   **Pl. 11**
Identification: Head and body 5-6 in. (127-152 mm); tail 3½-4⅕ in. (89-107 mm); wt. 2-3 oz. (57-85 g). Gray with indistinct dark stripes down middle of back and along sides. Lower sides and feet washed with yellow. Skull has 22 teeth. There are 8 mammae.
Similar species: (1) Least, (2) Uinta, (3) Panamint, and Gray-neck Chipmunks all have distinct dark and light stripes.
Habitat: Piñon pine-juniper slopes and lower edge of pines.
                                              Map p. 112

SONOMA CHIPMUNK *Eutamias sonomae*
Identification: Head and body 4⅘-6 in. (122-152 mm); tail 4-5 in. (102-127 mm). A *large, dark* chipmunk. Backs of ears uniform color; body stripes indistinct, the light ones yellowish. Skull has 22 teeth.
Similar species: (1) In the Yellow Pine Chipmunk the stripes are bright; black and white. (2) In the Townsend Chipmunk the backs of ears are bicolored, dusky in front and gray behind.
Habitat: Chaparral, brushy clearings, streamside thickets; warm slopes, sea level to 6000 ft. (1829 m).
Habits: Sits on limb, stump, or rock while eating. Forages among small branches of bushes as well as on ground.
                                              Map p. 112

YELLOW PINE CHIPMUNK *Eutamias amoenus*
Identification: Head and body 4½-5⅕ in. (114-132 mm); tail 3-4¼ in. (76-108 mm); wt. 1⅓-2½ oz. (38-71 g). Colors bright; black and white (or grayish) back and side stripes *distinct;* ears blackish in front, whitish behind; underside of tail tawny, as are the sides. Skull has 22 teeth. There are 8 mammae.
Similar species: (1) In the Least Chipmunk the fronts of ears are tawny. (2) In the Alpine Chipmunk the dark side stripes are tawny. (3) Redtail Chipmunk has dark reddish underside of tail. (4) In the Lodgepole and (5) Uinta Chipmunks the side stripes are dark brown. (6) Townsend, (7) Merriam, (8) Long-eared, and (9) Sonoma Chipmunks are larger; stripes indistinct.
Habitat: Open coniferous forests, chaparral, rocky areas with brush or scattered pines, burned-over areas with stumps and brush.
Habits: Strictly diurnal. Climbs trees. Eats great variety of plant material, mostly seeds, and a few insects; eats meat in

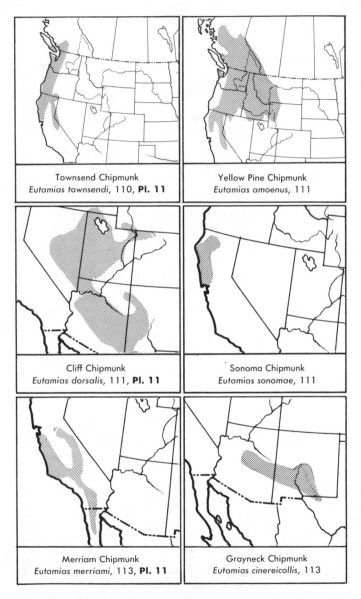

Townsend Chipmunk
Eutamias townsendi, 110, **Pl. 11**

Yellow Pine Chipmunk
Eutamias amoenus, 111

Cliff Chipmunk
Eutamias dorsalis, 111, **Pl. 11**

Sonoma Chipmunk
Eutamias sonomae, 111

Merriam Chipmunk
Eutamias merriami, 113, **Pl. 11**

Grayneck Chipmunk
Eutamias cinereicollis, 113

captivity. Nests in ground burrows up to 3 ft. (1 m) long; no loose soil at entrances; stores food in nest chamber. Hibernates Nov.–March in North. Lives 5 years or more in wild. Mates in April.

Young: Born May; 5–7; 1 litter a year. Naked; blind. Above-ground in June; weaned at 6 weeks. Breed following spring.

Economic status: Found usually in nonagricultural country; an attractive animal in several parks. May be seen at Craters of the Moon Natl. Monument (larger and darker of 2 species), Mt. Rainier and Olympic Natl. Parks (smaller and brighter-colored of 2 kinds). Map opposite

MERRIAM CHIPMUNK *Eutamias merriami* **Pl. 11**
Identification: Head and body $4\frac{2}{3}$–$6\frac{1}{2}$ in. (118–165 mm); tail $3\frac{1}{2}$–$5\frac{3}{5}$ in. (89–142 mm); wt. $2\frac{1}{2}$–4 oz. (71–113 g). A large grayish-brown chipmunk with *indistinct stripes*. Stripe below ear brownish. Skull has 22 teeth. There are 8 mammae.
Similar species: (1) Long-eared Chipmunk has a black stripe under each ear; a white patch behind the ear. (2) Yellow Pine and (3) Lodgepole Chipmunks have distinct white stripes.
Habitat: Chaparral slopes, mixed oak and digger pine forests, streamside thickets, rock outcroppings, foothills.
Map opposite

GRAYNECK CHIPMUNK *Eutamias cinereicollis*
Identification: Head and body $4\frac{3}{4}$–$5\frac{1}{2}$ in. (121–140 mm); tail $3\frac{3}{5}$–$4\frac{3}{5}$ in. (91–117 mm); wt. 2–3 oz. (57–85 g). Body *dark gray* washed on sides with tawny and with *pale gray neck and shoulders;* lateral dark stripes dark brown, median one black. Skull (Plate 27) has 22 teeth. There are 8 mammae.
Similar species: (1) Least Chipmunk is smaller; neck not noticeably gray. (2) Cliff Chipmunk has indistinct side stripes.
Habitat: Coniferous forests, high mts. Map opposite

LONG-EARED CHIPMUNK *Eutamias quadrimaculatus*
Identification: Head and Body 5–6 in. (127–152 mm); tail $3\frac{1}{2}$–$4\frac{2}{3}$ in. (89–118 mm); wt. $2\frac{1}{2}$–$3\frac{1}{2}$ oz. (71–100 g). This *large, high-Sierra* chipmunk is grayish or tawny, with indistinct body stripes. Behind each ear is a large, clearly defined *white patch;* stripe below ear black. Skull has 22 teeth.
Similar species: (1) Yellow Pine, (2) Lodgepole, and (3) Uinta Chipmunks are smaller; stripes distinct. (4) Townsend and (5) Merriam Chipmunks have brownish stripe below ear.
Habitat: Forests and brush thickets; 3600–7300 ft. (1097–2225 m) elevation. Map p. 115

REDTAIL CHIPMUNK *Eutamias ruficaudus*
Identification: Head and body $4\frac{3}{5}$–$5\frac{4}{5}$ in. (117–147 mm); tail 4–$4\frac{4}{5}$ in. (102–122 mm). *Large;* brilliantly colored; shoulders

and sides bright tawny; rump gray; underside of tail dark reddish. Skull has 22 teeth. There are 8 mammae.
Similar species: (1) Yellow Pine Chipmunk has tawny underside of tail. (2) Least Chipmunk is smaller; rump does not contrast with sides and head.
Habitat: Coniferous forests, talus slides, mts. up to timberline.
Map opposite

COLORADO CHIPMUNK *Eutamias quadrivittatus* **Pl. 11**
Identification: Head and body $4\frac{1}{2}$–5 in. (114–127 mm); tail $3\frac{1}{5}$–$4\frac{1}{2}$ in. (81–114 mm); wt. 2–3 oz. (57–85 g). Head, rump, and sides gray with an overwash of tawny on sides; color bright; side stripes dark brown; ears blackish in front, white behind. Tail tawny beneath, tipped with black, and bordered with white or pale tawny. Skull has 22 teeth. There are 8 mammae.
Similar species: Least Chipmunk is smaller; dorsal stripes continue to base of tail.
Habitat: Coniferous forests, rocky slopes and ridges.
Map opposite

UINTA CHIPMUNK *Eutamias umbrinus*
Identification: Head and body $4\frac{1}{2}$–5 in. (114–127 mm); tail $3\frac{1}{2}$–$4\frac{3}{5}$ in. (89–117 mm); wt. 2–3 oz. (57–85 g). Characters as in Colorado Chipmunk. Skull has 22 teeth. There are 8 mammae.
Some authors have included this with *E. quadrivittatus*.
Similar species: (1) Least Chipmunk has front of ears tawny. (2) Yellow Pine Chipmunk has black side stripes. (3) Lodgepole Chipmunk has top of head brown; subterminal black area on underside of tail more than $\frac{1}{2}$ in. (12 mm) long. (4) Panamint Chipmunk has bright tawny shoulders and sides; ears tawny in front. (5) Townsend, (6) Long-eared, and (7) Cliff Chipmunks have indistinct side stripes.
Habitat: Coniferous forests (yellow pine zone) up to timberline; rocky slopes; 6000–11,000 ft. (1829–3353 m) elevation.
Map opposite

PANAMINT CHIPMUNK *Eutamias panamintinus*
Identification: Head and body $4\frac{1}{2}$–$4\frac{2}{3}$ in. (114–118 mm); tail $3\frac{1}{2}$–4 in. (89–102 mm); wt. $1\frac{1}{2}$–$2\frac{1}{3}$ oz. (42–66 g). Brightly colored; head and rump gray; sides, back, and front of ears tawny; median line dusky. Skull has 22 teeth. There are 8 mammae.
Similar species: (1) In the Least Chipmunk the rump is similar to back. (2) In the Lodgepole and (3) Uinta Chipmunks the ears are blackish in front, white behind. (4) Charleston Mountain Chipmunk occurs in yellow pine belt and above. (5) Cliff Chipmunk has no white side stripe.
Habitat: Piñon pines and junipers; semiarid areas.
Map opposite

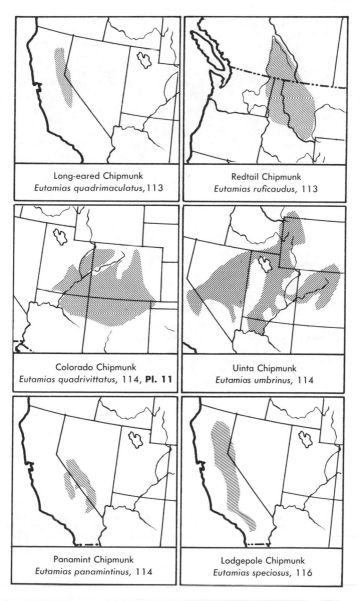

Long-eared Chipmunk
Eutamias quadrimaculatus, 113

Redtail Chipmunk
Eutamias ruficaudus, 113

Colorado Chipmunk
Eutamias quadrivittatus, 114, **Pl. 11**

Uinta Chipmunk
Eutamias umbrinus, 114

Panamint Chipmunk
Eutamias panamintinus, 114

Lodgepole Chipmunk
Eutamias speciosus, 116

LODGEPOLE CHIPMUNK   *Eutamias speciosus*

Identification: Head and body 4 3/5 – 5 1/3 in. (117 – 135 mm); tail 2 4/5 – 4 in. (71 – 102 mm); wt. 1 4/5 – 2 1/5 oz. (51 – 62 g). Brightly colored; light and dark colors contrast; *top of head brown* sprinkled with gray; side stripes white and dark brown, distinct; median dorsal stripe *black;* ears blackish in front, whitish behind; *subterminal black area* on underside of tail 1/2 to 4/5 in. (13 – 20 mm) long. Skull has 22 teeth. There are 8 mammae.
Similar species: (1) Uinta Chipmunk has top of head gray and subterminal black area on underside of tail less than 1/2 in. (12 mm) long. (2) Yellow Pine Chipmunk has black side stripes. (3) Panamint Chipmunk is smaller, shoulders and sides bright tawny; ears tawny in front. (4) Least and (5) Alpine Chipmunks are smaller. (6) Merriam, (7) Townsend, and (8) Long-eared Chipmunks are larger; side stripes indistinct.
Habitat: Lodgepole pine forests and adjacent chaparral.

Map p. 115

CHARLESTON MOUNTAIN CHIPMUNK
Eutamias palmeri

Identification: Head and body 5 in. (127 mm); tail 3 1/2 – 4 in. (89 – 102 mm). Skull has 22 teeth.
Similar species: Panamint Chipmunk is smaller; occurs in piñon-juniper belt.
Habitat: Coniferous forest, rocky slopes, from yellow pine belt to timberline.
Range: Charleston Mts., Nevada.

WESTERN GRAY SQUIRREL   *Sciurus griseus*   Pl.12

Identification: Head and body 9 – 12 in. (23 – 30 cm); tail 10 – 12 in. (25 – 30 cm); wt. 1 1/4 – 1 3/4 lb. (567 – 794 g). A *large, gray* tree squirrel with a long, very *bushy tail, white belly,* and *dusky feet.* Skull has 22 teeth. There are 8 mammae.
Similar species: (1) California Ground Squirrel (p. 97) has less bushy tail; whitish shoulders. (2) Chickaree has yellowish or rusty belly. (3) Eastern Fox Squirrel is rusty yellowish, not gray.
Habitat: Oak and pine-oak forests; fairly open.
Habits: Most active during mornings. Arboreal, but often seen on the ground. Feeds mostly on acorns and seeds of conifers. Nests in cavities in trees or in tree nest made of sticks and shredded bark; nest usually 20 ft. (6 m) or more from ground. Home range 1/2 – 2 acres (0.2 – 0.8 ha). Populations vary from 2 squirrels per acre (5 per ha) to 1 squirrel for 10 acres (4 ha). Has lived 11 years in captivity. Voice, a rather rapid barking sound. Female displays territorial behavior when young are in nest.
Young: Born Feb. – June; 3 – 5; gestation period probably more than 43 days; 1 litter a year.

Economic status: A fair game mammal; also attractive to visitors of parks such as Yosemite Natl. Park and several state and city parks. Walnut and almond crops are often damaged by these squirrels.   Map below

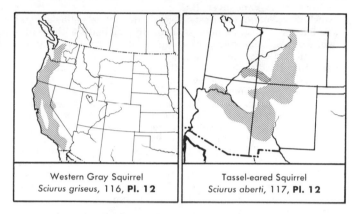

| Western Gray Squirrel | Tassel-eared Squirrel |
| *Sciurus griseus*, 116, **Pl. 12** | *Sciurus aberti*, 117, **Pl. 12** |

TASSEL-EARED SQUIRREL *Sciurus aberti*   **Pl. 12**
(Abert Squirrel, Kaibab Squirrel)
Identification: Head and body 11–12 in. (28–30 cm); tail 8–9 in. (20–23 cm); wt. $1\frac{1}{2}$–2 lb. (681–908 g). This is the most colorful of our tree squirrels. Tail either *all-white* or *white beneath* and broadly bordered with white; belly either *white or black;* prominent black, or blackish, *ear tufts* except late summer; sides gray; back reddish. Skull has 22 teeth. The only squirrel with these markings.
    Some authors consider the squirrels north of the Grand Canyon (*S. kaibabensis*) as a distinct species; they have *all-white tails*.
Habitat: Yellow pine forests, 7000–8500 ft. (2133–2590 m) elevation.
Habits: Feeds primarily on pinecones and the cambium layer of small pine twigs; also eats fungi. Builds bulky nest high in pines; may be heard barking when excited, but usually rather quiet. Mates March–April.
Young: Born April–May; 3–4.
Economic status: Does not interfere with man's activities; a wonderful tourist attraction over most of its range, but rare on North Rim in Grand Canyon Natl. Park.   Map above

EASTERN GRAY SQUIRREL *Sciurus carolinensis*   **Pl. 12**
Identification: Head and body 8–10 in. (20–25 cm); tail $7\frac{3}{4}$–10 in. (20–25 cm); wt. $\frac{3}{4}$–$1\frac{3}{5}$ lb. (340–726 g). Its general *grayish* color, washed with tawny in summer, and *very bushy*

tail bordered with white-tipped hairs will usually serve to distinguish this squirrel. Black squirrels (a melanistic color phase) are common in some parts of its range. Skull has 22 teeth. There are 8 mammae. Introduced in Seattle, Washington, and Stanley Park, Vancouver, B.C.

Similar species: (1) Eastern Fox Squirrel is yellowish; tail bordered with hairs tipped with tawny; or body with distinct white or black markings, or steel-gray all over. (2) Red Squirrel is small; yellowish or reddish.

Habitat: Hardwood forests with nut trees, river bottoms.

Habits: Primarily arboreal, rarely ventures far from trees. Apparently has homing instinct. Feeds on a great variety of nuts, seeds, fungi, fruits, and often the cambium layer beneath the bark of trees; stores nuts and acorns singly in small holes in ground, many are never recovered and some sprout to grow into trees. Nests in holes in trees or builds leaf nest in branches, usually 25 ft. (7.6 m) or more from ground. Home range 2–7 acres (0.8–2.8 ha). Populations of 2–20 per acre (5–50 per ha). Formerly emigrated in great masses when populations were high. May be detected by a series of short barks when excited. Has lived 15 years in captivity. Mates Jan.–Feb., and July in North, Dec. and June in South.

Young: 3–5; gestation period 44 days; 2 litters a year. Naked, blind. Weaned at 2 months.

Economic status: In some parts of range one of the most important small game mammals; important as a reforestation agent by planting many nuts; an attractive mammal in many towns; does little harm to crops.   Map opposite

ARIZONA GRAY SQUIRREL   *Sciurus arizonensis*
Identification: Head and body 10–11 in. (25–28 cm); tail 10–12 in. (25–30 cm); wt. 1⅓–1⅔ lb. (605–756 g). The common tree squirrel in the mts. of se. Arizona. A large *gray* squirrel, sometimes washed with yellowish on the back; *belly* and *tail fringe white*. Skull has 20 teeth. There are 8 mammae.

Similar species: (1) Tassel-eared Squirrel has prominent tufts (except late summer) on ears. (2) Apache Fox Squirrel is yellowish brown. (3) Red Squirrel is smaller; yellowish or reddish on sides and back.

Habitat: Oak and pine forests.

Habits: Chiefly arboreal. Feeds on acorns, nuts, seeds; behavior similar to that of Eastern Gray Squirrel as far as known.

Economic status: Probably neutral; not found in large numbers; range restricted.   Map opposite

EASTERN FOX SQUIRREL   *Sciurus niger*   **Pl. 12**
Identification: Head and body 10–15 in. (25–38 cm); tail 9–14 in. (23–35 cm); wt. 1⅕–3 lb. (544–1362 g). Wherever

there are nut trees in its range the Eastern Fox Squirrel is found. Over most of its extensive range, this squirrel is *rusty yellowish* with a pale *yellow to orange belly,* and with the bushy tail *bordered with tawny-tipped hairs.* In Southeast, body may be variously sprinkled with mixtures of yellow, white, and black, and the head more or less black with white on nose and ears. In a small area on Atlantic Coast (Delaware, Maryland) and adjoining parts of Virginia, West Virginia, and Pennsylvania, they may be pure steel-gray with no tawny. Skull (Plate 27) has 20 teeth. There are 8 mammae.

Similar species: (1) Eastern Gray Squirrel is smaller; gray with slight overwash of tawny (summer) and with white border on tail. (2) Western Gray Squirrel is gray, not rusty or yellowish. (3) Red Squirrel is smaller with whitish belly.

Habitat: Open hardwood woodlots in North and pine forests in South, both with clearings interspersed.

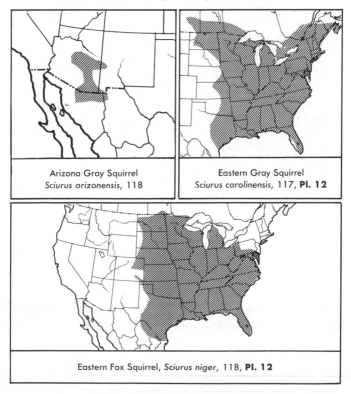

Arizona Gray Squirrel
Sciurus arizonensis, 118

Eastern Gray Squirrel
Sciurus carolinensis, 117, **Pl. 12**

Eastern Fox Squirrel, *Sciurus niger,* 118, **Pl. 12**

Habits: Spends much time on ground foraging, sometimes in open several rods from trees. Feeds on great variety of nuts, acorns, seeds, fungi, bird eggs, and cambium beneath bark of small branches of trees; buries nuts singly, many of which are not retrieved. Nests in cavities in trees or builds twig and leaf nest in crotch or branches, usually 30 ft. (9.1 m) or more from ground. Home range 10–40 acres (4–16 ha). Populations of 1 squirrel per 2 acres (0.8 ha) to 3 squirrels per acre (0.4 ha). Lives 10 years or more. Mates Jan.–Feb. and June–July in North, about 1 month earlier in South; females breed at 1 year.

Young: Born Feb.–April and Aug.–Sept. in North, a month earlier in South; 2–5; gestation period 44 days; yearling females have 1 litter, old females 2 litters. Weaned at 2–3 months.

Economic status: An important small game mammal; does some damage to grain crops near woodlots; an attractive mammal in many small cities and parks. Introduced in several western cities — i.e., Seattle, Washington, and Fresno, Sacramento, and San Francisco, California.   Map p. 119

APACHE FOX SQUIRREL *Sciurus apache*

Identification: Head and body 10½–11½ in. (27–29 cm); tail 10½–11½ in. (27–29 cm); wt. 1⅛–1⅘ lb. (510–817 g). Barely enters U. S. in mts. of se. Arizona. A large, *yellowish-brown* squirrel with an *ochraceous belly*. Skull has 20 teeth. The only tree squirrel in the area with above characters.

Habitat: Thickets of canyon bottoms.

Range: Known only from Chiricahua Mts., se. Arizona, in U.S.

RED SQUIRREL *Tamiasciurus hudsonicus*   **Pl. 11**
(Spruce Squirrel)

Identification: Head and body 7–8 in. (178–203 mm); tail 4–6 in. (102–152 mm); wt. 7–8⅘ oz. (198–250 g). This *noisy* little squirrel is usually heard before seen. Its *ratchet-like call* reveals it, usually sitting on a branch 10 or 20 ft. (3 or 6 m) aboveground. Color uniformly *yellowish or reddish,* paler on back in winter (ear tufts), a *black line* along side in summer; whitish belly. Tail bushy. Smallest of the tree squirrels in its range. Skull (Plate 27) has 20 teeth (rarely 22). There are 8 mammae.

Similar species: (1) Eastern Gray Squirrel is larger; gray or black. (2) Eastern Fox Squirrel is larger, no black line on side in summer; no ear tufts in winter. (3) Arizona Gray Squirrel is gray. (4) Tassel-eared Squirrel has gray sides or is black; white or gray tail. (5) Golden-mantled Squirrel (p. 105) has copper-colored head; white stripe on side.

Habitat: Pine and spruce or mixed hardwood forests, swamps.

Habits: Active throughout year. Primarily diurnal, but occasionally out after dark. Tunnels in snow. Feeds on great variety of seeds, nuts, eggs, fungi; stores conifer cones and nuts in caches, not singly; fungi may be stored in crotches of trees, singly; usually has favorite feeding stump where shucks from pinecones or nuts may accumulate in piles of a bushel or more. Nest either in cavity in tree or outside in branches, built of leaves, twigs, and shredded bark, usually near tree trunk. Home range less than 200 yd. (183 m) across. Populations of 2 squirrels to 3 acres (1.2 ha) probably average, may be as high as 10 per acre (25 per ha). May live 10 years. Displays territorial behavior. Mates Feb.–March and again June–July.

Young: Born April–May and Aug.–Sept.; 2–7; gestation period 38 days.

Economic status: May damage cabins while unattended; affords pleasure to campers and hikers; too small for a game species. Map below

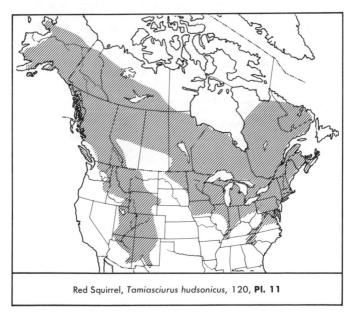

Red Squirrel, *Tamiasciurus hudsonicus*, 120, **Pl. 11**

CHICKAREE *Tamiasciurus douglasi* **Pl. 11**
(Douglas Squirrel)

Identification: Head and body 6–7 in. (152–178 mm); tail 4¾–5 in. (121–127 mm); wt. 6–7⅕ oz. (170–204 g). This *noisy* little squirrel of the *evergreen forests* of the West is a counterpart of the Red Squirrel. It is dark *reddish olive,* grayer in winter, with a *yellowish or rusty belly*. Distinct *black line* along each side in summer, absent or indistinct in winter. Skull has 20 teeth. There are 8 mammae.

Similar species: (1) Western Gray Squirrel (p. 116) is larger; gray with white belly. (2) Golden-mantled Squirrel has copper–colored head, white stripe on side.

Habitat: Coniferous forests.

Habits: Similar to those of the Red Squirrel.

Young: Born June and Oct.; 4–8.

Economic status: Does little if any harm; affords pleasure to campers and visitors of parks within its range.   Map below

SOUTHERN FLYING SQUIRREL *Glaucomys volans* **Pl. 12**

Identification: Head and body 5½–5⅔ in. (140–144 mm); tail 3½–4½ in. (89–114 mm); wt. 1¾–2⅘ oz. (50–79 g). Flying squirrels are seldom seen. Thick soft fur is glossy *olive-brown above, white to the skin below*. A folded layer of *loose skin along each side* of body, from front leg to hind leg, is found in no other mammals (except bats) here considered. When outstretched, this skin supports body as animal glides from tree to tree. Eyeshine is a reddish orange. Skull has 22 teeth. There are 8 mammae.

Similar species: The Northern Flying Squirrel is larger; belly hairs are lead color at bases near skin.

Habitat: Woodlots and forests of deciduous or mixed deciduous-coniferous trees.

Habits: This and the next species are the only strictly nocturnal squirrels. Appears in open at deep dusk. Gregarious in winter. Apparently has homing instinct. Feeds on variety of seeds, nuts, insects, bird eggs; will eat meat if available; stores some food in nest chamber, also in crotches in trees. Makes nest in an old

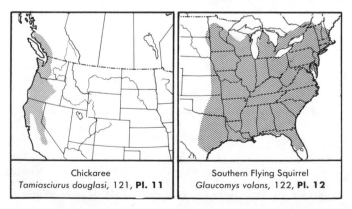

Chickaree
Tamiasciurus douglasi, 121, **Pl. 11**

Southern Flying Squirrel
Glaucomys volans, 122, **Pl. 12**

woodpecker hole, or builds outside nest of leaves, twigs, and bark; also occupies attics of buildings; 20 or more may den together in winter. Home range about 4 acres (1.6 ha). Populations of 1-2 per acre (2-5 per ha) in summer. Has lived 13 years in captivity; makes good pet. Voice, a high-pitched twitter. Mates Feb.-March and June-July.

Young: Born April-May and Aug.-Sept.; 2-6; gestation period about 40 days.

Economic status: Unless its home is in the attic of a house, does not interfere with man's activities.   Map opposite

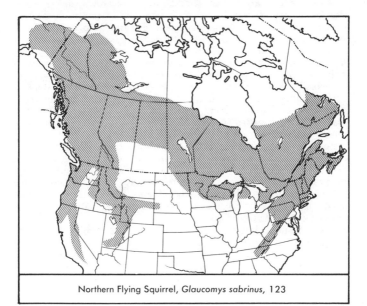

Northern Flying Squirrel, *Glaucomys sabrinus*, 123

NORTHERN FLYING SQUIRREL   *Glaucomys sabrinus*

Identification: Head and body 5½-6⅖ in. (140-162 mm); tail 4⅓-5½ in. (110-140 mm); wt. 4-6½ oz. (113-185 g). Characters similar to those for Southern Flying Squirrel except that it is larger and belly hairs are *white* only at tips, lead color at bases near skin. Skull (Plate 27) has 22 teeth. There are 8 mammae.

Similar species: Southern Flying Squirrel has belly hairs white to bases near skin.

Habitat: Coniferous and mixed forests.

Habits: Probably similar to those of the Southern Flying Squirrel; not too well known.

Young: Born May – June; 2 – 5.
Economic status: Serves as food for some furbearers; may
enter traps set for furbearers with meat bait.   Map p. 123

Pocket Gophers: Geomyidae

MEMBERS of this family are small to medium-sized; head and
body, $4\frac{3}{4}$ – 9 in. (120 – 229 mm); they have external *cheek pouches*
(pockets) which are fur-lined and reversible and open on either
side of mouth. Their large, yellowish incisor teeth are *always
exposed* in front of the mouth opening; skin, with hair, extends
behind the incisors and the teeth are exposed when mouth is
closed. Front claws large and curved for efficient digging tools;
tail *always shorter than head and body* and naked or scantily
haired. Eyes and ears small. Presence of pocket gophers is easily
detected by *mounds* of earth which they push out as they excavate
their subterranean tunnels. Mounds characteristically *fan-
shaped;* position of opening indicated by a round earth plug, the
last of the dirt pushed to surface. They never leave their burrows
open for long.

Some of the species are difficult to distinguish without resorting
to internal structures. Rarely are 2 kinds found in the same field,
but the general ranges of some interdigitate. If in doubt, specimens should be sent to a museum for positive identification. Color
varies from nearly white to nearly black; mostly they are some
shade of brown. Strictly N. American family of rodents. Known
as fossils from Middle Oligocene.

Habits: General habits of all members of this family similar, as
far as known. Solitary for much of their lives, they are active day
and night throughout the year. All are burrowers, seldom seen
aboveground. Prefer soil that is slightly moist and easy to work,
but some are found in rocky situations, especially in mts. In
winter, particularly in mts., they tunnel through snow and push
loose dirt into tunnels. When snow melts, long ropelike cores of
dirt settle to surface of ground. Pocket gophers feed largely on
roots and tubers as well as some surface vegetation. Sometimes
come aboveground to forage, but often pull plants down through
surface soil into burrow system. Home range about 2200 sq. ft.
(204 sq. m) for males and 1300 sq. ft. (120 sq. m) for females of *T.
bottae.* In some at least, territorial behavior is displayed. They
are polygamous and may breed once a year in the North and 2
or more times a year in the South.

Economic status: Considered harmful wherever they occur in
cultivated areas; particularly bad in alfalfa fields, where not only
do they consume some of the vegetation but their mounds hinder
harvesting the crop. Root crops also suffer from their depreda-

tions. In wilderness areas pocket gophers are probably important as soil-forming agents; they bring subsoil to the surface and aid in water conservation and aeration of the soil. Biologically they are interesting animals. If control is necessary, it is best to consult a farm agent.

VALLEY POCKET GOPHER *Thomomys bottae* **Pl. 13**
   Identification: Head and body 4⅘–7 in. (122–178 mm); tail 2–3¾ in. (51–95 mm); wt. 2½–8⅘ oz. (71–250 g). Throughout its range this pocket gopher is extremely variable in size and coloration: small on some of the southern desert mts., large in the valleys; nearly white in the Imperial Desert, nearly black along parts of Pacific Coast. Usually some shade of brown. Best identified by where it lives. Differences given below apply to those parts of the population where ranges interdigitate. A single indistinct groove near inner border of each upper incisor. Skull has 20 teeth. There are 8 mammae.
   Similar species: (1) Bailey Pocket Gopher is smaller; in mts. (2) Northern Pocket Gopher is smaller, grayish; female has 10 mammae; high in mts. (3) Sierra Pocket Gopher is smaller; high in mts. (4) Townsend Pocket Gopher is larger, grayish. (5) Pygmy Pocket Gopher is smaller; in mts. (6) Mexican Pocket Gopher is larger, yellowish; a deep groove down middle of each upper incisor. (7) Plains Pocket Gopher is larger; 2 grooves down front of each upper incisor.
   Habitat: Valleys and mt. meadows; it prefers a loam soil, but some occur in sandy or rocky situations.
   Young: Born Oct.–June; usually 5–7 (extremes, 3–13); gestation period about 19 days; peaks in breeding activity, Nov. 1 and April 1. Map p. 126

BAILEY POCKET GOPHER *Thomomys baileyi*
   Identification: Head and body 6 in. (152 mm); tail 2½ in. (64 mm). Wt.: males, 6⅓–8⅘ oz. (180–250 g); females, 5–6⅓ oz. (142–179 g). This tawny pocket gopher, found in the *foothills,* is similar to the Valley Pocket Gopher. It may be the same species, but is treated here separately. Skull has 20 teeth. There are 8 mammae.
   Similar species: (1) Valley Pocket Gopher is difficult to distinguish; lowlands. (2) Pygmy Pocket Gopher has 6 mammae; high in mts. (3) Mexican and (4) Plains Pocket Gophers have prominent grooves in upper incisors.
   Habitat: Hard, clayey soils. Map p. 126

PYGMY POCKET GOPHER *Thomomys umbrinus*
   Identification: Head and body 4⅗–5 in. (117–127 mm); tail 2–2⅖ in. (51–61 mm). This small pocket gopher, *yellowish*

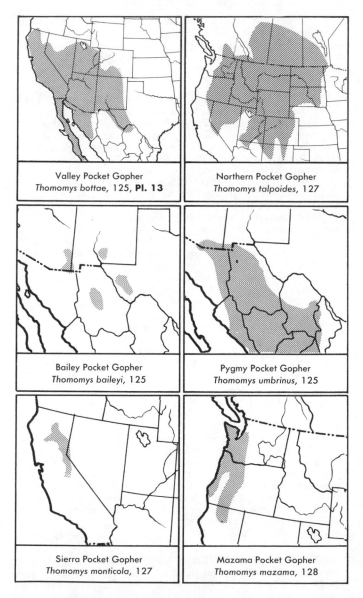

Valley Pocket Gopher
Thomomys bottae, 125, **Pl. 13**

Northern Pocket Gopher
Thomomys talpoides, 127

Bailey Pocket Gopher
Thomomys baileyi, 125

Pygmy Pocket Gopher
Thomomys umbrinus, 125

Sierra Pocket Gopher
Thomomys monticola, 127

Mazama Pocket Gopher
Thomomys mazama, 128

brown to deep *chestnut* in color, is found only in the *mts.* Other pocket gophers with which it might be confused are usually found in valleys. A single indistinct groove near inner border of each incisor. Skull has 20 teeth. There are 6 mammae.

Similar species: (1) Valley Pocket Gopher is larger; lowlands. (2) Bailey Pocket Gopher females have 8 mammae. (3) Mexican Pocket Gopher is larger, yellowish; deep groove down middle of each upper incisor; lowlands.

Habitat: Oaks and pines, sometimes rocky soil.

Map opposite

NORTHERN POCKET GOPHER   *Thomomys talpoides*

Identification: Head and body $5-6\frac{1}{2}$ in. (127–165 mm); tail $1\frac{3}{4}-3$ in. (44–76 mm); wt. $2\frac{3}{4}-4\frac{3}{5}$ oz. (78–130 g). Males are larger than females. This gopher, where it occurs close to ranges of others, is usually found in the *high mts. Grayish,* sometimes washed with brown; nose brown or blackish; black patches behind rounded ears. A single indistinct groove near inner border of each upper incisor. Skull (Plate 27) has 20 teeth. There are 10 mammae.

Similar species: (1) Valley Pocket Gopher is usually not grayish; female has 8 mammae; foothills and valleys. (2) Sierra Pocket Gopher is brown, not grayish; ears pointed. (3) Townsend Pocket Gopher is larger; along river valleys. (4) Giant Pocket Gopher is larger; lowlands. (5) Plains Pocket Gopher is larger; prominent groove in each upper incisor; lowlands.

Habitat: Grassy prairies, alpine meadows, brushy areas, and open pine forests.

Young: Born Feb.–June; usually 4–7; 1 or 2 litters a year.

Map opposite

SIERRA POCKET GOPHER   *Thomomys monticola*

Identification: Head and body $5\frac{3}{5}-6$ in. (142–152 mm); tail $2-3$ in. (51–76 mm); wt. $2\frac{1}{2}-3\frac{1}{5}$ oz. (71–91 g). Small; *bay to yellowish brown;* nose black or blackish, as are patches behind the pointed ears; tail with some white; feet and wrists often white. A single indistinct groove near inner border of each upper incisor. Skull has 20 teeth. There are 8 mammae.

Similar species: (1) Northern Pocket Gopher is grayish; female has 10 mammae. (2) Valley Pocket Gopher occurs in low foothills and valleys. (3) Giant Pocket Gopher is larger; lowlands.

Habitat: Mt. meadows.

Habits: In wet meadows, tunnels through snow; builds winter nest aboveground in snow; length of burrow system, 20–120 ft. (6–36 m). Populations of 4–14 per acre (10–35 per ha). May live 4 years in wild.

Young: Born July–Aug.; 3–4; 1 litter a year.   Map opposite

MAZAMA POCKET GOPHER *Thomomys mazama*
Identification: Head and body 5½-6⅗ in. (140-167 mm); tail 2⅛-2⅞ in. (54-73 mm); wt. 2⅘-4½ oz. (79-127 g). Males slightly larger than females; similar in external appearance to Northern Pocket Gopher; ranges separate. Skull has 20 teeth.
Similar species: Giant Pocket Gopher is larger; in valleys.

Map p. 126

TOWNSEND POCKET GOPHER *Thomomys townsendi*
Identification: Head and body 7-7½ in. (178-190 mm); tail 2-3⅘ in. (51-97 mm); wt. 8½-10¼ oz. (240-291 g). Largest pocket gopher within its range; *grayish* faintly washed with buff; tail, feet, and area around mouth may be white. A single indistinct groove near inner border of each upper incisor. Skull has 20 teeth. There are 8 mammae.
Similar species: (1) Valley Pocket Gopher is smaller, usually brownish. (2) Northern Pocket Gopher is smaller; high mts.
Habitat: Deep soils of river valleys.
Young: Born March-April; 3-8; 2 litters a year. Map below

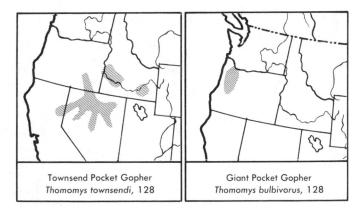

Townsend Pocket Gopher
Thomomys townsendi, 128

Giant Pocket Gopher
Thomomys bulbivorus, 128

GIANT POCKET GOPHER *Thomomys bulbivorus*
Identification: Head and body 7⅗-8½ in. (193-216 mm); tail 3¼-3⅗ in. (82-91 mm). This is by far the *largest* pocket gopher in Oregon. It is sooty brown. A single indistinct groove near inner border of each upper incisor. Skull has 20 teeth. There are 8 mammae.
Similar species: (1) Sierra, (2) Mazama, and (3) Northern Pocket Gophers are all smaller and all mt. dwellers.
Habitat: Deep soils of Willamette Valley, Oregon; does not enter pines.
Young: Born April-July; 3-5; 1 litter a year. Map above

Color Plates

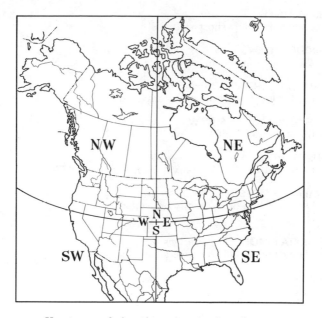

Key to area designations given on legend pages

Plate I

SHREWS AND MOLES

	Map	Text
MASKED SHREW *Sorex cinereus*	4	3

Grayish brown; long tail; pointed nose. N.

MERRIAM SHREW *Sorex merriami* — Map 7, Text 6
Pale gray; underparts whitish; small size. W.

LEAST SHREW *Cryptotis parva* — Map 14, Text 15
Cinnamon color; short tail. SE.

ARCTIC SHREW *Sorex arcticus* — Map 4, Text 5
Tricolored pattern in winter; darkest on back. N.

SHORTTAIL SHREW *Blarina brevicauda* — Map 15, Text 15
Lead color; short tail; no external ears. E.

NORTHERN WATER SHREW *Sorex palustris* — Map 13, Text 12
Blackish gray; stiff hairs on hind feet. N.

SHREW-MOLE *Neurotrichus gibbsi* — Map 14, Text 16
Body and tail black; hairy tail; naked nose. NW.

STARNOSE MOLE *Condylura cristata* — Map 18, Text 17
Dark brown or black; fleshy projections around nose.
NE.

HAIRYTAIL MOLE *Parascalops breweri* — Map 20, Text 18
Slate color; broad front feet; hairy tail. NE.

EASTERN MOLE *Scalopus aquaticus* — Map 18, Text 17
Broad front feet; naked tail. SE.
Pale phase: Light golden color.
Dark phase: Slate color.

TOWNSEND MOLE *Scapanus townsendi* — Map 20, Text 19
Blackish brown to black; broad front feet; tail
slightly haired. NW.

Shrew-Mole snout
top view

h.f., Water Shrew
fringe of stiff hairs

Surface mole tunnel from above

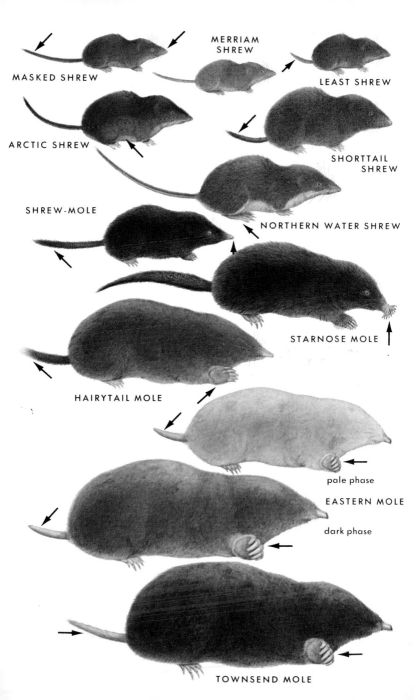

MASKED SHREW

MERRIAM SHREW

LEAST SHREW

ARCTIC SHREW

SHORTTAIL SHREW

SHREW-MOLE

NORTHERN WATER SHREW

STARNOSE MOLE

HAIRYTAIL MOLE

pale phase

EASTERN MOLE

dark phase

TOWNSEND MOLE

Plate 2

BATS

	Map	Text
LITTLE BROWN MYOTIS *Myotis lucifugus*	26	25

Brown, with glossy sheen; medium-sized ears; small size. N, S, E, W.

	Map	Text
LONG-EARED MYOTIS *Myotis evotis*	30	29

Pale brown; large black ears. W.

EASTERN BIG-EARED BAT *Plecotus rafinesquei*   42   41
Lumps on nose; large ears joined in middle. SE.

CALIFORNIA MYOTIS *Myotis californicus*   31   31
Bases of hairs dark; small size. W.

SMALL-FOOTED MYOTIS *Myotis subulatus*   34   32
Yellowish fur; black mask; small size. W, Central, NE.

EASTERN PIPISTREL *Pipistrellus subflavus*   35   34
Yellowish brown to drab brown; blunt tragus. E.

WESTERN PIPISTREL *Pipistrellus hesperus*   35   33
Pale ashy or yellowish gray; blunt tragus; small size. W.

PALLID BAT *Antrozous pallidus*   44   42
Pale yellowish gray; large ears not joined; simple muzzle. W.

BIG BROWN BAT *Eptesicus fuscus*   36   35
Pale brown to dark brown; blunt tragus; large size. N, S, E, W.

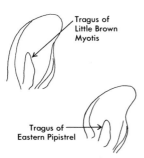

Tragus of Little Brown Myotis

Tragus of Eastern Pipistrel

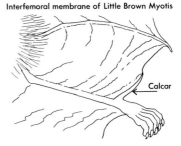

Interfemoral membrane of Little Brown Myotis

Calcar

LITTLE BROWN
MYOTIS

LONG-EARED MYOTIS

EASTERN
BIG-EARED BAT

EASTERN PIPISTREL

CALIFORNIA
MYOTIS

SMALL-FOOTED
MYOTIS

WESTERN PIPISTREL

PALLID BAT

BIG BROWN BAT

Plate 3

OTHER BATS

	Map	Text

SILVER-HAIRED BAT *Lasionycteris noctivagans* — Map 34, Text 33
Blackish brown, with white-tipped hairs. N, S, E, W.

MEXICAN FREETAIL BAT *Tadarida brasiliensis* — Map 44, Text 43
Chocolate-brown; tail beyond membrane; ears not joined; small size. S.

LEAFNOSE BAT *Macrotus californicus* — Map 23, Text 22
Grayish; projection on tip of nose; large ears. SW.

EASTERN YELLOW BAT *Lasiurus intermedius* — Map 40, Text 38
Yellowish brown; tail membrane furred on basal 3rd. SE.

SPOTTED BAT *Euderma maculata* — Map 40, Text 39
White spots on shoulders and rump; large ears. W.

HOGNOSE BAT *Choeronycteris mexicana* — Map 23, Text 22
Light brown; long nose with projection on end; small ears. SW.

RED BAT *Lasiurus borealis* — Map 36, Text 37
Tail membrane furred above. N, S, E, W.
Male: Brick-red, frosted.
Female: Pale reddish, frosted.

SEMINOLE BAT *Lasiurus seminolus* — Map 40, Text 37
Tail membrane furred above; mahogany-brown, frosted. SE.

HOARY BAT *Lasiurus cinereus* — Map 38, Text 37
Tail membrane furred above; buffy throat; frosted body. N, S, E, W.

WESTERN MASTIFF BAT *Eumops perotis* — Map 42, Text 45
Chocolate-brown; tail beyond membrane; large size. SW.

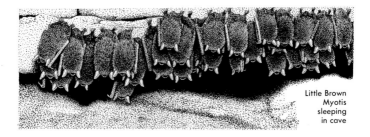

Little Brown Myotis sleeping in cave

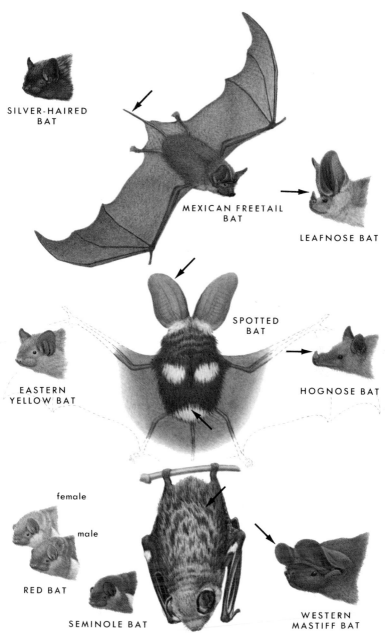

SILVER-HAIRED BAT

MEXICAN FREETAIL BAT

LEAFNOSE BAT

SPOTTED BAT

EASTERN YELLOW BAT

HOGNOSE BAT

female

male

RED BAT

SEMINOLE BAT

HOARY BAT

WESTERN MASTIFF BAT

Plate 4

BEARS

Grizzly Bear claw marks sometimes show in tracks

Big Brown Bear

Front foot middle claws of bears
× ½

Black Bear

	Map	Text

ALASKAN BROWN BEAR *Ursus middendorffi* — Map 48, Text 47
Hump on shoulders; large size; face dished; moderate front claws. NW.

GRIZZLY BEAR *Ursus horribilis* — Map 48, Text 46
Hump on shoulders; face dished; large front claws. NW.

POLAR BEAR *Thalarctos maritimus* — Map 49, Text 50
White, sometimes with pale yellowish wash. Arctic, Subarctic.

BLACK BEAR *Ursus americanus* — Map 49·, Text 46
Blue phase, cinnamon phase, black phase.
Nearly white on Gribble I., B.C.
No hump on shoulders; face brown, not dished; claws small. N, S, E, W.

9 in. ±

r. f.

r. h.

12 in. ±

Black Bear

ALASKAN BROWN BEAR

GRIZZLY BEAR

POLAR BEAR

blue phase   cinnamon phase   black phase

BLACK BEAR

Plate 5

FUR-BEARING MAMMALS

	Map	Text
MARTEN *Martes americana*	55	54

Yellowish brown to dark brown; pale buff on breast; bushy tail. N.

	Map	Text
FISHER *Martes pennanti*	55	54

Blackish brown; frosted with white-tipped hairs on head and shoulders. N.

	Map	Text
WOLVERINE *Gulo luscus*	62	63

Dark brown; broad yellowish stripes from shoulders to rump. N.

	Map	Text
SEA OTTER *Enhydra lutris*		63

Head and neck grayish or yellowish; floats on back; seacoast. W.

	Map	Text
RIVER OTTER *Lutra canadensis*	61	60

Rich brown upperparts, silvery underparts; tail thick at base. N, S, E, W.

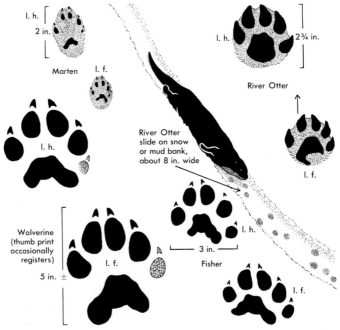

l. h.
2 in.

Marten

l. f.

l. h.
2¾ in.

River Otter

River Otter slide on snow or mud bank, about 8 in. wide

l. f.

l. h.

Wolverine (thumb print occasionally registers)
5 in. ±

l. f.

l. h.
3 in.

Fisher

l. f.

MARTEN

FISHER

WOLVERINE

SEA OTTER

RIVER OTTER

Plate 6

WEASELS AND MINK

	Map	Text
LEAST WEASEL *Mustela rixosa*	57	56

No black tip on short tail. N.

SHORTTAIL WEASEL *Mustela erminea*   57   55
Winter: White; medium-sized; tail with black tip.
Summer: Brown; white down hind leg to foot. N.

LONGTAIL WEASEL *Mustela frenata*   59   58
Hind legs brownish; black tip on long tail. N, S, E,
W.
Northeast: No white on face.
Southwest: White on face.

BLACK-FOOTED FERRET *Mustela nigripes*   61   58
Yellowish-brown to buffy body; black forehead and
feet. W Central.

MINK *Mustela vison*   59   60
Rich dark brown; white on chin. E, NW.

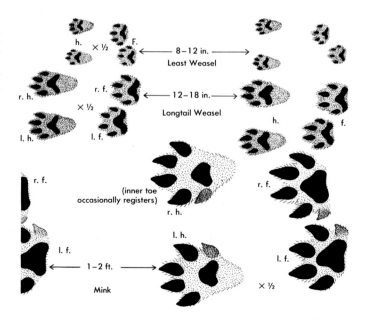

h.   × ½   F.   ← 8–12 in. →
Least Weasel

r. h.   r. f.   ← 12–18 in. →
× ½   Longtail Weasel
l. h.   l. f.   h.   f.

r. f.
(inner toe occasionally registers)   r. f.
r. h.

l. f.   l. h.
← 1–2 ft. →   l. f.
Mink   × ½

LEAST WEASEL

winter

summer
male

SHORTTAIL
WEASEL

northeast
female

LONGTAIL WEASEL

southwest

BLACK-FOOTED FERRET

MINK

Plate 7

DOGLIKE MAMMALS

	Map	Text
RED FOX *Vulpes fulva*	74	72

White tip on bushy tail. N, S, E, W.
Red phase: Reddish yellow; feet black.
Black phase: Black with white-tipped hairs.
Cross phase: Reddish yellow to brown; dark cross over shoulders.

GRAY FOX *Urocyon cinereoargenteus*   76   75
Black stripe down top of tail; feet and legs rusty. S, E, W.

ARCTIC FOX *Alopex lagopus*   76   75
Blue phase: Bluish brown; no white tip on tail.
White phase: White.
Arctic, Subarctic.

SWIFT FOX *Vulpes velox*   74   73
Black tip on tail. W Central.

COYOTE *Canis latrans*   69   69
Rusty legs, feet, and ears; nose pad less than 1 in. (25 mm) wide; tail down when running. W, NE.

GRAY WOLF *Canis lupus*   71   70
Usually gray; nose pad more than 1 in. (25 mm) wide; tail high when running. N, W.

RED WOLF *Canis niger*   71   72
Reddish or blackish; tail high when running. SE.

h. f.

11 in.
Gray Fox trotting

h. f.

1¾ in.
Red Fox

13 in.
Coyote trotting

2½ in.
Coyote (outer toes larger)

Wolf walking   10 in. ±

5 in. ±

h. f.
Staggered prints (wild canines, prints in straight line)

Dog   (variable)

h. f.

Wolf   (middle toes larger)

red phase

black phase

cross phase

RED FOX

GRAY FOX

blue phase

white phase

ARCTIC FOX

SWIFT FOX

COYOTE

GRAY WOLF

RED WOLF

Plate 8

CATS

	Map	Text
LYNX *Lynx canadensis*	81	80

LYNX *Lynx canadensis*
Short tail with tip black all way around. N.

BOBCAT *Lynx rufus*   81   81
Short tail with tip black only on top. N, S, E, W.

MOUNTAIN LION *Felis concolor*   78   77
Young: Spotted.
Adult: Tawny to grayish; large; long tail with dark brown tip.
W, SE.

OCELOT *Felis pardalis*   79   78
Spots arranged in rows; long tail; small size. S.

JAGUARUNDI CAT *Felis yagouaroundi*   79   80
Long tail; short legs. SW.
Red phase: Reddish.
Gray phase: Bluish gray.

JAGUAR *Felis onca*   79   77
Spots in form of rosettes; large size. SW.

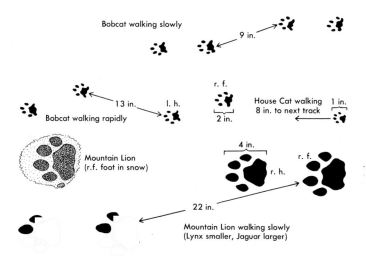

Bobcat walking slowly

9 in.

Bobcat walking rapidly

13 in.   l. h.

r. f.

House Cat walking
8 in. to next track   1 in.

2 in.

Mountain Lion
(r.f. foot in snow)

4 in.

r. h.

r. f.

22 in.

Mountain Lion walking slowly
(Lynx smaller, Jaguar larger)

LYNX

BOBCAT

young

MOUNTAIN LION

adult

red
phase

gray
phase

OCELOT

JAGUARUNDI CAT

JAGUAR

Plate 9

MEDIUM-SIZED MAMMALS

	Map	Text
WOODCHUCK *Marmota monax*	93	92

Yellowish brown or brown, frosted; feet dark brown or black. NW, E.

| **YELLOWBELLY MARMOT** *Marmota flaviventris* | 93 | 92 |

Belly yellow; white between eyes. W.

| **HOARY MARMOT** *Marmota caligata* | 91 | 94 |

Head and shoulders black and white; feet black. NW.

| **RINGTAIL** *Bassariscus astutus* | 53 | 52 |

Yellowish gray; long tail with rings. SW.

| **RACCOON** *Procyon lotor* | 51 | 50 |

Black mask; tail with rings. N, S, E, W.

| **COATI** *Nasua narica* | 53 | 52 |

Grizzled brown; white spots above and below each eye; long tail; long snout. SW.

| **BADGER** *Taxidea taxus* | 62 | 64 |

Yellowish gray; white stripe on forehead; feet black. W, N Central.

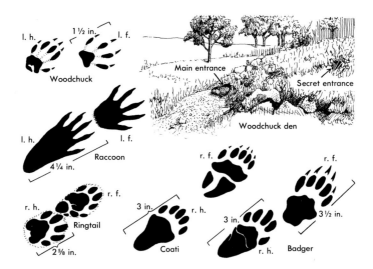

l. h.   1 ½ in.   l. f.
Woodchuck

Main entrance

Secret entrance

Woodchuck den

l. h.   l. f.
4 ¼ in.   Raccoon

r. f.

r. h.   r. f.
Ringtail
2 ⅝ in.

3 in.   r. h.
Coati

3 in.
r. h.   Badger

r. f.
3 ½ in.

WOODCHUCK

YELLOWBELLY
MARMOT

HOARY
MARMOT

RINGTAIL

RACCOON

COATI

BADGER

Plate 10
GROUND SQUIRRELS AND PRAIRIE DOGS

	Map	Text

SPOTTED GROUND SQUIRREL *Citellus spilosoma*   106 103
Indistinct squarish spots not in rows. S Central.

WASHINGTON GROUND SQUIRREL   96   98
Citellus washingtoni
Smoke-gray dappled with whitish; blackish tip on
short tail. NW.

THIRTEEN-LINED GROUND SQUIRREL   104 102
Citellus tridecemlineatus
Broken stripes on sides and back. Central.

COLUMBIAN GROUND SQUIRREL   101 100
Citellus columbianus
Upperparts mottled gray; feet and legs dark rufous.
NW.

CALIFORNIA GROUND SQUIRREL *Citellus beecheyi*
Sides of neck and shoulders whitish; dark on back
between shoulders. W.   96   97

ROCK SQUIRREL *Citellus variegatus*   96   97
Mottled grayish; large; tail slightly bushy; rocky
areas. SW.

ARCTIC GROUND SQUIRREL *Citellus parryi*   101 100
Top of head reddish; back flecked with white; feet
and legs tawny. NW.

FRANKLIN GROUND SQUIRREL *Citellus franklini*   106 105
Dark gray; large; open prairies. N Central.

WHITETAIL PRAIRIE DOG *Cynomys gunnisoni*   96   95
Body yellowish; tip of tail white. W Central.

BLACKTAIL PRAIRIE DOG *Cynomys ludovicianus*   96   94
Body yellowish; tip of tail black. W Central.

Prairie dog town

SPOTTED GROUND SQUIRREL

WASHINGTON GROUND SQUIRREL

THIRTEEN-LINED GROUND SQUIRREL

CALIFORNIA GROUND SQUIRREL

COLUMBIAN GROUND SQUIRREL

ROCK SQUIRREL

ARCTIC GROUND SQUIRREL

FRANKLIN GROUND SQUIRREL

WHITETAIL PRAIRIE DOG

BLACKTAIL PRAIRIE DOG

Plate 11

SQUIRRELS WITH STRIPES

	Map	Text

RED SQUIRREL *Tamiasciurus hudsonicus* — 121 120
  Upperparts yellowish or reddish; belly white. N, SW.
  Winter: Ear tufts.
  Summer: Black line along side.

CHICKAREE *Tamiasciurus douglasi* — 122 121
  Upperparts reddish olive; belly yellowish or rusty.
  NW.
  Winter: Ear tufts.
  Summer: Black line along side.

CLIFF CHIPMUNK *Eutamias dorsalis* — 112 111
  Gray; indistinct dark stripes down back and sides.
  SW.

COLORADO CHIPMUNK *Eutamias quadrivittatus* — 115 114
  Bright colors; stripes distinct; white behind ear. SW.

LEAST CHIPMUNK *Eutamias minimus* — 109 110
  East: Stripes on face; back stripes to base of tail.
  West: Pale yellowish gray; small size.
  W, N Central.

EASTERN CHIPMUNK *Tamias striatus* — 109 108
  Stripes on face; body stripes end at reddish rump;
  bushy tail. E.

TOWNSEND CHIPMUNK *Eutamias townsendi* — 112 110
  Dark brown; stripes on face and body indistinct.
  NW.

MERRIAM CHIPMUNK *Eutamias merriami* — 112 113
  Stripes indistinct; stripe below ear brownish. SW.

YUMA ANTELOPE SQUIRREL — 106 107
Ammospermophilus harrisi
  Pinkish cinnamon to mouse-gray; white stripes on
  body only. SW.

WHITETAIL ANTELOPE SQUIRREL — 106 107
Ammospermophilus leucurus
  Pinkish gray, with white stripes on body only; tail
  white beneath. SW.

GOLDEN-MANTLED SQUIRREL *Citellus lateralis* — 104 105
  Stripes on body only; coppery head. W.

Chipmunk at food cache

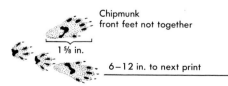

Chipmunk front feet not together

1 ⅝ in.

6–12 in. to next print

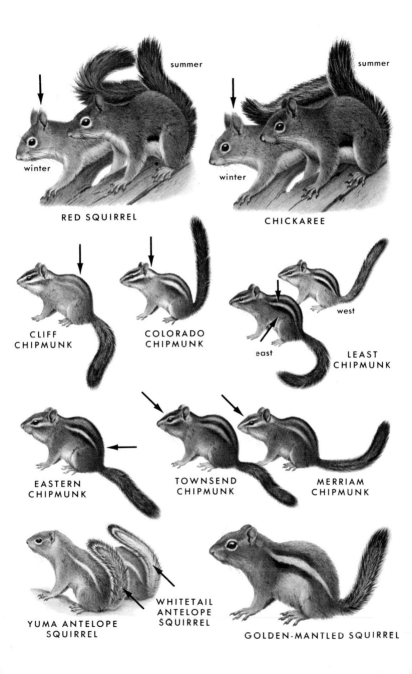

RED SQUIRREL
summer
winter

CHICKAREE
summer
winter

CLIFF
CHIPMUNK

COLORADO
CHIPMUNK

LEAST
CHIPMUNK
west
east

EASTERN
CHIPMUNK

TOWNSEND
CHIPMUNK

MERRIAM
CHIPMUNK

YUMA ANTELOPE
SQUIRREL

WHITETAIL
ANTELOPE
SQUIRREL

GOLDEN-MANTLED SQUIRREL

Plate 12

TREE SQUIRRELS

	Map	Text
WESTERN GRAY SQUIRREL *Sciurus griseus*	117	116

Body gray, feet dusky; very bushy tail. W.

EASTERN GRAY SQUIRREL *Sciurus carolinensis* 119 117
Body gray, washed with fulvous in summer. E.
Winter: White behind ears.
Summer: Tail bordered with white.

SOUTHERN FLYING SQUIRREL *Glaucomys volans* 122 122
Fur soft; olive-brown above, white on belly; loose
skin between front and hind legs. E.

TASSEL-EARED SQUIRREL *Sciurus aberti* 117 117
Ears tufted except in late summer. SW.
South of Grand Canyon: Tail white beneath.
North of Grand Canyon: Tail all-white.

EASTERN FOX SQUIRREL *Sciurus niger* 119 118
South: Head blackish, body grayish.
North: Rusty; tail bordered with fulvous.
East: Steel-gray; no fulvous.
E.

Leaf nest of
Tree Squirrel

Flying Squirrel gliding
from den-tree hole

2¼ in.
Gray Squirrel
bounding

Fox Squirrel,
h.f. 2⅞ in.

(front feet paired)

Red Squirrel
h.f. 1¾ in.

24 in.

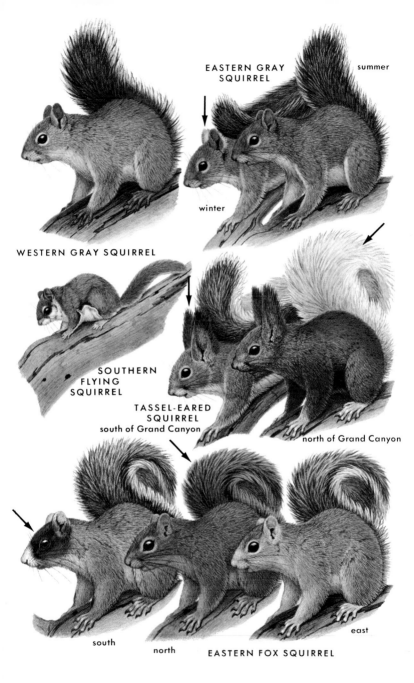

EASTERN GRAY SQUIRREL

winter

summer

WESTERN GRAY SQUIRREL

SOUTHERN FLYING SQUIRREL

TASSEL-EARED SQUIRREL
south of Grand Canyon

north of Grand Canyon

south

north

EASTERN FOX SQUIRREL

east

Plate 13

POCKET MICE, JUMPING MICE, POCKET GOPHERS

(Fur-lined cheek pouches or with long hind legs and tails)

	Map	Text
SILKY POCKET MOUSE *Perognathus flavus*	135	134

SILKY POCKET MOUSE *Perognathus flavus*   135   134
Yellowish; soft fur; tail not crested; small size. W Central.

APACHE POCKET MOUSE *Perognathus apache*   135   136
Buffy; tail more than $2\frac{1}{2}$ in. (64 mm). SW.

ROCK POCKET MOUSE *Perognathus intermedius*   138   139
Gray to black, sprinkled with fulvous; tail crested. SW.

CALIFORNIA POCKET MOUSE   141   140
Perognathus californicus
Spinelike hairs on rump. SW.

LONGTAIL POCKET MOUSE *Perognathus formosus*   141   140
Soft fur; tail long and crested; medium-sized. SW.

GREAT BASIN POCKET MOUSE *Perognathus parvus*   138   137
Olive-gray; soft fur. W.

HISPID POCKET MOUSE *Perognathus hispidus*   143   142
Fur coarse, mixed yellowish and brownish; tail medium-sized, not crested. Central.

BAILEY POCKET MOUSE *Perognathus baileyi*   141   142
Large; fur soft; tail crested. SW.

MEXICAN POCKET MOUSE *Liomys irroratus*   135   133
Dark gray; spinelike hairs on rump; no grooves on upper incisors. S.

MEADOW JUMPING MOUSE *Zapus hudsonius*   197   196
Olive-yellow, dark back, pale sides; large hind feet; no pouches; long tail; upper incisors grooved. N.

WOODLAND JUMPING MOUSE   198   199
Napaeozapus insignis
Brownish back, bright yellowish sides; white tip on long tail. NE.

PLAINS POCKET GOPHER *Geomys bursarius*   132   131
Two grooves down front of each upper incisor. Central.

MEXICAN POCKET GOPHER *Pappogeomys castanops*   132   132
One distinct groove down middle front of each upper incisor. SW.

VALLEY POCKET GOPHER *Thomomys bottae*   126   125
Three color phases; 1 indistinct groove near inner border of each incisor. SW.

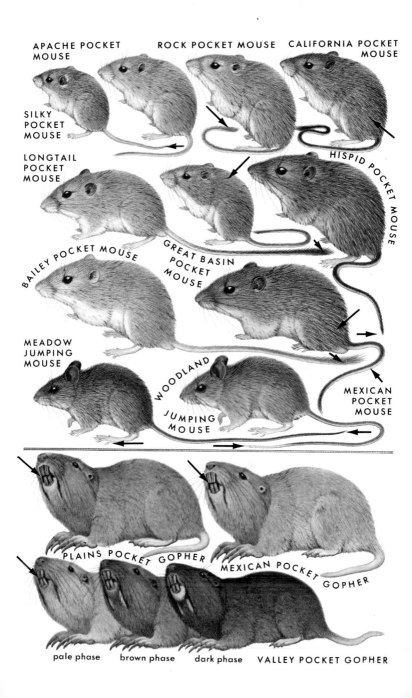

APACHE POCKET MOUSE

ROCK POCKET MOUSE

CALIFORNIA POCKET MOUSE

SILKY POCKET MOUSE

LONGTAIL POCKET MOUSE

HISPID POCKET MOUSE

BAILEY POCKET MOUSE

GREAT BASIN POCKET MOUSE

MEADOW JUMPING MOUSE

WOODLAND JUMPING MOUSE

MEXICAN POCKET MOUSE

PLAINS POCKET GOPHER

MEXICAN POCKET GOPHER

pale phase   brown phase   dark phase   VALLEY POCKET GOPHER

Plate 14

KANGAROO RATS AND MICE

(Fur-lined cheek pouches; deserts)

| | | *Map* | *Text* |

MERRIAM KANGAROO RAT *Dipodomys merriami* — 149 150
Four toes on hind foot; small size. SW.

BANNERTAIL KANGAROO RAT *Dipodomys spectabilis* 145 144
White tip on tail. SW.

PALE KANGAROO MOUSE *Microdipodops pallidus* — 145 143
Tail swollen in middle; not crested. SW.

DESERT KANGAROO RAT *Dipodomys deserti* — 149 150
Pale yellowish; white-tipped tail; large size. SW.

PACIFIC KANGAROO RAT *Dipodomys agilis* — 149 148
Five toes on hind foot. SW.

HEERMANN KANGAROO RAT *Dipodomys heermanni* 145 144
Normally 4 toes on hind foot; valleys and foothills.
W.

ORD KANGAROO RAT *Dipodomys ordi* — 147 147
Dark tail stripes broader than white ones. W.

GIANT KANGAROO RAT *Dipodomys ingens* — 145 146
Five toes on hind foot; large size. SW.

BIG-EARED KANGAROO RAT *Dipodomys elephantinus* — 148
Large ears; end of tail heavily crested. SW.

Kangaroo Rat den in desert

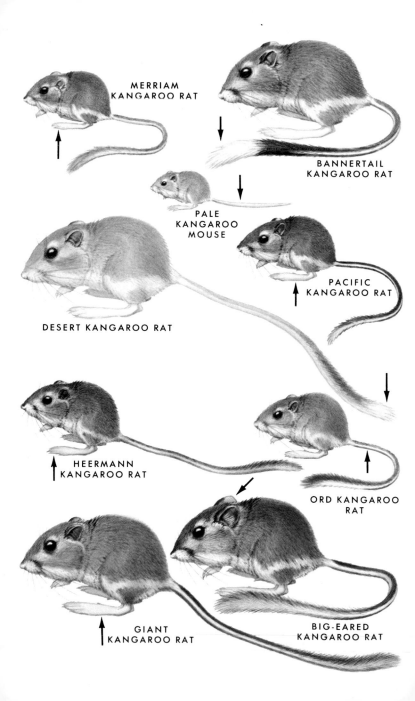

MERRIAM
KANGAROO RAT

BANNERTAIL
KANGAROO RAT

PALE
KANGAROO
MOUSE

DESERT KANGAROO RAT

PACIFIC
KANGAROO RAT

HEERMANN
KANGAROO RAT

ORD KANGAROO
RAT

GIANT
KANGAROO RAT

BIG-EARED
KANGAROO RAT

Plate 15

SMALL MICE

	Map	Text
EASTERN HARVEST MOUSE *Reithrodontomys humulis*	154	153

Color rich brown; grooves down front of upper incisors. SE.

	Map	Text
WESTERN HARVEST MOUSE	155	154

Reithrodontomys megalotis
Color gray, washed with fulvous, to brown; grooves on upper incisors. W, Central.

		Text
SALT MARSH HARVEST MOUSE		155

Reithrodontomys raviventris
Belly fulvous; salt marshes. W.

	Map	Text
FULVOUS HARVEST MOUSE	155	156

Reithrodontomys fulvescens
Sides fulvous; tail long; upper incisors grooved. S.

		Text
HOUSE MOUSE *Mus musculus*		195

Grayish brown with gray or buffy belly; tail scaly; incisors smooth. N, S, E, W.

	Map	Text
PYGMY MOUSE *Baiomys taylori*	164	165

Dark grayish brown; incisors smooth; small size. S.

	Map	Text
NORTHERN GRASSHOPPER MOUSE	166	166

Onychomys leucogaster
Two color phases; tail short with white tip. W.

Harvest Mouse
and nest

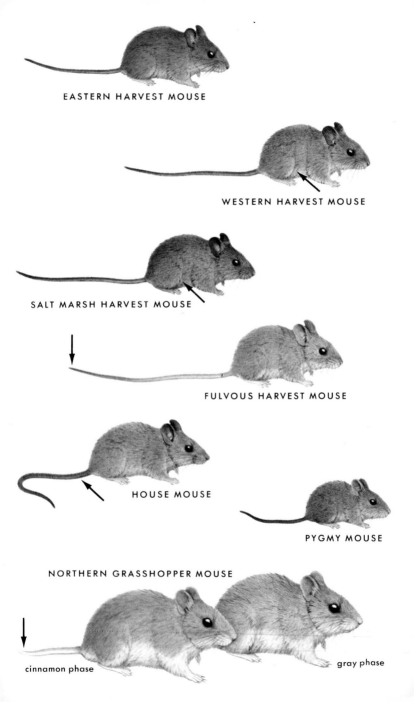

EASTERN HARVEST MOUSE

WESTERN HARVEST MOUSE

SALT MARSH HARVEST MOUSE

FULVOUS HARVEST MOUSE

HOUSE MOUSE

PYGMY MOUSE

NORTHERN GRASSHOPPER MOUSE

cinnamon phase

gray phase

Plate 16

MICE WITH LONG TAILS

(Usually with white bellies and feet)

	Map	Text

CANYON MOUSE *Peromyscus crinitus* 158 157
  Buffy gray to buff; tuft on end of long tail. W.

BRUSH MOUSE *Peromyscus boylei* 162 162
  Tail well haired. SW, S Central.

CACTUS MOUSE *Peromyscus eremicus* 158 156
  Pale gray faintly washed with fulvous; long tail slightly haired; desert. SW.

OLDFIELD MOUSE *Peromyscus polionotus* 158 159
  Whitish to pale cinnamon; tail short and bicolored; small size. SE.

PIÑON MOUSE *Peromyscus truei* 164 163
  Large ears; tail bicolored. SW.

DEER MOUSE *Peromyscus maniculatus* 160 158
  Variations in color; tail bicolored. N, S, E, W.

GOLDEN MOUSE *Peromyscus nuttalli* 164 165
  Rich golden cinnamon; nests in trees and vines. SE.

WHITE-FOOTED MOUSE *Peromyscus leucopus* 160 161
  Tail usually shorter than head and body. N, S, E, W.

CALIFORNIA MOUSE *Peromyscus californicus* 158 157
  Dark brown; top of tail blackish; big ears; large size. SW.

RICE RAT *Oryzomys palustris* 172 172
  Body grayish brown, sometimes washed with fulvous; feet whitish; tail scaly; near water. SE.

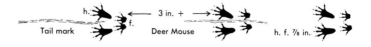

Tail mark   h.   f.   ← 3 in. + →   Deer Mouse   h. f. ⅞ in.

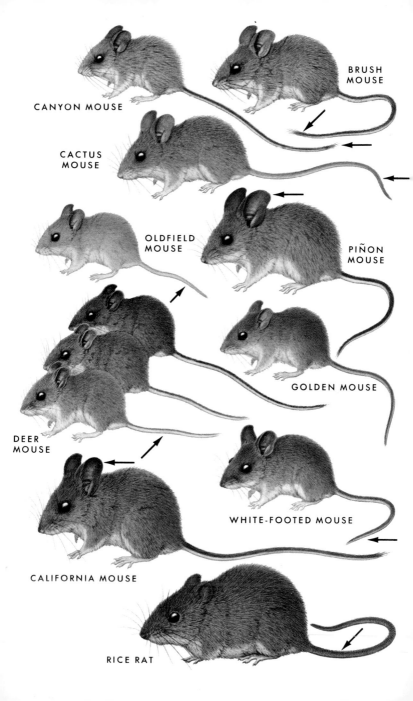

CANYON MOUSE

BRUSH MOUSE

CACTUS MOUSE

OLDFIELD MOUSE

PIÑON MOUSE

DEER MOUSE

GOLDEN MOUSE

CALIFORNIA MOUSE

WHITE-FOOTED MOUSE

RICE RAT

Plate 17

SMALL VOLE-LIKE MAMMALS

(With short tails and long fur, nearly concealing ears)

	Map	Text

PINE VOLE *Pitymys pinetorum*   190   192
  Auburn; soft fur; short tail; smooth upper incisors.
  E.

BOREAL REDBACK VOLE *Clethrionomys gapperi*   180   181
  Usually reddish down middle of back; upper incisors
  not grooved. N, SE, SW.

SOUTHERN BOG LEMMING *Synaptomys cooperi*   176   176
  Upper incisors grooved in front; short tail. NE.

TREE PHENACOMYS *Phenacomys longicaudus*   187   179
  Body reddish; tail blackish, long. NW.

MOUNTAIN PHENACOMYS *Phenacomys intermedius* 180   179
  Gray washed with brown to dark brown; incisors
  smooth. N, SW.

SAGEBRUSH VOLE *Lagurus curtatus*   190   192
  Pale ash-gray; sagebrush. NW.

HISPID COTTON RAT *Sigmodon hispidus*   174   173
  Coarse fur, mixed buff and black above, whitish below;
  large size. S.

PRAIRIE VOLE *Microtus ochrogaster*   189   191
  Grayish to dark brown, with mixture of fulvous;
  short tail; smooth incisors; prairies. Central.

TOWNSEND VOLE *Microtus townsendi*   187   185
  Blackish tail; dusky feet; large size. NW.

YELLOWNOSE VOLE *Microtus chrotorrhinus*   189   188
  Yellow on nose. NE.

MEADOW VOLE *Microtus pennsylvanicus*   184   183
  Grayish brown; long tail; upper incisors not grooved.
  N, SE, SW.

BROWN LEMMING *Lemmus trimucronatus*   177   178
  Body reddish-brown, never white; tail short. NW, N
  Central.

GREENLAND COLLARED LEMMING   177   175
Dicrostonyx groenlandicus
  Dark stripe down back in summer; white in winter.
  Arctic, Subarctic.

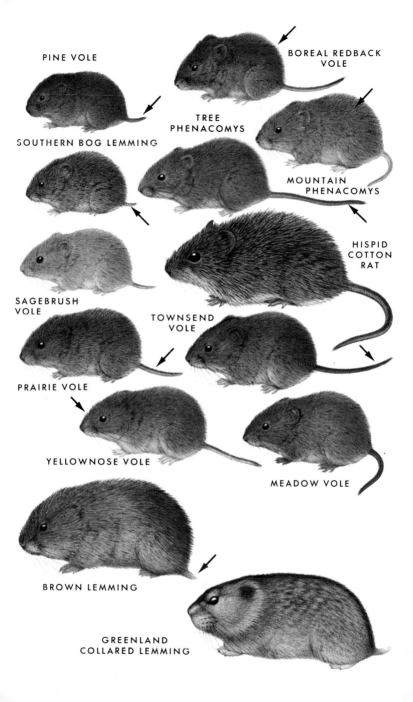

PINE VOLE

BOREAL REDBACK VOLE

TREE PHENACOMYS

SOUTHERN BOG LEMMING

MOUNTAIN PHENACOMYS

HISPID COTTON RAT

SAGEBRUSH VOLE

TOWNSEND VOLE

PRAIRIE VOLE

YELLOWNOSE VOLE

MEADOW VOLE

BROWN LEMMING

GREENLAND COLLARED LEMMING

Plate 18

WOODRATS AND OTHERS

WHITETHROAT WOODRAT *Neotoma albigula*   170   168
Gray washed with fulvous; hairs of throat white to skin; tail haired. SW.

DESERT WOODRAT *Neotoma lepida*   170   169
Gray washed with fulvous; hairs of belly slaty near skin; desert. SW.

MEXICAN WOODRAT *Neotoma mexicana*   170   169
Belly grayish white; tail white below; rocky areas. SW.

DUSKY-FOOTED WOODRAT *Neotoma fuscipes*   171   171
Body grayish brown; hind feet dusky; large size. W.

SOUTHERN PLAINS WOODRAT *Neotoma micropus*   170   168
Gray, no fulvous; tail haired. S Central.

BUSHYTAIL WOODRAT *Neotoma cinerea*   171   171
Tail squirrel-like, bushy. W.

EASTERN WOODRAT *Neotoma floridana*   170   167
Feet and belly whitish; tail haired. Central, NE, SE.

NORWAY RAT *Rattus norvegicus*   195
Grayish brown; tail scaly, long, but shorter than head and body. N, S, E, W.

BLACK RAT *Rattus rattus*   195
Tail longer than head and body; scaly. S.
Brown phase: Body brown.
Black phase: Body black.

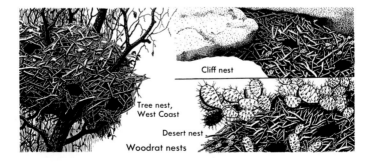

Cliff nest

Tree nest,
West Coast

Desert nest

Woodrat nests

WHITETHROAT WOODRAT

DESERT WOODRAT

MEXICAN WOODRAT

SOUTHERN PLAINS WOODRAT

DUSKY-FOOTED WOODRAT

EASTERN WOODRAT

BUSHYTAIL WOODRAT

brown phase

black phase

NORWAY RAT

BLACK RAT

Plate 19

SOME ODD MAMMALS

Muskrat houses in marsh

Tree cut by Beaver

	Map	Text
FLORIDA WATER RAT *Neofiber alleni*	190	193

Rich brown fur; round tail; water. SE.

	Map	Text
MUSKRAT *Ondatra zibethica*	194	193

Rich brown fur; scaly tail flattened on sides; water.
N, S, E, W.

	Map	Text
APLODONTIA *Aplodontia rufa*	91	90

Dark brown; no apparent tail; moist situations. NW.

	Map	Text
NUTRIA *Myocastor coypus*		200

Body grayish brown; tail long, round, scantily haired;
water. S, NW.

	Map	Text
ARMADILLO *Dasypus novemcinctus*	228	228

Covered with armor plate. S Central, SE.

	Map	Text
OPOSSUM *Didelphis marsupialis*	2	1

White face, naked tail; size of House Cat. S, E, W.

	Map	Text
BEAVER *Castor canadensis*	152	151

Tail scaly, paddle-shaped, flattened on top and
bottom. N, S, E, W.

	Map	Text
PORCUPINE *Erethizon dorsatum*	200	199

Long sharp spines on body and tail. N, W.

	Map	Text
PECCARY *Pecari angulatus*	214	213

Piglike; 3 toes on hind foot. SW, S Central.

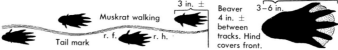

3 in. ±
Muskrat walking
Tail mark r. f. r. h.

Beaver 3–6 in.
4 in. ±
between
tracks. Hind
covers front.

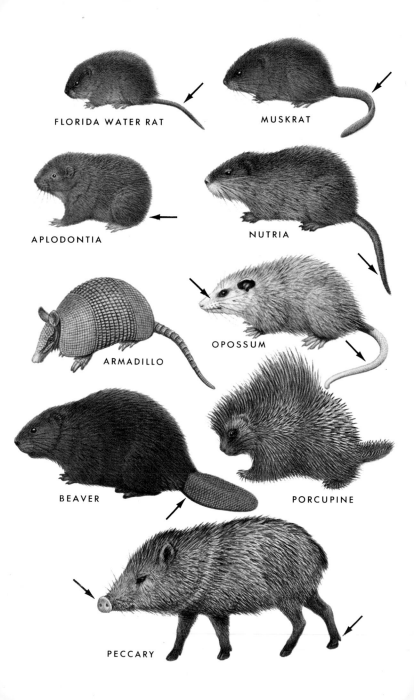

FLORIDA WATER RAT

MUSKRAT

APLODONTIA

NUTRIA

ARMADILLO

OPOSSUM

BEAVER

PORCUPINE

PECCARY

Plate 20

JACKRABBITS AND HARES

	Map	Text

WHITETAIL JACKRABBIT *Lepus townsendi*   204   204
  Winter: White or pale gray; large; tail usually white.
  Summer: Brownish gray; tail usually white above
  and below.
  N Central, NW.

SNOWSHOE HARE *Lepus americanus*   203   205
  Winter: White; hairs dark at bases; large hind feet.
  Summer: Dark brown; large hind feet.
  N, E, W.

BLACKTAIL JACKRABBIT *Lepus californicus*   206   207
  Black on top of tail and rump; ears black-tipped. W,
  S Central.

ANTELOPE JACKRABBIT *Lepus alleni*   206   206
  Whitish sides and hips; ears huge. SW.

EUROPEAN HARE *Lepus europaeus*   206   205
  Black on top of tail; large size; open areas. NE.

ARCTIC HARE *Lepus arcticus*   203   203
  Winter: Body hairs white to skin; tips of ears black.
  Summer: Gray, brown, or white; tail always white;
  tips of ears black.
  Arctic, Subarctic.

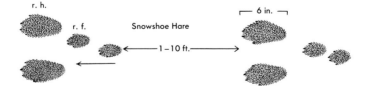

l. h.   l. f.   7 – 12 ft.

2¾ in. +   Jackrabbit

r. h.   r. f.   Snowshoe Hare   6 in.

1 – 10 ft.

winter

summer

WHITETAIL JACKRABBIT

winter

summer

SNOWSHOE HARE

BLACKTAIL JACKRABBIT

ANTELOPE JACKRABBIT

EUROPEAN HARE

winter

summer

ARCTIC HARE

Plate 21

COTTONTAILS AND PIKAS

Pika and haystack in rockslide

	Map	Text
PYGMY RABBIT *Sylvilagus idahoensis*	210	212

Body slate-gray with pinkish tinge; ears short; small size; desert brush. NW.

BRUSH RABBIT *Sylvilagus bachmani*	210	211

Body brown; ears relatively short; small, inconspicuous tail; brush. W.

PIKA *Ochotona princeps*	202	201

No visible tail; rounded ears; small size; rockslides. W.

DESERT COTTONTAIL *Sylvilagus auduboni*	210	209

Pale gray washed with yellow; large ears. W.

MOUNTAIN COTTONTAIL *Sylvilagus nuttalli*	208	209

Grayish; mts. W.

EASTERN COTTONTAIL *Sylvilagus floridanus*	208	208

Feet whitish; nape patch rusty and distinct. E, Central, SW.

MARSH RABBIT *Sylvilagus palustris*	210	211

Body dark brown; fur coarse; marshes. SE.

SWAMP RABBIT *Sylvilagus aquaticus*	210	212

Body brownish gray; feet rusty above; fur coarse. SE.

l. f. l. h. Cottontail 1–7 ft. 4 in. ±

PYGMY RABBIT

BRUSH RABBIT

PIKA

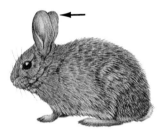

DESERT COTTONTAIL

MOUNTAIN COTTONTAIL

EASTERN
COTTONTAIL

MARSH RABBIT

SWAMP RABBIT

Plate 22

NORTHERN BIG GAME MAMMALS

BARREN GROUND CARIBOU *Rangifer arcticus*
Whitish; small antlers. Arctic.

WOODLAND CARIBOU *Rangifer caribou*
Body dark chocolate color; neck whitish; white on rump and above hoofs. Arctic, Subarctic.

MUSKOX *Ovibos moschatus*
Long, silky, brown hair reaches nearly to ground. Arctic.

ELK *Cervus canadensis*
Neck chestnut-brown; rump patch pale yellowish. W, Central.

MOOSE *Alces alces*
Body dark brown; antlers (on male) palmate; overhanging snout; "bell" on throat; no white; large size. N.

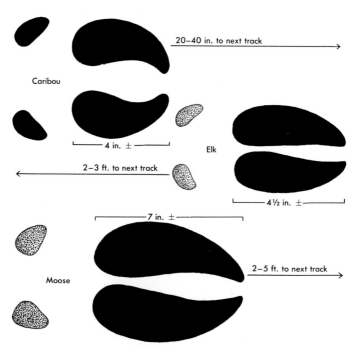

Caribou

20–40 in. to next track

4 in. ±

Elk

2–3 ft. to next track

4½ in. ±

7 in. ±

Moose

2–5 ft. to next track

BARREN GROUND CARIBOU

WOODLAND CARIBOU

MUSKOX

ELK

MOOSE

Plate 23

PRONGHORN AND DEER

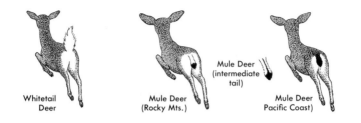

Whitetail Deer

Mule Deer (Rocky Mts.)

Mule Deer (intermediate tail)

Mule Deer Pacific Coast)

	Map	Text

PRONGHORN *Antilocapra americana* — Map 223, Text 223
Body pale tan; bands on throat, rump patch, and lower sides white. W.

MULE DEER *Odocoileus hemionus* — Map 217, Text 216
Northwest Pacific Coast: Winter, black on tip of tail.
Rocky Mts.: Winter, whitish rump, large ears, black-tipped tail.
Antlers in velvet, summer.
W.

WHITETAIL DEER *Odocoileus virginianus* — Map 217, Text 218
Winter, male: Body blue-gray; large tail white beneath; antlers branch from main beam.
Summer, female: Body reddish; large tail white beneath.
Fawn: Spotted, tail white beneath.
N, S, E, W.

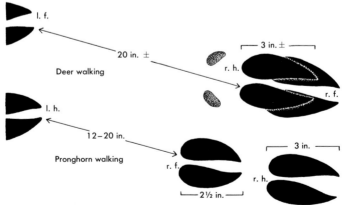

l. f.

20 in. ±

Deer walking

r. h.

3 in. ±

r. f.

l. h.

12–20 in.

Pronghorn walking

r. f.

2½ in.

3 in.

r. h.

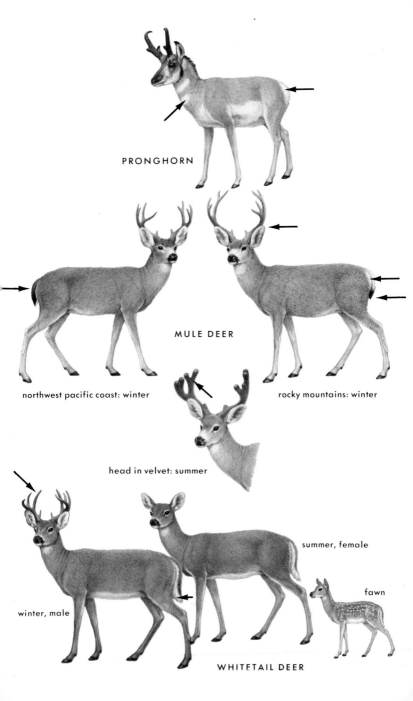

PRONGHORN

MULE DEER

northwest pacific coast: winter

rocky mountains: winter

head in velvet: summer

winter, male

summer, female

fawn

WHITETAIL DEER

Plate 24

GOAT, SHEEP, AND BISON

	Map	Text
MOUNTAIN GOAT *Oreamnos americanus*	223	224

    White; horns and hoofs black; beard. NW.

WHITE SHEEP *Ovis dalli*   227   227
    Horns massive, yellowish, coiled. NW.
    Gray phase: Grayish.
    Black phase: Blackish.
    White phase: White.

BIGHORN SHEEP *Ovis canadensis*   227   226
    Creamy-white rump; massive coiled horns. W.

BISON *Bison bison*   225   224
    Body dark brown all over; hump over shoulders;
    massive head; horns in both sexes. W.

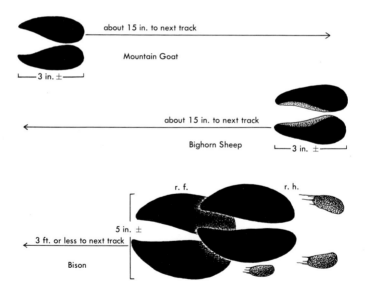

about 15 in. to next track

Mountain Goat

— 3 in. ± —

about 15 in. to next track

Bighorn Sheep
— 3 in. ± —

r. f.   r. h.

5 in. ±

3 ft. or less to next track

Bison

MOUNTAIN GOAT

gray phase

WHITE
SHEEP

black phase

BIGHORN
SHEEP

WHITE SHEEP
white phase

BISON

PLAINS POCKET GOPHER   *Geomys bursarius*   **Pl. 13**
   Identification: Head and body 5½–9 in. (140–229 mm); tail
   2–4½ in. (51–113 mm); wt. 4½–12½ oz. (127–354 g). Largest
   in the North, smallest in the South; males larger than females.
   Color varies from yellowish tawny to browns; nearly black in
   Illinois. Spotted and albino individuals fairly common. May
   be distinguished from other pocket gophers (except South Texas
   Pocket Gopher) by the *2 distinct grooves down* front of each
   upper incisor. Skull (Plate 27) has 20 teeth. There are 6
   mammae.
      The species *G. arenarius,* from w. Texas and s. New Mexico,
   is considered a distinct species by some authors; it is included
   with *G. bursarius* on the distribution map.
   Similar species: (1) South Texas Pocket Gopher is slightly
   larger; ranges separate for most part. (2) Mexican Pocket
   Gopher has 1 distinct groove in middle (front) of each upper
   incisor. (3) Bailey, (4) Northern, and (5) Valley Pocket Gophers
   have 1 indistinct groove near inner border of each upper incisor.
   Habitat: Grassland, alfalfa fields, pastures, roadsides, and rail-
   road rights-of-way.
   Habits: Burrows to 300 ft. (91 m) long; nests in underground
   tunnels in North; in South some nest, in winter, in large mounds
   that they build up on surface. Breeds April–July in North,
   Feb.–Aug. in South.
   Young: Usually 3–5 (1–8); 1 litter a year in North, 2 or more
   in South; gestation period, 18–19 days.   Map p. 132

SOUTH TEXAS POCKET GOPHER   *Geomys personatus*
   Identification: Head and body 7–8⅕ in. (178–208 mm); tail
   2½–4⅘ in. (64–122 mm); wt. 10–14 oz. (284–397 g). Pale,
   grayish brown; tail scantily haired; belly whitish to dusky.
   Similar to Plains Pocket Gopher.
   Similar species: Plains Pocket Gopher is similar, but smaller
   where they meet; ranges separate for most part.
   Habitat: Deep, sandy soils.   Map p. 132

SOUTHEASTERN POCKET GOPHER   *Geomys pinetis*
(Salamander)
   Identification: Head and body 6½–8 in. (165–203 mm); tail
   3–4 in. (76–102 mm). This is the only mammal in its area that
   has *fur-lined external cheek pouches.* Skull has 20 teeth.
      Formerly known as *G. tuza.*
      In current literature, 3 other species are recognized (all oc-
   curring in Georgia). They are: *G. colonus* in Camden Co.,
   G. fontanelus in Chatham Co., and *G. cumberlandius* on Cum-
   berland I., Camden Co. In this *Field Guide* they are treated
   together on the distribution map for *G. pinetis.*
   Habitat: Pine woods and fields.

Young: May appear in any month; 1–3; at least 2 litters a year.
Map below

MEXICAN POCKET GOPHER   Pl. 13
Pappogeomys castanops

Identification: Head and body 7¼–8 in. (184–203 mm); tail
3–4 in. (76–102 mm); wt. 7½–11⁷⁄₁₀ oz. (212–330 g). This
large, yellowish pocket gopher may be distinguished from other
pocket gophers by the distinct *single groove down middle*
(front) *of each upper incisor.* Skull (Plate 27) has 20 teeth.
Formerly known as *Cratogeomys.*
Similar species: (1) Plains Pocket Gopher has 2 grooves on
front of each upper incisor. (2) Bailey, (3) Pygmy, and (4)
Valley Pocket Gophers are smaller; an indistinct groove down
front of each upper incisor, near inner border.
Habitat: Deep, easily worked (preferably sandy) soil.
Young: 1–3; possibly 2 litters a year.   Map below

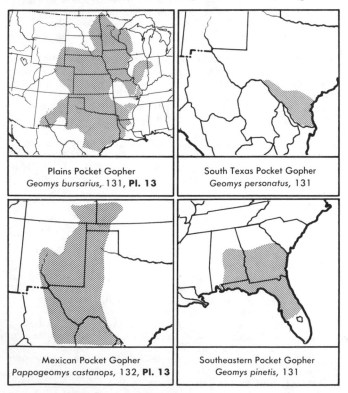

Plains Pocket Gopher
Geomys bursarius, 131, **Pl. 13**

South Texas Pocket Gopher
Geomys personatus, 131

Mexican Pocket Gopher
Pappogeomys castanops, 132, **Pl. 13**

Southeastern Pocket Gopher
Geomys pinetis, 131

Pocket Mice, Kangaroo Mice, and Kangaroo Rats: Heteromyidae

MEMBERS of this family are mostly *small* with *fur-lined cheek pouches* that open on either side of the mouth. Front feet are *weak* and hind feet and legs are strong and well developed. Tail is generally as long as or longer than head and body. Except for the genus *Liomys,* the upper incisors are grooved on front faces. All are adapted for arid or semiarid conditions; they do not need drinking water. Burrow into ground for nest sites. Usually prefer pliable, *sandy soil.* All are nocturnal; may be seen dead along the highway or hopping across in front of headlights. Eyeshine dull amber. Known as fossils from Oligocene.

Pocket mice include the smallest members of this family; head and body not more than 5 in. (127 mm). They vary from pale yellowish to dark gray, with paler belly, but *never* have striking color patterns on face or body. Tail never swollen along its middle. Possibly some hibernate or remain in den during severe weather. All store food, chiefly seeds.

Kangaroo mice are small silky-haired members of this group; head and body, 3 in. (76 mm). Tail *swollen* along its middle, smaller at base and tip, and *never crested* with long hairs at tip. Head is large for the animal.

Kangaroo rats are largest members of this family; head and body to 6½ in. (165 mm). They have extremely *long hind legs* and small front legs and front feet. Belly always *white;* upperparts vary from pale yellow to dark brownish. *Long tail* usually dark above and below, with side stripes of white and with a crest of long hairs on terminal ⅕ or more. There are distinct *facial markings* of white and usually black. On most of them, a definite *white band crosses thigh region* and joins the tail. Variation is mostly in intensity of coloration, not pattern.

Economic status: Members of this family, for the most part, occupy uncultivated areas. They do no harm, and by eating many weed seeds may be beneficial.

MEXICAN POCKET MOUSE *Liomys irroratus*   Pl. 13
Identification: Head and body 4–5 in. (102–127 mm); tail 4–5 in. (102–127 mm); wt. 1⅕–1¾ oz. (34–50 g). This large pocket mouse barely enters the *Brownsville* area of Texas. It is dark gray, white on belly, and has a pale yellow line along the side; hair on back and rump *stiff and spinelike.* Upper incisors not grooved on front faces. Skull (Plate 27) has 20 teeth. There are 6 mammae.
Similar species: (1) Hispid Pocket Mouse has tail shorter than head and body; upper incisors with grooves on front faces.

(2) Merriam Pocket Mouse is smaller, yellowish; fur silky.
Habitat: Dense thickets on low ridges.   Map opposite

WYOMING POCKET MOUSE   *Perognathus fasciatus*
Identification: Head and body $2\frac{4}{5}$ in. (71 mm); tail $2\frac{1}{2}$ in. (64 mm); wt. $\frac{1}{4}$–$\frac{1}{3}$ oz. (7–9 g). Found on the plains, this is one of the *silky* pocket mice; the fur is soft. Color *olive-gray,* with pale *yellow on ears* and a yellow wash along sides. Skull has 20 teeth. There are 6 mammae.
Similar species: (1) Plains and (2) Silky Pocket Mice are smaller; yellowish above or with yellow patches behind ears. (3) Hispid Pocket Mouse is larger; fur coarse.
Habitat: Shortgrass prairies, sandy loam.
Young: 4–6; gestation period about 4 weeks; 1 litter a year.
                                                   Map opposite

PLAINS POCKET MOUSE   *Perognathus flavescens*
Identification: Head and body $2\frac{1}{4}$–$2\frac{3}{4}$ in. (57–70 mm); tail 2–$2\frac{3}{5}$ in. (51–66 mm); wt. $\frac{1}{4}$–$\frac{1}{3}$ oz. (7–9 g). A small *pale-yellowish* pocket mouse with *white belly;* no clear yellow patches behind ears. Skull has 20 teeth. There are 6 mammae.
Similar species: (1) Wyoming Pocket Mouse is gray. (2) Merriam and (3) Silky Pocket Mice have clear yellow patches behind ears. (4) Bailey and (5) Hispid Pocket Mice are larger.
Habitat: Open areas with sparse vegetation and sandy soil.
Habits: Feeds mostly on small seeds; burrows usually beneath bushes; entrances plugged during day. Home range about $\frac{1}{10}$ acre (0.04 ha). Breeds April–July.
Young: 4–5; probably 2 litters a year.   Map opposite

MERRIAM POCKET MOUSE   *Perognathus merriami*
Identification: Head and body $2\frac{1}{4}$–$2\frac{3}{4}$ in. (57–70 mm); tail $1\frac{1}{2}$–2 in. (38–51 mm); wt. $\frac{1}{4}$–$\frac{1}{3}$ oz. (7–9 g). Fur soft and silky; rich *tawny* sprinkled with dark hairs on back, and with yellow patches behind ears; belly *white.* Difficult to distinguish this from Silky Pocket Mouse on external characters alone. Skull has 20 teeth.
Similar species: (1) Silky Pocket Mouse is less richly colored, difficult to distinguish. (2) Plains Pocket Mouse has no patches behind ears. (3) Other pocket mice are distinctly larger and have coarse pelage.
Habitat: Open plains, sandy or gravelly soil, short or sparse vegetation.
Habits: Burrows usually at base of shrub or cactus; breeding season April–Nov.
Young: 3–6; 2 or more litters a year.   Map opposite

SILKY POCKET MOUSE   *Perognathus flavus*   **Pl. 13**
Identification: Head and body 2–$2\frac{1}{2}$ in. (51–64 mm); tail

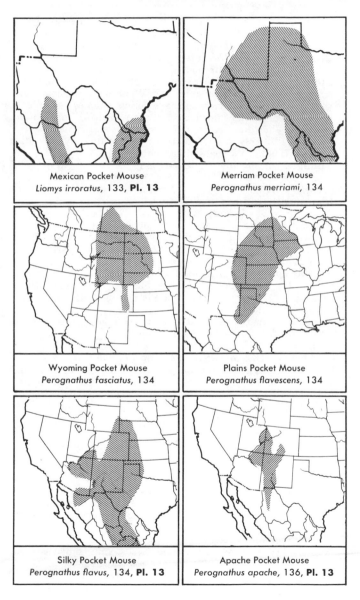

Mexican Pocket Mouse
Liomys irroratus, 133, **Pl. 13**

Merriam Pocket Mouse
Perognathus merriami, 134

Wyoming Pocket Mouse
Perognathus fasciatus, 134

Plains Pocket Mouse
Perognathus flavescens, 134

Silky Pocket Mouse
Perognathus flavus, 134, **Pl. 13**

Apache Pocket Mouse
Perognathus apache, 136, **Pl. 13**

1 $\frac{3}{4}$ - 2 $\frac{1}{4}$ in. (44 - 57 mm); wt. $\frac{1}{4}$ - $\frac{1}{3}$ oz. (7 - 9 g). Fur soft; upper-parts *pale yellow,* faintly to heavily sprinkled with black hairs; a clear *yellow patch behind each ear;* belly *white.* Tail usually slightly *shorter than head and body,* not crested. Skull has 20 teeth. There are 6 mammae.
Similar species: (1) Merriam Pocket Mouse is more richly colored; difficult to distinguish. (2) Wyoming (olive-gray) and (3) Plains Pocket Mice do not have yellow patches behind ears. (4) All other pocket mice have tail more than 2 $\frac{1}{2}$ in. (64 mm).
Habitat: Shortgrass prairies, sandy, occasionally rocky soils.
Habits: Probably similar to those of the directly preceding species. Has lived 5 years in captivity.
Young: 2 - 6; possibly 2 litters a year.   Map p. 135

APACHE POCKET MOUSE *Perognathus apache*   **Pl. 13**
   Identification: Head and body 2 $\frac{2}{5}$ - 3 in. (61 - 76 mm); tail 2 $\frac{2}{5}$ - 2 $\frac{4}{5}$ in. (61 - 71 mm); wt. $\frac{1}{4}$ - $\frac{2}{5}$ oz. (7 - 11 g). The soft fur of this inhabitant of some of our sparsely populated areas in the West is usually *buff,* slightly sprinkled with black. On the white sands, Otaro Co., New Mexico, they are nearly white. Belly is *white.* Skull has 20 teeth.
   Similar species: (1) Arizona Pocket Mouse is similar; slightly larger. (2) Silky Pocket Mouse has tail less than 2 $\frac{1}{2}$ in. (64 mm). (3) Other pocket mice are larger and with longer hairs toward tip of tail.
   Habitat: Sparse brush, scattered junipers and pines; usually 5000 - 7200 ft. (1524 - 2195 m) elevation.   Map p. 135

LITTLE POCKET MOUSE *Perognathus longimembris*
   Identification: Head and body 2 $\frac{1}{5}$ - 2 $\frac{4}{5}$ in. (56 - 71 mm); tail 2 - 3 $\frac{2}{5}$ in. (51 - 86 mm); wt. $\frac{1}{4}$ - $\frac{1}{3}$ oz. (7 - 9 g). Fur *soft;* upper-parts *buffy* to grayish buff; belly white. Difficult to distinguish from San Joaquin Pocket Mouse, but the ranges, for the most part, are distinct. Skull has 20 teeth. There are 6 mammae.
   Similar species: (1) San Joaquin Pocket Mouse is confined to San Joaquin and Sacramento Valleys, California. (2) Arizona Pocket Mouse is larger; longer tail. (3) Great Basin Pocket Mouse is larger; dark olive-gray. (4) All other pocket mice are larger and have long hairs toward tip of tail. (5) Dark Kangaroo Mouse (p. 142) is brownish; tail swollen in middle. (6) Pale Kangaroo Mouse (p. 143) is whitish; tail swollen in middle.
   Habitat: Valleys and slopes; sandy soil covered with *desert pavement* of small pebbles; sagebrush, creosote bush, and cactus; occasionally scattered piñon pines and junipers.
   Habits: Feeds primarily on small seeds; may range 350 yd. (320 m) in 24 hr.; has lived 7 $\frac{1}{2}$ years in captivity.
   Young: Born April - July; 3 - 7; 1 or 2 litters a year.
                                                         Map p. 138

ARIZONA POCKET MOUSE   *Perognathus amplus*
  Identification: Head and body $2\frac{4}{5}$–3 in. (71–76 mm); tail 3–$3\frac{4}{5}$ in. (76–97 mm); wt. $\frac{3}{7}$–$\frac{1}{2}$ oz. (12–14 g). Upperparts *pinkish buff,* sparsely sprinkled with black hairs on back; belly *white;* fur *soft and silky.* Tail *longer than head and body.* Skull has 20 teeth.
  Similar species: (1) Apache and (2) Little Pocket Mice are smaller. (3) Silky Pocket Mouse is smaller; tail less than $2\frac{1}{2}$ in. (64 mm). (4) Bailey, (5) Rock, and (6) Desert Pocket Mice are all larger and with long hairs toward tip of tail.
  Habitat: Arid desert, scattered vegetation.   Map p. 138

SAN JOAQUIN POCKET MOUSE   *Perognathus inornatus*
  Identification: Head and body $2\frac{1}{2}$–$3\frac{1}{5}$ in. (64–81 mm); tail $2\frac{4}{5}$–3 in. (71–76 mm). This soft-haired, buffy pocket mouse is confined to the *San Joaquin and Sacramento Valleys,* California. Only other pocket mouse of similar size and coloration with which this mouse might be confused is the Little Pocket Mouse, but ranges distinct for the most part. Skull has 20 teeth.
  Similar species: (1) Little Pocket Mouse is difficult to distinguish; should be sent to a museum for identification. (2) White-eared Pocket Mouse occurs in pine zone. (3) California Pocket Mouse is olive-brown.
  Habitat: Dry, open, grassy or weedy areas; fine-textured soil.
                                                      Map p. 138

GREAT BASIN POCKET MOUSE   **Pl. 13**
Perognathus parvus
  Identification: Head and body $2\frac{1}{2}$–3 in. (64–76 mm); tail $3\frac{1}{4}$–4 in. (82–102 mm); wt. $\frac{2}{3}$–1 oz. (19–28 g). Olive-gray, usually washed with tawny on belly; fur soft; tail paler below than above, not particularly bushy on the end. Skull has 20 teeth. There are 6 mammae.
  Similar species: (1) Little Pocket Mouse is smaller; buffy. (2) Longtail and (3) Desert Pocket Mice have long hairs on tail, distinctly bushy near tip. (4) Kangaroo mice (pp. 142–143) have white bellies and tail swollen near middle.
  Habitat: Sagebrush, chaparral, piñon and yellow pines.
  Habits: Inactive in winter. Solitary for most of life. Burrows beneath bushes, closed during day; stores seeds in den. Has lived $4\frac{1}{2}$ years in captivity.
  Young: Born late spring and early summer; 3–8, usually 4–5; probably 1 litter a year.   Map p. 138

WHITE-EARED POCKET MOUSE   *Perognathus alticolus*
  Identification: Head and body 3–$3\frac{2}{5}$ in. (76–86 mm); tail 3–$3\frac{3}{5}$ in. (76–91 mm). Hair soft; upperparts olive-green buff; *ears* and underparts *white* or *whitish.* Skull has 20 teeth.
  Similar species: (1) San Joaquin Pocket Mouse does not have

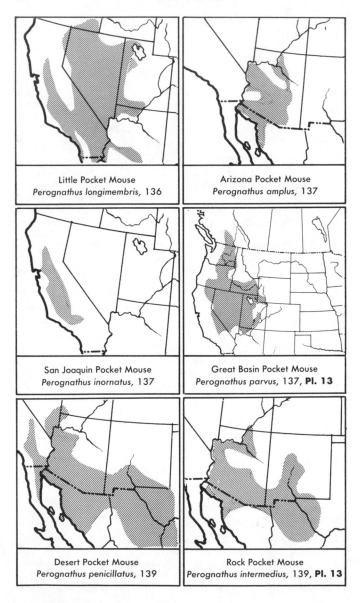

Little Pocket Mouse
Perognathus longimembris, 136

Arizona Pocket Mouse
Perognathus amplus, 137

San Joaquin Pocket Mouse
Perognathus inornatus, 137

Great Basin Pocket Mouse
Perognathus parvus, 137, **Pl. 13**

Desert Pocket Mouse
Perognathus penicillatus, 139

Rock Pocket Mouse
Perognathus intermedius, 139, **Pl. 13**

whitish ears; below pines. (2) California and (3) San Diego Pocket Mice have harsh fur; usually below pines.
Habitat: Scattered pines with undergrowth of grass or bracken ferns; 5400–6000 ft. (1646–1829 m) elevation.
Range: Mt. Pinos and western part of San Bernardino Mts., California.

WALKER PASS POCKET MOUSE
Perognathus xanthonotus
Identification: Head and body 3⅖ in. (86 mm); tail 3⅖ in. (86 mm). Skull has 20 teeth.
Similar species: Other pocket mice within its range either have harsh fur or occur in low valleys.
Habitat: Chaparral, sagebrush, bunchgrass; 4600–5300 ft. (1402–1615 m) elevation.
Range: Known only from eastern slope of Walker Pass, Kern Co., California.

DESERT POCKET MOUSE *Perognathus penicillatus*
Identification: Head and body 3–3⅘ in. (76–97 mm); tail 3⅕–4 in. (81–102 mm); wt. ⅖–⅘ oz. (11–22 g)? Usually *grayish* brown to yellowish gray; *tail crested, longer than head and body;* hair slightly harsh, but *no rump spines.* Skull has 20 teeth.
Similar species: (1) Rock Pocket Mouse prefers rocky situations. (2) Bailey Pocket Mouse is larger, grayish. (3) Longtail Pocket Mouse is slate-gray. (4) San Diego, (5) Spiny, and (6) Nelson Pocket Mice have spinelike hairs on rump. (7) All other pocket mice without crest on tail.
Habitat: Open, sandy desert floors preferred; sparse vegetation.
Habits: Inactive in winter; home range less than 1 acre (0.4 ha).
Young: Born May–Sept.; 2–5.   Map opposite

ROCK POCKET MOUSE *Perognathus intermedius* **Pl. 13**
Identification: Head and body 3–3⅘ in. (76–97 mm); tail 3⅕–4 in. (81–102 mm); wt. ⅖–⅘ oz. (11–22 g). Usually *gray* sprinkled with tawny; on some lava areas nearly *black;* tail *crested.* Some have indistinct spinelike hairs on rump. Skull (Plate 27) has 20 teeth.
Similar species: (1) Desert Pocket Mouse is found on sandy soils. (2) Bailey Pocket Mouse is larger. (3) All other pocket mice within its range have no crest on tail.
Habitat: Rocky slopes, old lava flows, sparse vegetation.
Young: Born May–July; 3–6.   Map opposite

NELSON POCKET MOUSE *Perognathus nelsoni*
Identification: Head and body 3–3⅖ in. (76–86 mm); tail 4–4⅗ in. (102–117 mm); wt. ½–⅗ oz. (14–17 g). Upperparts

mixed fulvous and light brown; hair hispid, *spinelike* on rump; *tail crested,* longer than head and body. Similar to Rock Pocket Mouse and may belong to same species. No other pocket mouse within its range has spinelike hairs on rump.

Habitat: Rocky areas with sparse vegetation; 2300–4800 ft. (701–1463 m) elevation. Map opposite

SAN DIEGO POCKET MOUSE *Perognathus fallax*

Identification: Head and body $3\frac{1}{5}$–$3\frac{1}{2}$ in. (81–89 mm); tail $3\frac{1}{2}$–$4\frac{4}{5}$ in. (89–122 mm). Upperparts dark *rich brown* flecked *with* deep *tawny;* definite *spinelike hairs on rump;* belly white; a deep tawny line along each side; tail crested. Skull has 20 teeth.

Similar species: (1) California Pocket Mouse is similar; difficult to distinguish; usually found in chaparral or live-oak belt, not on low desert. (2) Spiny Pocket Mouse is pale yellowish. (3) No other pocket mice within its range have spinelike hairs on rump.

Habitat: Open, sandy areas grown to weeds. Map opposite

CALIFORNIA POCKET MOUSE Pl. 13
Perognathus californicus

Identification: Head and body $3\frac{1}{5}$–$3\frac{3}{5}$ in. (81–91 mm); tail 4–$5\frac{4}{5}$ in. (102–147 mm). This is the common pocket mouse along the coast of the southern part of California. Color *olive-brown* flecked *with fulvous.* Tail *crested, longer than head and body.* Spinelike hairs on rump. Skull has 20 teeth.

Similar species: (1) San Diego Pocket Mouse is difficult to distinguish; usually found at lower altitude on desert. (2) Other pocket mice within its range are without rump spines.

Habitat: Slopes covered with chaparral or live oaks.

Map opposite

SPINY POCKET MOUSE *Perognathus spinatus*

Identification: Head and body 3–$3\frac{3}{5}$ in. (76–91 mm); tail $3\frac{1}{5}$–5 in. (81–127 mm). Upperparts *pale yellowish* mixed with light brown; *tail long and crested;* distinct *spinelike hairs on rump.* Skull has 20 teeth.

Similar species: (1) San Diego Pocket Mouse is dark brownish. (2) All other pocket mice within its range are without spines on rump.

Habitat: Rough-surfaced mesas and rocky slopes, sparse vegetation, hot desert. Map opposite

LONGTAIL POCKET MOUSE Pl. 13
Perognathus formosus

Identification: Head and body $3\frac{1}{5}$–$3\frac{4}{5}$ in. (81–97 mm); tail $3\frac{4}{5}$–$4\frac{4}{5}$ in. (97–122 mm); wt. $\frac{1}{2}$–$\frac{5}{6}$ oz. (14–24 g). Upperparts *gray; hair soft; tail* long and conspicuously *crested with long*

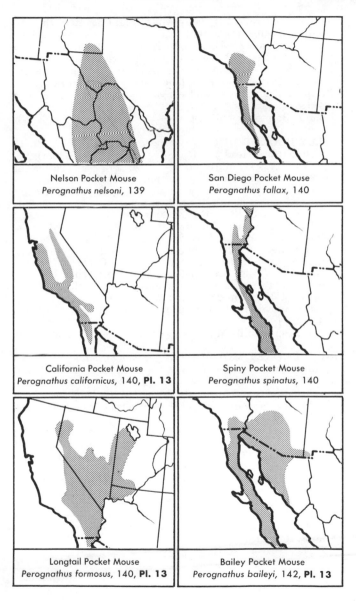

Nelson Pocket Mouse
Perognathus nelsoni, 139

San Diego Pocket Mouse
Perognathus fallax, 140

California Pocket Mouse
Perognathus californicus, 140, **Pl. 13**

Spiny Pocket Mouse
Perognathus spinatus, 140

Longtail Pocket Mouse
Perognathus formosus, 140, **Pl. 13**

Bailey Pocket Mouse
Perognathus baileyi, 142, **Pl. 13**

hairs on its terminal ⅓; belly white. Skull has 20 teeth.
Similar species: (1) Little Pocket Mouse is yellowish; tail not crested. (2) Bailey Pocket Mouse is larger; yellowish admixture of hairs. (3) Desert Pocket Mouse is yellowish. (4) Great Basin Pocket Mouse does not have crested tail. (5) San Diego and (6) Spiny Pocket Mice have long spinelike hairs on rump.
Habitat: Rocky slopes and canyons, gravelly soil; to 8000 ft. (2438 m) elevation.
Young: Born May – July; 4 – 6.   Map p. 141

BAILEY POCKET MOUSE *Perognathus baileyi*   **Pl. 13**
  Identification: Head and body 3⅗ – 4⅕ in. (91 – 107 mm); tail 4⅖ – 5 in. (112 – 127 mm); wt. ⅚ – 1⅓ oz. (24 – 38 g). This is the *largest* of the *soft-haired* pocket mice with crested tails. It is in general grayish with a good sprinkling of yellowish hairs. Belly and underside of tail white; tail has distinct *crest* of long hairs on *terminal* ⅓. Skull has 20 teeth.
  Similar species: (1) Longtail Pocket Mouse is smaller; no yellowish mixture. (2) Hispid Pocket Mouse has no crest on tail. (3) Desert Pocket Mouse is smaller; yellowish. (4) Rock Pocket Mouse is smaller. (5) San Diego, (6) California, and (7) Spiny Pocket Mice are smaller and have spinelike hairs on rump. (8) Other pocket mice have no crest on tail.
  Habitat: Rocky slopes with sparse vegetation.
  Habits: Active all winter; home range probably less than 1 acre (0.4 ha).
  Young: Born April – May; 3 – 4 embryos recorded. Map p. 141

HISPID POCKET MOUSE *Perognathus hispidus*   **Pl. 13**
  Identification: Head and body 4½ – 5 in. (114 – 127 mm); tail 3½ – 4½ in. (89 – 114 mm); wt. 1 – 1⅔ oz. (28 – 47 g). *Harsh* hair, mixed yellowish and brownish. *Large size, and noncrested tail shorter than head and body* will distinguish this pocket mouse. Skull has 20 teeth.
  Similar species: (1) Mexican Pocket Mouse has tail as long as or longer than head and body; upper incisors not grooved on front faces. (2) Other pocket mice are either very much smaller or have crested tails.
  Habitat: Shortgrass prairies where soil is friable and vegetation rather sparse; fence rows and roadsides in cultivated areas.
  Habits: Active all year in South, inactive part of winter in North. Feeds on seeds and insects. Burrows appear to go straight down, usually in open and mostly without pile of dirt.
  Young: Born any time of year in South; usually 2 – 6; probably 2 litters a year in North.   Map opposite

DARK KANGAROO MOUSE *Microdipodops megacephalus*
  Identification: Head and body 2⅘ – 3 in. (71 – 76 mm); tail 2⅔ – 4 in. (67 – 102 mm); wt. ⅓ – ⅔ oz. (9 – 18 g). This *small*

brownish or blackish kangaroo mouse usually has bases of hairs lead color and tip of tail blackish. Tail *swollen* in middle. Skull has 20 teeth.

Similar species: (1) Pale Kangaroo Mouse has whitish or light buffy upperparts. (2) Great Basin Pocket Mouse (p. 137) has belly washed with tawny; tail not swollen in middle. (3) Little Pocket Mouse (p. 136) is yellowish.

Habitat: Fine sandy soil with sagebrush and rabbitbrush.

Habits: Nocturnal; feeds mostly on seeds, but takes some insects; closes openings to burrows during day.

Young: Born May to early July; 1–7 embryos reported.

Map p. 145

PALE KANGAROO MOUSE   Pl. 14
Microdipodops pallidus

    Identification: Head and body 3 in. (76 mm); tail 3–4 in. (76–102 mm); wt. ⅓–⅔ oz. (9–18 g). Upperparts *whitish* or *pale*

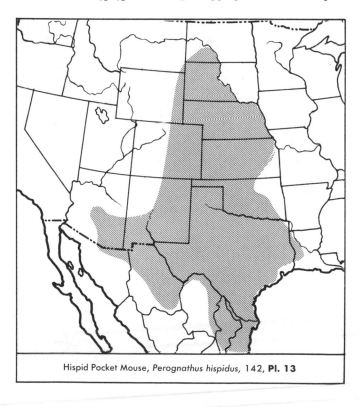

Hispid Pocket Mouse, *Perognathus hispidus*, 142, **Pl. 13**

buff; hairs of belly and underside of tail *white to bases;* tail *swollen* in middle, no black tip. Skull (Plate 27) has 20 teeth.
Similar species: (1) Dark Kangaroo Mouse is brownish or blackish; tail has blackish tip. (2) Great Basin Pocket Mouse is olive-gray. (3) Little Pocket Mouse is yellowish.
Habitat: Fine sand and scattered brush.
Habits: Probably similar to those of Dark Kangaroo Mouse.
Map opposite

BANNERTAIL KANGAROO RAT   Pl. 14
Dipodomys spectabilis
Identification: Head and body 5-6 in. (127-152 mm); tail 7-9 in. (178-229 mm); wt. 4-6⅕ oz. (113-176 g). Most spectacularly marked of any of the kangaroo rats. A *large, 4-toed* species with *prominent white tip on tail.* Narrow white side stripes on tail end about ⅔ distance to tip; there is then a black band followed by the white tip. Skull has 20 teeth. There are 6 mammae.
Similar species: (1) Ord and (2) Merriam Kangaroo Rats are smaller; no white tip on tail.
Habitat: Arid or semiarid grassland with scattered brush, mesquite, or junipers.
Habits: Active throughout year. Nocturnal. Builds mounds of mixed earth and plant debris up to 10 ft. (3 m) across and 3 ft. (1 m) high; up to 12 burrow openings in mound. Stores seeds in den; more than 12 lb. (5.4 kg) removed from 1 den. Home range usually not more than 600 ft. (183 m) across; may move nearly a mile (1.6 km). Populations of 1-2 per acre (2.5-5 per ha). Has lived longer than 2 years in wild.
Young: Born Jan.-Aug.; 1-4; gestation period, 27± days; 1-3 litters a year.   Map opposite

HEERMANN KANGAROO RAT   Pl. 14
Dipodomys heermanni
Identification: Head and body 4-5 in. (102-127 mm); tail 6½-8½ in. (165-215 mm); wt. 1¾-3⅓ oz. (50-94 g). A medium-sized kangaroo rat; either 4 or 5 toes on each hind foot; normally 4. Tip of tail white or dusky. The species is difficult to characterize on external characters; in some parts of its range the skull must be examined for certain identification. Skull has 20 teeth.
Similar species: (1) Giant Kangaroo Rat is larger; head and body over 5 in. (127 mm); 5 toes. (2) Santa Cruz Kangaroo Rat has 5 toes on hind foot and a white band across outer flank. (3) Big-eared Kangaroo Rat has heavily crested tail. (4) Fresno Kangaroo Rat has tail usually less than 6 in. (152 mm).
Habitat: Dry grassy plains and partly open gravelly ground on slopes with sparse chaparral.

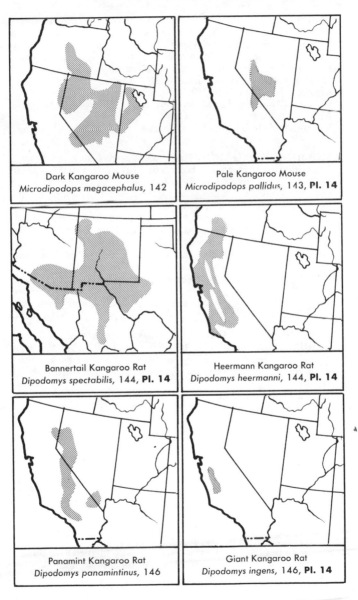

Dark Kangaroo Mouse
Microdipodops megacephalus, 142

Pale Kangaroo Mouse
Microdipodops pallidus, 143, **Pl. 14**

Bannertail Kangaroo Rat
Dipodomys spectabilis, 144, **Pl. 14**

Heermann Kangaroo Rat
Dipodomys heermanni, 144, **Pl. 14**

Panamint Kangaroo Rat
Dipodomys panamintinus, 146

Giant Kangaroo Rat
Dipodomys ingens, 146, **Pl. 14**

Habits: Active throughout year. Nocturnal, prefers moonless nights. Stores seeds, but in small amounts; eats much green vegetation. Mounds at den entrances, long and narrow; many burrow entrances without mounds; 1-6 entrances to each burrow system; burrows 6-24 in. (15-61 cm) deep, 10-40 ft. (3-12 m) long. Home range usually less than 400 ft. (122 m) across; some move ½ mi. (0.8 km) or more. Populations of 1-7 per acre (2.5-16 per ha). Breeding season Feb.-Oct., height in April.

Young: 2-5; 1-3 litters a year. Naked. Females breed 1st year.

Map p. 145

PANAMINT KANGAROO RAT *Dipodomys panamintinus*
Identification: Head and body 5 in. (127 mm); tail 6⅖-7⅗ in. (162-192 mm); wt. 2¼-3⅓ oz. (64-94 g). There are 5 *toes* on each hind foot. Dark stripe on underside of tail tapers to point near end. Skull has 20 teeth.
Similar species: (1) Great Basin Kangaroo Rat occurs chiefly in sagebrush and greasewood. (2) In the Pacific Kangaroo Rat the dark stripe on underside of tail continues to tip. (3) Ord Kangaroo Rat is smaller; tail not more than 6 in. (151 mm). (4) Merriam Kangaroo Rat is smaller; 4 toes on hind foot. (5) Desert Kangaroo Rat is larger, pale; no black markings; 4 toes on hind foot.
Habitat: Sandy or gravelly soil, tree yuccas, piñon pines, scattered sagebrush.

Map p. 145

STEPHENS KANGAROO RAT *Dipodomys stephensi*
Identification: Head and body 5½ in. (140 mm); tail 6½-7⅕ in. (165-182 mm); wt. 2⅔ oz. (75 g). This 5-*toed* kangaroo rat is found only in the *San Jacinto Valley,* California. Skull has 20 teeth.
Similar species: (1) Pacific Kangaroo Rat is difficult to distinguish without skull. (2) Merriam Kangaroo Rat is smaller and has 4 toes on hind foot.
Habitat: Dry, open, or sparsely brushy areas; sandy or gravelly soil.
Range: San Jacinto Valley, w. Riverside and s. San Bernardino Cos., California.

GIANT KANGAROO RAT *Dipodomys ingens* **Pl. 14**
Identification: Head and body 5⅗-6 in. (142-152 mm); tail 7-8 in. (177-203 mm); wt. 4½-6⅓ oz. (127-179 g). This is the *largest* of the kangaroo rats. It has *5 toes on each hind foot.* Skull has 20 teeth. There are 6 mammae.
Similar species: (1) Heermann, (2) Fresno (4-toed), (3) Pacific, and (4) Santa Cruz Kangaroo Rats all have head and body less than 5½ in. (140 mm).
Habitat: Fine sandy loam with sparse vegetation.

Habits: Nocturnal. Eats mostly green food when available, also
seeds. Burrows in groups of 2 – 4 and widely spaced. May display territorial behavior. Breeding season Jan. – May.
Young: Usually 3 – 4, occasionally 6.   Map p. 145

ORD KANGAROO RAT *Dipodomys ordi*   Pl. 14
Identification: Head and body 4 – 4 ½ in. (102 – 114 mm); tail
5 – 6 in. (127 – 152 mm); wt. 1 ½ – 2 ½ oz. (42 – 72 g). This is the
most widely distributed of the kangaroo rats. May have either
4 or 5 toes on each hind foot. *Dark tail stripes broader* than
white ones; ventral stripe *tapers to a point* near tip of tail.
Lower incisors rounded, not flat across front. Skull has 20 teeth.
Similar species: (1) Panamint Kangaroo Rat has a tail more

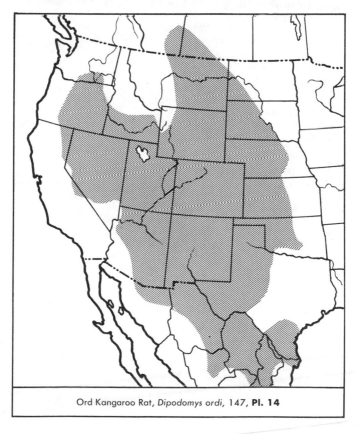

Ord Kangaroo Rat, *Dipodomys ordi*, 147, **Pl. 14**

than 6 in. (152 mm) long. (2) Merriam Kangaroo Rat has 4 toes; light tail stripes are broader than dark ones. (3) Great Basin Kangaroo Rat has flat, chisel-like lower incisors. (4) Texas, (5) Bannertail, and (6) Desert Kangaroo Rats have white tip on tail.

Habitat: Sandy soils preferred, but it is sometimes found on rather hard soils.

Habits: Active throughout year; nocturnal. Will drink water when available; stores seeds.

Young: Born May – June; 2 – 5; may be 2 litters a year.

Map p. 147

PACIFIC KANGAROO RAT *Dipodomys agilis* **Pl. 14**
Identification: Head and body 4⅖–5 in. (112–127 mm); tail 6⅕–8 in. (157–203 mm); wt. 1⅗–2⁷⁄₁₀ oz. (45–77 g). This is the common kangaroo rat of the Pacific Coast of s. California. Dark ventral stripe continues to tip of tail; *5 toes* on each hind foot. Skull has 20 teeth.

Similar species: (1) Stephens Kangaroo Rat is difficult to distinguish without skull. (2) Merriam and (3) Fresno Kangaroo Rats are smaller; 4 toes. (4) Giant Kangaroo Rat is larger. (5) In the Panamint Kangaroo Rat the dark ventral stripe tapers to a point near tip of tail.

Habitat: Gravelly or sandy soil, slopes or washes, open chaparral; from near sea level to 7500 ft. (2286 m) elevation.

Map opposite

SANTA CRUZ KANGAROO RAT *Dipodomys venustus*
Identification: Head and body 4⅘–5⅕ in. (122–132 mm); tail 7–8 in. (178–203 mm); wt. 2⁷⁄₁₀–3⅕ oz. (77–91 g). Along a narrow strip of the Pacific Coast of California, this *5-toed, richly colored* kangaroo rat may be found. Has *large ears* and a white band across flank. Skull has 20 teeth.

Similar species: (1) In the Heermann Kangaroo Rat there are usually 4 toes on hind foot; no white band across flank. (2) In the Giant Kangaroo Rat the head and body are longer than 5½ in. (140 mm).

Habitat: Slopes with chaparral, oaks, pines; also flat areas; up to 5900 ft. (1798 m) elevation.   Map opposite

BIG-EARED KANGAROO RAT   **Pl. 14**
Dipodomys elephantinus
Identification: Head and body 5 in. (127 mm); tail 7–8 in. (177–203 mm); wt. 2⅘–3⅕ oz. (79–91 g). A handsome, *big-eared* kangaroo rat; 5 toes on each hind foot; end of tail heavily crested with long hairs. Skull has 20 teeth.

Similar species: The Heermann Kangaroo Rat may have only 4 toes; tail is not heavily crested.

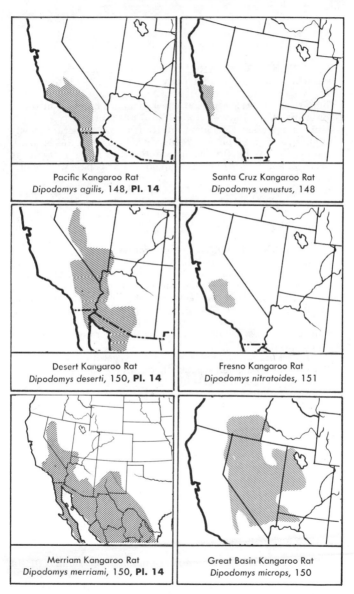

Pacific Kangaroo Rat
Dipodomys agilis, 148, **Pl. 14**

Santa Cruz Kangaroo Rat
Dipodomys venustus, 148

Desert Kangaroo Rat
Dipodomys deserti, 150, **Pl. 14**

Fresno Kangaroo Rat
Dipodomys nitratoides, 151

Merriam Kangaroo Rat
Dipodomys merriami, 150, **Pl. 14**

Great Basin Kangaroo Rat
Dipodomys microps, 150

Habitat: Chaparral-covered slopes.
Range: Southern part of Gabilan Range, vicinity of Pinnacles, San Benito and Monterey Cos., California.

GREAT BASIN KANGAROO RAT *Dipodomys microps*
Identification: Head and body 4–5 in. (102–127 mm); tail 5⅗–7⅓ in. (142–186 mm); wt. 2½–3⅕ oz. (72–91 g). Medium-sized; 5 toes; insides of cheek pouches blackish in some; lower incisors flat across front. Skull has 20 teeth.
Similar species: (1) Panamint Kangaroo Rat occurs chiefly in yucca and piñon pines. (2) Merriam Kangaroo Rat is small; 4 toes. (3) In the Ord Kangaroo Rat the lower incisors are rounded, not flat. (4) Desert Kangaroo Rat is pale with white-tipped tail.
Habitat: Sandy or gravelly soil, desert floor or rocky slopes, areas sparsely covered with sagebrush and greasewood.
Habits: Feeds on green vegetation as well as seeds.
Young: Born May–June; 1–4.   Map p. 149

DESERT KANGAROO RAT *Dipodomys deserti*   **Pl. 14**
Identification: Head and body 5–6½ in. (127–165 mm); tail 7–8½ in. (178–216 mm); wt. 3–5⅕ oz. (85–147 g). Pale *yellowish;* 4 toes; *no* dark markings except in front of white tail tip, where there may be dusky band. By *large size, pale coloration,* and *white tip on tail,* this species may be distinguished. Skull (Plate 27) has 20 teeth. There are 6 mammae.
Similar species: No other species within its range has a white tip on the tail.
Habitat: Fine sandy areas with sparse vegetation, low deserts.
Habits: Feeds on green vegetation and seeds; has lived 5½ years in captivity. Breeds Feb.–June.
Young: Usually 3 (2–5); gestation period 29–30 days.
                                                              Map p. 149

TEXAS KANGAROO RAT *Dipodomys elator*
Identification: Head and body 5¾ in. (146 mm); tail 8 in. (203 mm). This large *4-toed* kangaroo rat, with a *white tip* on the end of its tail, has a limited range in Texas and Oklahoma. Skull has 20 teeth.
Similar species: Ord Kangaroo Rat does not have white tip on tail.
Habitat: Mesquite, cactus, grama grass.
Range: Comanche Co., Oklahoma, and Clay, Wichita, Baylor, Archer, and Wilbarger Cos., Texas.

MERRIAM KANGAROO RAT *Dipodomys merriami*   **Pl. 14**
Identification: Head and body 4 in. (102 mm); tail 5–6⅖ in. (127–162 mm); wt. 1⅕–1¾ oz. (34–50 g). This is the *smallest*

of the kangaroo rats. It has *4 toes* on each hind foot. Color varies from pale yellowish to dark brownish above. Skull has 20 teeth. There are 6 mammae.

Similar species: (1) Ord Kangaroo Rat may have 5 toes, or ventral tail stripe broad at base and tapering to point near tip of tail. (2) Bannertail and (3) Desert Kangaroo Rats are larger; white tip on tail. (4) Other kangaroo rats have 5 toes on each hind foot.

Habitat: Sandy to rocky soils, mostly low desert with scattered vegetation.

Habits: Nocturnal. Feeds mostly on seeds, but includes green vegetation. Makes shallow burrows, 6–13 in. (15–33 cm) deep. Home range $\frac{1}{3}$–$\frac{1}{2}$ acre (0.1–0.2 ha) in Arizona. Has lived $5\frac{1}{2}$ years in captivity. Females display territorial behavior. Breeds Feb.–Oct.

Young: 1–4; 1–2 litters a year. Naked; eyes open at 13 days.
Map p. 149

FRESNO KANGAROO RAT *Dipodomys nitratoides*
Identification: Head and body $3\frac{3}{5}$–4 in. (91–102 mm); tail $4\frac{4}{5}$–6 in. (122–152 mm); wt. 1–$1\frac{3}{4}$ oz. (28–50 g). By its *small size* and *4 toes* on each hind foot, this inhabitant of the *San Joaquin Valley,* California, may be distinguished from other kangaroo rats. Skull has 20 teeth.

Similar species: (1) Heermann Kangaroo Rat is larger; tail longer than 6 in. (152 mm). (2) Other kangaroo rats have 5 toes.

Habitat: Arid, often alkaline, plains with sparse growths of grass and low brush.
Map p. 149

Beaver: Castoridae

THERE is but one living genus (*Castor*) in this family. The Beaver is the largest rodent here considered. Fossils date back to Lower Oligocene.

BEAVER *Castor canadensis* **Pl. 19**
Identification: Head and body 25–30 in. (63–76 cm); tail 9–10 in. (23–25 cm); wt. 30–60 lb. (13.5–27 kg). A stick-and-mud *dam across a stream,* or a large *conical* house of similar material at the edge of a lake and stumps of small trees in the vicinity showing tooth marks will reveal the presence of the Beaver. A loud report, caused by the tail as the Beaver dives below the surface of the water, will also indicate its presence. Rich brown in color; tail naked, scaly, *shaped like a paddle,* flat, about 6 in. (15 cm) wide. Huge front teeth chestnut-colored

on front faces; hind feet webbed, 2nd claw double. Skull (Plate 28) has 20 teeth. There are 4 mammae.

Similar species: (1) River Otter (p. 60) has tail covered with fur. (2) Muskrat (p. 193) is smaller; tail slender and flattened from side to side. (3) Nutria (p. 200) has a rounded tail that is haired.

Habitat: Streams and lakes with trees or alders on banks.

Habits: Chiefly nocturnal, occasionally seen by day; appears shortly after sundown. Preferred food is aspen, poplar, birch, maple, willow, and alder; feeds on bark and small twigs; stores branches and small sections of logs underwater near lodge. Family groups of parents, yearlings, and kits may occupy a lodge; 2-year-olds are driven out or leave parental home. May burrow in bank for den along swift streams. Colony defends territory against other colonies; all may share in repairing dam. Has moved 150 mi. (240 km) or more from birth place, usually under 6 mi. (9.6 km). Lives 11 years in wild, 19 years in captivity. Females breed at $2\frac{1}{2}$ years.

Young: Born April – July; usually 2 – 4, occasionally 8; gestation

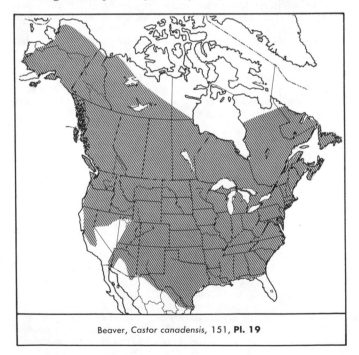

Beaver, *Castor canadensis*, 151, **Pl. 19**

period about 128 days; 1 litter a year. Kits furred and with eyes open.

Economic status: An important fur animal and water conservationist; timber destroyed is mostly low-grade; occasionally floods roads or fields; meat edible. Exterminated in much of former range, now being reintroduced widely. May be seen in most of the northern parks — Algonquin Provincial and Jasper Natl. Parks in Canada; Glacier, Yellowstone, Grand Teton, Mt. Rainier, Olympic, and Rocky Mt. Natl. Parks in U.S.

Map opposite

Mice, Rats, Lemmings, and Voles: Cricetidae

THIS family includes small to medium-sized rodents, with head and body 2–10 in. (51–254 mm); tail $\frac{2}{5}$–8 in. (10–203 mm), except Muskrat, which may have head and body 14 in. (356 mm). Most of them have 4 toes on the front foot, some have 5, and all have 5 toes on the hind foot. Tails rarely bushy, mostly covered with short hair. Mice and rats have large ears and eyes and long tails; lemmings and voles have short tails, small ears and eyes, and usually long fur on body. They live mostly on and in the ground, some in trees (in part), and some in rocky situations; some are partially aquatic. A representative of this family will be found wherever one is in N. America. Fossils date back to Oligocene, possibly Upper Eocene time. All have 2 gnawing teeth and 6 cheek teeth in upper and lower jaws (16 teeth).

Harvest Mice

EXTERNALLY, these small brown mice resemble House Mice. One certain way to distinguish them from all other small brownish mice is to examine the upper incisors. If each of these has a distinct *groove* down the front, lengthwise, it is probably a harvest mouse. Other mice with grooved teeth have external cheek pouches, or extremely long scaly tails, or tails less than 1 in. (25 mm) long. Skull has 16 teeth. There are 6 mammae.

Economic status: In most of range very little competition with man; probably neutral.

EASTERN HARVEST MOUSE   **Pl. 15**
Reithrodontomys humulis

    Identification: Head and body $2\frac{3}{5}$–3 in. (66–76 mm); tail $1\frac{4}{5}$–$2\frac{1}{2}$ in. (46–64 mm); wt. $\frac{1}{3}$–$\frac{1}{2}$ oz. (9–14 g). This *rich-brown* mouse, with belly and underside of tail slightly paler

than back, is the only kind of harvest mouse over most of its range.
Similar species: (1) The Fulvous Harvest Mouse has a longer tail and white belly. (2) Pygmy Mouse (p. 165) is smaller; upper incisors not grooved.
Habitat: Old fields, marshes, wet meadows.
Young: Born May – Nov.; 2 – 5.   Map below

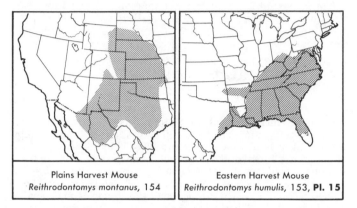

Plains Harvest Mouse
Reithrodontomys montanus, 154

Eastern Harvest Mouse
Reithrodontomys humulis, 153, **Pl. 15**

PLAINS HARVEST MOUSE   *Reithrodontomys montanus*

Identification: Head and body $2\frac{1}{5}$–3 in. (56–76 mm); tail 2–$2\frac{3}{5}$ in. (51–66 mm); wt. $\frac{1}{5}$–$\frac{1}{3}$ oz. (5–9 g). This is a *pale grayish* mouse, faintly *washed with tawny* and often with an indistinct dark area down middle of back. Belly, feet, and underside of tail white.
Similar species: (1) Western Harvest Mouse may be difficult to distinguish; tail usually more than $2\frac{1}{2}$ in. (64 mm). (2) Fulvous Harvest Mouse has tail longer than 3 in. (76 mm). (3) Pygmy Mouse (p. 165) has shorter tail, upper incisors are not grooved.
Habitat: Chiefly uplands; well-drained soil, shortgrass and other low vegetation, often sparse.
Habits: Breeds throughout year in South.
Young: 2–5; gestation period 21 days. Weaned at 2 weeks.

Map above

WESTERN HARVEST MOUSE   Pl. 15
Reithrodontomys megalotis

Identification: Head and body $2\frac{4}{5}$–3 in. (71–76 mm); tail $2\frac{1}{3}$–$3\frac{1}{5}$ in. (59–81 mm); wt. $\frac{1}{3}$–$\frac{3}{5}$ oz. (9–17 g). This wide-ranging harvest mouse is found from the Great Lakes to the Pacific Coast. Color ranges from *pale gray,* slightly washed with tawny, to *brown.* Belly and underside of tail range from white to deep gray. Occurs on Santa Catalina and Santa Cruz Is., California. Skull (Plate 26) has 16 teeth.

Similar species: (1) Plains Harvest Mouse may be difficult to distinguish; tail usually less than 2½ in. (64 mm). (2) Salt Marsh Harvest Mouse has deep tawny belly. (3) Fulvous Harvest Mouse has bright fulvous (tawny) sides; tail usually more than 3⅓ in. (85 mm). (4) Pygmy Mouse (p. 165) has shorter tail, upper incisors not grooved.

Habitat: Grassland, open desert, weed patches; usually dense vegetation and near water.

Habits: Active throughout year. Feeds mostly on seeds, but eats some insects. Nests usually on surface of ground or aboveground in vines, tall vegetation, woodpecker hole in fence post or small tree. Breeds every month of year in some part of its range; usually 2 months when not breeding (Jan. and March in California).

Young: Usually 2–4 (1–9); gestation period 23–24 days. Naked, blind. Females breed at 4½ months.   Map below

SALT MARSH HARVEST MOUSE   **Pl. 15**
Reithrodontomys raviventris

Identification: Head and body 2⅗–3⅕ in. (66–81 mm); tail 2⅕–3⅖ in. (56–86 mm). Body *rich brown* washed with deep *tawny,* especially on belly; tail about same color all around; found only in *salt marshes* in San Francisco Bay area.

Similar species: Western Harvest Mouse has white or gray belly, not rusty.

Habitat: Salt marshes.

Habits: Appropriates old nest of song sparrow above high-water level.

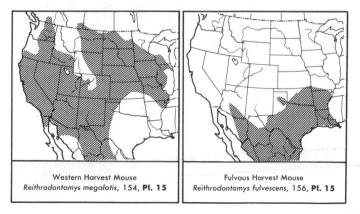

Western Harvest Mouse
Reithrodontomys megalotis, 154, **Pl. 15**

Fulvous Harvest Mouse
Reithrodontomys fulvescens, 156, **Pl. 15**

Range: Bayside marshlands around San Francisco Bay, including lower part of the Sacramento River, California.

FULVOUS HARVEST MOUSE   Pl. 15
Reithrodontomys fulvescens

Identification: Head and body 2⅘–3⅕ in. (71–81 mm); tail 3⅓–4 in. (84–102 mm); wt. ½–1 oz. (14–28 g). This is the most strikingly colored as well as the *largest* of the harvest mice here considered. *Grayish brown,* with *bright fulvous (tawny) along sides* and with a *white belly.* Tail paler below than above.

Similar species: (1) Eastern Harvest Mouse is smaller; dark brown with gray belly. (2) Plains Harvest Mouse has tail less than 3 in. (76 mm). (3) In the Western Harvest Mouse the sides are not bright fulvous; tail usually 3 in. (76 mm) or less. (4) Pygmy Mouse (p. 165) has shorter tail, upper incisors not grooved.

Habitat: Grasslands with scattered brush and mesquite; weedy fields and fence rows.

Habits: Nests in underground burrow, converted bird nest, or nest of own making in bushes or tall grass. Breeding season probably Feb.–Oct.

Young: 2–5; probably more than 1 litter a year. Naked, blind.

Map p. 155

White-footed and Pygmy Mice

THESE medium-sized mice all have *white feet,* usually white bellies, and some shade of brown or tawny backs. Tails relatively *long,* as long as head and body in many. They are nocturnal, live in woods, prairies, rocks, and occasionally around buildings. Most are ground dwellers, but some nest in trees. Gestation period is 21–27 days. Young are born naked and blind. Skull has 16 teeth.

Similar species: (1) Grasshopper Mice (pp. 166–167) have short tail with white tip. (2) Harvest Mice (above) have a groove down front of each upper incisor tooth. (3) The Rice Rat (p. 172) has woolly fur on belly and a long, scantily haired tail with scales showing through. (4) In the House Mouse (p. 195) the belly is not white, or tail is naked and long.

Economic status: Neutral for the most part; sometimes enters dwellings and does some damage; easily eliminated with a few snap traps baited with rolled oats.

CACTUS MOUSE   *Peromyscus eremicus*   Pl. 16

Identification: Head and body 3⅕–3⅗ in. (81–91 mm); tail 3⅘–5⅖ in. (97–137 mm); wt. ⅗–1⅖ oz. (17–40 g). Body *pale gray,* faintly washed with tawny; belly whitish; tail long, thinly haired, and faintly bicolored. There are 4 mammae.

Similar species: (1) Merriam Mouse is slightly larger; difficult to distinguish. (2) White-ankled Mouse has head and body usually smaller; ankles white. (3) In the Canyon Mouse the tail has a slight tuft of long hair at the tip. (4) The Deer Mouse has a well-haired, distinctly bicolored tail. (5) The White-footed Mouse has a relatively shorter tail. (6) In the Brush Mouse the tail has long hairs toward the tip. (7) The Piñon Mouse has huge ears; found in foothills. (8) The Rock Mouse has huge ears and a well-haired tail.

Habitat: Low deserts with sandy soil and scattered vegetation; rocky outcrops; may go as high as piñon pine zone.

Habits: Normally lives in burrows in ground or among rocks; climbs trees for food; feeds on seeds, insects, and possibly some green vegetation.

Young: 1–4; may be 3–4 litters a year.   Map p. 158

MERRIAM MOUSE *Peromyscus merriami*

Identification: Head and body 3⅘–4 in. (97–102 mm); tail 4–4⅘ in. (102–122 mm). Similar to Cactus Mouse; ranges overlap very little.

Similar species: (1) Cactus Mouse is slightly smaller; difficult to distinguish. (2) Deer Mouse has well-haired tail which is distinctly bicolored. (3) White-footed Mouse has relatively shorter tail. (4) In the Brush Mouse the tail has long hairs toward the tip.

Habitat: Mesquite and scattered brush, low desert.

Range: Pinal, Pima, and Santa Cruz Cos., Ariz.

CALIFORNIA MOUSE *Peromyscus californicus*   Pl. 16

Identification: Head and body 3⅘–4⅗ in. (96–117 mm); tail 5–5⅘ in. (127–147 mm); wt. 1½–1¾ oz. (42–50 g). This is the *largest* mouse of this genus here considered. *Dark brown,* with *top of tail blackish;* feet and belly whitish; ears large. Size alone will serve to distinguish this species. There are 4 mammae.

Similar species: All other mice are smaller and with tail usually under 5 in. (127 mm).

Habitat: Slopes grown with live oaks and dense chaparral.

Habits: Stores acorns in nests that are often in houses of Dusky-footed Woodrat; also uses buildings for nesting sites. Nest of twigs and sticks, lined with fine grasses. Breeds throughout year, mostly spring, summer, and fall.

Young: Usually 2 (1–3); may be several litters a year.

Map p. 158

CANYON MOUSE *Peromyscus crinitus*   Pl. 16

Identification: Head and body 3–3⅖ in. (76–86 mm); tail 3½–4⅓ in. (89–110 mm). Body *buffy gray to buff;* fur long and lax; the long *well-haired tail* has a slight *tuft* on the end; belly and underside of tail whitish. There are 4 mammae.

Similar species: (1) In the Cactus Mouse the tail is not tufted. (2) Deer Mouse, where they occur together, has tail less than $3\frac{1}{2}$ in. (89 mm). (3) Brush Mouse is brown. (4) Piñon and (5) Rock Mice have huge ears, nearly 1 in. (25 mm) high; head and body longer than $3\frac{1}{2}$ in. (89 mm). (6) In the California Mouse the tail is 5 in. (127 mm) or longer.

Habitat: Rocky canyons and slopes and old lava-covered areas; arid conditions.

Habits: Nests among the rocks or in burrow beneath them.

Young: Born spring and probably summer; 3–5. Map below

DEER MOUSE *Peromyscus maniculatus*   **Pl. 16**

Identification: Head and body $2\frac{4}{5}$–4 in. (71–102 mm); tail 2–5 in. (51–127 mm); wt. $\frac{2}{3}$–$1\frac{1}{4}$ oz. (18–35 g). The most

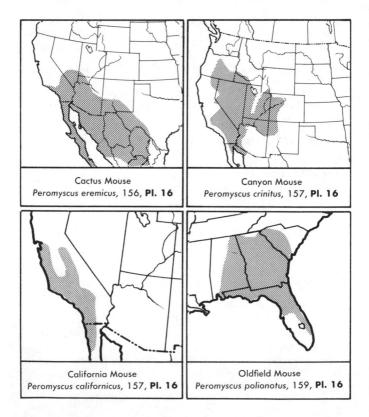

Cactus Mouse
Peromyscus eremicus, 156, **Pl. 16**

Canyon Mouse
Peromyscus crinitus, 157, **Pl. 16**

California Mouse
Peromyscus californicus, 157, **Pl. 16**

Oldfield Mouse
Peromyscus polionotus, 159, **Pl. 16**

widely distributed and most variable of members of the genus. Color ranges from pale grayish buff to deep reddish brown. Tail always *sharply bicolored,* white below, dark above. Often difficult to distinguish from similar species. Skull (Plate 26) has 16 teeth. There are 6 mammae.

Similar species: (1) White-footed Mouse, in South, has tail not distinctly bicolored; in northeastern forests, tail less than $3\frac{3}{5}$ in. (91 mm), difficult to distinguish. (2) Cactus and (3) Merriam Mice have scantily haired tail, not distinctly bicolored. (4) Canyon Mouse has tail longer than head and body; fur long and lax. (5) In the Cotton Mouse the head and body are larger; dark brown. (6) Brush and (7) White-ankled Mice have the tail as long as, or longer than, head and body. (8) Piñon and (9) Rock Mice have huge ears, nearly 1 in. (25 mm) high. (10) In the Golden Mouse the head and body are uniform cinnamon. (11) California Mouse is larger.

Habitat: Nearly every dry-land habitat within its range is occupied by this species; forests in some areas, grassland in others, a mixture in still others.

Habits: Nests in burrow in ground, in trees, stumps, and buildings. Feeds on seeds, nuts, acorns, insects; stores food. Home range $\frac{1}{2}$ – 3 acres (0.2 – 1.2 ha) or more. Summer population of 10 – 15 per acre (25 – 37 per ha) is high; some congregate in winter. Rarely lives more than 2 years in wild, 5 – 8 years in captivity. Females may display territorial behavior in breeding season. Breeding season normally Feb. – Nov.; varies with latitude.

Young: Usually 3 – 5 (1 – 8); 2 – 4 litters a year. Breed at 5 – 6 weeks.   Map p. 160

SITKA MOUSE   *Peromyscus sitkensis*
   Identification: Head and body $4\frac{1}{3}$ – $4\frac{3}{5}$ in. (109 – 117 mm); tail $3\frac{4}{5}$ – $4\frac{1}{2}$ in. (97 – 114 mm); wt. $1\frac{1}{5}$ – $1\frac{3}{5}$ oz. (34 – 45 g). This large white-footed mouse is found only on islands. There are 6 mammae.
   Habits: Feeds largely on spruce seeds and small invertebrate animals.
   Young: Average of 6 per litter; probably 2 litters a year.
   Range: Baranof, Chichagof, and Forrester Is., Alaska; Kunghit, Frederick, and Hippa Is., B.C.

OLDFIELD MOUSE   *Peromyscus polionotus*   **Pl. 16**
   Identification: Head and body $3\frac{2}{5}$ – $3\frac{4}{5}$ in. (86 – 97 mm); tail $1\frac{3}{5}$ – $2\frac{2}{5}$ in. (41 – 61 mm). Upperparts *whitish* to *pale cinnamon;* belly and feet white. There are 6 mammae.
   Similar species: (1) White-footed, (2) Cotton, and (3) Florida Mice are dark brown or with tail more than $2\frac{2}{5}$ in. (61 mm).

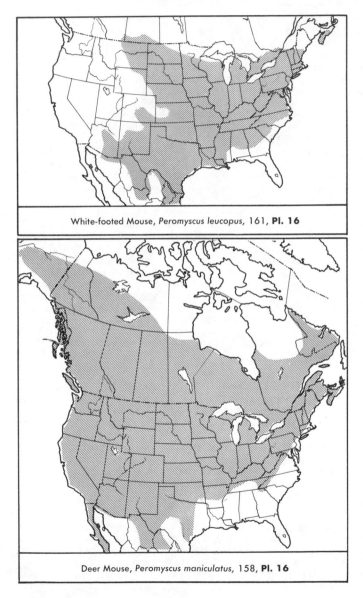

White-footed Mouse, *Peromyscus leucopus*, 161, **Pl. 16**

Deer Mouse, *Peromyscus maniculatus*, 158, **Pl. 16**

(4) Golden Mouse is bright cinnamon over head and body; tail 3 in. (76 mm) or longer.

Habitat: Sand beaches and fallow sandy fields.

Habits: Feeds on seeds and berries. Makes own burrows with mounds of earth at entrances; burrow openings usually closed during day. Home range up to 900 ft. (274 m) in greatest diam. Populations up to 6 per acre (15 per ha), usually fewer. Has lived 5 years, 3 months in captivity. Females may display territorial behavior during breeding season. Breeds all year, mostly in winter.

Young: Average of 4 per litter; probably 2 or more litters a year. Map p. 158

WHITE-FOOTED MOUSE *Peromyscus leucopus* **Pl. 16**

Identification: Head and body $3\frac{3}{5}$–$4\frac{1}{5}$ in. (91–107 mm); tail $2\frac{2}{5}$–4 in. (61–102 mm); wt. $\frac{1}{2}$–$1\frac{1}{10}$ oz. (14–31 g). Upperparts pale to rich reddish brown; belly and feet white; tail usually *shorter than head and body*. In parts of its range it is difficult to distinguish from other species. There are 6 mammae.

Similar species: (1) In the Deer Mouse the tail is always bicolored; in northeastern forests tail more than $3\frac{3}{5}$ in. (91 mm); difficult to distinguish. (2) Cotton Mouse is slightly larger; difficult to distinguish. (3) Brush Mouse has tail longer than head and body. (4) Cactus and (5) White-ankled Mice have distinctly longer hairs on terminal 1 in. (25 mm) of tail. (6) Oldfield Mouse has tail less than $2\frac{2}{5}$ in. (61 mm). (7) Piñon and (8) Rock Mice have ears nearly 1 in. (25 mm) high. (9) Merriam Mouse has scantily haired tail. (10) Golden Mouse has rich cinnamon head and body.

Habitat: Wooded or brushy areas preferred; sometimes open areas.

Habits: Feeds on seeds, nuts, insects; stores seeds and nuts. Nests any place that affords shelter — belowground, in old bird or squirrel nests, buildings, stumps, and logs. Home range, $\frac{1}{2}$–$1\frac{1}{2}$ acres (0.2–0.6 ha). Populations of 4–12 per acre (10–30 per ha). Lives 5 years or more in captivity, 2–3 years in wild. Females display territorial behavior during breeding season. Breeding season in North, March–June and Sept.–Nov.; in South probably all year.

Young: 2–6; 2–4 litters a year. Females breed at 10–11 weeks. Map opposite

COTTON MOUSE *Peromyscus gossypinus*

Identification: Head and body $3\frac{3}{5}$–$4\frac{3}{5}$ in. (91–117 mm); tail $2\frac{4}{5}$–$3\frac{3}{5}$ in. (71–91 mm); wt. 1–$1\frac{4}{5}$ oz. (28–51 g). Upperparts *dark brown* with a slight tawny mixture, whitish below; tail may or may not be bicolored. There are 6 mammae.

Similar species: (1) White-footed Mouse is slightly smaller;

difficult to distinguish. (2) Deer Mouse is smaller. (3) Oldfield Mouse is pale; tail less than 2 ½ in. (64 mm). (4) Golden Mouse is bright cinnamon. (5) Florida Mouse is larger; sandy ridges.
Habitat: Wooded areas, along streams or bordering fields, swampland.
Habits: Climbs trees. Feeds on seeds and possibly on insects. Nests in trees, under logs, in buildings. Breeds Aug.–May.
Young: Usually 3–4 (1–7); 4 or more litters a year.

Map below

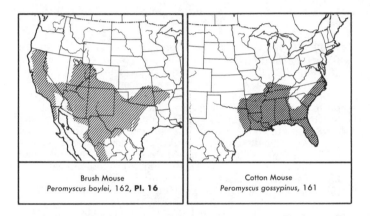

Brush Mouse
Peromyscus boylei, 162, **Pl. 16**

Cotton Mouse
Peromyscus gossypinus, 161

BRUSH MOUSE *Peromyscus boylei* **Pl. 16**
Identification: Head and body 3⅗–4⅕ in. (91–107 mm); tail 3⅗–4⅖ in. (91–112 mm); wt. ¾–1¼ oz. (22–36 g). Color ranges from *grayish brown* to fairly *dark brown* washed with *tawny* on the sides; *well-haired tail* about as long as head and body, often slightly longer. There are 6 mammae.
Similar species: (1) White-ankled Mouse is slightly smaller; ankles white. (2) Piñon and (3) Rock Mice have ears nearly 1 in. (25 mm) high; in California some may be difficult to distinguish. (4) Cactus and (5) Merriam Mice have scantily haired tails. (6) California Mouse is large; tail 5 in. (127 mm) or more. (7) Canyon Mouse is pale gray or buffy. (8) Deer and (9) White-footed Mice have tail shorter than head and body. (10) Golden Mouse is bright cinnamon.
Habitat: Chaparral areas of arid and semiarid regions; rocky situations.
Habits: Good climber. Feeds on pine nuts, acorns, seeds, berries. Nests under rocks, in crevices, and under debris. Breeds throughout most of year, height of season spring and summer.
Young: 2–6; probably 4 or more litters a year.   Map above

WHITE-ANKLED MOUSE *Peromyscus pectoralis*
Identification: Head and body 3²/₅ in. (86 mm); tail 3⅘ – 4²/₅ in. (97 – 112 mm); wt. ¾ – 1²/₅ oz. (22 – 40 g). Body *pale grayish;* tail *longer* than head and body; ankles white. There are 6 mammae.
Similar species: (1) Brush Mouse slightly larger, ankles dusky. (2) Cactus Mouse is usually larger, ankles dusky. (3) Deer and (4) White-footed Mice have tail shorter than head and body.
Habitat: Rocky areas with scattered oaks and junipers; chaparral.
Habits: Sometimes occupies buildings. Feeds on seeds, berries, acorns. Breeds April – Oct.
Young: 3 – 7; probably more than 1 litter a year. Map p. 164

PIÑON MOUSE *Peromyscus truei* **Pl. 16**
Identification: Head and body 3⅗ – 4 in. (91 – 102 mm); tail 3²/₅ – 4⅘ in. (86 – 122 mm); wt. ⅔ – 1¹/₁₀ oz. (19 – 31 g). A *large-eared* mouse, ears nearly 1 in. (25 mm) high; *grayish brown,* heavily washed with tawny; tail slightly shorter to slightly longer than head and body, *distinctly bicolored.* There are 6 mammae.
Similar species: (1) Rock Mouse is difficult to distinguish. (2) Brush Mouse has smaller ears, less than ¾ in. (19 mm) high; in California some difficult to distinguish. (3) Cactus Mouse has tail not conspicuously hairy; low desert. (4) California Mouse has tail 5 in. (127 mm) or more. (5) Canyon Mouse is smaller; pale gray or buff. (6) Deer and (7) White-footed Mice have small ears, less than ½ in. (12 mm) high.
Habitat: Rocky terrain with scattered piñon pines and junipers.
Habits: A good climber. Feeds chiefly on seeds and nuts. May nest in trees and among rocks. Breeds principally in spring and summer.
Young: 3 – 6; probably more than 1 litter a year. Map p. 164

ROCK MOUSE *Peromyscus difficilis*
Identification: Head and body 3⅗ – 4 in. (91 – 102 mm); tail 3⅗ – 4²/₅ in. (91 – 112 mm); wt. ⅚ – 1¹/₇ oz. (24 – 32 g). The Rock Mouse is similar to the Piñon Mouse, is intermediate between it and the Brush Mouse, and is difficult to distinguish, even in a museum. See Piñon Mouse for characters and similar species. There are 6 mammae.
  Formerly known as *P. nasutus.*
Habitat: Rock outcrops, cliffs, canyon walls.
Young: Born early spring to Oct.; usually 3 – 4 (1 – 6).
Map p. 164

FLORIDA MOUSE *Peromyscus floridanus*
Identification: Head and body 4²/₅ – 5 in. (112 – 127 mm); tail

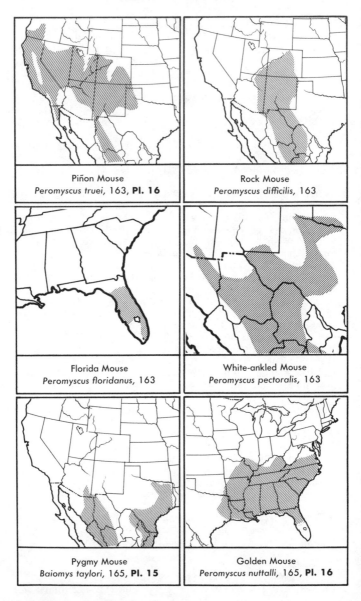

Piñon Mouse
Peromyscus truei, 163, **Pl. 16**

Rock Mouse
Peromyscus difficilis, 163

Florida Mouse
Peromyscus floridanus, 163

White-ankled Mouse
Peromyscus pectoralis, 163

Pygmy Mouse
Baiomys taylori, 165, **Pl. 15**

Golden Mouse
Peromyscus nuttalli, 165, **Pl. 16**

3 ⅕ – 3 ⅘ in. (81 – 97 mm). A *large* mouse with nearly naked ears and large hind feet. There are 6 mammae.
Similar species: (1) Cotton Mouse is smaller; occurs in woods. (2) Oldfield Mouse is smaller; whitish to pale cinnamon. (3) Golden Mouse is bright cinnamon.
Habitat: High sandy ridges, blackjack and turkey oaks, scrub palmetto.
Habits: Shares burrows with gopher turtle; in captivity breeds throughout year.
Young: 1 – 3; several litters a year.   Map opposite

GOLDEN MOUSE   *Peromyscus nuttalli*   Pl. 16
Identification: Head and body 3 ⅖ – 3 ⅘ in. (86 – 97 mm); tail 3 – 3 ⅗ in. (76 – 91 mm); wt. ⅔ – ⁶⁄₇ oz. (19 – 25 g). This is a handsome, bright *golden-cinnamon* mouse with a *white belly*. There are 6 mammae.
Some authors consider this a distinct genus (*Ochrotomys*).
Similar species: No other mouse has the striking golden coloration of this one. Others found within its range are: (1) Deer, (2) Oldfield, (3) White-footed, (4) Cotton, (5) Brush, and (6) Florida Mice.
Habitat: Forests, edges of canebrakes, moist thickets, honeysuckle, greenbrier, Spanish moss.
Habits: Gregarious on occasion; at home in trees, vines, brush. Builds leaf and shredded-bark nest, 6 – 8 in. (152 – 203 mm) diam. and 5 – 10 ft. (1.5 – 3 m) aboveground, in vines, thickets, Spanish moss. Breeds throughout spring and summer.   Map opposite

PYGMY MOUSE   *Baiomys taylori*   Pl. 15
Identification: Head and body 2 – 2 ½ in. (51 – 64 mm); tail 1 ⅖ – 1 ⅘ in. (36 – 46 mm); wt. ¼ – ⅓ oz. (7 – 9 g). This, *smallest* of our mice, is *dark grayish brown,* with the belly slightly paler than the back. Has somewhat the appearance of a young House Mouse, but tail is *paler below than above* and covered with short hair. Skull (Plate 26) has 16 teeth.
Similar species: (1) House Mouse (p. 195) is larger; tail naked. (2) Harvest mice (p. 153–156) have grooved upper incisors.
Habitat: Grassy or weedy areas.
Habits: Partially colonial. Feeds mostly on seeds. Nest may be on the surface or underground. Home range less than 100 ft. (30.5 m) across. Populations 6 – 8 per acre (15 – 20 per ha). Breeds Jan. – Oct.
Young: 1 – 5; gestation period about 20 days; several litters a year.   Map opposite

Grasshopper Mice

THESE mice are inhabitants chiefly of the *prairies* and south-western *desert* areas. They are either *gray* or *pinkish cinnamon* above, white beneath. The fur is short. The only mice that they might be confused with are members of the genus *Peromyscus*. The *short, white-tipped* tail and stout body will usually be sufficient to distinguish the grasshopper mouse. There are 6 mammae.
Habitat: Open country; grass, sagebrush, greasewood; sandy or gravelly soil.
Habits: Carnivorous; eat insects, scorpions, other mice, lizards; also eat some seeds. Live mostly in burrows of other animals such as ground squirrels, prairie dogs, pocket gophers. Voice, a shrill whistle, apparently a call note.
Young: Born Feb.–Sept.; usually 4–5 (2–7); gestation period 32–47 days; 2–3 litters a year. Naked, blind.
Economic status: Beneficial or neutral; destroy many insects and do little harm.

NORTHERN GRASSHOPPER MOUSE   Pl. 15
Onychomys leucogaster
   Identification: Head and body 4–5 in. (102–127 mm); tail 1–2⅖ in. (25–61 mm); wt. ⁶⁄₇–1⅖ oz. (25–40 g). This is a stocky, heavy-bodied, *gray* or *pinkish-cinnamon* mouse with

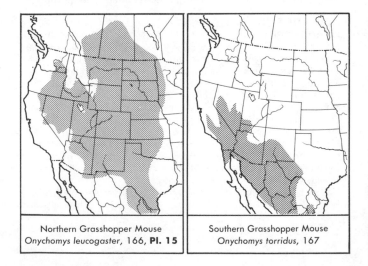

Northern Grasshopper Mouse
Onychomys leucogaster, 166, **Pl. 15**

Southern Grasshopper Mouse
Onychomys torridus, 167

a relatively *short, white-tipped tail.* Skull (Plate 26) has 16 teeth.

Similar species: Southern Grasshopper Mouse is smaller; tail usually more than ½ length of head and body; low valleys.

Map opposite

SOUTHERN GRASSHOPPER MOUSE *Onychomys torridus*
Identification: Head and body 3½–4 in. (89–102 mm); tail 1⅗–2 in. (41–51 mm); wt. ⅝–⅝ oz. (20–24 g). Body *grayish* or *pinkish cinnamon;* belly *white;* tip of tail *white.* Skull has 16 teeth.

Similar species: Northern Grasshopper Mouse is larger; usually above valley floors where the two overlap.   Map opposite

Woodrats

THE WOODRATS, also known as "packrats" or "trade rats," are about the size of ordinary house rats, but are easily distinguished from the latter by the *hairy,* not scaly, tail, and soft, fine fur covering the body. Further, their ears are *larger* and usually they have *white* feet and bellies. In the mts. they are commonly found along rock cliffs, where small piles of sticks and rubbish on rock ledges indicate their presence. On the plains they build stick and cactus houses, 2–4 ft. (61–122 cm) in diam. at base and nearly as high, in clumps of cactus, yucca, or brush. On the West Coast their nests (houses) may be in live oak trees. They are nocturnal; seldom seen by day. Skull has 16 teeth. There are 4 mammae.

Similar species: (1) Norway and (2) Black Rats (p. 195) have scaly tail, not covered with hair. (3) Cotton rats (pp. 173–174) have coarse fur; blackish brown mixed with buff or whitish, and small ears.

Economic status: Neutral, live mostly in wild areas; may cause some damage to unattended cabins.

EASTERN WOODRAT *Neotoma floridana*   Pl. 18
Identification: Head and body 8–9 in. (203–229 mm); tail 6–8 in. (152–203 mm); wt. 7–13½ oz. (200–382 g). This is a large, *grayish-brown* woodrat with *white or grayish belly* and with the tail, which is *shorter* than head and body, *white or gray beneath, brown above.*

Similar species: (1) Southern Plains Woodrat is steel-gray, not washed with brown. (2) Bushytail Woodrat has squirrel-like tail. (3) Norway and (4) Black Rats have scaly tail.

Habitat: Rocky cliffs in Northeast; hummocks, swamps, and cabbage palmetto in Southeast; yuccas and cacti in West.

Habits: May be partially colonial. Feeds chiefly on seeds, nuts, and fruits. Usually builds houses of sticks, rocks, bones, and debris; nest inside house, in burrow beneath, or in rock crevice; sometimes house and nest in tree. Home range rarely more than 100 yd. (91.5 m) across. Populations of 2-3 adults per acre (5-8 per ha) probably high. Has lived 33 months in the wild. Breeds throughout year in South; spring, summer, and fall in North. **Young:** Normally 2-4; gestation period 30-37 days; 2-3 litters a year.   Map p. 170

SOUTHERN PLAINS WOODRAT *Neotoma micropus* **Pl. 18**
Identification: Head and body $7\frac{1}{2}$-$8\frac{1}{2}$ in. (190-216 mm); tail $5\frac{1}{2}$-$6\frac{1}{2}$ in. (140-165 mm); wt. 7-11 oz. (200-311 g). Upperparts *steel-gray;* belly gray; hairs on *throat, breast,* and feet *white to bases;* tail blackish above, gray below.
Similar species: (1) Whitethroat Woodrat has back mixed with tawny. (2) Desert Woodrat is smaller; throat hairs not white at bases; back has tawny mixture. (3) Mexican and (4) Stephens Woodrats have throat hairs slate at bases. (5) Eastern Woodrat has grayish-brown upperparts.
Habitat: Semiarid brushland, cacti, mesquite, thornbush; low valleys and plains.
Habits: Feeds on cactus, seeds, acorns. Houses, made of cactus, brush, and rubbish, are 3-5 ft. (0.9-1.5 m) high and usually placed among cactus or thorny vegetation. Breeds in early spring.
Young: 2-4; gestation period about 33 days; probably 1 litter a year.   Map p. 170

WHITETHROAT WOODRAT *Neotoma albigula* **Pl. 18**
Identification: Head and body $7\frac{1}{2}$-$8\frac{1}{2}$ in. (190-216 mm); tail $5\frac{1}{2}$-$7\frac{1}{3}$ in. (140-186 mm); wt. $4\frac{4}{5}$-10 oz. (135-283 g). Body *gray* washed with *tawny* above; belly *white or grayish;* hairs of throat *white to their bases;* feet *white;* tail whitish below, brown above. Skull (Plate 26) has 16 teeth.
Similar species: (1) Southern Plains Woodrat is steel-gray above. (2) Desert, (3) Stephens, and (4) Mexican Woodrats have throat hairs slate at bases. (5) In the Dusky-footed Woodrat the tail is blackish above; hind feet dusky near ankles. (6) Bushytail Woodrat has squirrel-like tail; high mts.
Habitat: Brushland and rocky cliffs with shallow caves.
Habits: Feeds on cactus, mesquite beans, and various seeds; may store some food in house. Houses 2-3 ft. (61-91 cm) high, built usually among cactus, brush, or in caves in cliffs. Home range probably under 100 ft. (30.5 m) across in most instances. Populations of 10-20 adults per acre (25-50 per ha). Breeds Jan.-Aug.
Young: Usually 2 (1-3); probably more than 1 litter a year.
                                   Map p. 170

DESERT WOODRAT   *Neotoma lepida*   **Pl. 18**
  Identification: Head and body 5⅘–7 in. (147–178 mm); tail
  4⅓–6⅖ in. (110–162 mm); wt. 3⅓–6 oz. (94–170 g). Body pale
  to dark *gray* variously *washed with tawny;* belly *grayish to
  tawny;* bases of hairs everywhere *slate color.*
  Similar species: (1) In the Mexican Woodrat the tail is white,
  not gray, below; difficult to distinguish without skull. (2)
  Stephens Woodrat has hind foot with dusky patch on top, below
  ankle; tail slightly bushy. (3) Southern Plains and (4) Whitethroat Woodrats have hairs of throat white to bases. (5)
  Dusky-footed Woodrat is larger; hind feet dusky above. (6)
  Bushytail Woodrat has squirrel-like tail.
  Habitat: Desert floors or rocky slopes with scattered cactus,
  yucca, or other low vegetation.
  Habits: Feeds mostly on seeds, fruits, acorns, cactus. Houses
  of rubbish usually on ground or along cliffs, occasionally in
  trees. Has lived 5 years 7 months in captivity.
  Young: Usually 2–3 (1–5); gestation period 30–36 days; 4 or
  more litters a year. Partially pigmented at birth; eyes open at
  13 days; sexually mature at 60 days.   Map p. 170

STEPHENS WOODRAT   *Neotoma stephensi*
  Identification: Head and body 6–8⅖ in. (152–213 mm); tail
  4⅕–5⅗ in. (107–142 mm). Body grayish buff, darker on top;
  belly washed with buff; *dusky wedge* on *top of hind foot,* ¼–⅓
  distance below ankle; tail *slightly bushy* on end, whitish below,
  blackish above.
  Similar species: (1) Desert, (2) Whitethroat, and (3) Mexican
  Woodrats have top of hind foot white to ankle; tail not slightly
  bushy. (4) Bushytail Woodrat has tail squirrel-like, not blackish
  above, where ranges meet. (5) Southern Plains Woodrat has
  steel-gray upperparts.   Map p. 170

MEXICAN WOODRAT   *Neotoma mexicana*   **Pl. 18**
  Identification: Head and body 6½–7¾ in. (165–197 mm); tail
  6–6½ in. (152–165 mm). Normally *gray* with a *tawny wash,*
  nearly black in some lava areas; belly grayish white; tail distinctly bicolored, *whitish below, blackish above.*
  Similar species: (1) Desert Woodrat is hardly distinguishable
  without inspection of skull; tail less sharply bicolored. (2)
  Stephens Woodrat has slightly bushy tail; hind foot dusky on
  top below ankle, may be difficult to distinguish. (3) Southern
  Plains and (4) Whitethroat Woodrats have hairs on throat white
  to bases; valleys and plains. (5) Bushytail Woodrat has squirrel-like tail.
  Habitat: Rocks and cliffs, mts.
  Habits: Feeds on acorns, nuts, seeds, fruits, mushrooms, and
  cactus plants when available; may store some food. Does not

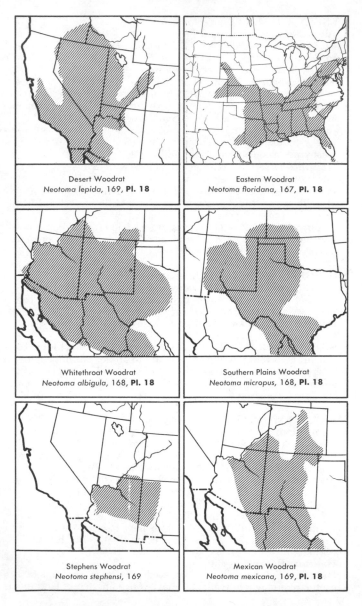

Desert Woodrat
Neotoma lepida, 169, **Pl. 18**

Eastern Woodrat
Neotoma floridana, 167, **Pl. 18**

Whitethroat Woodrat
Neotoma albigula, 168, **Pl. 18**

Southern Plains Woodrat
Neotoma micropus, 168, **Pl. 18**

Stephens Woodrat
Neotoma stephensi, 169

Mexican Woodrat
Neotoma mexicana, 169, **Pl. 18**

normally build houses like most other woodrats, but deposits sticks and rubbish among crevices in rocks and cliffs, under logs or tree roots, and in deserted buildings.

Young: Born in spring and summer; 2–4.   Map opposite

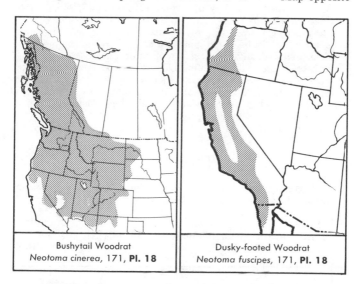

Bushytail Woodrat
Neotoma cinerea, 171, **Pl. 18**

Dusky-footed Woodrat
Neotoma fuscipes, 171, **Pl. 18**

DUSKY-FOOTED WOODRAT   *Neotoma fuscipes*   **Pl. 18**
Identification: Head and body 7⅗–9 in. (193–229 mm); tail 6⅘–8⅔ in. (173–220 mm); wt. 8–13¾ oz. (227–390 g). Body *grayish brown above, grayish to whitish below;* tail may be slightly paler below than above; hind feet sprinkled on top with *dusky* hairs; a large rat.
Similar species: (1) Whitethroat Woodrat is usually smaller; hind feet white above. (2) Desert Woodrat is smaller; hind feet white. (3) Bushytail Woodrat has squirrel-like tail; hind feet white.
Habitat: Heavy chaparral, streamside thickets, deciduous or mixed woods.
Habits: Feeds on variety of seeds, nuts, acorns, fruits, green vegetation, and fungi; stores food in house near nest. Builds large stick houses on ground or in trees. Shows ownership of house (territorial). Has lived 4 years in wild.
Young: Most born May and June, but few from Jan. to Oct.; 1–3 per litter.   Map above

BUSHYTAIL WOODRAT   *Neotoma cinerea*   **Pl. 18**
Identification: Head and body 7–9⅔ in. (178–245 mm); tail

$5\frac{1}{5}-7\frac{2}{5}$ in. (132–188 mm); wt. $7\frac{1}{2}-20\frac{2}{5}$ oz. (212–580 g). Body varies from *pale gray* washed with tawny to *nearly black* above; hind feet white. May be distinguished from all other woodrats by its *long, bushy, squirrel-like tail.*

Similar species: (1) Whitethroat, (2) Desert, (3) Mexican, (4) Eastern, and (5) Dusky-footed Woodrats all have short-haired tail tapering toward tip. (6) In the Stephens Woodrat the tail is not squirrel-like, but blackish above where ranges meet.

Habitat: High mts.; rimrock, rockslides, pines.

Habits: Climbs about cliffs easily. Feeds on green vegetation, twigs, shoots; may store some food as dry hay. Does not normally build large houses, but accumulates sticks, bones, and other material in rock crevices or under logs. Usually 1 family to a rockslide. Breeding season, May–Sept.

Young: Usually 2–4 (1–5); 1 litter a year.   Map p. 171

Rice Rats

RICE RATS, primarily tropical and subtropical in distribution, range south into S. America. One species is found in U.S.

RICE RAT *Oryzomys palustris*   **Pl. 16**
   Identification: Head and body $4\frac{3}{4}-5\frac{1}{5}$ in. (121–132 mm); tail $4\frac{1}{3}-7\frac{1}{5}$ in. (110–183 mm); wt. $1\frac{2}{5}-2\frac{4}{5}$ oz. (40–80 g). Body

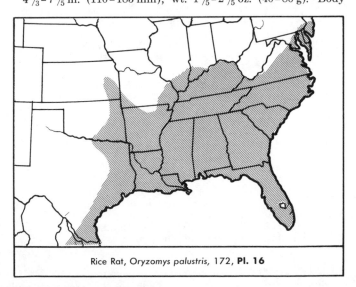

Rice Rat, *Oryzomys palustris*, 172, **Pl. 16**

grayish brown, sometimes washed with tawny; *gray or tawny* belly; *long, scaly tail* slightly paler below than above; feet *whitish;* fur short and soft. Skull (Plate 26) has 16 teeth. There are 8 mammae.

Similar species: (1) Hispid Cotton Rat has long coarse fur; tail black above. (2) In the Norway and (3) Black Rats (p. 195) the tail is not paler below. (4) All mice are smaller.

Habitat: Marshy areas, grasses, sedges.

Habits: Chiefly nocturnal; semiaquatic; makes surface runways. Feeds on green vegetation and seeds. Nests under debris above high-water level. Breeds throughout year.

Young: Usually 3–4 (1–7); gestation period about 25 days; several litters a year. Nearly naked, blind. Sexually mature at 50 days.

Economic status: Rarely interferes with man's activities; can do damage in a rice field.   Map opposite.

Cotton Rats

COTTON RATS are medium-sized, with grayish-brown to blackish-brown coarse fur *heavily mixed* with *pale buff.* Finely haired tail, blackish above, pale below, shorter than head and body. Feet gray; ears nearly concealed by long fur. Young cotton rats are similar in appearance to some voles.

Similar species: Woodrats (pp. 167–171) are grayish with large ears.

Habitat: Tall grass, sedges, and weeds; moist areas.

Economic status: May do damage to alfalfa and other green crops.

HISPID COTTON RAT   *Sigmodon hispidus*   **Pl. 17**
Identification: Head and body 5–8 in. (127–203 mm); tail $3\frac{1}{5}$–6 in. (81–152 mm); wt. 4–7 oz. (113–198 g). Long coarse body fur mixed buff and black above, *whitish below;* pale in West, dark in East. Skull (Plate 26) has 16 teeth. There are 8–10 mammae.

Similar species: (1) Least Cotton Rat has buff belly; in mts. (2) Yellownose Cotton Rat is yellowish around nose. (3) Rice Rat has scaly tail as long as head and body.

Habits: Makes surface runways along which may be found small piles of cut grass stems. Feeds chiefly on green vegetation, also eats eggs of ground-nesting birds. Nests either on surface or in burrow. Home range 100–200 ft. (30.5–61 m) across. Populations 10–12 per acre (25–30 per ha), fluctuate from year to year. Rarely lives more than 1 year in wild. Has extended range northward in recent years. Breeds all year.

Young: Usually 5–6 (2–12); gestation period about 27 days;

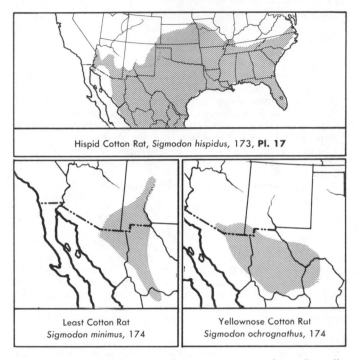

Hispid Cotton Rat, *Sigmodon hispidus*, 173, **Pl. 17**

Least Cotton Rat
Sigmodon minimus, 174

Yellownose Cotton Rat
Sigmodon ochrognathus, 174

as many as 9 litters a year. Leave nest at 4–7 days. Sexually
mature in 40 days.   Map above

LEAST COTTON RAT   *Sigmodon minimus*
Identification: Head and body 5–6 in. (127–152 mm); tail
$3\frac{4}{5}$–$4\frac{1}{5}$ in. (97–107 mm). This rat may be distinguished by the
mixture of black and pale buff hairs of upperparts, and the *buff
belly*. Those from N. Mexico known as *S. fulviventer* by some
authors. Skull has 16 teeth.
Similar species: (1) Hispid Cotton Rat has a whitish belly;
in valleys. (2) Yellownose Cotton Rat has a gray belly.
                                                      Map above

YELLOWNOSE COTTON RAT   *Sigmodon ochrognathus*
Identification: Head and body 5–6 in. (127–152 mm); tail
4–$4\frac{3}{5}$ in. (102–117 mm); wt. 2–4 oz. (57–114 g). This is a *foothills* or *mt.* form. Upperparts mixed buffy and blackish, washed
with *tawny* on *nose, face,* and *rump; belly gray*. Skull has 16
teeth.

Similar species: (1) Hispid Cotton Rat has no buff on nose.
(2) Least Cotton Rat has buff belly.
Habitat: Dense vegetation; foothills and mts.   Map opposite

Lemmings

THESE SMALL, vole-like mammals are found mostly in the Far
North. Their fur is long and soft and nearly conceals the small
thin ears. The tail is usually less than 1 in. (25 mm) long. Relationships of lemmings are uncertain. The 3 genera are grouped
here for convenience.
Economic status: Important food for foxes, especially those on
tundra, so that their abundance means money to the Eskimo fur
trapper.

HUDSON BAY COLLARED LEMMING
Dicrostonyx hudsonius
   Identification: Head and body $4\frac{3}{4}$–$5\frac{2}{5}$ in. (121–137 mm); tail
   $\frac{3}{4}$–$\frac{9}{10}$ in. (19–23 mm); wt. $1\frac{3}{5}$–$2\frac{2}{5}$ oz. (45–68 g). Found on
   several islands in Hudson Bay. Upperparts buffy gray with a
   dark stripe along middle of back and a tawny band across
   throat in summer. Ears and tail barely show through the long
   fur, which is *white in winter;* 3rd and 4th claws on front feet
   greatly enlarged, especially in winter. Skull (Plate 26) has 16
   teeth.
   Similar species: (1) Northern Bog Lemming is uniform brownish gray; teeth grooved. (2) Voles (pp. 181–192) and (3) phenacomys (p. 179) have tail more than 1 in. (25 mm) long.
   Habitat: Tundra of Ungava and islands in Hudson Bay.
   Habits: More active by day than at night during summer.
   Probably feeds on available vegetation. Nest (diam. about 8 in.;
   203 mm) may be underground, among rocks, or, in winter,
   aboveground and beneath the snow. Digs numerous refuge
   burrows 1–2 ft. (30–61 cm) long; deposits feces in selected locations, may be 2–3 qt. (1.9–2.8 l) of tiny fecal pellets in a pile.
   Populations may fluctuate widely. Has lived more than 2 years
   in captivity. Both parents care for young.
   Young: Usually 3–4 (1–7); gestation period 19–21 days; 1–2
   litters a year.   Map p. 176

GREENLAND COLLARED LEMMING   Pl. 17
Dicrostonyx groenlandicus
   Identification: Head and body 4–$5\frac{1}{2}$ in. (102–140 mm); tail
   $\frac{2}{5}$–$\frac{4}{5}$ in. (10–20 mm); wt. $1\frac{3}{5}$–$2\frac{2}{5}$ oz. (45–68 g). See Hudson
   Bay Collared Lemming for description. This lemming occupies
   the *tundra* west and north of Hudson Bay and a strip in Greenland.

Those on St. Lawrence I., Alaska, considered as a distinct species (*D. exsul*) by most authors.

Similar species: (1) Brown Lemming has no dark streak down back; brown in winter. (2) Northern Bog Lemming is brownish gray; upper incisors grooved. (3) Voles (pp. 181–192) and (4) phenacomys (p. 179) have tail longer than 1 in. (25 mm).

Map opposite

SOUTHERN BOG LEMMING *Synaptomys cooperi* **Pl. 17**
Identification: Head and body $3\frac{2}{5}$–$4\frac{2}{5}$ in. (86–112 mm); tail $\frac{3}{5}$–$\frac{7}{8}$ in. (15–22 mm); wt. $\frac{1}{2}$–$1\frac{2}{5}$ oz. (14–40 g). Upperparts brownish gray, belly grayish; ears *nearly concealed;* tail less than 1 in. (25 mm) long; *shallow groove* near outer edge of upper incisor. Skull (Plate 26) has 16 teeth. There are 6–8 mammae.

Similar species: (1) Meadow Vole has tail more than 1 in. (25 mm). (2) Yellownose Vole has yellow nose. (3) In the Prairie Vole the front teeth are not grooved. (4) Pine Vole is uniform auburn color. (5) Boreal Redback Vole has tail more than 1 in. (25 mm); reddish on middle of back.

Habitat: Low damp bogs and meadows with heavy growth of vegetation.

Habits: Active day or night; feeds primarily on green vegetation; cuts grass stems 1–2 in. (25–51 mm) long and deposits in small piles along runways through heavy grass; nests both above and below ground. Home range about $\frac{1}{3}$ acre (0.1 ha). Populations fluctuate widely, to 35 per acre (87 per ha). Breeds throughout year in southern part of range.

Young: Usually 3–4 (2–6); gestation period about 23 days; 2–3 litters a year. Map below

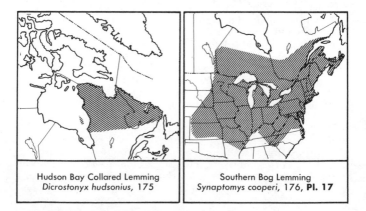

Hudson Bay Collared Lemming
Dicrostonyx hudsonius, 175

Southern Bog Lemming
Synaptomys cooperi, 176, **Pl. 17**

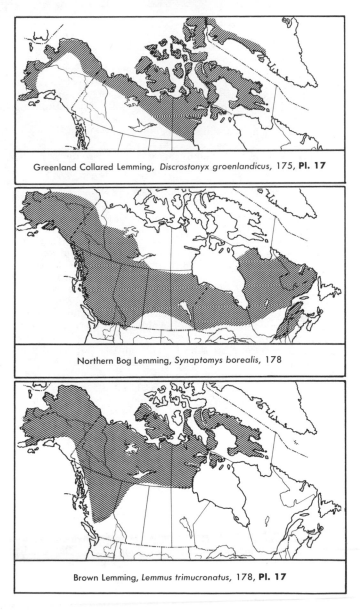

Greenland Collared Lemming, *Discrostonyx groenlandicus*, 175, **Pl. 17**

Northern Bog Lemming, *Synaptomys borealis*, 178

Brown Lemming, *Lemmus trimucronatus*, 178, **Pl. 17**

NORTHERN BOG LEMMING *Synaptomys borealis*
  Identification: Head and body 4–4⅗ in. (102–117 mm); tail
  ⅘–1 in. (20–25 mm). As described for Southern Bog Lemming
  but slightly larger.
  Similar species: (1) Brown Lemming has hairy soles of feet;
  teeth not grooved. (2) Collared Lemming has tawny band across
  throat, summer; white, winter. (3) In voles and (4) phenacomys
  the front teeth are not grooved and/or tail is longer than 1 in.
  (25 mm).
  Habitat: Wet alpine and subalpine meadows, muskeg, heaths,
  and sedges.
  Habits: Winter nest usually aboveground, summer nest beneath surface; leaves small piles of cuttings along runways;
  deposits droppings in special places.
  Young: Born May–Aug.; usually 4–5 (2–8).   Map p. 177

BROWN LEMMING *Lemmus trimucronatus*   **Pl. 17**
  Identification: Head and body 4½–5½ in. (114–140 mm); tail
  ⅘–1⅙ in. (20–28 mm); wt. 2½–4 oz. (70–113 g). Back and
  rump reddish brown; head and shoulders *grayish;* fur *long and
  soft; tail short.* Does not turn white in winter. Soles of feet
  hairy; upper incisors not grooved. Skull has 16 teeth.
      Population on St. George I., Pribilofs, is considered a distinct
  species (*L. nigripes*).
  Similar species: (1) Greenland Collared Lemming has dark
  median stripe down back, or all white. (2) Northern Bog Lemming is brownish gray; incisors grooved. (3) Voles and (4) phenacomys have tail more than 1 in. (25 mm), or not brightly colored; soles of feet not furred.
  Habitat: Tundra and alpine meadows.
  Habits: Active day and night. Feeds mostly on vegetation;
  nests aboveground in winter, underground in summer. Populations may fluctuate widely, with peaks every 3–4 years. Breeds
  June–Aug.
  Young: Usually 2–6 (2–11); probably 2 or more litters a year.
                                                        Map p. 177

Phenacomys

THESE vole-like rodents are inhabitants of grassy areas within the
cold forested regions of Canada, the high mountaintops of w. U.S.,
and the humid nw. Pacific Coast. They occur where people seldom
go, and therefore are not likely to be encountered. Most of them
are ground-living, have relatively short tails, and rather long, soft,
grayish-brown fur. The belly is pale grayish. The Tree Phenacomys is quite different from the others; it has a relatively long

blackish tail, which contrasts with the bright rufous body; and it is arboreal.

Economic status: Neutral; occur mostly in wild areas.

MOUNTAIN PHENACOMYS   **Pl. 17**
Phenacomys intermedius
(Heather Phenacomys)
   Identification: Head and body $3\frac{1}{2}$–$4\frac{3}{5}$ in. (89–117 mm); tail 1–$1\frac{2}{3}$ in. (25–42 mm); wt. 1–$1\frac{2}{5}$ oz. (28–40 g). Body *gray* washed with *brown to dark brown, white* feet and *silvery* belly sometimes tinged with buff; nose or face yellowish in some; tail bicolored. Skull (Plate 26) has 16 teeth. There are 8 mammae.
   Similar species: (1) In the Mountain Vole the tail is usually longer; difficult to distinguish. (2) Longtail Vole has tail longer than 2 in. (51 mm). (3) Yellow-cheeked and (4) Yellownose Voles have tail longer than $1\frac{2}{3}$ in. (42 mm). (5) Tundra Vole is larger. (6) In Redback Voles the nose is not yellowish; back reddish. (7) Others are not found near mountaintops, or measurements differ.
   Habitat: Open grassy areas near mountaintops; pine and spruce forests, rocky slopes, tundra, dry areas or near water; not restricted, but occupies several habitats.
   Habits: Most active at twilight and night. Feeds on bark of dwarf birch and willows, seeds, lichens, berries, green vegetation; caches food items. Nests aboveground in winter; below surface, under rocks, stumps, debris in summer.
   Young: Born June–Sept.; 2–8; gestation period about 21 days; 2 or more litters a season. Naked, blind. Females sexually mature at 4–6 weeks, breed 1st year.   Map p. 180

PACIFIC PHENACOMYS   *Phenacomys albipes*
   Identification: Head and body $3\frac{4}{5}$–$4\frac{2}{5}$ in. (97–112 mm); tail $2\frac{1}{2}$–$2\frac{4}{5}$ in. (64–71 mm). Body dark, *rich brown* above; gray washed with buff on belly; tail brown above, paler below. Skull has 16 teeth.
   Similar species: (1) Mountain Vole lives in high mt. meadows. (2) Townsend and (3) Longtail Voles have head and body over $4\frac{1}{2}$ in. (114 mm). (4) Oregon Vole has tail under 2 in. (51 mm). (5) California Redback Vole has chestnut back. (6) Tree Phenacomys is reddish with blackish tail. (7) California Vole is larger, grayish brown.
   Habitat: Dense forests; near small streams.   Map p. 182

TREE PHENACOMYS   *Phenacomys longicaudus*   **Pl. 17**
   Identification: Head and body 4–$4\frac{1}{3}$ in. (102–110 mm); tail $2\frac{2}{5}$–$3\frac{1}{3}$ in. (61–85 mm); wt. 1 oz. (28 g). A bright *reddish-brown* to *cinnamon* phenacomys with a blackish, *well-haired* tail. Color and size serve to distinguish this species from all others in area.

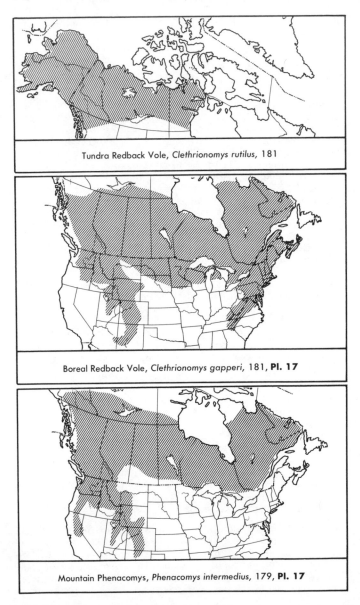

Tundra Redback Vole, *Clethrionomys rutilus*, 181

Boreal Redback Vole, *Clethrionomys gapperi*, 181, **Pl. 17**

Mountain Phenacomys, *Phenacomys intermedius*, 179, **Pl. 17**

Authors have thought there are 2 species in Oregon; the other is *P. silvicola*. Externally it is difficult to distinguish them, so they are treated as one here. Further study is needed to resolve this problem. Some authors consider the tree-inhabiting phenacomys to belong to the genus *Arborimus*. Skull has 16 teeth. There are 4 mammae.

Habitat: Spruce, hemlock, and fir forests.

Habits: Arboreal. Food consists almost entirely of leaves of tree in which they are living; spruce, hemlock, or fir. Bulky nest, up to the size of a half-bushel measure or larger, is built on branches, usually near the trunk, 15–100 ft. (4.6–30.5 m) up in the trees; nest becomes larger with age, some probably occupied by many generations.

Young: Born any time of year; 1–3. Naked, blind.

Map p. 187

Redback Voles

THESE small forest rodents, 5–6 in. (127–152 mm) overall length, usually have long, soft fur, *gray* or washed with *yellowish on sides* and *reddish down the back*. In southern part of the range they may be deep brown with little, if any, contrast between sides and back. Belly always *gray or silvery,* and tail bicolored. There are 8 mammae.

TUNDRA REDBACK VOLE   *Clethrionomys rutilus*
  Identification: Head and body 4–4½ in. (102–114 mm); tail 1⅕–1⅗ in. (30–41 mm); wt. 1–1⅕ oz. (28–34 g). Sides washed with yellowish; bright *reddish* (sometimes brown) *down middle of back;* belly silvery or washed with yellow; tail yellowish beneath, dark brown on top; winter pelage paler than that of summer. Skull has 16 teeth. There are 8 mammae.
    Formerly known as *C. dawsoni.*
  Similar species: (1) Lemmings are larger; no distinct reddish stripe down back. (2) In other voles the color of sides and back do not contrast.
  Habitat: Tundra and damp forest floors, alpine conditions.
  Young: Born May–Sept.; 4–9; probably 2 litters a year.

Map opposite

BOREAL REDBACK VOLE   *Clethrionomys gapperi*   **Pl. 17**
  Identification: Head and body 3⅔–4⅔ in. (93–118 mm); tail 1⅕–2 in. (30–51 mm); wt. ½–1⅖ oz. (14–40 g). In North and East there are 2 color phases, red and gray (palest in Labrador). For most part, may be distinguished from all other voles of its area by *reddish back* and *gray sides,* but in North and East the gray phase may not have a reddish back and may be difficult to distinguish from other voles of the area without examination

of the skull. No grooves on upper incisors. Skull (Plate 26) has 16 teeth. There are 8 mammae.

Similar species: (1) Lemmings are larger and have shorter tail. In (2) phenacomys and (3) other voles there is no contrast between color of sides and back.

Habitat: Coniferous, deciduous, or mixed forests; it prefers damp situations.

Habits: Active day or night; good climber for a vole. Feeds chiefly on green vegetation, but adds seeds, nuts, bark, fungi, and a few insects. Nest usually under roots or logs, simple platform. Home range about $\frac{1}{4}$ acre (0.1 ha). Populations to 10 per acre (25 per ha), usually fewer.

Young: Born March – Oct.; usually 4 – 6 (3 – 8); gestation period 17 – 19 days; probably 2 or more litters a year. Naked, blind.

Map p. 180

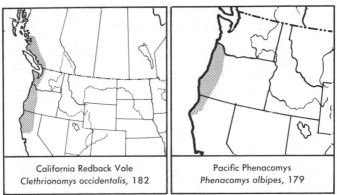

California Redback Vole
Clethrionomys occidentalis, 182

Pacific Phenacomys
Phenacomys albipes, 179

CALIFORNIA REDBACK VOLE   *Clethrionomys occidentalis*
Identification: Head and body $4\frac{1}{3}$ in. (110 mm); tail $2 - 2\frac{1}{5}$ in. (51 – 56 mm). Body *dark sepia;* back *dark chestnut,* but does not contrast strikingly with sides; belly *buffy* or *soiled whitish;* feet *whitish* or *dusky.* Skull has 16 teeth. There are 8 mammae.
    Formerly known as *C. californicus.*

Similar species: (1) Mountain Vole is grayish; occurs in high mt. meadows. (2) California Vole is grayish brown. (3) Townsend, (4) Richardson, and (5) Longtail Voles have head and body $4\frac{1}{2}$ in. (114 mm) or more. (6) Oregon Vole has tail less than 2 in. (51 mm). (7) Mountain Phenacomys has tail less than 2 in. (51 mm); high mts. (8) Pacific and (9) Tree Phenacomys have tail more than $2\frac{1}{5}$ in. (56 mm).

Habitat: Forest floors, moist and strewn with logs.

Young: Embryos reported for July and Aug.; 2 – 4.

Map above

Other Voles

THROUGHOUT Canada and the U.S. where there is good *grass cover,* 1 or more species of voles are likely to be found. Their presence often may be detected by *narrow runways,* 1–2 in. (25–51 mm) wide, through the matted grasses. Small piles of brownish droppings and short pieces of grass stems along these runways are further evidence. In a few places, these voles are found among rocks or on forest floors where there is no grass. In areas of winter snow, their *round openings* to the surface of the snow also reveal their presence. They are active by day as well as by night. Mostly they are *brownish gray* with *long fur, small ears,* and relatively *short tail,* always less than length of head and body. They have small, black, beadlike eyes. Skull has 16 teeth.

Similar species: (1) In the bog lemmings the upper incisors have grooves down their front surfaces, tail never longer than 1 in. (25 mm). (2) Collared and (3) Brown Lemmings are brightly colored. (4) Phenacomys are difficult to distinguish as a group; see special accounts. (5) Redback voles usually have reddish back contrasting with gray sides.

Young: Hairless, blind.

Economic status: Voles can do severe damage to fruit trees by girdling the trunks or removing bark from roots, especially in winter under a protective covering of snow. Also, they may do damage to hay and grain crops, particularly if these are left in the shock during winter. On the credit side, they serve as a buffer species to predators and supply the food for many fur-bearing mammals as well as for hawks and owls.

MEADOW VOLE *Microtus pennsylvanicus*   **Pl. 17**
  Identification: Head and body $3\frac{1}{2}$–5 in. (89–127 mm); tail $1\frac{2}{5}$–$2\frac{3}{5}$ in. (35–66 mm); wt. 1–$2\frac{1}{2}$ oz. (28–70 g). The most widely distributed of the voles, this species varies from a gray, faintly washed with brown, in the West, to dark brown in the East. Belly *silvery to slightly buffy or dark gray,* and tail *bicolored.* Fur is *long* and soft. Upper incisors not grooved. Skull (Plate 26) has 16 teeth. There are 8 mammae.
  The voles on Muskeget I., Massachusetts, *M. breweri,* and Gull I., off Long I., New York, *M. nesophilus* (probably extinct), may be distinct species.
  Similar species: (1) In the Mountain Vole the characters are not distinct; occurs in high mt. meadows. (2) Tundra Vole is larger where ranges meet. (3) Longtail Vole has tail more than 2 in. (51 mm); may be difficult to distinguish. (4) Prairie Vole has tail usually less than $1\frac{2}{5}$ in. (36 mm); sometimes difficult to distinguish. (5) Alaska Vole has tail less than $1\frac{2}{5}$ in. (36 mm);

occurs above timberline. (6) Yellow-cheeked and (7) Yellownose Voles have yellow nose. (8) Richardson Vole has head and body longer than 5 ½ in. (140 mm). (9) Redback voles have reddish back; sides are gray or yellowish. (10) In the Mountain Phenacomys (p. 179) the tail is usually less than 1 ⅖ in. (36 mm); occurs in high mts. (11) In others the tail is never longer than 1 in. (25 mm).

Habitat: Low moist areas or high grasslands with rank growths of vegetation; near streams, lakes, swamps, occasionally in forests with little ground cover; orchards with grass undergrowth.
Habits: Active day or night. A good swimmer. Feeds on grasses, sedges, seeds, grain, bark, and probably some insects. Nests either above or below ground; makes burrows along surface runways. Home range ¹⁄₁₀–1 acre (0.04–0.4 ha). Populations fluctuate markedly with highs at 3– to 4–year intervals. Lives 1–3 years in wild. A good fighter; probably displays territorial behavior during part of year. Breeds throughout year.
Young: Born any month of year; 1–9 (usually 3–5); gestation period 21 days; several litters a year (in captivity, a female had 17 litters in 1 year).   Map below

MOUNTAIN VOLE   *Microtus montanus*
    Identification: Head and body 4–5 ½ in. (102–140 mm); tail

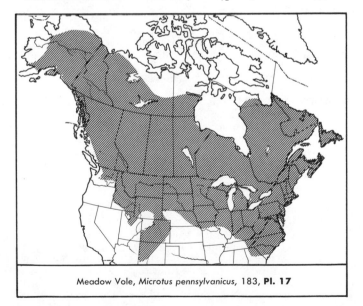

Meadow Vole, *Microtus pennsylvanicus*, 183, **Pl. 17**

1 $\frac{1}{5}$ – 2 $\frac{3}{5}$ in. (30 – 66 mm); wt. 1 – 3 oz. (28 – 85 g). Upperparts *grayish brown to blackish,* belly whitish; *feet* usually *dusky;* found primarily in the *valleys* of the mountainous Great Basin area. There are 8 mammae.
Similar species: (1) In the Longtail Vole the tail is usually longer; may be difficult to distinguish. (2) Meadow and (3) California Voles usually not in high mt. meadows; difficult to distinguish. (4) Mountain Phenacomys occurs near tops of mts.; difficult to distinguish. (5) Oregon Vole is dark brown, hair short. (6) Richardson Vole has head and body 5 $\frac{1}{2}$ in. (140 mm) or more. (7) Prairie Vole is found in low prairies. (8) Mexican Vole has yellowish, not whitish, belly. (9) Townsend Vole has blackish tail. (10) California Redback Vole is dark sepia and chestnut. (11) Pacific Phenacomys is not found in high mts.
Map p. 187

CALIFORNIA VOLE *Microtus californicus*
Identification: Head and body 4 $\frac{3}{4}$ – 5 $\frac{2}{3}$ in. (120 – 143 mm); tail 1 $\frac{3}{5}$ – 2 $\frac{4}{5}$ in. (40 – 71 mm).; wt. 1 $\frac{1}{2}$ – 3 $\frac{1}{2}$ oz. (42 – 100 g). This is a *grayish-brown* (blackish toward the coast, reddish in the desert) vole with *bicolored tail* and *pale feet* that contrast with the color of the back. There are 8 mammae.
Similar species: (1) In the Longtail Vole the tail is usually longer; may be difficult to distinguish. (2) Mountain Vole has dusky feet; occurs in high mt. meadows. (3) Townsend Vole has blackish tail; feet dusky. (4) Oregon Vole is dark brown; fur short. (5) California Redback Vole has sepia body and chestnut back. (6) Mountain Phenacomys has tail usually under 1 $\frac{3}{5}$ in. (41 mm); high mts. (7) Pacific Phenacomys is smaller, rich brown. (8) Tree Phenacomys is reddish with blackish tail.
Habitat: Marshy ground, saltwater and fresh; wet meadows, dry, grassy hillsides. Seashore to mts.
Habits: Feeds on grasses, sedges, and other green vegetation. Breeds throughout year.
Young: 4 – 8; gestation period 21 days; more than 1 litter a year.
Map p. 187

TOWNSEND VOLE *Microtus townsendi*   **Pl. 17**
Identification: Head and body 4 $\frac{3}{4}$ – 6 $\frac{2}{5}$ in. (120 – 162 mm); tail 2 – 3 in. (51 – 76 mm). A large, *blackish-brown* vole with *gray belly, blackish tail,* and *dusky feet.* Ears project well above fur. Found also on San Juan and Shaw Is., Washington, and Bowen I., B.C. (not shown on map). May be distinguished from all others by size and color. There are 8 mammae.
Habitat: Moist fields; sedges, tules, meadows; from tidewater to alpine meadows. Usually near water.
Young: Born March – Sept.; usually 4 – 5 (1 – 9); gestation period 21 days.   Map p. 187

TUNDRA VOLE   *Microtus oeconomus*
Identification: Head and body 5–6⁴⁄₅ in. (127–173 mm); tail
1²⁄₅–2¹⁄₈ in. (36–54 mm); wt. 1¹⁄₃–2⁴⁄₅ oz. (37–79 g). *Body dull
brown* washed with buffy or fulvous. Belly *grayish,* tail *bicolored.* Its fairly uniform color above, and size, will distinguish
it from most other small rodents in the area. There are 8
mammae. Occurs on St. Lawrence, Big Punuk, Amak, Unalaska, Popof, Afognak, Kodiak, Chichagof, Montague, Baranof,
and Barter Is., Alaska.
Similar species: (1) Yellow-cheeked Vole is large and has
yellowish nose. (2) Meadow Vole is smaller where ranges meet.
(3) Alaska Vole has tail usually under 1²⁄₅ in. (36 mm). (4)
Longtail Vole has tail longer than 2 in. (51 mm). (5) Redback
voles have reddish back. (6) Mountain Phenacomys is smaller.
(7) Lemmings have tail no longer than 1 in. (25 mm) or body
brightly colored.
Habitat: Moist to wet tundra.
Habits: Makes runways through tundra vegetation; may store
some food. Nests in shallow burrows or under debris.
Young: 3–11 embryos reported.   Map opposite

LONGTAIL VOLE   *Microtus longicaudus*
Identification: Head and body 4¹⁄₂–5¹⁄₃ in. (114–135 mm); tail
2–3¹⁄₂ in. (51–89 mm); wt. 1¹⁄₃–2 oz. (37–57 g). A rather *large*
vole with a *long tail.* Fur *dark gray washed with brown or
blackish;* feet *soiled whitish;* tail *bicolored.* There are 8
mammae.
Similar species: (1) In the Meadow Vole the tail is usually
under 2 in. (51 mm); may be difficult to distinguish. (2) California Vole usually has shorter tail; mostly in foothills and
valleys; may be difficult to distinguish. (3) Mountain Vole has
whitish belly; sometimes difficult to differentiate. (4) In the
Mexican, (5) Prairie, (6) Oregon, (7) Alaska, and (8) Tundra
Voles the tail is usually under 2 in. (51 mm). (9) Townsend Vole
is large, with blackish tail. (10) Richardson Vole has head and
body longer than 5¹⁄₂ in. (140 mm). (11) Phenacomys are either
reddish or rich brown, or with tail under 2 in. (51 mm). (12)
Redback voles have reddish back, grayish or yellowish sides.
(13) Others have tail less than 2 in. (51 mm).
Habitat: Streambanks and mt. meadows, occasionally in dry
situations; brushy areas in winter.
Habits: Feeds on grasses, bulbs, bark of small twigs. Nests
aboveground in winter, in burrows in summer.
Young: Born May–Sept.; 4–8.   Map p. 189

CORONATION ISLAND VOLE   *Microtus coronarius*
Identification: Head and body 5–5³⁄₅ in. (127–142 mm); tail
2⁴⁄₅–3³⁄₅ in. (71–91 mm). Similar to Longtail Vole.
Range: Coronation, Forrester, and Warren Is., Alaska.

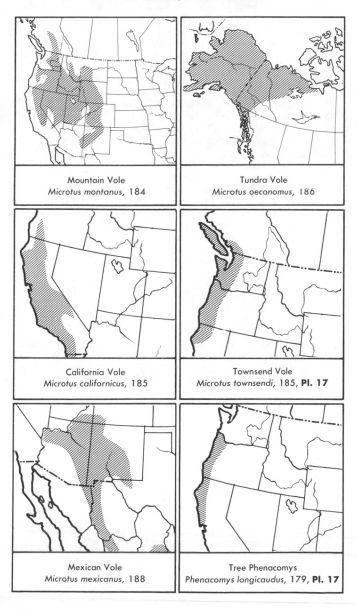

Mountain Vole
Microtus montanus, 184

Tundra Vole
Microtus oeconomus, 186

California Vole
Microtus californicus, 185

Townsend Vole
Microtus townsendi, 185, **Pl. 17**

Mexican Vole
Microtus mexicanus, 188

Tree Phenacomys
Phenacomys longicaudus, 179, **Pl. 17**

MEXICAN VOLE   *Microtus mexicanus*
   Identification: Head and body 4–4⅗ in. (102–117 mm); tail
   1–1⅖ in. (25–36 mm); wt. 1–1½ oz. (28–42 g). A *small,
   brownish* vole. Feet *dusky;* tail *short.* There are 4 mammae.
   Similar species: (1) Mountain Vole has whitish belly. (2)
   Longtail Vole has tail 2 in. (51 mm) or more. (3) Boreal Redback Vole has red back and gray sides.
   Habitat: Mt. meadows and parklike yellow pine forests; usually
   dry situations.
   Habits: Active by day. May nest aboveground in winter, below
   in summer; makes runways and burrows through grass or herbaceous cover.
   Young: Usually 3–4 (2–5).   Map p. 187

YELLOW-CHEEKED VOLE   *Microtus xanthognathus*
   Identification: Head and body 6–7 in. (152–178 mm); tail
   1⅘–2 in. (46–51 mm); wt. 4–6 oz. (113–170 g). A large, yel-
   low-cheeked, dull brown vole. There are 8 mammae.
   Similar species: (1) Lemmings have tail no longer than 1 in.
   (25 mm). (2) Other voles are smaller; cheeks not yellowish. (3)
   Mountain Phenacomys has tail under 1⅘ in. (46 mm).
   Habitat: Spruce forests and bordering tundra.
   Habits: Chiefly crepuscular, but may be active day or night.
   May construct dirt mounds 2–10 ft. (61–305 cm) in diam. and
   1–2 ft. (30–61 cm) high; runways through sphagnum.
   Young: 7–10 embryos reported.   Map opposite

YELLOWNOSE VOLE   *Microtus chrotorrhinus*   **Pl. 17**
   Identification: Head and body 4–4⅘ in. (102–122 mm); tail
   1⅘–2 in. (46–51 mm); wt. 1–2 oz. (28–57 g). A medium-sized,
   grayish-brown vole with a rich *yellow nose.* There are 8
   mammae.
   Similar species: (1) The Meadow Vole, (2) Pine Vole, (3)
   Boreal Redback Vole, and (4) bog lemmings do not have grayish-brown body and rich yellow nose. (5) Mountain Phenacomys has tail under 1⅘ in. (46 mm).
   Habitat: Cool, moist, rocky woodlands.   Map opposite

RICHARDSON VOLE   *Microtus richardsoni*
   Identification: Head and body 5⅗–6½ in. (142–165 mm); tail
   2⅖–3⅗ in. (61–91 mm); wt. 2½–3½ oz. (71–100 g). The *largest* vole within its range. Body dull *grayish brown* with a *pale
   gray belly* and a *bicolored tail.* May be recognized by large size.
   There are 8 mammae.
   Similar species: (1) In the Oregon Vole the tail is under 2 in.
   (51 mm). (2) Longtail, (3) Mountain, and (4) Meadow Voles
   have head and body no longer than 5½ in. (140 mm). (5) Boreal
   Redback Vole has reddish back and gray sides. (6) In others
   the tail is less than 2 in. (51 mm).

Habitat: Creekbanks and marshes; mts., to above timberline.
Habits: Semiaquatic; swims well and takes to water readily.
Burrows along streambanks; some entrances below water. Nests
beneath roots, old stumps, logs.
Young: Usually 4–6; breeding season not known.

Map p. 190

OREGON VOLE   *Microtus oregoni*
Identification: Head and body $4-4\frac{2}{5}$ in. (102–112 mm); tail
$1\frac{1}{5}-1\frac{3}{5}$ in. (30–41 mm); wt. $\frac{3}{5}-\frac{7}{10}$ oz. (17–20 g).   A small,

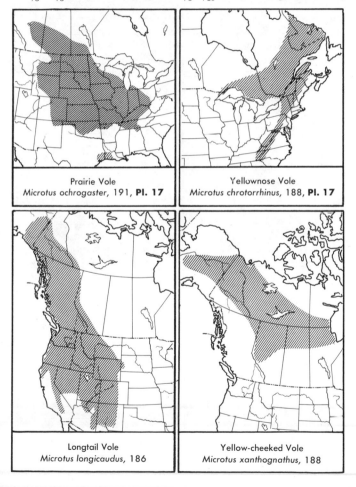

Prairie Vole
Microtus ochrogaster, 191, **Pl. 17**

Yellownose Vole
Microtus chrotorrhinus, 188, **Pl. 17**

Longtail Vole
Microtus longicaudus, 186

Yellow-cheeked Vole
Microtus xanthognathus, 188

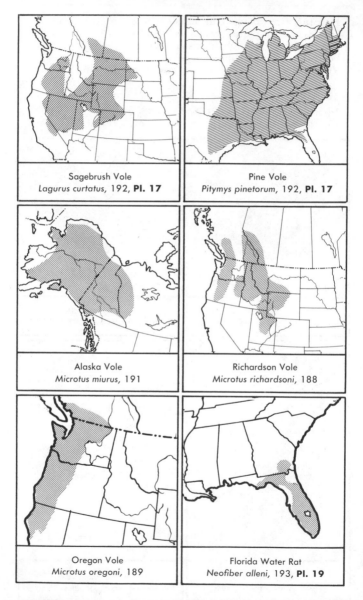

Sagebrush Vole
Lagurus curtatus, 192, **Pl. 17**

Pine Vole
Pitymys pinetorum, 192, **Pl. 17**

Alaska Vole
Microtus miurus, 191

Richardson Vole
Microtus richardsoni, 188

Oregon Vole
Microtus oregoni, 189

Florida Water Rat
Neofiber alleni, 193, **Pl. 19**

brown, short-haired vole; tail *bicolored;* belly *silvery.* There are 8 mammae.
Similar species: (1) California and (2) Mountain Voles have long fur. (3) Townsend, (4) Longtail, (5) Richardson, and (6) California Redback Voles, and (7) Pacific and (8) Tree Phenacomys have tail longer than 2 in. (51 mm). (9) Mountain Phenacomys occurs near mountaintops.
Habitat: Forests, brush, grassy areas; usually on dry slopes.
Habits: Burrows through the duff on the forest floor or among the grass roots; seldom comes aboveground. Breeding season, May – Aug., possibly longer.
Young: Report of 3–5 per litter.   Map opposite

ALASKA VOLE *Microtus miurus*
  Identification: Head and body $3\frac{1}{2}$–5 in. (89–127 mm); tail 1–$1\frac{2}{5}$ in. (25–36 mm); wt. 1–2 oz. (28–57 g). Tail short; body *buffy.* May be distinguished by *small size* and *short tail.* There are 8 mammae.
  Similar species: (1) Lemmings are larger; tail no longer than 1 in. (25 mm) or body brightly colored. (2) In the Mountain Phenacomys the body is not buffy. (3) Other voles either have reddish back or are larger; tail usually more than $1\frac{3}{5}$ in. (40 mm).
  Habitat: High, well-drained slopes, tundra benches, scattered dwarf willows.
  Habits: Active day or night. In autumn, constructs forage piles of 1 qt. to 8 gal. (0.9–30 l) in volume. Digs own burrows, but may also occupy those of ground squirrels. Breeds June–Aug.
  Young: 4–12 embryos reported.   Map opposite

INSULAR VOLE *Microtus abbreviatus*
  Identification: Head and body $5\frac{2}{5}$–$5\frac{4}{5}$ in. (137–147 mm); tail 1–$1\frac{1}{5}$ in. (25–30 mm).
  Range: Hall and St. Matthew Is., Bering Sea, Alaska.

PRAIRIE VOLE *Microtus ochrogaster*   **Pl. 17**
  Identification: Head and body $3\frac{1}{2}$–5 in. (89–127 mm); tail $1\frac{1}{5}$–$1\frac{3}{5}$ in. (30–41 mm); wt. 1–$1\frac{1}{2}$ oz. (28–42 g). In the extensive *prairie* region, this is the typical vole. It is *grayish to dark brown,* with a good mixture of tawny-tipped hairs; darkest in South and East, palest in Northwest. Tail *short* for a vole; belly either *whitish or yellowish.* There are 6 mammae.
  Some authors consider this a separate genus (*Pedomys*). The populations in Louisiana and Texas are considered distinct by some (*M. ludovicianus*).
  Similar species: (1) Meadow Vole has a tail that is usually more than $1\frac{3}{5}$ in. (41 mm); sometimes difficult to distinguish. (2) Longtail Vole has tail 2 in. (51 mm) or more. (3) Mountain

Vole and (4) Mountain Phenacomys occur in mts. (5) Boreal
Redback Vole has a red back. (6) Sagebrush Vole is ash-gray.
(7) Pine Vole is auburn; tail 1 in. (25 mm) or less. (8) Southern
Bog Lemming has grooved upper incisors.

Habitat: Open prairies; fence rows, railway rights-of-way, and
old cemeteries; usually fairly dry places.

Habits: Active day and night. Has extensive underground
burrow system as well as runways on surface; nests more often
underground.

Young: Born mostly March–Sept.; usually 3–4 (2–6); gestation period 21 days; 3–4 litters a season. Females breed at 30
days.   Map p. 189

PINE VOLE   *Pitymys pinetorum*   **Pl. 17**
Identification: Head and body $2\frac{4}{5}$–$4\frac{1}{5}$ in. (71–107 mm); tail
$\frac{2}{3}$–1 in. (17–25 mm); wt. $\frac{3}{4}$–$1\frac{1}{3}$ oz. (22–37 g). This handsome
little vole is rarely found in pines, as the name would imply,
but is more characteristic of the eastern *deciduous forest. Auburn fur thick and soft,* does not have the scattered long guard
hairs found in most other voles. Ears small; tail *short.* Upper
incisors smooth. Skull (Plate 26) has 16 teeth. There are 4
mammae.

Some authors place this in the genus *Microtus.* The Pine Vole
in Florida is considered a distinct species (*P. parvulus*) by some.
Similar species: (1) Meadow and (2) Yellownose Voles have
tail longer than 1 in. (25 mm). (3) Prairie Vole is not auburn.
(4) Boreal Redback Vole has longer tail. (5) Southern Bog
Lemming has grooved upper incisors.

Habitat: Usually a forest floor with a thick layer of duff, deciduous in North, pines in South; occasionally found in other
situations, particularly in orchards.

Habits: Active day or night. Tunnels through leaf mold and
loose soil, near surface; may burrow around orchard trees and
eat bark from roots; also eats bulbs, tubers, seeds. Nests beneath
stumps, logs, or other protection. Home range about $\frac{1}{4}$ acre
(0.1 ha). Populations fluctuate widely. Breeds Jan–Oct. in
North, probably all year in South.

Young: Usually 3–4 (2–7); gestation period about 21 days; 3–4
litters a year.   Map p. 190

SAGEBRUSH VOLE   *Lagurus curtatus*   **Pl. 17**
Identification: Head and body $3\frac{4}{5}$–$4\frac{1}{2}$ in. (97–114 mm); tail
$\frac{3}{5}$–$1\frac{1}{8}$ in. (15–29 mm); wt. $\frac{4}{5}$–$1\frac{1}{3}$ oz. (23–37 g). An extremely
pale, *ash-gray* vole with *whitish belly and feet;* tail usually *less
than 1 in.* (25 mm). If found living in *sagebrush* it is without
doubt this species. Palest of the voles; also the one found in
driest places. Skull (Plate 26) has 16 teeth. There are 8 mammae.

Similar species: (1) Prairie Vole has a tail longer than 1 ⅛ in. (29 mm). (2) Other voles have longer tail; not found in sagebrush.
Habitat: Scattered sagebrush, loose soil; arid conditions.
Habits: Active day or night. Makes shallow burrows, usually close to a sagebrush. Feeds on green vegetation, particularly sagebrush. Breeds throughout year.
Young: Usually 4–6 (3–8); more than 1 litter a year.

Map p. 190

Water Rat and Muskrat

THESE are the largest and most nearly aquatic members of this family of rodents. Most of their lives are spent in or near water. There is but 1 species in each genus.

FLORIDA WATER RAT *Neofiber alleni* **Pl. 19**
Identification: Head and body 7⅘–8⅗ in. (20–22 cm); tail 4⅕–6⅘ in. (11–17 cm); wt. 5½–11⅔ oz. (156–330 g). A small round-tailed edition of the Muskrat; *rich brown fur,* with *coarse guard hairs* over dense underfur, and size will distinguish it from any other water-living rodent in the area. Skull (Plate 26) has 16 teeth. There are 6 mammae.
Habitat: Bogs, marshes, weedy borders of lakes; savannas bordering streams.
Habits: Builds bulky nest in stumps, mangroves, or open savannas. Constructs feeding platform in shallow water; feeds on water plants, crayfish. Probably breeds throughout year.
Young: 1–3 recorded.
Economic status: Of no importance; may do occasional damage to crops; an interesting part of our native fauna.

Map p. 190

MUSKRAT *Ondatra zibethica* **Pl. 19**
Identification: Head and body 10–14 in. (25–36 cm); tail 8–11 in. (20–28 cm); wt. 2–4 lb. (908–1816 g). *Fur dense, rich brown,* overlaid with coarse guard hairs; belly *silvery;* tail long, *naked,* scaly, and black; *flattened from side to side.* Character of tail alone is sufficient to distinguish the Muskrat from all other mammals. Their presence in marshes may be detected by the *conical houses,* 2–3 ft. (61–91 cm) above water, which are built of marsh vegetation. Skull (Plate 26) has 16 teeth. There are 6 mammae.

The Muskrat on Newfoundland may be a distinct species (*O. obscura*).
Habitat: Marshes, edges of ponds, lakes, and streams; cattails, rushes, water lilies, open water.

Habits: Chiefly aquatic; moves overland, especially in autumn. Feeds on aquatic vegetation, also clams, frogs, and fish on occasion. Builds house in shallow water; also burrows in banks; entrances usually underwater; 1 family to each house. Breeds April–Aug. in North, in winter in South.

Young: Usually 5–6 (1–11); gestation period 22–30 days; 2–3 litters a year. Naked, blind.

Economic status: One of our most valuable fur animals; may cause some damage to dikes by burrowing.   Map below

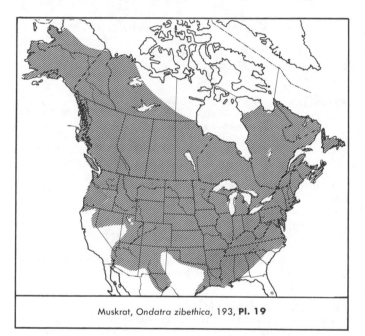

Muskrat, *Ondatra zibethica*, 193, **Pl. 19**

Old World Rats and Mice: Muridae

THESE include the Norway Rat, Black Rat, and House Mouse, none of which commonly occurs far from man-made structures. They are *dull grayish brown to black, with long naked tail* fairly uniform in color. Albino mutants of the Norway Rat and the House Mouse are standard laboratory mammals for genetic and medical experimentation. Skull has 16 teeth.

Habitat: Warehouses, farm buildings, wherever food is stored; closely associated with man and his structures.
Economic status: In the wild, entirely detrimental; destroy stored foods and damage buildings; also carry diseases communicable to man; damage runs into millions of dollars each year. Although they were not knowingly released in this country, the results of their introduction should be a lesson in the release of foreign species without thorough investigation beforehand. The laboratory strains serve a useful purpose.

NORWAY RAT   *Rattus norvegicus*   **Pl. 18**
(Brown Rat, House Rat)
   Identification: Head and body 7–10 in. (178–254 mm); tail 5–8 in. (127–203 mm); wt. 7–10 oz. (200–283 g). Primarily an inhabitant of *cities and farmyards,* this rat may be distinguished by its *grayish-brown color* and rather *long scaly tail.* Belly grayish, not white. Skull (Plate 26) has 16 teeth. There are 12 mammae.
   Similar species: (1) Woodrats usually have white belly and feet, tail covered with hair. (2) Black Rat has tail longer than head and body. (3) Rice Rat has bicolored tail.
   Habits: Colonial. Burrows along foundations of buildings or beneath rubbish piles. Feeds on anything edible. Home range usually less than 100 ft. (30.5 m) across. Populations of 1 rat to 5 or 6 people is common in larger cities, probably higher populations in small communities.
   Young: Usually 8–10 (6–22); gestation period 21–22 days; 12 litters a year possible. Females breed at 3 months.
   Range: Throughout the continent where people are concentrated.

BLACK RAT (Roof Rat)   *Rattus rattus*   **Pl. 18**
   Identification: Head and body 7–8 in. (178–203 mm); tail 8⅖–10 in. (214–253 mm); wt. 5–10 oz. (142–283 g). There are 2 color phases (*brown* and *black*) in this species. Belly may be grayish but *never white. Naked* tail is *longer* than head and body. Found chiefly around *buildings;* rare in North, common in extreme South. Skull has 16 teeth. There are 10 mammae.
   Similar species: (1) Norway Rat has tail shorter than head and body. (2) Woodrats and (3) Rice Rat have bicolored tail.
   Habits: Lives mostly in tops of buildings; does not require soil to burrow into; occasionally found in fields some distance from buildings.
   Range: Chiefly seaports; has been reported as far inland as Urbana, Illinois.

HOUSE MOUSE   *Mus musculus*   **Pl. 15**
   Identification: Head and body 3⅕–3⅖ in. (81–86 mm); tail

$2\frac{4}{5}-3\frac{4}{5}$ in. (71–97 mm); wt. $\frac{2}{5}-\frac{4}{5}$ oz. (11–22 g). A small *grayish-brown* mouse with *gray or buffy belly* and a *scaly tail* about the *same color above and below;* fur fairly short. Upper incisors not grooved. Skull (Plate 26) has 16 teeth. There are 10 mammae.

Similar species: (1) White-footed and (2) Deer Mice have white belly. (3) Pygmy Mouse is smaller; has haired tail. (4) Harvest mice have grooved upper incisors. (5) Jumping mice have white belly.

Habits: Occasionally found in fields, but usually in buildings. Eats anything edible. A prolific species; breeds year round.

Young: 3–11; gestation period 18–21 days; several litters a year. First breed at 6 weeks.

Range: Throughout the continent, wherever there are concentrations of people.

Jumping Mice: Zapodidae

MEMBERS of this family are rather small to *medium-sized* mice with extremely *long tails* and *large hind feet.* Body *yellowish to orange* along sides, darker on back, *belly white;* ears small, narrowly *edged with buff or white.* No external cheek pouches. Upper incisors have *grooves* down front surfaces. They prefer damp meadows and forests, and hibernate during the winter.

Similar species: (1) Pocket mice and (2) kangaroo rats have external cheek pouches.

Economic status: Neutral; rarely sufficiently numerous to do damage.

MEADOW JUMPING MOUSE *Zapus hudsonius*   **Pl. 13**
  Identification: Head and body $3-3\frac{1}{3}$ in. (76–85 mm); tail $4-5\frac{4}{5}$ in. (102–147 mm); wt. $\frac{1}{2}-\frac{4}{5}$ oz. (14–22 g). If seen jumping through the grass, these *olive-yellow* mice might be mistaken for frogs. On close inspection, the *2-toned body* and *long,* scantily haired tail, plus the *large hind feet,* will serve to distinguish this from most other small mammals. Skull (Plate 26) has 18 teeth. There are 8 mammae.

  Similar species: (1) Woodland Jumping Mouse has white tip on tail. (2) Western Jumping Mouse has head and body over $3\frac{1}{3}$ in. (85 mm); in mts.

  Habitat: This mouse prefers low meadows for feeding, but appears in various land habitats; not restricted.

  Habits: Primarily nocturnal. Feeds on seeds, insects, fruits. Winter nest 2–3 ft. (61–91 cm) beneath surface, in well-drained site; hibernates in Oct. or Nov., emerges April–May; summer nest on surface or beneath brush, logs, stumps. Home range

$\frac{1}{2}$ – 2 acres (0.2 – 0.8 ha). Populations fluctuate, never very high. Lives 1 – 2 years in wild. Breeds June – Aug.

Young: Usually 4 – 5 (3 – 7); gestation period 18 – 21 days; 2 – 3 litters a season.   Map below

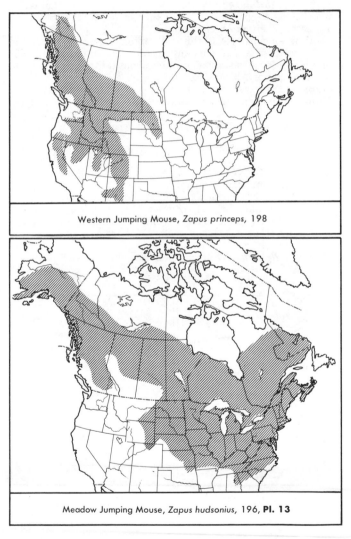

Western Jumping Mouse, *Zapus princeps*, 198

Meadow Jumping Mouse, *Zapus hudsonius*, 196, **Pl. 13**

WESTERN JUMPING MOUSE   *Zapus princeps*

Identification: Head and body $3\frac{1}{2}$–4 in. (89–102 mm); tail 5–6 in. (127–152 mm); wt. $\frac{2}{3}$–$1\frac{1}{3}$ oz. (18–37 g). This is chiefly a *mt.* species. *Yellowish sides, darker back, white* (or buffy) *belly, long tail, large hind feet,* and absence of external cheek pouches set it apart from most other small rodents. Skull has 18 teeth. There are 8 mammae.

Similar species: (1) Meadow Jumping Mouse has head and body less than $3\frac{1}{2}$ in. (89 mm); usually not in mts. (2) Pacific Jumping Mouse is similar but more colorful; ranges known to overlap only at Allison Pass, B.C.

Habitat: Near streams, lush growths of grasses and herbs.

Habits: Chiefly nocturnal. Good swimmer. Feeds primarily on seeds. Hibernates Sept. or Oct. to April or May. Nests on surface under protection of grasses or herbs. Can jump 4–6 ft. (1.2–1.8 m).

Young: Born June–July; 2–7; 1 litter a season.   Map p. 197

PACIFIC JUMPING MOUSE   *Zapus trinotatus*

Identification: Head and body $3\frac{3}{5}$–$3\frac{4}{5}$ in. (91–97 mm); tail $5\frac{1}{5}$–$6\frac{1}{5}$ in. (132–157 mm). Similar to the Western Jumping Mouse but is more brightly colored. *Long tail, large hind feet,* and no external cheek pouches will identify this species. Range separate, except at Allison Pass, B.C., from ranges of other jumping mice.

Habitat: Wet, marshy areas, open meadows, woods; to timberline.   Map below

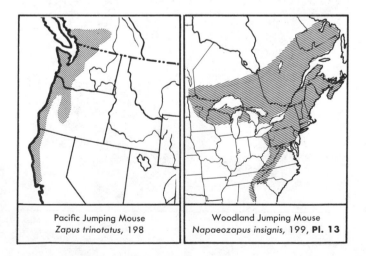

Pacific Jumping Mouse
Zapus trinotatus, 198

Woodland Jumping Mouse
Napaeozapus insignis, 199, **Pl. 13**

WOODLAND JUMPING MOUSE   **Pl. 13**
Napaeozapus insignis
  Identification: Head and body $3\frac{3}{5}$–4 in. (91–102 mm); tail
  5–$6\frac{1}{5}$ in. (127–157 mm); wt. $\frac{7}{10}$–$1\frac{1}{10}$ oz. (20–30 g). A handsome jumping mouse; *bright yellowish sides, brownish back,*
  white belly, large hind feet, and a *long white-tipped tail* should
  serve to identify it within its range. Skull (Plate 26) has 16
  teeth. There are 8 mammae.
  Similar species: Meadow Jumping Mouse does not have white
  tip on tail.
  Habitat: Forested or brushy areas near water; wet bogs, stream
  borders.
  Habits: Nocturnal. Feeds on seeds, fruits, and insects. Hibernates Nov.–April. Home range 1–2 acres. (0.4–0.8 ha). Populations of 3 per acre (7 per ha) normal.
  Young: Born June–Sept.; usually 3–5 (1–6); gestation period
  29 days or more; possibly 2 litters a season.   Map opposite

Porcupine: Erethizontidae

LARGE, blackish rodent with an overlay of yellow-tipped hairs;
size of small dog; most of body, especially rump and tail, *thickly*
set with long sharp spines. Known as fossils from Oligocene.

PORCUPINE   *Erethizon dorsatum*   **Pl. 19**
  Identification: Head and body 18–22 in. (46–56 cm); tail
  7–9 in. (18–23 cm); wt. 10–28 lb. (4.5–12.7 kg). A *heavy-*
  bodied, short-legged, clumsy animal that may be seen lumber-
  ing through the forest or hunched into what appears to be a
  large black ball high in a tree. Often seen along shoulders of
  highways, especially where salt has been used, in evening or
  early morning. Many are killed by autos. Trees with tops
  barked indicate presence of Porcupines nearby. Only N. American mammal with long sharp quills. Eyeshine deep red. Skull
  (Plate 28) has 20 teeth. There are 4 mammae.
  Habitat: Usually forested areas, but occasionally away from
  trees if brush is available.
  Habits: Most active at night, but may be seen during day,
  especially in top of tree; climbs awkwardly, but is more at home
  in tree than on ground. Solitary in summer; may be colonial
  in winter. Feeds on buds, small twigs, and inner bark of trees;
  fond of salt. Dens in hollow trees or natural caves in rocks;
  does not hibernate. Grunts, groans, and high-pitched cries may
  be heard for $\frac{1}{4}$ mi. (0.4 km), especially in fall rutting season.
  Breeds Sept.–Oct.
  Young: Born April–May; 1; gestation period about 7 months;

wt. about 1 lb. (454 g). Furred, and eyes open; quills soft and about $\frac{1}{4}$ in. (6 mm) long at birth, become hard and effective within a few minutes. Able to climb trees and eat solid foods a few hours after birth. Sexually mature at 3 years.

Economic status: May damage buildings, communication lines, and trees. Quills used for decorative purposes by Indians; meat edible, best if animal had not been feeding on pines. May be seen in many of the western parks and throughout Canada.

Map below

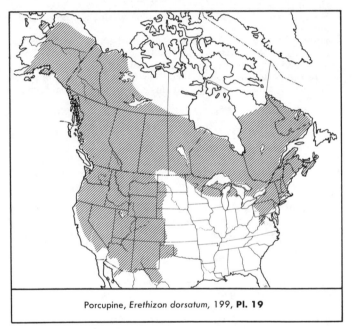

Porcupine, *Erethizon dorsatum*, 199, **Pl. 19**

Nutria: Capromyidae

A LARGE S. AMERICAN rodent that was introduced first into Louisiana as a possible fur-bearing mammal; now spread over much of U.S. Some raised in captivity for breeding stock and fur. Probably most numerous in marshes of Louisiana and Oregon.

NUTRIA (Coypu)   *Myocastor coypus*   **Pl. 19**
    Identification: Head and body 22–25 in. (56–63 cm); tail 12–

17 in. (30-43 cm); wt. 15-20 lb. (6.7-9 kg). A *large grayish-brown* rodent with *long, round, scantily haired* tail. Hind feet webbed. Skull has 20 teeth.

Similar species: (1) Beaver (p. 151) and (2) Muskrat (p. 193) have flattened, naked tail. (1) Opossum (p. 1) has a white face, pointed nose, and no webs between toes.

Habitat: Marshes, swamps, ponds, and lakes.

Habits: Nocturnal. Feeds on nearly every kind of aquatic plant available; carries food to feeding station: log, brush, or vegetation that will support the animal. Burrows in banks with entrance above water; builds winter resting platforms 20-30 in. (51-75 cm) wide and 6-9 in. (15-23 cm) above water, in dense vegetation; builds simple nest in vegetation growing in shallow water. Lives 4 years in wild to 12 years in captivity. Breeds throughout year in South.

Young: 2-11; gestation period 127-132 days; wt. about ½ lb. (225 g). Swim and feed on solids 24 hrs. after birth. Sexually mature at 5 months.

Economic status: Wild-caught Nutria fur is of little value. The Nutria competes for food in the wild with the more valuable Muskrat. This is a case of an introduced foreign species that has become a liability rather than an asset.

Range: Found locally in many states where it has been released or where it has escaped from Nutria ranches.

Pikas, Hares, and Rabbits: Lagomorpha

Pikas: Ochotonidae

SMALL, *rat-sized,* grayish to buffy or brownish, with short, broad, rounded ears and *no visible tail.* Found only in the *rockslides* and near timberline in high mts. Known as fossils from Upper Oligocene.

PIKA (Cony) *Ochotona princeps*   **Pl. 21**
   Identification: Head and body 6⅕-8½ in. (157-216 mm); wt. 4-6⅓ oz. (113-180 g). Small piles of *fresh hay* in the *rockslides* means that Pikas are around. One of these *grayish* to *buffy* or *brownish* mammals may be sitting hunched up on a boulder of nearly the same color. A series of peculiar short squeaks is

further evidence. *No visible tail.* Other mammals seen in similar situations during daytime are marmots, Golden-mantled Squirrels, and chipmunks. All have bushy tails. Skull (Plate 28) has 26 teeth. There are 6 mammae.

Habitat: Talus slopes, rockslides; usually near timberline in mts., down to sea level in North.

Habits: Active only by day. Colonial. Feeds on grasses and herbs; stores food in small piles of "hay" beneath boulders; does not hibernate. Each Pika has its territory within the colony, at least in autumn. Breeds in spring and possibly in summer.

Young: Born May – June and July – Aug.; 2 – 5; gestation period 30 – 31 days.

Economic status: Lives where few people ever go; does no harm; an interesting part of our native fauna. May be seen at some of the talus slopes along highway in Glacier Natl. Park; also in Crater Lake, Kings Canyon, Mt. Rainier, Rocky Mt., Sequoia, Yellowstone, and Yosemite Natl. Parks.   Map below

COLLARED PIKA   *Ochotona collaris*
Identification: Similar to *O. princeps;* may be same species; geographic range separate.   Map below

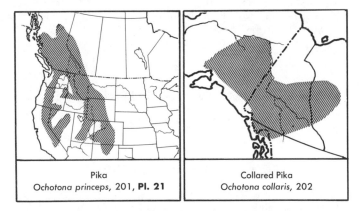

Pika
Ochotona princeps, 201, **Pl. 21**

Collared Pika
Ochotona collaris, 202

Hares and Rabbits: Leporidae

MEMBERS of this family usually have *long ears, long hind legs,* soft fur, and a *short cottony tail.* Most species, particularly in warmer climates, carry tularemia, or "rabbit disease." Sick rabbits should be avoided. Meat should be well cooked; if in doubt, rubber gloves should be worn when dressing-out. Skull has 28 teeth. Known as fossils from Upper Eocene.

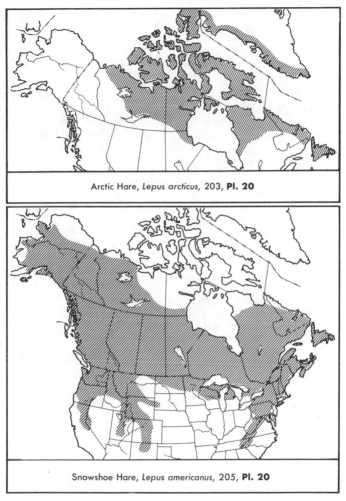

Arctic Hare, *Lepus arcticus*, 203, **Pl. 20**

Snowshoe Hare, *Lepus americanus*, 205, **Pl. 20**

ARCTIC HARE   *Lepus arcticus*   **Pl. 20**

Identification: Head and body 17–24 in. (43–61 cm); ear 3–4 in. (76–102 mm); wt. 6–12 lb. (2.7–5.4 kg). A truly *arctic* mammal, this large hare occupies the barren grounds. In Elles- mere and n. Baffin Is. and Greenland, these hares remain *white throughout year;* elsewhere *gray or brown in summer,* but tail remains *white.* In winter, fur *white to the base* (except tips of ears, which are black).

Similar species: Snowshoe Hare is smaller; tail brown in summer, fur not white to base in winter.
Habitat: Tundra of Far North.
Habits: Active throughout year; somewhat gregarious. Often stands up on hind feet, also hops kangaroo-fashion without touching forefeet to ground. Feeds on low-growing tundra plants. Populations fluctuate widely.
Young: Born June–July; 4–8. Fully furred, eyes open.
Economic status: Serves as food for foxes and dogs; also eaten by Eskimos, but meat not nourishing; skins used for clothing and robes. Map p. 203

TUNDRA HARE *Lepus othus*
Identification: Head and body 20–24 in. (51–61 cm); ear 3–3½ in. (76–89 mm); wt. 9–10 lb. (4–4.5 kg). This is the western representative of the Arctic Hare and probably should be in the same species. It turns *brown in summer,* but *tail remains white.* In winter, fur *white to the skin.*
Similar species: Snoeshoe Hare has head and body less than 20 in. (51 cm); tail brown in summer, fur not white to skin in winter.
Habits: Probably similar to those of Arctic Hare; young huddle together in a small depression; no nest. Map below

WHITETAIL JACKRABBIT *Lepus townsendi* Pl. 20
Identification: Head and body 18–22 in. (46–56 cm); ear 5–6 in. (13–15 cm); wt. 5–10 lb. (2.2–4.5 kg). On our northern *plains* and in the *western mts.* this is the largest hare. *Brownish gray* in summer, *white or pale gray* in winter. Tail nearly always *white above and below.* There are 8 mammae.
Similar species: (1) The Snowshoe Hare is smaller; dark

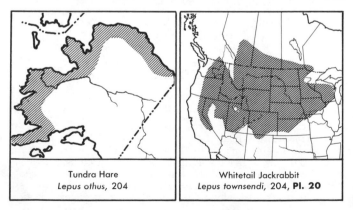

Tundra Hare
Lepus othus, 204

Whitetail Jackrabbit
Lepus townsendi, 204, **Pl. 20**

brown in summer; prefers forests and swamps. (2) Blacktail
Jackrabbit has top of tail black. (3) Cottontails are smaller;
do not turn white in winter.
Habitat: Open, grassy or sagebrush plains.
Habits: Nocturnal. Sits in lair during day; does not burrow
in soil, but makes tunnels in deep snow. Feeds mostly on grasses
and other green vegetation in summer; may add buds, bark, and
small twigs in winter. When running, can clear 17 ft. (5.2 m)
at a jump; has been clocked at 40 mph (64 kmph).
Young: 3–6. Furred, eyes open. Concealed in vegetation, not
in nest.
Economic status: Causes some damage to hay crops and small
trees; a good game mammal; meat edible.   Map opposite

SNOWSHOE HARE *Lepus americanus*   **Pl. 20**
(Varying Hare, Jackrabbit)
  Identification: Head and body 13–18 in. (33–46 cm); ear
  3½–4 in. (89–102 mm); wt. 2–4 lb. (0.9–1.8 kg). A *large-footed*
  hare that turns *white* in winter; in summer, *dark brown*. The
  white of winter is only on tips of hairs; beneath these is a
  yellowish band. Ears relatively small for a hare. Eyeshine
  orange. There are 8–10 mammae.
  Similar species: (1) Arctic and (2) Tundra Hares have tail
  always white; fur is white to skin in winter. (3) Whitetail Jackrabbit is larger; tail nearly always white; long ears. (4) Cottontails are brownish or grayish throughout year; feet usually
  whitish; nape patch rusty. (5) Blacktail Jackrabbit has black
  stripe down rump and on top of tail; occurs in open areas. (6)
  European Hare is larger; top of tail black; open areas.
  Habitat: Swamps, forests, thickets; mts. in West.
  Habits: Nocturnal. Sits in its lair beneath brush or trees during
  day. Feeds on succulent vegetation in summer, twigs, buds, bark
  in winter; fond of frozen meat. Does not build nest. Home
  range about 10 acres (4 ha), but may travel up to 1 mi. (1.6 km).
  Populations fluctuate tremendously, with highs about every 11
  years. Few live more than 3 years in the wild, up to 8 years
  in captivity. May display territorial behavior during breeding
  season. Runs in circle in front of dogs.
  Young: Born April–Aug.; usually 2–4 (1–7); gestation period
  36–37 days; 2–3 litters. Leverets furred, eyes open.
  Economic status: An important game mammal; causes some
  damage to new forest plantations and gardens.   Map p. 203

EUROPEAN HARE *Lepus europaeus*   **Pl. 20**
  Identification: Head and body 25–27 in. (63–68 cm); ear
  4½–5 in. (11–13 cm); wt. 7–10 lb. (3.1–4.5 kg). This large introduced hare is *brownish gray;* does not turn white in winter.
  Top of tail black. Within its present range, by far the *largest*

member of its group; may easily be distinguished by size alone.
Habitat: Open fields and low, unforested hills.
Economic status: A good game mammal, but if sufficiently
numerous could cause considerable damage to crops.

Map below

ANTELOPE JACKRABBIT   *Lepus alleni*   **Pl. 20**
Identification: Head and body 19–21 in. (48–53 cm); ear
7–8 in. (18–20 cm); wt. 6–13 lb. (2.7–5.9 kg). A bounding white
flash among the mesquite, giant cactus, and other desert vegetation, or a pair of *huge ears, without black* on them, erect and
supported by a relatively small head, may be your introduction
to this large, long-legged hare of the desert. Its pale *whitish*

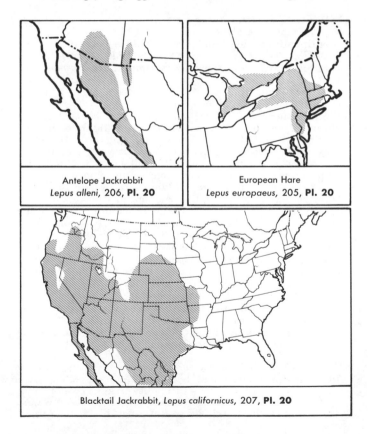

Antelope Jackrabbit
Lepus alleni, 206, **Pl. 20**

European Hare
Lepus europaeus, 205, **Pl. 20**

Blacktail Jackrabbit, *Lepus californicus*, 207, **Pl. 20**

sides and hips will serve for identification. There are 6 mammae.

The population in extreme s. New Mexico may be of a distinct species (*L. gaillardi* or *L. callotis*)

Similar species: (1) Blacktail Jackrabbit has brown on sides and hips; ear tips bordered with blackish. (2) Cottontails are smaller; brownish or grayish; have smaller ears.

Habitat: Grasses, mesquites, and catclaws; on slopes at moderate elevations; creosote desert.

Habits: Active from early evening to well after sunrise; sits in shade of a bush during day; may be seen in groups of 2–25 or more. May move some distance from daytime resting spot to feeding area. Feeds on various desert plants, including cacti. Home range usually no more than 1000 ft. (305 m) across. Does not build nest. Populations fluctuate, occasionally seen in concentrations of 10 per acre (25 per ha). May run 30–40 mph. (48–64 kmph). Many infected with tapeworm cysts (bladder worm). Breeding season, Dec.–Sept.

Young: Usually 1–3 (1–5). Furred, eyes open; scattered among bushes.

Economic status: An average of 8 rabbits will eat as much as 1 sheep, 41 as much as 1 cow; on desert grazing range these large jackrabbits compete with livestock. A fair game mammal.

Map opposite

BLACKTAIL JACKRABBIT *Lepus californicus* **Pl. 20**

Identification: Head and body 17–21 in. (43–53 cm); ear 6–7 in. (15–18 cm); wt. 3–7 lb. (1.3–3.1 kg). Throughout the *grasslands* and *open areas* of the West this is the common jackrabbit. Its grayish-brown body, *large black-tipped ears,* and *black streak* on top of the tail will serve to distinguish it from all near-relatives. Eyeshine reddish. Skull (Plate 28) has 28 teeth. There are 6 mammae.

Similar species: (1) Antelope Jackrabbit has white sides and no black on ears. (2) Whitetail Jackrabbit usually has no black on top of tail; whitish in winter. (3) Snowshoe Hare does not have black tail; body white in winter; occurs in forests. (4) Cottontails are much smaller; ears not black-tipped. (5) Swamp Rabbit is smaller; no black on ears or tail. (6) Brush Rabbit is smaller.

Habitat: Open prairies and sparsely vegetated deserts.

Habits: Most active early evenings through early mornings; sits in lair at base of bush or clump of grass during day. Often feeds on green vegetation along edges of highways. Populations may fluctuate. Can run 30–35 mph. (48–56 kmph). Breeds Dec.–Sept. in South.

Young: Usually 2–4 (1–6). Fully furred, eyes open. Probably no nest prepared.

Economic status: Average of 12 rabbits will eat as much as 1 sheep, 59 as much as 1 cow. Consumes considerable vegetation that could be utilized by stock. A fair game animal. Commonly seen along highways in early morning and evenings.

Map p. 206

EASTERN COTTONTAIL *Sylvilagus floridanus* **Pl. 21**
Identification: Head and body 14–17 in. (35–43 cm); ear 2½–3 in. (64–76 mm); wt. 2–4 lb. (0.9–1.8 kg). Body brownish or grayish; *cottony tail white;* nape patch rusty, feet whitish. Skull (Plate 28) has 28 teeth. There are 8 mammae.
Similar species: (1) Desert Cottontail is smaller and has longer ears; not found in forests. (2) New England Cottontail has pale rusty nape patch, if present; reddish in summer; mts. (3) Swamp and (4) Marsh Rabbits do not have distinct rusty nape patches; feet not pale whitish. (5) Snowshoe Hare is larger; dark

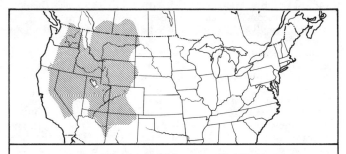

Mountain Cottontail, *Sylvilagus nuttalli,* 209, **Pl. 21**

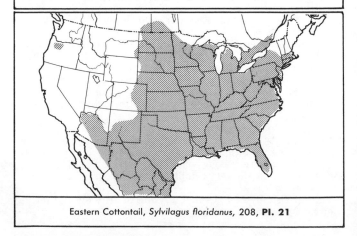

Eastern Cottontail, *Sylvilagus floridanus,* 208, **Pl. 21**

brown in summer, white in winter. (6) European Hare and (7) jackrabbits are larger, have longer ears, and occur in open areas.
Habitat: Heavy brush, strips of forest with open areas nearby, edges of swamps, weed patches.
Habits: Active from early evening to late morning; spends day in partially concealed form (slight depression in ground), burrow in ground, or beneath brush pile. Feeds on green vegetation in summer, bark and twigs in winter. Home range 3–20 acres (1.2–8 ha). Populations fluctuate from 1 cottontail per 4 acres (1.6 ha) to several per acre especially in winter concentrations. Females may display territorial behavior during breeding season.
Young: Born mostly March–May, also to Sept.; 4–7; gestation period 26.5–30 days; 3–4 litters a year. Blind, placed in nest in depression in ground; mother visits nest to suckle young.
Economic status: Most important small game mammal; can do considerable damage to gardens, shrubs, and small trees.

Map opposite

MOUNTAIN COTTONTAIL *Sylvilagus nuttalli* **Pl. 21**
Identification: Head and body 12–14 in. (30–36 cm); ear 2 $\frac{1}{5}$ – 2 $\frac{3}{5}$ in. (56–66 mm); wt. 1 $\frac{1}{2}$ – 3 lb. (0.7–1.3 kg). Similar to the Eastern Cottontail, but somewhat paler. Over most of its range it is the only cottontail. There are 8 mammae.
Similar species: (1) Desert Cottontail found in valleys and low deserts; has longer ears. (2) Snowshoe Hare is brown or white, not gray. (3) Pygmy Rabbit is smaller; found in low *desert.* (4) Jackrabbits are larger, with longer ears.
Habitat: Thickets, sagebrush, loose rocks, and cliffs; forests in South; mts.
Habits: In general, similar to those of Eastern Cottontail.
Young: Born April–July; 4–6.
Economic status: An important small game mammal; meat edible. Map opposite

NEW ENGLAND COTTONTAIL *Sylvilagus transitionalis*
Identification: Head and body 17 in. (43 cm); ear 2 $\frac{1}{2}$ in. (64 mm); wt. 2 $\frac{1}{4}$ – 3 lb. (1–1.3 kg). This mt. cottontail is *reddish* in summer and sprinkled with white to give it a *reddish-gray* appearance in winter; nape patch behind ears *pale, small, or absent; a dark patch* between ears.
Similar species: (1) Eastern Cottontail has distinct rusty nape patch; occurs in lower areas. (2) Snowshoe Hare has brown feet in summer; white in winter. (3) European Hare is larger; top of tail black.
Habitat: Brushy areas, open forests, rough mt. terrain.

Map p. 210

DESERT COTTONTAIL *Sylvilagus auduboni* **Pl. 21**
Identification: Head and body 12–15 in. (30–38 cm); ear

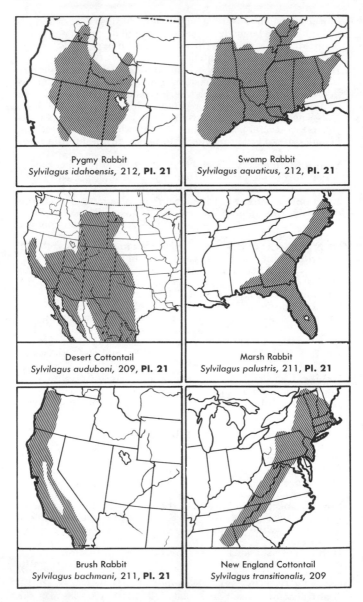

Pygmy Rabbit
Sylvilagus idahoensis, 212, **Pl. 21**

Swamp Rabbit
Sylvilagus aquaticus, 212, **Pl. 21**

Desert Cottontail
Sylvilagus auduboni, 209, **Pl. 21**

Marsh Rabbit
Sylvilagus palustris, 211, **Pl. 21**

Brush Rabbit
Sylvilagus bachmani, 211, **Pl. 21**

New England Cottontail
Sylvilagus transitionalis, 209

3–4 in. (76–102 mm); wt. 1⅖–2¾ lb. (0.6–1.2 kg). This is the common cottontail of the *valleys* in the arid Southwest. Body *pale gray washed with yellow.* Ears large. There are 8 mammae.

Similar species: (1) Mountain Cottontail has shorter ears; mts. (2) Eastern Cottontail is larger, but ears are shorter. (3) Brush Rabbit is smaller; dark brown; has shorter ears; occurs in heavy brush. (4) Snowshoe Hare is dark brown or white; found high in mts. (5) Pygmy Rabbit is smaller; occurs in heavy brush. (6) Jackrabbits are larger; found in open areas.

Habitat: Open plains, foothills, and low valleys; grass, sagebrush, scattered piñons and junipers.

Habits: Most active from late afternoon throughout the night, but may be seen at any time of day. Seeks safety in thickets or burrows. Home range from 1 (females) to 15 (males) acres (0.4–6 ha). May live 2 years or more in wild.

Young: Born throughout year in some part of range; 2–6. Blind. Deposited in grass-lined nest in depression in ground; female returns to nest to suckle young.

Economic status: An important small game mammal; does little damage to gardens and green crops.   Map opposite

BRUSH RABBIT *Sylvilagus bachmani*   **Pl. 21**
Identification: Head and body 11–13 in. (28–33 cm); ear 2–2⅗ in. (51–66 mm); wt. 1¼–1⅘ lb. (0.6–0.8 kg). A *small brown* rabbit; ears and tail relatively *small.* There are 8 mammae.

Similar species: (1) Desert Cottontail is larger; grayish; ears longer. (2) Blacktail Jackrabbit is larger; occurs in open areas.

Habitat: Chaparral or thick brush.

Habits: Least active in middle of day, but may be seen feeding on green vegetation at any time. Never ventures far from thick cover. Rarely uses burrows; makes runways through thick vegetation. Home range ¼–1 acre (0.1–0.4 ha). Populations of 1–3 per acre (2–7 per ha). Breeding season, Jan.–June.

Young: 2–5. Covered with fine, short hair; blind.

Economic status: Meat excellent, but small size discourages hunters; does little damage; in cities, feeds mostly on lawns near dense cover.   Map opposite

MARSH RABBIT *Sylvilagus palustris*   **Pl. 21**
Identification: Head and body 14–16 in. (35–41 cm); ear 2½–3 in. (64–76 mm); wt. 2½–3½ lb. (1.1–1.6 kg). A *dark brown,* coarse-haired, *small-footed* rabbit; feet *reddish brown* above, darker below; tail small and inconspicuous, dingy white below.

Similar species: Eastern Cottontail has whitish hind feet and large rusty nape patch; also conspicuous white tail.

Habitat: Wet bottomlands, swamps, hummocks.
Habits: Chiefly nocturnal. Feeds on various marsh vegetation, including rhizomes and bulbs. Breeding season, Feb.–Sept.
Young: Usually 2–4 (2–5). Placed in nest in depression in ground.
Economic status: A good game mammal; does little damage.
Map p. 210

SWAMP RABBIT *Sylvilagus aquaticus*   **Pl. 21**
(Cane-cutter)
   Identification: Head and body 14–17 in. (35–43 cm); ear 3½–4 in. (89–102 mm); wt. 3½–6 lb. (1.6–2.7 kg). This is a rich *brownish-gray* rabbit with coarse hair; feet *rusty;* nape patch *small* and indistinct.
   Similar species: (1) Eastern Cottontail has distinct rusty nape patch and whitish hind feet. (2) Blacktail Jackrabbit is larger and has black on ears and tail.
   Habitat: Swamps, marshes, wet bottomlands.
   Habits: Takes to water readily, a good swimmer; rarely uses burrows; nests beneath logs, at bases of stumps, or in depression in ground. Runs in circles in front of dogs. Home range 11–27 acres (4.4–10.8 ha). Lives 1–4 years. Breeds Jan.–Sept.
   Young: Usually 2–3 (1–5); gestation period 36–40 days. Furred, eyes open in 2–3 days.
   Economic status: Does some damage to crops near swamps; a good game mammal.   Map p. 210

PYGMY RABBIT *Sylvilagus idahoensis*   **Pl. 21**
   Identification: Head and body 8½–11 in. (22–28 cm); ear 2¼–2½ in. (57–64 mm); wt. ½–1 lb. (0.2–0.5 kg). Small, *slate-gray* rabbit with a *pinkish tinge;* difficult to see in dense cover; *smallest* of the rabbits; may be distinguished from all others by size alone. Skull (Plate 28) has 28 teeth. There are 10 mammae.
   Considered by some to belong to a distinct genus (*Brachylagus*).
   Similar species: Cottontails are larger and have conspicuous white tail.
   Habitat: Tall sagebrush growing in clumps.
   Habits: Appears throughout the day, but is chiefly nocturnal and crepuscular. Digs simple burrows, generally 2 or more entrances. Feeds primarily on sagebrush. Home range usually within 30 yd. (27.4 m) of burrow or other home site. May issue a barking sound while sitting at burrow mouth.
   Young: Born June–July; 5–8.   Map p. 210

Even-toed Hoofed Mammals: Artiodactyla

WEIGHT distributed equally on digits 3 and 4; 2 or 4 toes on each foot (except peccaries); medium-sized to large mammals; young able to walk a few minutes after birth.

Peccaries: Tayassuidae

PECCARIES are truly wild pigs of the New World. Primarily tropical and subtropical, they occur south into S. America.

PECCARY (Javelina)   *Pecari angulatus*   **Pl. 19**
   Identification: Head and body 34–36 in. (86–91 cm); height 20–24 in. (51–61 cm); wt. 40–50 lb. (18–22.5 kg). *Piglike* mammal. Hair coarse, mixed black and gray, lighter over front of shoulder; *3 toes* on each hind foot. Upper tusks pointed downward. Young, reddish with black stripe down back. Skull (Plate 31) has 38 teeth. There are 2 mammae.
      Sometimes known as *Dicotyles tajacu;* also *Tayassu tajacu.*
   Similar species: In the Wild Boar the upper tusks curve upward and there are 4 toes on each hind foot.
   Habitat: Brushy, semidesert; cacti, oaks, chaparral, mesquite; along cliffs; near waterholes.
   Habits: Most active mornings and late afternoons; usually seen in bands of 2–25. Omnivorous; feeds on nuts, mesquite beans, berries, fruits, cacti, grubs, bird eggs. Apparently breeds throughout year.
   Young: Usually 2 (1–5); gestation period 142–48 days. Able to follow mother 1 day after birth.
   Economic status: Beneficial; does not compete with grazing animals for food; destroys much prickly pear cactus; a good game mammal. Musk gland on rump should be removed, or meat will be tainted. Hides make fine leather. May be seen in Organ Pipe Cactus and Saguaro Natl. Monuments, Arizona.
Map p. 214

Old World Swine: Suidae

MEMBERS of this family have been introduced mostly as domesticated farm animals. Some of these have become feral. Also, wild

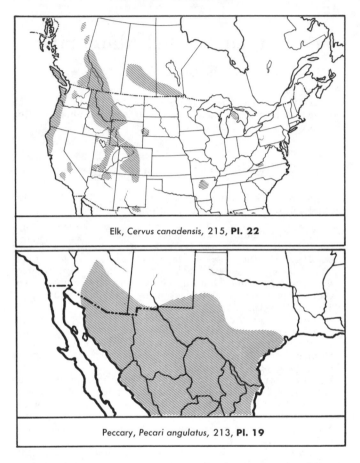

Elk, *Cervus canadensis*, 215, **Pl. 22**

Peccary, *Pecari angulatus*, 213, **Pl. 19**

stock (same species) from Europe has been released in several places as big game.

WILD BOAR (Swine) *Sus scrofa*
   Identification: Head and body 3½–5 ft. (107–152 cm); height to 3 ft. (91 cm); wt. to 400 lb. (180 kg). Hair coarse and thin; *upper tusks curve upward;* 4 toes on each foot. Skull has 44 teeth. Normally 12 mammae.
   Similar species: In the Peccary the upper tusks point downward; there are 3 toes on each hind foot.
   Young: 4–12; gestation period 16–17 weeks.

Range: Feral domestic swine or the introduced Wild Boar from Europe may be found in the following states: New Hampshire, North Carolina, Missouri, Arkansas, Tennessee, Georgia, Texas, Oregon, and California.

Deer: Cervidae

THIS FAMILY includes *hoofed* mammals that have *antlers* which are shed *each year*. They all chew their cud. There are no upper incisors. It includes our deer, Elk, Moose, and caribou. Known as fossils from Lower Oligocene.

ELK (Wapiti)   *Cervus canadensis*   **Pl. 22**
  Identification: Height 4–5 ft. (122–152 cm). Wt.: males, 700–1000 lb. (315–450 kg); females, 500–600 lb. (225–270 kg). Beam length of antlers to 64¾ in. (164 cm); record spread 74 in. (188 cm). A large deer with pale yellowish rump patch, small white tail, general *reddish-brown* body (chestnut-brown neck with a mane in males), and *huge spreading antlers* on males in late summer and autumn. Skull (Plate 32) has 34 teeth. There are 4 mammae.
  The Dwarf, or Tule Elk, now confined to a reserve in Kern Co., California, is considered a distinct species (*C. nannodes*) by some authors. Some would place the N. American Elk in the Old World species *elaphus*.
  Similar species: (1) Moose has a large overhanging snout and brown rump. (2) Mule Deer is smaller and has black on the tail. (3) Whitetail Deer is smaller; no rump patch. (4) Woodland Caribou has whitish neck.
  Habitat: Semiopen forest, mt. meadows (in summer), foothills, plains, and valleys.
  Habits: Most active mornings and evenings. Usually seen in groups of 25 or more; both sexes together in winter, old bulls in separate groups during summer. Feeds on grasses, herbs, twigs, bark. Migrates up mts. in spring, down in fall; males shed antlers Feb.–March; velvet shed in Aug. Attains adult dentition at 2½–3 years. Calf has high-pitched squeal when in danger; cow has similar squeal, also sharp bark when traveling with herd; males have high-pitched bugling call that starts with a low note and ends with a few low-toned grunts, heard during rutting season, especially at night. Lives 14 years (25 in captivity). Females breed at 2½ years. Rut starts in Sept.; old males round up harems.
  Young: Born May–June; normally 1, rarely 2; gestation period about 8½ months. Spotted. Able to walk a few minutes after birth.
  Economic status: Can do considerable damage to vegetables,

pastures, grainfields, and haystacks; a prize game mammal for meat and trophies; formerly ranged over much of continent, now restricted. There have been numerous attempts to reestablish them, some successful, others not. May be seen commonly in following national parks: Grand Teton, Yellowstone, Olympic, Glacier, Rocky Mt., Banff, and Jasper; also other places where they have been introduced. Apparently established on Afognak I., Alaska (not on map).   Map p. 214

MULE DEER (Blacktail Deer) *Odocoileus hemionus*   **Pl. 23**
   Identification: Height 3–3½ ft. (91–107 cm). Wt.: males, 125–400 lb. (56.2–180 kg); females, 100–150 lb. (45–67.5 kg). Largest in Rocky Mts. Record antler spread 47½ in. (121 cm). *Reddish* in summer, *blue-gray* in winter; some have whitish rump patch. Tail either *black-tipped or black on top*. Ears *large*. Antlers, on males, branch *equally,* are not prongs from a main beam. Skull has 32 teeth. There are 4 mammae.
   The deer of the nw. Pacific Coast (Blacktail Deer, *O. hemionus*), formerly regarded as a distinct species (*O. columbianus*), is now considered a subspecies of the Mule Deer.
   Similar species: (1) Whitetail Deer has a broad tail that is white below; antlers with main beam and prongs from it. (2) Elk is larger; there is no black on tail. (3) In the Woodland and (4) Barren Ground Caribou there is no black on the tail; their necks are whitish. (5) Moose is larger, dark brown, and has an overhanging snout. (6) Pronghorn has no black on tail, but has white on sides.
   Habitat: Coniferous forests, desert shrubs, chaparral, grassland with shrubs; occupies several types of habitat; browse plants necessary.
   Habits: Most active mornings, evenings, and moonlight nights; occurs singly or in small groups; more gregarious in winter. A browser, feeds mostly on shrubs and twigs, but adds grass and herbs. In mts. may migrate up in spring, down in fall; on plains does not migrate. Males shed antlers Jan.–Feb. Voice of fawns and does, a bleat — seldom heard; bucks have guttural grunt, especially during rut; both sexes snort when alarmed. Follows definite trails, noticeably in winter. Home range 90–600 acres (36–240 ha) or more. Normal life span about 16 years (25 in captivity). Females breed at 1½ years. Rutting season, Oct.–Dec.
   Young: Born June–July; usually 2 (1–3); gestation period about 7 months. Spotted. Able to walk a few minutes after birth.
   Economic status: The most important big game mammal of the West; can do considerable damage to crops, range, and forest land if allowed to become too numerous. May be seen in most western parks.   Map opposite

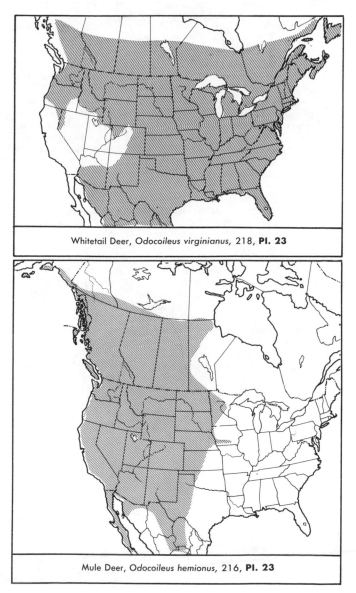

Whitetail Deer, *Odocoileus virginianus*, 218, **Pl. 23**

Mule Deer, *Odocoileus hemionus*, 216, **Pl. 23**

WHITETAIL DEER   *Odocoileus virginianus*   **Pl. 23**
(Virginia Deer, Whitetail)
Identification: Height 3–3½ ft. (91–107 cm). Wt.: males,
75–400 lb. (33.7–180 kg); females, 50–250 lb. (22.5–112.5 kg).
Largest in North. Record antler spread 33½ in. (85 cm). A large
white flag wagging back and forth and disappearing into the
woods indicates a Whitetail Deer on the move. *Reddish* in
summer, *blue-gray* in winter. Antlers, on males, consist of a
main beam with prongs issuing from it. A loud *whistling snort*
from the woods, in morning or evening, means a deer has scented
you. Skull (Plate 32) has 32 teeth. There are 4 mammae.
   The Key Deer, a "toy" race of the Whitetail Deer, weighing
around 50 lb. (22.5 kg) or less, was once endangered. Con-
servationists have been successful in having a preserve set aside
for it in the Florida Keys.
Similar species: (1) Mule Deer has a black tip on tail; prongs
of antlers not from a main beam. (2) Elk is larger and has a
yellowish rump patch. (3) Woodland Caribou has a whitish
rump patch and white on the neck. (4) Moose is larger; no
white; has overhanging snout. (5) Pronghorn has a large white
rump.
Habitat: Forests, swamps, and open brushy areas nearby.
Habits: Similar to those of the Mule Deer but more of a forest
mammal. A browser; eats twigs, shrubs, fungi, acorns, and grass
and herbs in season. Occurs in groups up to 25 or more in winter,
usually singly or 2–3 (doe and fawns) in summer and fall; some
in North migrate to swamps in winter. Home range rarely more
than 1 mi. (1.6 km) across. Voice rarely heard, low bleat by
fawns, guttural grunts by old bucks in rut; both sexes snort
when alarmed. Full dentition at 13 months; males occasionally
have upper canine teeth. Can run 35–40 mph (56–64 kmph)
and jump 30 ft. (9 m) horizontally, 8½ ft. (2.5 m) vertically.
Lives to 16½ years in wild. Females breed at 1½ years (rarely
at ½); breeding season, Nov.–Feb.
Young: Usually 2 (1–3) to adult does; gestation period about
6½ months. Weaned at 4 months. May run with mother for
nearly 1 year.
Economic status: The most important big game mammal of
the East; can do considerable damage to young orchards and
vegetable crops if populations are not controlled. Tame deer
are common along the road through Algonquin Provincial Park,
Ontario. May be seen along back roads mornings and evenings.
                                              Map p. 217

MOOSE   *Alces alces*   **Pl. 22**
   Identification: Height 5–6½ ft. (152–198 cm). Wt.: males,
850–1180 lb. (382.5–531 kg); females 600–800 lb. (270–360 kg).
Record antler spread 77⅝ in. (197 cm). A large, dark brown
animal with gray legs. By its *large size, overhanging snout,* and

pendent *"bell"* on throat, as well as its ungainly appearance, it may be distinguished from all other mammals. Males have massive, *palmate, flat antlers* with small prongs projecting from the borders. Often seen *in or near water.* Skull (Plate 32) has 32 teeth. There are 4 mammae.

Similar species: (1) Elk has pale yellow rump patch, snout is not enlarged. (2) Deer are smaller and have white on some part of body. (3) Caribou have whitish rump and neck, no overhanging snout.

Habitat: Forests with lakes and swamps.

Habits: Maximum activity at night, but may be seen at any time. Occurs singly or by twos (cow and calf) or threes (bull, cow, calf), rarely in small groups. Browses on many woody plants in winter, twigs, bark, saplings; feeds primarily on aquatic vegetation in summer. Males shed antlers mostly Dec.–Feb.; velvet shed Aug.–Sept. Voice, seldom heard, low *moo* with upward inflection at end, also low grunts. Attains full dentition at about 16 months. Can swim as fast as 2 men can paddle a canoe; speeds up to 35 mph (56 kmph) on land. Populations of 4 per sq. mi. (259 ha) are high. Lives 20 years or more in wild. Females first breed at 2–3 years. Rutting season, Sept.–Oct.

Young: Born May–June; usually 1, rarely 2; gestation period about 8 months. Light reddish brown, with dark stripe down back; follows mother after 3 days.

Economic status: A magnificent game mammal, for meat and trophies, where hunting is allowed; chiefly of scenic and scien-

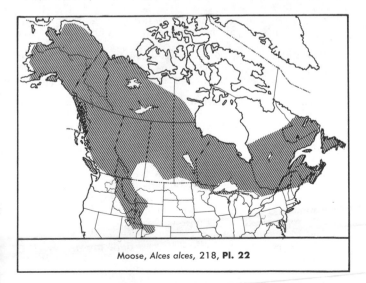

Moose, *Alces alces*, 218, **Pl. 22**

tific value in U.S. May be seen either at edge of forest or feeding
in shallow lake in following parks: Grand Teton, Yellowstone,
Glacier, Banff, Jasper, Isle Royale, Algonquin Provincial.

Map p. 219

WOODLAND CARIBOU *Rangifer caribou*   **Pl. 22**
   Identification: Height $3\frac{1}{2}$–4 ft. (107–122 cm). Wt.: males,
   250–600 lb. (112.5–270 kg); females, 150–350 lb. (67.5–
   157.5 kg). Antler spread to 60 in. (152 cm). A heavyset "deer"
   with *large feet* and *rounded* hoofs. All males and more than
   half of females have *antlers, semipalmated* with 1 prominent
   brow tine down over the nose; antlers dark mahogany-brown,
   beams flattened; velvet dark brown. Body dark chocolate-brown
   with *whitish on neck* and *rump* and *white above each hoof.*
   Skull has 32 or 34 teeth. There are 4 mammae.
      Recent authors have placed all species of caribou and the
   reindeer in one species, *R. tarandus.*
   Similar species: (1) Mule Deer has a black-tipped tail. (2)
   In the Whitetail Deer the neck and rump are not whitish. (3)
   Elk has chestnut-brown neck. (4) Moose is dark brown, no
   white; has overhanging snout; wholly palmate antlers and
   pointed hoofs.
   Habitat: Coniferous forests, muskegs.
   Habits: Moderately gregarious; usually in small bands. May
   migrate short distances, especially up and down mts. Feeds on
   a great variety of plants; chiefly a browser. Polygamous; rutting
   season, late Sept.
   Young: Born late May; usually 1, rarely 2; gestation period
   about 8 months. Grayish-brown fawn follows mother as soon
   as dry.
   Economic status: Occurs in wildest areas; an excellent game
   mammal; supplies food for Indians and white trappers; skins
   used for tents, clothing, and bedding.   Map opposite

BARREN GROUND CARIBOU *Rangifer arcticus*   **Pl. 22**
   Identification: Height $3\frac{1}{4}$–4 ft. (99–122 cm). Wt.: males,
   250–400 lb. (112.5–180 kg); females, 150–250 lb. (67.5–
   112.5 kg). Record antler spread 44 in. (112 cm). Similar, in
   general, to Woodland Caribou, but paler (in Far North *nearly
   white*). Antlers on both sexes; pale brown or ivory, beams cylin-
   drical, velvet light brown to gray. After the southward migration in autumn this and the Woodland Caribou may occur
   together, in winter, in n. Manitoba and n. Saskatchewan, but
   in summer, after the northward migration, their ranges are
   usually separate. Skull (Plate 32) has 32 or 34 teeth. There
   are 4 mammae.
   Similar species: (1) Moose is larger, dark brown; and has
   overhanging snout; antlers wholly palmate. (2) Mule Deer has

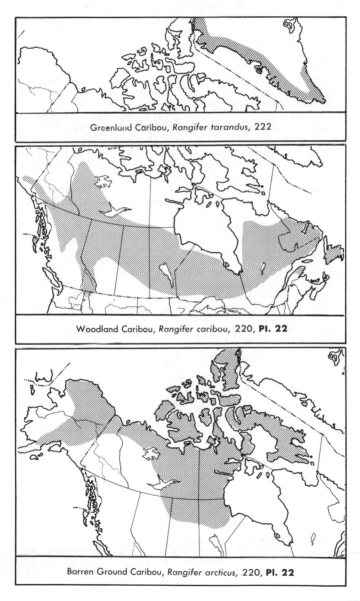

Greenland Caribou, *Rangifer tarandus*, 222

Woodland Caribou, *Rangifer caribou*, 220, **Pl. 22**

Barren Ground Caribou, *Rangifer arcticus*, 220, **Pl. 22**

black on tail. (3) Reindeer (introduced, domesticated animals from Siberia) are smaller; have larger antlers, with prominent brow tine in female; color often variable, white or spotted. (4) Muskox has massive unbranched horns; hair of body reaches nearly to ground.

Habitat: Tundra in summer, partially open coniferous forest in winter.

Habits: Always in large herds, some numbering in the tens of thousands; migratory; never stays in one place for long; an excellent swimmer, will often cross a lake rather than go around. Feeds mostly on lichens (reindeer moss), but also takes herbs, mosses, willows, and grasses. Voice, a coughlike grunt. Foot joints make clicking noise as animal walks. Females breed in 2nd year. Polygamous; rutting season, Sept.–Oct.

Young: Born May–June; usually 1, rarely 2; gestation period about 8 months. Grayish-brown fawn follows mother as soon as dry.

Economic status: Eskimos and trappers living inland in the Far North could not exist without caribou meat for themselves and their dogs; skins are used for bedding, clothing, and tents. The Eskimo tradition is to kill all you can, when you can. Now that he has the high-power rifle, he often slaughters more than he can retrieve or use. In addition, fire and overgrazing by introduced domesticated Reindeer have destroyed much of the Barren Ground Caribou range, particularly in Alaska. Some of the herds have decreased or disappeared, and this is of real concern to those in charge. If the caribou go the way of the Bison, much of the Far North may again revert to the wild creatures that remain there.   Map p. 221

GREENLAND CARIBOU (Reindeer)   *Rangifer tarandus*
  Identification: Height $3\frac{1}{2}$ ft. (107 cm); wt. 150–300 lb. (67.5–135 kg). Found chiefly along coast of *Greenland*. The domesticated Reindeer (*R. tarandus*) from Siberia has been introduced in parts of Alaska and Canada without too much success. It is considered to be the same species as the Greenland Caribou.
  Similar species: Muskox has massive unbranched horns; hair of body reaches nearly to ground.   Map p. 221

Pronghorn: Antilocapridae

THERE is but one species in this family. It is a strictly N. American mammal. The Pronghorn has true horns, bone cores covered with horny sheaths made up of agglutinated hair, but peculiar in that the sheaths are shed each year. *Both sexes have horns.* Known as fossils from Middle Miocene.

PRONGHORN (Antelope)   *Antilocapra americana*   **Pl. 23**
Identification: Height 3 ft. (91 cm); wt. 75–130 lb. (33.7–58.5 kg); record spread of horns $22\frac{5}{16}$ in. (57 cm). A pale tan, medium-sized mammal; distinguished by its *large white rump patch,* white lower sides, 2 broad *white bands across throat,* and slightly curved horns, each with a single *prong projecting forward;* 2 toes on each foot. Skull (Plate 32) has 32 teeth. There are 4 mammae.
Similar species: (1) The Bighorn Sheep has massive coiled horns; no white bands across throat. (2) Mule Deer has black on tail; no white along sides. (3) Whitetail Deer does not have large white rump patch; no white along sides.
Habitat: Open prairies and sagebrush plains.
Habits: Chiefly diurnal, most active mornings and evenings, but may be seen at any time. Usually occurs in small bands. Mainly a browser; eats many weeds, some grass, but fond of sagebrush. In some areas migrates between summer and winter ranges. Home range for a band usually 2–4 mi. (3.2–6.4 km) across. May attain speed of 40 mph. (64 kmph). Hair on large white rump patch erects and makes animal more conspicuous; usually done only when fleeing from danger. Full dentition acquired at $3\frac{1}{2}$ years. Lives to 14 years in wild. Breeds at $1\frac{1}{2}$ years, Aug.–Oct.; some males collect small harems. Horn coverings shed after breeding season.
Young: Born April–May in South, May–June in North; usually 2 (1–3); gestation period 230–240 days. Grayish-brown kids are left alone for a few days, except at nursing time, then follow mother.

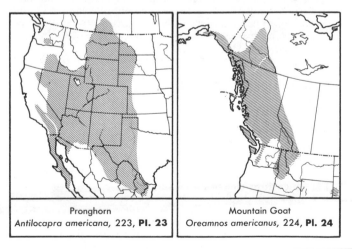

Pronghorn	Mountain Goat
Antilocapra americana, 223, **Pl. 23**	*Oreamnos americanus,* 224, **Pl. 24**

Economic status: Slight competition for food with cattle and sheep, but feeds mostly on vegetation not eaten by domestic stock. A big game mammal, but more important as an interesting element in our fauna. Commonly seen on western plains and in Yellowstone and Wind Cave Natl. Parks; also Petrified Forest Natl. Monument.   Map p. 223

Bison, Goats, Muskox, and Sheep: Bovidae

THIS is the family to which our domestic cattle, sheep, and goats belong. Members have *true horns,* which are *never shed* and are *not branched.* Horns are present in *both sexes.* Known as fossils from Lower Miocene.

BISON (Buffalo)   *Bison bison*   **Pl. 24**
Identification: Height 5–6 ft. (152–183 cm); wt. 800–2000 lb. (360–900 kg); record spread of horns 35 ⅜ in. (90 cm). This is a large, dark brown beast with *massive head,* a *high hump on its shoulders,* and *long shaggy hair on shoulders and front legs.* Skull (Plate 32) has 32 teeth. There are 4 functional mammae.
Similar species: Domestic Cattle are normally not dark brown.
Habitat: Open plains; grasslands in South, woodlands and openings in North.
Habits: Diurnal; gregarious. Formerly migrated north in spring and south in fall. Forms wallows, where it rolls in dust or mud. A grazing animal, feeds mostly on grasses, but takes some browse. May live nearly 30 years, normally 15–20. Breeds at 2–3 years, July–Oct.
Young: Normally 1; gestation period about 9 months. Yellowish-red calf follows mother soon after birth.
Economic status: Now confined to zoos and national or state lands. Some are harvested as a control measure; chiefly of scenic and scientific value. May be seen at the following national parks: Platt, Wind Cave, Yellowstone, and Wood Buffalo Park, Alberta. Also, Natl. Bison Range, Moiese, Mont.
                                                    Map opposite

MOUNTAIN GOAT   *Oreamnos americanus*   **Pl. 24**
Identification: Height 3–3½ ft. (91–107 cm); wt. 100–300 lb. (45–135 kg); record spread of horns 11 ⅜ in. (289 mm). On the *rocky crags near snowline,* this *white* goat with long fur, a definite beard, and short, *smooth, black horns* that curve slightly backward may be seen at a distance by the adventurer.

The hoofs are black. Skull has 32 teeth. There are 4 mammae.
Similar species: (1) Bighorn and (2) White Sheep have horns
that are massive, yellowish, and spiral-shaped.
Habitat: Steep slopes and benches along cliffs; usually at or
above timberline.
Habits: Primarily diurnal. Usually seen in groups of fewer than
10. Part grazer and part browser, feeds on various high-mt.
vegetation; usually above timberline in summer, moves to lower

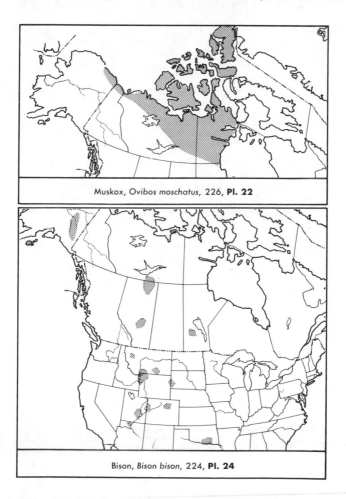

Muskox, *Ovibos moschatus*, 226, **Pl. 22**

Bison, *Bison bison*, 224, **Pl. 24**

elevations in winter. Remains in an area 3–6 mi. (4.8–9.6 km) across. Attains full dentition at $3\frac{1}{2}$–4 years. May live 12 years or more in wild. First breeds at $2\frac{1}{2}$ years; breeding season, Oct.–Dec.

Young: Born May–June; usually 1–2 kids, occasionally 3.

Economic status: Does no damage; an interesting mammal that has real scenic as well as scientific value. May be seen in Black Hills, S. Dakota, and following national parks: Mt. Rainier, Glacier, Olympic, Banff, Jasper. Map p. 223

MUSKOX *Ovibos moschatus* **Pl. 22**

Identification: Height 3–5 ft. (91–152 cm); wt. 500–900 lb. (225–405 kg); record spread between tips of horns $29\frac{3}{4}$ in. (76 cm). In the *Far North,* this brownish ox may be recognized by long, silky, brown hair that *hangs skirtlike nearly to its feet.* Broad flat horns are *plastered close to skull,* with curved tips pointing forward; both sexes have horns. Skull has 32 teeth. There are 4 mammae.

Similar species: (1) In the Barren Ground and (2) Greenland Caribou the hair does not reach nearly to the ground; antlers, not horns.

Habitat: Tundra of Far North; introduced on Nunivak I., Alaska (not shown on map).

Habits: May occur singly, but usually in small groups. Form circle with heads facing outward when attacked by wolves. Feeds on tundra grasses, willows, forbs, sedges, and probably any other food available. Sexually mature at 3–4 years; breeding season, July–Aug.

Young: Usually 1, every other year.

Economic status: Formerly an important item in the Eskimo economy; easily killed and, therefore exterminated over much of their range; may be recovering under strict protection.

Map p. 225

BIGHORN SHEEP (Bighorn) *Ovis canadensis* **Pl. 24**

Identification: Height $2\frac{1}{2}$–$3\frac{1}{2}$ ft. (76–107 cm). Wt.: males, 125–275 lb. (56.2–123.7 kg); females, 75–150 lb. (33.7–67.5 kg). Record spread of horns 33 in. (84 cm). This brown to grayish-brown sheep has a *creamy white rump* and *massive coiled horns* (small, not coiled in females) that spiral back, out, and then forward to complete an arc. Skull has 32 teeth. There are 2 mammae.

Similar species: (1) Mountain Goat is white and has black horns. (2) Deer have branched antlers or none. (3) Pronghorn has branched horns and white bands across throat.

Habitat: Mt. slopes with sparse growths of trees, rugged terrain.

Habits: Gregarious. Sexes usually separate in summer; rams join ewes and lambs in fall. May move to lower elevations in

winter. Both a browser and grazer, feeds on great variety of
plants. Full dentition attained at 4 years. Probably lives to 15
years in wild. Females breed at 2½ years. Rutting season,
Nov.–Dec.

Young: Born May–June; 1, occasionally 2; gestation period
about 180 days. Lambs follow mother soon after birth.

Economic status: Little competition with domestic stock for
food; has been exterminated in much of former range. Most
likely to be seen in Yellowstone and Glacier Natl. Parks and
in Death Valley Natl. Monument.   Map below

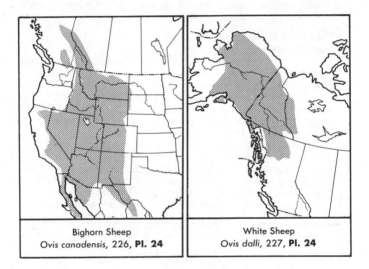

Bighorn Sheep
Ovis canadensis, 226, **Pl. 24**

White Sheep
Ovis dalli, 227, **Pl. 24**

WHITE SHEEP (Dall Sheep)   *Ovis dalli*   **Pl. 24**
  Identification: Height 3–3⅓ ft. (91–102 cm); wt. 125–200 lb.
  (56.2–90 kg); record spread of horns 35 in. (89 cm). This stocky
  white or whitish to nearly black (in the south of its range) sheep
  is found in the *inaccessible mt. areas* of the Northwest. Horns
  are yellowish, massive in males, smaller in females. Usually seen
  in bands of 6 or more. Included here are the "Stone Sheep,"
  a blackish color phase, and the "Fannin Sheep," an intermediate
  phase. Skull (Plate 32) has 32 teeth. There are 2 mammae.
  Similar species: The Mountain Goat has long fur and a beard;
  also small, slender, black horns that curve slightly backward.
  Habitat: Rough terrain, mt. slopes.
  Habits: Similar to those of the Bighorn Sheep.   Map above

Sloths and Armadillos: Xenarthra

Armadillos: Dasypodidae

THIS is chiefly a tropical family. They have *degenerate teeth* (simple pegs), and the body is covered with a *protective "armor" of horny material.* Small, scattered hairs grow from between the plates. Known as fossils from Paleocene.

ARMADILLO *Dasypus novemcinctus*   **Pl. 19**
   Identification: Head and body 15–17 in. (38–43 cm); tail 14–16 in. (36–41 cm); wt. 8–17 lb. (3.6–7.6 kg). This peculiar *"armored"* mammal is about the size of a House Cat. Body, tail, and top of head *covered with horny material.* The only mammal here included that has a protective cover of armor plate; commonly seen along highways at night; many killed by autos. Skull (Plate 31) usually has 32 (28–32) peglike teeth. There are 4 mammae.
   Habitat: Woodlands, brushy areas, rock outcrops and cliffs.
   Habits: Occasionally out by day, especially in winter, but mostly mornings, evenings, and at night in summer. Seeks safety by dashing to a burrow or dense thicket; rarely rolls into a ball for protection; frequents waterholes and streams for mud baths as well as drinking water. Feeds almost entirely on insects

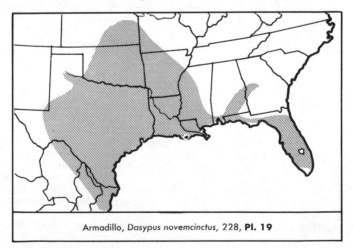

Armadillo, *Dasypus novemcinctus*, 228, **Pl. 19**

and other small invertebrates; eats a few berries, fruits, and bird eggs; roots in leaf mold for much of its food. Dens in openings in rock outcroppings or in burrows 10–15 ft (3–4.6 m) long that it digs. One Armadillo to 3–10 acres (1.2–4 ha) is normal population.

Young: Born March–April; always 4 of same sex; gestation period reported at about 150 days.

Economic status: Almost entirely beneficial; destroys many insects; burrows serve as home sites for other mammals; meat edible; shells made into baskets for tourist trade.

Map opposite

Dugong and Manatee: Sirenia

WHOLLY aquatic mammals, *not* related to whales. Two living species, each in a separate family.

Manatee: Trichechidae

THE 1 species in this family is confined to warm coastal waters. For characters see below. Known as fossils from Pleistocene.

MANATEE (Sea Cow)   *Trichechus manatus*   **p. 244**
Identification: Length 7–13 ft. (2.1–4 m); wt. up to 1300 lb. (585 kg). A large sluggish aquatic mammal with *broad head, thick, cleft upper lips,* front flippers, and a broad, horizontally flattened and rounded tail; no hind legs (flippers). Muzzle adorned with stiff bristles. Skull (p. 265) usually has 24 teeth (all alike) in use at one time; teeth move forward and are replaced from behind. There are 2 mammae.
Similar species: (1) Whales and (2) porpoises are seen usually in deep water some distance from shore; tail is not rounded.
Habitat: Brackish water, lagoons, mouths of rivers; generally shallow.
Habits: A sluggish animal, usually seen in small groups; cannot tolerate water temperatures below 46°F. (7.7°C); can remain underwater for 30 min. Feeds on aquatic vegetation.
Young: No definite season known; 1 calf; gestation period about 11 months.
Economic status: Does no harm; a most interesting part of our fauna; meat edible; protected in U.S.
Range: From Beaufort, N. Carolina, south to the Florida Keys, and along coast of Gulf of Mexico.

Whales, Dolphins, and
Porpoises: Cetacea

THESE are strictly *marine* mammals as far as N. America is concerned. They are *fishlike* in general appearance except that the *tail fluke is horizontal,* not vertical. Also, they breathe air and must come to the surface periodically. Just before or as they break water, they expel warm, moisture-laden air from the lungs, and the vapor one sees as they "blow" is mostly condensation of moisture in the expelled air. The large whales usually are not seen at close range, unless washed up on a beach, and are difficult for the novice to identify. Porpoises and dolphins play off bows of boats and may be seen at close range, thus making identification easier. They can maintain a speed of 16–20 mph (26–32 kmph). The large rorquals reach speeds of 23 mph (37 kmph). Some may remain submerged for 2 hr. Whales normally give birth to 1 young (calf) on alternate years; some migrate thousands of miles each year. There are 2 mammae. Known as fossils from Upper Eocene. **Economic status:** Whaling was a big and profitable industry in the past. With no restrictions on numbers or kinds taken, some of the large whales were threatened with extinction. Now there is international control over kinds, sizes, and numbers of whales taken. This is respected by most nations. It is regrettable that two nations continue to hunt these magnificent creatures. In addition to their commercial value, there is a definite scenic or aesthetic value. Who at sea has not been thrilled at seeing one of the large whales surface nearby — or at seeing a school of dolphins or porpoises coming toward the boat to play across the bow?

Toothed Whales: Odontoceti

THIS suborder contains the beaked and sperm whales and the large group of dolphins and porpoises. All have simple, peglike teeth (variable in number).

Beaked Whales: Ziphiidae

MEMBERS of this family have *vestigial teeth* in the upper jaw; functional teeth (2–4) in the lower jaw (some females and young have no teeth showing). Two grooves on throat converge anteriorly to form a V. Snout elongated into beak; small dorsal fin between tail and middle of back; flippers small and placed far forward. Food probably consists of fish and squids for most part. Known as fossils from Lower Miocene.

BAIRD BEAKED WHALE *Berardius bairdi* **p. 235**
Identification: Length to 42 ft. (12.8 m). This is a rare and little-known whale. It is black with a *whitish area on lower belly.* Snout is formed into a definite beak; lower jaw protrudes beyond upper; dorsal fin small and set far back on body. There are 4 functional teeth, 2-3 in. (51-76 mm) long and flattened laterally, in the lower jaw.
Similar species: (1) The Pacific Beaked Whale and (2) Goosebeak Whale are smaller.
Habits: Travels in schools of 20 or more. Raises flukes above water when diving. Feeds on rockfish, herring, squid, and octopus. Gestation period about 10 months.
Range: Pacific Coast south to California.

SOWERBY BEAKED WHALE *Mesoplodon bidens*
Identification: Length to 16 ft. (4.9 m). A rare and little-known species. Dorsal fin well back on the body. Extremely pointed head and snout; no median notch in flukes. *Dark gray* above, paler on sides and belly. There are 2 *small,* laterally flattened teeth near tip of lower jaw.
Similar species: (1) The True Beaked Whale is slaty black on the back. (2) The Atlantic Beaked Whale has 2 large teeth, about 6 in. (151 mm) long, near front of lower jaw.
Range: North Atlantic Coast, south to Massachusetts.

ATLANTIC BEAKED WHALE *Mesoplodon densirostris*
(Blainville Whale)
Identification: Length to 15 ft. (4.6 m); wt. to 2400 lb. (1088 kg). Nearly completely black; pale patches beneath flippers and on belly. Male has 2 *large* teeth about 6 in. (152 mm) long near front of lower jaw. Forehead hardly evident.
Similar species: (1) The Sowerby Beaked Whale and (2) the True Beaked Whale have 2 small teeth near front of lower jaw.
Range: Atlantic Coast.

GERVAIS BEAKED WHALE *Mesoplodon europaeus*
Identification: Length to 22 ft. (6.7 m). Black above, paler on sides and belly. Male has 2 small teeth near front of lower jaw. Forehead barely evident; no median notch in fluke.
Formerly known as *M. gervaisi.*
Similar species: Other species of *Mesoplodon* are smaller.
Range: Atlantic Coast from New York south.

TRUE BEAKED WHALE *Mesoplodon mirus* **p. 235**
Identification: Length to 17 ft. (5.2 m). Slaty black on top, paler on belly. Male has 2 *small* teeth, laterally compressed, at

tip of lower jaw. Forehead evident; no median notch in fluke.
Similar species: (1) Sowerby Beaked Whale not slaty black
on back. (2) The Atlantic Beaked Whale has 2 *large* teeth,
about 6 in. (152 mm) long, near front of lower jaw.
Range: North Atlantic Coast, occasionally south to Florida.

PACIFIC BEAKED WHALE *Mesoplodon stejnegeri*
    Identification: Length to 17 ft. (5.2 m). Blackish, with anterior
body, especially head, grayish to whitish. 2 *large* laterally compressed teeth about 8 in. (203 mm) long near tip of lower jaw.
Similar species: (1) The Baird Beaked Whale is much larger.
(2) Archbeak Whale has a whitish beak.
Range: Pacific Coast south to California.

JAPANESE BEAKED WHALE *Mesoplodon ginkgodens*
(Ginkgo Beaked Whale)
    Identification: Length to 17 ft. (5.2 m). A pair of large
$2\frac{1}{2}$ x 4 in. (63 x 102 mm) "onion-shaped" teeth in lower jaw
show outside mouth. Adult is dark gray; whitish underneath
when immature. No median notch in flukes, which spread 30
percent of body length.
Similar species: (1) Pacific Beaked Whale has grayish or
whitish head. (2) The Archbeak Whale has a whitish beak.
Range: Known from 1 stranded individual near Delmar, California.

ARCHBEAK WHALE *Mesoplodon carlhubbsi*
    Identification: Length to 17 ft. (5.2 m). *Body black* over most
of surface except for *whitish beak*. Lower jaw definitely protrudes beyond upper. Upper and lower edges of peduncle
sharply keeled. Dorsal fin far back on body; posterior edge
concave.
Similar species: (1) The Pacific Beaked Whale has anterior
body and head grayish; may be difficult to distinguish. (2) The
Japanese Beaked Whale does not have white beak.
Range: Pacific Coast from Washington to California.

GOOSEBEAK WHALE *Ziphius cavirostris*   **p. 235**
(Cuvier Whale)
    Identification: Length to 28 ft. (8.5 m). Variable in color; gray
to black on back, with occasional white on head and middle
of back; sides black to brownish or spotted; belly usually whitish. Body thick; a distinct *keel from dorsal fin to tail;* distance
from tip of snout to blowhole $\frac{1}{8}$-$\frac{1}{10}$ total length. 2 teeth $2\frac{1}{2}$ in.
(64 mm) long in lower jaw of male, occasionally in female.
Similar species: The Baird Beaked Whale is larger.
Habits: Swims in groups of 30-40 individuals. Feeds on squids.
Gestation period about 1 year.

Range: Atlantic Coast from Rhode Island south; Pacific Coast south to California.

BOTTLENOSE WHALE   *Hyperoodon ampullatus*   **p. 235**
Identification: Length to 30 ft. (9.1 m); at birth, 10 ft. (3 m). Grayish black to light brown or yellowish, with *whitish about head* and a whitish belly. Forehead of male *rises abruptly* from short beak; old males may be recognized by *whitish patch on forehead* and *white dorsal fin.* Distance from tip of snout to blowhole ⅕-⅐ total length. There are 2 *small* teeth about 1½ in. (38 mm) long at *tip* of lower jaw.
Similar species: The Common Blackfish has large dorsal fin on front half of body.
Habits: Swims in small schools of 4-10.
Range: Arctic and North Atlantic Coasts.

Sperm Whale: Physeteridae

THIS FAMILY contains but 1 species. Occurs in all oceans. For characters, see below. Known as fossils from Lower Miocene.

SPERM WHALE (Cachalot)   *Physeter catodon*   **p. 240**
Identification: Length: males to 60 ft. (18.3 m); females to 30 ft. (9.1 m); at birth 12-14 ft. (3.6-4.3 m). Wt. to 53 tons (48,000 kg). *Snout square;* head large, about ⅓ length of animal; *lower jaw small, narrow. No dorsal fin;* pectoral fin ½ total length; row of bumps on posterior half of back. Bluish gray above, paler below. 20-25 teeth in each lower jaw; teeth up to 8 in. (203 mm) long. The spout is prolonged and *directed forward* at a distinct angle. The above characters are found in no other whale.
Habits: Females and young tend to remain in warmer waters, males in colder waters in summer. Reaches sexual maturity in 8 years. Gestation period about 16 months. Can remain submerged 75 min. Feeds mostly on squids and octopuses.
Economic status: This is one of the large whales that have been hunted for centuries, and still are. It is the whale that produces ambergris. Spermaceti oil is located in the head. About 25,000 are killed annually.
Range: Atlantic and Pacific Coasts.

Pygmy Sperm Whales: Kogiidae

THIS FAMILY contains 2 species. They occur in the Atlantic and Pacific Oceans. Sexual maturity is attained in 2 years. Gestation period about 9 months. Known as fossils from Lower Pliocene.

PYGMY SPERM WHALE   *Kogia breviceps*   **p. 240**
   Identification: Length to 13 ft. (4 m). One of the smallest
   whales; *snout broad, protruding; lower jaw narrow;* body black
   above, grayish white below; a pale bracket-shaped mark behind
   eye. A small dorsal fin is present. There are 18–30 needlelike
   teeth in lower jaws.
   Similar species: (1) In the bottlenose dolphins the lower jaw
   projects slightly beyond the upper jaw. (2) The Grampus has
   a prominent dorsal fin and the body is marked with several
   irregular streaks. (3) The Dwarf Sperm Whale is smaller and
   does not have a bracket-shaped mark behind the eye.
   Range: Warm waters of both coasts from Nova Scotia and
   Washington south.

DWARF SPERM WHALE   *Kogia simus*
   Identification: Length to 8½ ft. (2.6 m). Body black above,
   whitish below with *gray mottling* from the upper lip to the
   insertion of the flipper and from the axilla and above the flipper
   midlaterally to the flukes. Dorsal *fin high,* near middle of back.
   There are 9 pairs of teeth in the lower jaw, 2 pairs in the upper.
   The *smallest whale* described here.
   Similar species: The Pygmy Sperm Whale is larger and has
   a pale bracket-shaped mark behind the eye.
   Range: Central coasts of Atlantic and Pacific.

White Whale and Narwhal:
Monodontidae

No DORSAL fin is present in these whales. The snout is blunt;
no grooves on throat. Inhabit cold arctic waters. Feed mostly on
fish and cuttlefish. Gestation period about 14 months. Teeth
present. Known as fossils from Pleistocene.

WHITE WHALE   *Delphinapterus leucas*   **p. 235**
(Beluga)
   Identification: Length to 14 ft. (4.3 m). This small *white* whale
   may be recognized by size and color. No other cetaceans have
   these characters. Young are bluish gray. Very short snout and
   high forehead. Skull (p. 265) has 32–40 small, pointed teeth;
   both jaws have teeth.
   Similar species: The male Narwhal has long forward-project-
   ing tusk; both sexes are mottled on back.
   Habits: Usually in schools of 5–30, but occasionally in pairs.
   Swims at speed of 6 mph. (9.6 kmph). May go far up rivers,
   usually in shallow water.
   Young: Born March–May; gestation period 14 months.

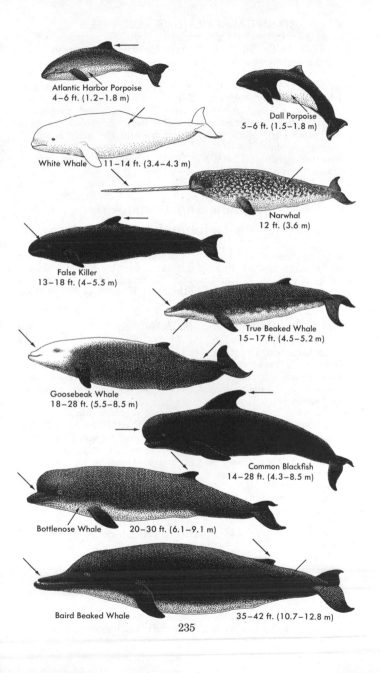

Atlantic Harbor Porpoise
4–6 ft. (1.2–1.8 m)

Dall Porpoise
5–6 ft. (1.5–1.8 m)

White Whale 11–14 ft. (3.4–4.3 m)

Narwhal
12 ft. (3.6 m)

False Killer
13–18 ft. (4–5.5 m)

True Beaked Whale
15–17 ft. (4.5–5.2 m)

Goosebeak Whale
18–28 ft. (5.5–8.5 m)

Common Blackfish
14–28 ft. (4.3–8.5 m)

Bottlenose Whale   20–30 ft. (6.1–9.1 m)

Baird Beaked Whale   35–42 ft. (10.7–12.8 m)

235

Range: Arctic and North Atlantic Coasts; Hudson Bay; Alaska; chiefly in cold waters, rarely south as far as Cape Cod.

NARWHAL   *Monodon monoceros*   **p. 235**
Identification: Length to 12 ft. (3.6 m). Peculiar in that the male has a *long, spirally twisted "unicorn" tusk projecting forward* from the blunt snout. This tusk may reach a length of 9 ft. (2.7 m). Back is mottled gray and the belly is white; young are bluish gray.
Similar species: The White Whale is white in adult.
Range: Arctic Coast.

Dolphins and Porpoises:
Delphinidae

SMALL REPRESENTATIVES of the order, length to 30 ft. (9.1 m). Tail fluke notched in middle; dorsal fin usually well developed. Feed primarily on fish and squids. Commonly travel in groups up to 50 or more. Teeth in both jaws. Known as fossils from Lower Miocene.

SPOTTED DOLPHIN   *Stenella dubia*   **p. 240**
(Cuvier Dolphin)
   Identification: Length to 7 ft. (2.1 m). Back blackish or grayish black with numerous *white spots;* belly pale gray or whitish; *long snout* separated from forehead by distinct *transverse groove;* dorsal fin present; 35 – 44 teeth on each side of upper and lower jaws.
   Formerly known as *S. frontalis* and *S. plagiodon.*
   Similar species: (1) The Rough-toothed Dolphin does not have transverse groove between beak and forehead. (2) The Longbeak Dolphin has 46 – 56 teeth in each tooth row.
   Range: Atlantic Coast N. Carolina to Texas.

STRIPED DOLPHIN   *Stenella caeruleoalba*
(Longsnout Dolphin)
   Identification: Length to 8 ft. (2.4 m). Black above, white below; narrow black streak from eye along lower side, another from eye to flipper; 44 – 50 teeth on each side of upper and lower jaws.
   Formerly known as *S. styx.*
   Similar species: The Common Dolphin is colored differently.
   Range: Atlantic Coast from Greenland south; Pacific Coast from Bering Sea to Oregon.

LONGBEAK DOLPHIN   *Stenella longirostris*
Identification: Length to 7 ft. (2.1 m). Dark gray mottled with

light gray above; white blotched with grayish below; flippers small; rostrum twice length of cranial portion of skull; 46–56 teeth in each tooth row.
Similar species: Spotted Dolphin has 35–44 teeth on each side of upper and lower jaws.
Range: Pacific and tropical Atlantic.

ROUGH-TOOTHED DOLPHIN   *Steno bredanensis*
Identification: Length to 8 ft. (2.4 m). Black above, white (including beak) below; sides spotted; *no transverse groove* between beak and forehead; slender beak *compressed* from side to side; 20–27 roughened and furrowed teeth on each side of upper and lower jaws.
   Formerly known as *S. rostratus.* Some authors place this in a separate family, Stenidae.
Similar species: The Spotted Dolphin has a transverse groove between beak and forehead.
Range: Atlantic and Pacific Coasts from Virginia and California south.

COMMON DOLPHIN   *Delphinus delphis*   p. 240
Identification: Length to 8½ ft. (2.6 m). Back and flippers black; flanks yellowish; belly white; 2 white lines across groove that separates beak from forehead; beak about 6 in. (152 mm) long; dorsal fin present. There are 30–40 small teeth on each side of upper and lower jaws.
   The Pacific Dolphin is considered a distinct species by some authors (*D. bairdi*).
Similar species: (1) The Pacific White-sided Dolphin has a blunt beak; no white between beak and forehead. (2) White-beak Dolphin has a blunt beak.
Habits: Usually seen in medium to large schools. Swims at speeds to 25 mph (40 kmph). Likely to be seen playing in front of a ship; leaps high out of water when traveling. This is one of the dolphins displayed at the Marinelands of California and Florida.
Range: Atlantic and Pacific Coasts; warm and temperate waters, usually some distance from shore.

ATLANTIC BOTTLENOSE DOLPHIN   *Tursiops truncatus*
Identification: Length to 12 ft. (3.6 m). This is the *commonest* dolphin along the Atlantic Coast. May be recognized by *large* size and general *grayish* coloration, slightly paler beneath than on back. The relatively *short beak,* about 3 in. (76 mm) long, is separated from the forehead by a *transverse groove.* Lower jaw is slightly longer than the upper; 20–26 teeth on each side of upper and lower jaws.
Similar species: Other dolphins are smaller or colored differently.

Habits: This species has been successfully maintained in captivity in the Marinelands of California and Florida; the dolphin that does most of the performing. Females are sexually mature at 4 years.
Young: 1 calf; gestation period 10–12 months.
Range: Atlantic Coast from Cape Cod south.

PACIFIC BOTTLENOSE DOLPHIN *Tursiops gilli*   **p. 240**
Identification: Length to 12 ft. (3.6 m). Similar to Atlantic Bottlenose Dolphin. Grayish black above, white beneath, except for dark area from vent to fluke; *white on upper lip*. May be seen off West Coast.
Similar species: Other dolphins are smaller or are colored differently.
Range: Pacific Coast from California south.

RIGHT WHALE DOLPHIN *Lissodelphis borealis*   **p. 240**
Identification: Length to 8 ft. (2.4 m). A small black dolphin with a narrow *white belly stripe* from breast to tail and *no dorsal fin* will most certainly be of this species. There are 43–45 teeth on each side of upper and lower jaws.
Similar species: Other dolphins have a dorsal fin.
Range: Pacific Coast from the Bering Sea south.

ATLANTIC WHITE-SIDED DOLPHIN
Lagenorhynchus acutus
Identification: Length to 9 ft. (2.7 m). This dolphin may be recognized by its blackish back, white belly, and a *pale area* along either side below the *prominent dorsal fin*. There are yellowish streaks along the sides. The *nose is short and blunt*. There are 30–37 teeth on each side of upper and lower jaws.
Similar species: (1) The Common Dolphin has a pointed beak and white at base of forehead. (2) The Whitebeak Dolphin has a white beak.
Range: Atlantic Coast south to Cape Cod.

PACIFIC WHITE-SIDED DOLPHIN   **p. 240**
Lagenorhynchus obliquidens
Identification: Length to 9 ft. (2.7 m); wt., 1 female 6 ft. (1.8 m) long, 190 lb. (85.5 kg). This dolphin has a greenish-black back, a *pale stripe along each side,* and a white belly. The dorsal fin is definitely hooked. Nose is blunt. There are 29–31 teeth on each side of upper and lower jaws.
Similar species: The Common Dolphin has a pointed beak and white at base of forehead.
Habits: Frequents near-shore waters in winter, moves offshore in summer; travels in groups of up to 1000. Feeds mostly on anchovies and sauries, also squids and other sea animals. Per-

forms well in captivity, but is not as versatile as Bottlenose Dolphin; may be seen at Marineland of Pacific.
Range: Pacific.

WHITEBEAK DOLPHIN *Lagenorhynchus albirostris* **p. 240**
Identification: Length to 10 ft. (3 m). In the North Atlantic one is likely to encounter this medium-sized blackish dolphin with a *pale stripe* along each side, a whitish belly, and a white beak about 2 in. (51 mm) long. There are 26–27 teeth on each side of upper and lower jaws.
Similar species: (1) The Atlantic White-sided Dolphin has no white on beak. (2) Common Dolphin has pointed beak.
Habits: May be seen in very large schools.
Range: North Atlantic Coast south to Labrador.

PYGMY KILLER WHALE *Feresa attenuata*
Identification: Length to 9 ft. (2.7 m). Black except for white lips and ventral patches. Prominent dorsal fin. 22 to 23 teeth on each side of upper and lower jaws. Snout broad; upper jaw slightly overhangs lower.
Range: Known from Gulf of Mexico.

KILLER WHALE (Sea Wolf) *Orcinus orca* **p. 240**
Identification: Length to 30 ft. (9.1 m). If seen at sea, the first indication of a Killer Whale would probably be the *large, exposed dorsal fin* cutting the surface of the water. If it shows a jet-black body with *white extending up on the side* posteriorly, it is this species. It also has a clear white spot behind each eye and white underparts. Nose is blunt. The broad flippers are about ⅙ of total length. There are 10–15 teeth on each side of upper and lower jaws.
Formerly known as *Grampus*. Pacific representative (*O. rectipina*) considered distinct species by some.
Similar species: (1) All dolphins are smaller. (2) Other whales colored differently.
Habits: Travels in packs of 5–40. Feeds on other whales (some much larger), seals, sea lions, and fish. This is the "wolf of the sea." Swims at speeds up to 23 mph (37 kmph). Gestation period about 1 year.
Range: Atlantic and Pacific Coasts.

GRAMPUS (Risso Dolphin) *Grampus griseus* **p. 240**
Identification: Length to 13 ft. (4 m); at birth 5 ft. (1.5 m). Rather *blunt-nosed,* with dark gray or blackish body marked with numerous *irregular streaks.* Head tinged with *yellow,* belly grayish white; *slender flippers* are mottled grayish. Dorsal fin prominent. There are 2–7 teeth in each lower jaw, usually none in uppers.
Formerly known as *Grampidelphis.*

Spotted Dolphin
5–7 ft. (1.5–2.1 m)

Common Dolphin
6½–8½ ft. (1.9–2.6 m)

Right Whale Dolphin
5–8 ft. (1.5–2.4 m)

Pacific White-sided Dolphin
7–9 ft. (2.1–2.7 m)

Pacific Bottlenose Dolphin
10–12 ft. (3–3.6 m)

Whitebeak Dolphin
7–10 ft. (2.1–3 m)

Pygmy Sperm Whale
9–13 ft. (2.7–4 m)

Grampus
9–13 ft. (2.7–4 m)

Atlantic
Killer Whale
15–30 ft.
(4.5–9.1 m)

Sperm Whale
40–60 ft. (12.2–18.3 m)

Similar species: (1) Dolphins are either smaller or differently colored. (2) Whales are either larger or lower jaw projects beyond upper.
Range: Atlantic and Pacific Coasts.

FALSE KILLER   *Pseudorca crassidens*   **p. 235**
Identification: Length to 18 ft. (5.5 m). This small black, *slender* whale has a relatively small, *recurved dorsal fin* just in front of the middle of the body. Snout is blunt and rounded, head flattened. 8–10 teeth on each side of upper and lower jaws.
Similar species: The Blackfish has a bulging forehead and prominent dorsal fin.
Habits: Usually seen in very large schools.
Range: Atlantic and Pacific Coasts from N. Carolina and Washington south.

COMMON BLACKFISH   *Globicephala melaena*   **p. 235**
(Pilot Whale)
Identification: Length to 28 ft. (8.5 m). *Uniformly black;* large recurved dorsal fin well forward of middle of body; flippers about ⅕ length of body. Forehead *high, bulges forward;* 7–12 teeth on each side of upper and lower jaws.
Formerly known as *G. ventricosa.*
Similar species: (1) The False Killer has neither a bulging forehead nor a prominent dorsal fin. (2) The Short-finned Blackfish has shorter fins, difficult to distinguish.
Habits: Normally travels in large schools; occasionally stranded on beach. Females are sexually mature in 6 or 7 years, males in 12 years; gestation period 16 months.
Range: Atlantic Coast south to Virginia.

SHORT-FINNED BLACKFISH   *Globicephala macrorhyncha*
(Pilot Whale)
Identification: Length to 20 ft. (6.1 m), flipper 2½–3 ft. (76–91 cm). This species is difficult to distinguish from the Common Blackfish. Flipper is about ⅙ as long as body.
Formerly known as *G. brachyptera* and *G. scammoni* (in part).
Similar species: For the Common Blackfish, see above.
Habits: Performs nearly as well as Bottlenose Dolphin in captivity.
Range: Atlantic Coast from New Jersey south; Pacific Coast.

HARBOR PORPOISE   *Phocoena phocoena*   **p. 235**
(Common Porpoise)
Identification: Length to 6 ft. (1.8 m); wt. 100–120 lb. (45–54 kg). A *small,* thick-bodied animal with a blunt snout, *black* back, triangular fin, *pinkish* sides, and *white* belly. A *dark line* runs from corner of mouth to flipper; 16–27 spade-shaped teeth

on each side of upper and lower jaws. Common near shore and in harbors.

Some authors place this and the Dall Porpoise in a separate family, Phocoenidae. The Pacific representative, *P. vomerina,* considered as a distinct species by some.

Similar species: All other cetaceans are larger or strikingly marked.

Range: Atlantic Coast south to Delaware River; Pacific Coast.

DALL PORPOISE   *Phocoenoides dalli*   **p. 235**
Identification: Length to 6 ft. (1.8 m). Strikingly marked; *black* except for a *large white area* across the vent region and extending slightly over halfway up the sides, the front edge about even with front of dorsal fin; 23–27 teeth on each side of upper and lower jaws.
Similar species: (1) Harbor Porpoise not strikingly marked. (2) All other cetaceans larger.
Range: Pacific Coast, south rarely to Long Beach, California.

Baleen Whales: Mysticeti

Whales *without teeth* (Skull, p. 265), but with *strips of whale-bone,* baleen, hanging from the roof of the mouth. These strips are frayed along the edges and serve to strain from the water the small organisms on which these largest of the whales feed. There are 2 blowholes on top of the head.

Known as fossils from Middle Oligocene.

Gray Whale: Eschrichtiidae

THIS FAMILY contains but 1 species. Occurs in the North Pacific Ocean. For characters, see below. Not known as fossils.

GRAY WHALE   *Eschrichtius gibbosus*   **p. 244**
Identification: Length to 45 ft. (13.7 m); wt. 17–37 tons (15,000–33,000 kg). Medium-sized, *blotched, grayish-black* whale, rather slender; spouts are *quick and low* (about 10 ft. (3 m) high). Has 2–4 *longitudinal folds* on throat; a slight hump, but *no fin,* on back. Baleen plates may be more than 1 ft. (305 mm) long. Estimated population (1971) 100,000–200,000.

Formerly known as *Rhachianectes glaucus.* Also known as *E. robustus.*
Similar species: (1) Right Whale and (2) Sperm Whale have large head, at least ⅓ length of animal. (3) Other whales have dorsal fin.

Habits: Migrates southward from latter part of Dec. to early Feb.; returns in March and April after about 3 months in breeding waters in Baja California, Mexico. May be seen in great numbers off coast of San Diego, California, during migrations. Attain sexual maturity at 8–9 years; gestation period about 12 months.
Range: Pacific Coast.

Finback Whales: Balaenopteridae

THIS FAMILY includes the largest whales. Each has many longitudinal grooves on its throat, and a small dorsal fin far back on the body. Gestation period is about 12 months.
Known as fossils from Upper Miocene.

FINBACK WHALE *Balaenoptera physalus* **p. 244**
(Common Rorqual)
Identification: Length to 70 ft. (21.3 m), length at birth, 22 ft. (6.7 m). This large *flat-headed* whale is *gray* with a *white* belly and white inner sides of flippers and underside of fluke. The columnar spout, 15–20 ft. (4.5–6.1 m) high, is accompanied by a loud *whistling sound;* it rises as a narrow column, then expands into an ellipse. Baleen is streaked *purple and white.* There are 320–420 baleen plates on each side of upper jaw.
Similar species: (1) The Rorqual is smaller and (2) the Blue Whale is larger; both have black baleen.
Range: Atlantic and Pacific.

RORQUAL (Sei Whale) *Balaenoptera borealis* **p. 244**
Identification: Length to 50 ft. (15.2 m) or more. Similar to the Finback Whale, but smaller and darker, and with a relatively larger dorsal fin; undersurface of fluke never white. Baleen is black except for the white frayed edges.
Similar species: (1) The Finback Whale has purple and white baleen. It and (2) the Blue Whale are both larger.
Range: Atlantic and Pacific.

PIKED WHALE *Balaenoptera acutorostrata* **p. 244**
(Lesser Rorqual, Minke Whale)
Identification: Length to 30 ft. (9.1 m); length at birth, 9 ft. (2.7 m). This small finback prefers coastal waters. It is bluish-gray above, white below. The dorsal fin has a *curved tip.* A broad *white band* crosses the upperside of the flipper. *Baleen* is *whitish.* There are 260–325 baleen plates on each side of upper jaw.
Similar species: All other baleen whales are larger, and none has a broad white band across the flipper.
Range: Atlantic and Pacific Coasts.

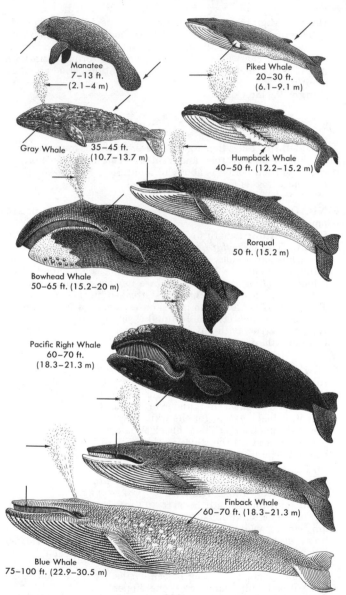

Manatee
7–13 ft.
(2.1–4 m)

Piked Whale
20–30 ft.
(6.1–9.1 m)

Gray Whale
35–45 ft.
(10.7–13.7 m)

Humpback Whale
40–50 ft. (12.2–15.2 m)

Rorqual
50 ft. (15.2 m)

Bowhead Whale
50–65 ft. (15.2–20 m)

Pacific Right Whale
60–70 ft.
(18.3–21.3 m)

Finback Whale
60–70 ft. (18.3–21.3 m)

Blue Whale
75–100 ft. (22.9–30.5 m)

BLUE WHALE   *Balaenoptera musculus*   **p. 244**
(Sulphurbottom)
   Identification: Length to 100 ft. (30.5 m); wt. to 150 tons
(136,000 kg); length at birth, 23–25 ft. (7–7.6 m). This is the
largest animal known to man, past or present. It is slaty to
bluish gray above, *yellowish* or *whitish* on belly; undersurface
of flippers white. Spout is *almost vertical* and may be 20 ft.
(6.1 m) high. Baleen is black; about 360 plates on each side of
upper jaw.
   Formerly known as *Sibbaldus.*
   Similar species: All other whales are smaller.
   Range: Atlantic and Pacific; commonest near pack ice.

BRYLE'S WHALE   *Balaenoptera edeni*
   Identification: Length to 49 ft. (15 m). Upperparts blue-black
and underparts bluish gray on throat and white or yellowish
white posteriorly. The flippers are dark bluish gray above and
below; baleen usually white, sometimes with gray stripes anteriorly and grayish black posteriorly. A pair of longitudinal,
lateral ridges on the dorsal part of the snout.
   Similar species: (1) The Finback and (2) Blue Whale are
larger. (3) The Rorqual has black baleen, except for white edges.
   Range: Known from one stranding on the Florida Coast.

HUMPBACK WHALE   *Megaptera novaeangliae*   **p. 244**
   Identification: Length to 50 ft. (15.2 m); length at birth about
16 ft. (4.9 m). This is a thick-bodied whale with long, narrow
flippers (nearly ⅓ length of animal) which are irregularly scal-
loped on posterior margin. Small dorsal fin well back on the
body. Black except for the *white throat, breast,* and undersides
of fluke and flippers. Flippers have *fleshy knobs* along front
borders and fluke is *irregular* in outline on posterior border.
Spout is an *expanding column* about 20 ft. (6.1 m) high. Baleen
is nearly black, and there are 300–320 plates on each side of
upper jaw.
   Similar species: Other whales have relatively shorter flippers
without knobs along front borders.
   Range: Atlantic and Pacific.

Right and Bowhead Whales:
Balaenidae

HEAD relatively large, about ⅓ length of animal; no dorsal fin;
no grooves on throat. Known as fossils from Lower Miocene.

RIGHT WHALE (Biscayan Whale)   *Balaena glacialis*   **p. 244**
   Identification: Length to 70 ft. (21.3 m). A large, *blackish*

whale, sometimes pale on the belly. Spout 10–15 ft. (3–4.6 m)
high, comes out in 2 columns that diverge to form a V. Baleen
plates about 8 ft. (2.4 m) long; black; 220–260 on each side of
upper jaw.
    Formerly known as *Eubalaena* and *E. sieboldi.*
Similar species: (1) The Humpback Whale has long, knobby
flippers. (2) The Bowhead Whale has front part of lower jaw
white.
Range: Atlantic and Pacific.

BOWHEAD WHALE   *Balaena mysticetus*   **p. 244**
    Identification: Length to 65 ft. (20 m). The Bowhead Whale
is found only in *polar* and *subpolar* seas, usually near *edge of
ice.* Head extremely large, *more than* $\frac{1}{2}$ *animal's length;* body
dark, grayish brown. When resting it may have part of its body
projecting above water. There are 300–360 black baleen plates
on each side of upper jaw.
    Similar species: The Right Whale does not have white on
front part of lower jaw.
    Range: Circumpolar; polar and subpolar seas.

Skulls
Dental Formulae
References
Index

Plate 25

BATS, SHREWS, AND MOLES

(Skulls natural size)

	Map	*Text*
1. **EASTERN PIPISTREL** *Pipistrellus subflavus*	35	34
2. **LITTLE BROWN MYOTIS** *Myotis lucifugus*	26	25
3. **LEAFNOSE BAT** *Macrotus californicus*	23	22
4. **PALLID BAT** *Antrozous pallidus*	44	42
5. **RED BAT** *Lasiurus borealis*	36	37
6. **EVENING BAT** *Nycticeius humeralis*	40	39
7. **LEAFCHIN BAT** *Mormoops megalophylla*	23	22
8. **WESTERN BIG-EARED BAT** *Plecotus townsendi*	41	39
9. **HOARY BAT** *Lasiurus cinereus*	38	37
10. **EASTERN YELLOW BAT** *Lasiurus intermedius*	40	38
11. **BIG BROWN BAT** *Eptesicus fuscus*	36	35
12. **MEXICAN FREETAIL BAT** *Tadarida brasiliensis*	44	43
13. **LONGNOSE BAT** *Leptonycteris nivalis*	23	23
14. **SILVER-HAIRED BAT** *Lasionycteris noctivagans*	34	33
15. **WESTERN MASTIFF BAT** *Eumops perotis*	41	45
16. **WESTERN MASTIFF BAT**		
17. **HOGNOSE BAT** *Choeronycteris mexicana*	23	22
18. **MASKED SHREW** *Sorex cinereus*	4	3
19. **PYGMY SHREW** *Microsorex hoyi*	13	12
20. **LEAST SHREW** *Cryptotis parva*	14	15
21. **SHORTTAIL SHREW** *Blarina brevicauda*	15	15
22. **HAIRYTAIL MOLE** *Parascalops breweri*	20	18
23. **SHREW-MOLE** *Neurotrichus gibbsi*	14	16
24. **STARNOSE MOLE** *Condylura cristata*	18	17
25. **TOWNSEND MOLE** *Scapanus townsendi*	20	19
26. **TOWNSEND MOLE**		
27. **EASTERN MOLE** *Scalopus aquaticus*	18	17

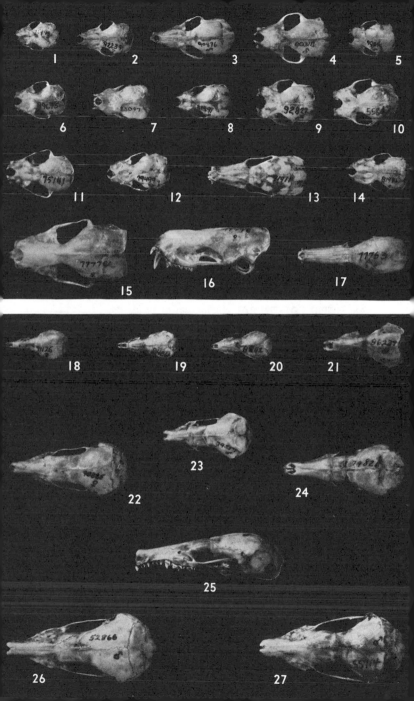

Plate 26

MICE, VOLES, AND RATS

(Skulls natural size)

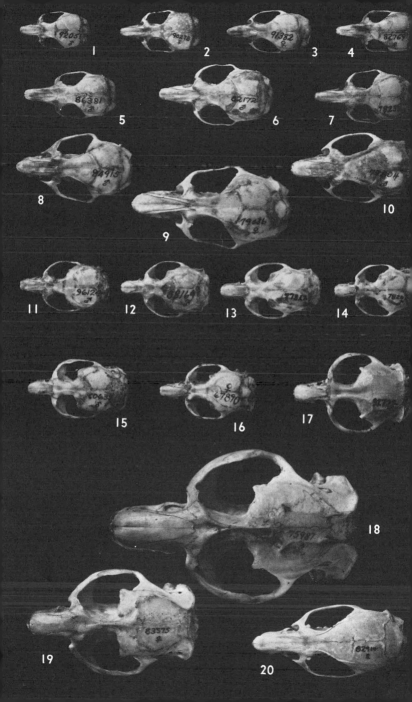

Plate 27

POCKET MICE, KANGAROO RATS, POCKET GOPHERS, CHIPMUNKS, AND SQUIRRELS

(Skulls natural size)

		Map	Text
1.	**MEXICAN POCKET MOUSE** *Liomys irroratus*	135	133
2.	**ROCK POCKET MOUSE** *Perognathus intermedius*	138	139
3.	**PALE KANGAROO MOUSE** *Microdipodops pallidus*	145	143
4.	**DESERT KANGAROO RAT** *Dipodomys deserti*	149	150
5.	**PLAINS POCKET GOPHER** *Geomys bursarius*	132	131
6.	**NORTHERN POCKET GOPHER** *Thomomys talpoides*	126	127
7.	**MEXICAN POCKET GOPHER** *Pappogeomys castanops*	132	132
8.	**EASTERN CHIPMUNK** *Tamias striatus*	109	108
9.	**GRAYNECK CHIPMUNK** *Eutamias cinereicollis*	112	113
10.	**RED SQUIRREL** *Tamiasciurus hudsonicus*	121	120
11.	**NORTHERN FLYING SQUIRREL** *Glaucomys sabrinus*	123	123
12.	**THIRTEEN-LINED GROUND SQUIRREL** *Citellus tridecemlineatus*	104	102
13.	**EASTERN FOX SQUIRREL** *Sciurus niger*	119	118

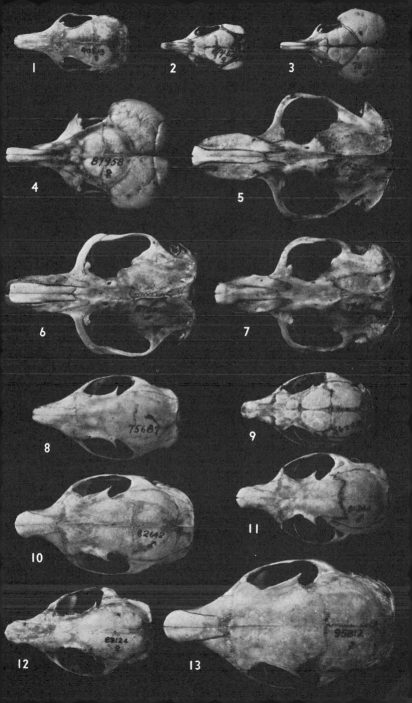

Plate 28

RABBITS, HARES, AND MISCELLANEOUS RODENTS

(Skulls one-half natural size)

	Map	Text
1. **PIKA** *Ochotona princeps*	202	201
2. **BLACKTAIL JACKRABBIT** *Lepus californicus*	206	207
3. **PYGMY RABBIT** *Sylvilagus idahoensis*	210	212
4. **EASTERN COTTONTAIL** *Sylvilagus floridanus*	208	208
5. **BLACKTAIL JACKRABBIT** *Lepus californicus*	206	207
6. **PORCUPINE** *Erethizon dorsatum*	200	199
7. **WOODCHUCK** *Marmota monax*	93	92
8. **APLODONTIA** *Aplodontia rufa*	91	90
9. **WHITETAIL PRAIRIE DOG** *Cynomys gunnisoni*	96	95
10. **BEAVER** *Castor canadensis*	152	151

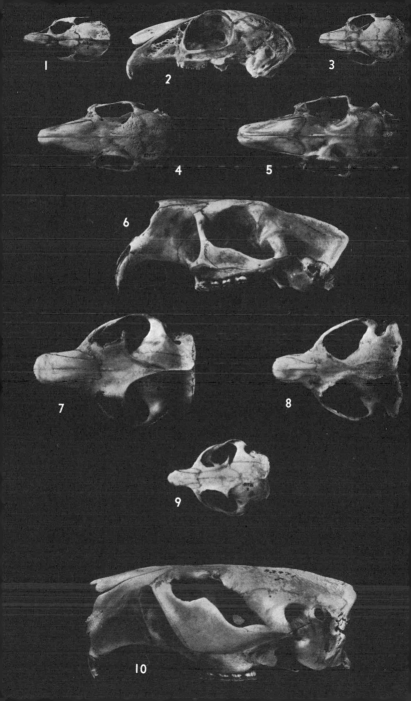

Plate 29
WEASEL AND RACCOON FAMILIES
(Skulls one-half natural size)

		Map	Text
1.	**MINK** *Mustela vison*	59	60
2.	**RIVER OTTER** *Lutra canadensis*	61	60
3.	**LONGTAIL WEASEL** *Mustela frenata*	59	58
4.	**STRIPED SKUNK** *Mephitis mephitis*	66	65
5.	**HOGNOSE SKUNK** *Conepatus leuconotus*	67	68
6.	**BADGER** *Taxidea taxus*	62	64
7.	**SPOTTED SKUNK** *Spilogale putoris*	66	64
8.	**MARTEN** *Martes americana*	55	54
9.	**RACCOON** *Procyon lotor*	51	50
10.	**COATI** *Nasua narica*	53	52
11.	**WOLVERINE** *Gulo luscus*	62	63

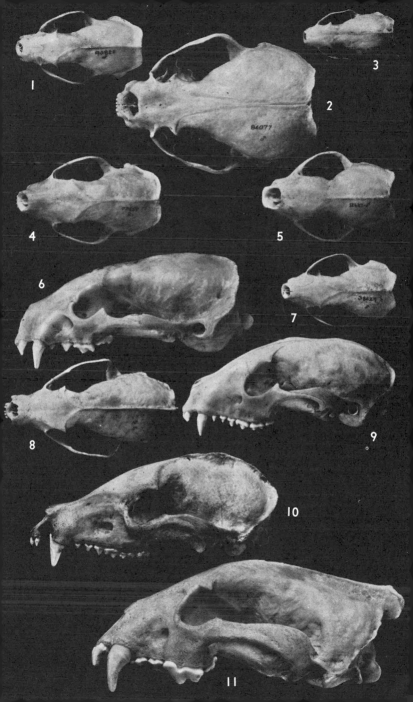

Plate 30

DOGS AND CATS

(Skulls one-half natural size)

		Map	Text
1. **COYOTE**	*Canis latrans*	69	69
2. **RED FOX**	*Vulpes fulva*	74	72
3. **GRAY FOX**	*Urocyon cinereoargenteus*	76	75
4. **BOBCAT**	*Lynx rufus*	81	81
5. **RINGTAIL**	*Bassariscus astutus*	53	52
6. **MOUNTAIN LION**	*Felis concolor*	78	77

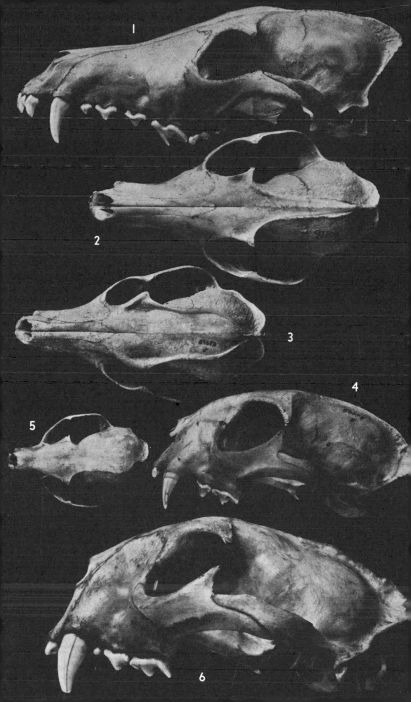

Plate 31

MISCELLANEOUS

(Skull Numbers 1–4, one-half natural size)

		Map	Text
1. **ARMADILLO**	*Dasypus novemcinctus*	228	228
2. **ARMADILLO**			
3. **OPOSSUM**	*Didelphis marsupialis*	2	1
4. **OPOSSUM**			

(Skull Numbers 5–7, one-fourth natural size)

		Map	Text
5. **PECCARY**	*Pecari angulatus*	214	213
6. **BLACK BEAR**	*Ursus americanus*	49	46
7. **ALASKAN BROWN BEAR**	*Ursus middendorffi*	48	47

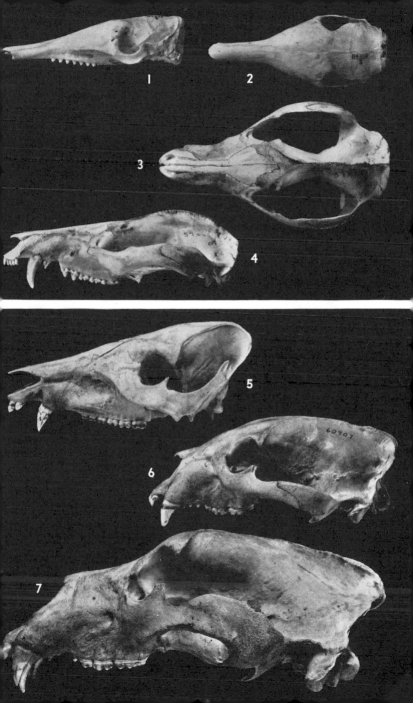

Plate 32

HOOFED MAMMALS

(Skulls one-sixth natural size)

		Map	Text
1.	**MOOSE** *Alces alces* (antlers shed)	219	218
2.	**BARREN GROUND CARIBOU** *Rangifer arcticus* (antlers removed)	221	220
3.	**WHITETAIL DEER** *Odocoileus virginianus* (antlers shed)	217	218
4.	**ELK** *Cervus canadensis* (female, no antlers)	214	215
5.	**PRONGHORN** *Antilocapra americana* (horn sheaths removed)	223	223
6.	**WHITE SHEEP** *Ovis dalli* (horn sheaths removed)	227	227
7.	**BISON** *Bison bison* (horn sheaths removed)	225	224

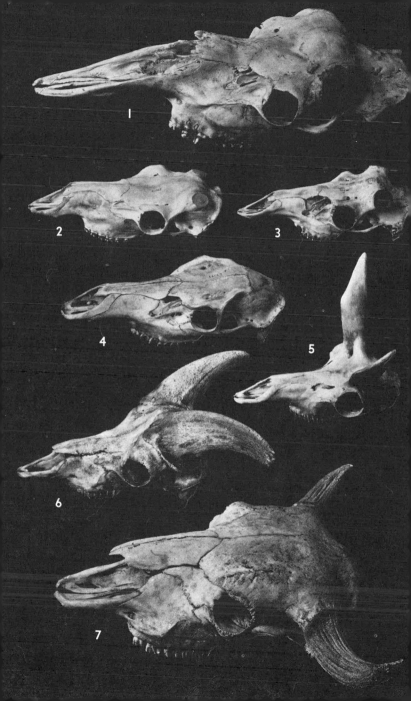

MARINE MAMMAL SKULLS

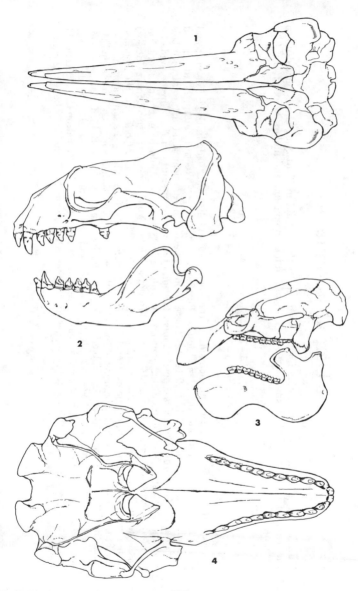

Dental Formulae

The following list of dental formulae for the land mammals may aid in identifying skulls picked up in the field. The symbols, I, C, P, and M refer to incisors, canines, premolars, and molars, respectively. The formula

$$I\frac{5-5}{4-4}, \quad C\frac{1-1}{1-1}, \quad P\frac{3-3}{3-3}, \quad M\frac{4-4}{4-4} = \frac{26}{24} = 50$$

means that there are 5 incisors on each side in the upper jaw and 4 on each side in the lower jaw; and similarly for the canines, premolars, and molars. Further, that there are 26 teeth in all in the upper and 24 in the lower jaw, or a total of 50 teeth. There is only one North American land mammal with this formula, the Opossum (*Didelphis*); positive identification of an Opossum skull can therefore be made by counting the teeth. Now suppose that you find a skull with 38 teeth. It could be either a myotis bat (*Myotis*), Peccary (*Pecari*), Marten (*Martes*), or Wolverine (*Gulo*). You examine the small front (incisor) teeth and find that there are 6 above and 6 below (total, 12). This eliminates *Myotis* and the Peccary, each of which has 4 above and 6 below (total, 10). The Marten and Wolverine have the same arrangement of teeth, so you turn to the photographs of the skulls (Plate 29) and find that the Marten skull is slightly more than $\frac{1}{2}$ the size of that of the Wolverine. You should be able to determine which your specimen is by its size. For many of the rodents with 16, 20, or 22 teeth, one cannot come so close to the species as in the above examples. The photographs, again, may help, but for positive identification the skull should be sent to a specialist. Scientific names of the genera are given after the dental formulae. The text location may be found in the Index.

DENTAL FORMULAE

		Incisors	Canines	Premolars	Molars	U and L	Total	Land Mammals
U		5-5	1-1	3-3	4-4	26	= 50	*Didelphis*
L		4-4	1-1	3-3	4-4	24		
U		3-3	1-1	4-4	3-3	22	= 44	*Condylura, Parascalops, Scapanus, Sus*
L		3-3	1-1	4-4	3-3	22		
U		3-3	1-1	4-4	2-2	20	= 42	*Alopex, Canis, Thalarctos, Urocyon, Ursus, Vulpes*
L		3-3	1-1	4-4	3-3	22		
U		3-3	1-1	4-4	2-2	20	= 40	*Bassariscus, Nasua, Procyon*
L		3-3	1-1	4-4	2-2	20		
U		2-2	1-1	3-3	3-3	18	= 38	*Myotis, Pecari*
L		3-3	1-1	3-3	3-3	20		
U		3-3	1-1	4-4	1-1	18	= 38	*Gulo, Martes*
L		3-3	1-1	4-4	2-2	20		
U		3-3	1-1	3-3	3-3	20	= 36	*Scalopus*
L		2-2	0-0	3-3	3-3	16		
U		2-2	1-1	3-3	3-3	18	= 36	*Neurotrichus*
L		1-1	1-1	4-4	3-3	18		
U		2-2	1-1	2-2	3-3	16	= 36	*Lasionycteris, Plecotus*
L		3-3	1-1	3-3	3-3	20		
U		3-3	1-1	4-4	1-1	18	= 36	*Lutra*
L		3-3	1-1	3-3	2-2	18		

DENTAL FORMULAE *(continued)*

	Incisors	Canines	Premolars	Molars	U and L	Total	Land Mammals
U	2-2	1-1	2-2	3-3	16	= 34	*Macrotus, Mormoops*
L	2-2	1-1	3-3	3-3	18		
U	2-2	1-1	2-2	3-3	16	= 34	*Euderma, Pipistrellus*
L	3-3	1-1	2-2	3-3	18		
U	3-3	1-1	3-3	1-1	16	= 34	*Mephitis, Mustela, Spilogale, Taxidea*
L	3-3	1-1	3-3	2-2	18		
U	0-0	1-1	3-3	3-3	14	= 34	*Cervus, Rangifer*
L	3-3	1-1	3-3	3-3	20		
U	3-3	1-1	3-3	3-3	20	= 32	*Blarina, Microsorex, Sorex*
L	1-1	1-1	1-1	3-3	12		
U	2-2	1-1	1-1	3-3	14	= 32	*Eptesicus*
L	3-3	1-1	2-2	3-3	18		
U	1-1	1-1	2-2	3-3	14	= 32	*Lasiurus borealis, L. cinereus, L. seminolus, Tadarida brasiliensis*
L	3-3	1-1	2-2	3-3	18		
U	3-3	1-1	3-3	1-1	16	= 32	*Enhydra*
L	2-2	1-1	3-3	2-2	16		
U	3-3	1-1	2-2	1-1	14	= 32	*Conepatus*
L	3-3	1-1	3-3	2-2	18		
U	0-0	0-0	3-3	3-3	12	= 32	*Alces, Antilocapra, Bison, Odocoileus, Oreamnos, Ovibos, Ovis, Rangifer*
L	3-3	1-1	3-3	3-3	20		

DENTAL FORMULAE (continued)

	Incisors	Canines	Premolars	Molars	U and L		Total	Land Mammals
U	0-0	0-0		{8-8}	16)	=	32	*Dasypus*
L	0-0	0-0		{8-8}	16)			
U	3-3	1-1	2-2	3-3	18)	=	30	*Cryptotis*
L	1-1	1-1	1-1	3-3	12)			
U	2-2	1-1	2-2	3-3	16)	=	30	*Choeronycteris*
L	0-0	1-1	3-3	3-3	14)			
U	2-2	1-1	2-2	2-2	14)	=	30	*Leptonycteris*
L	2-2	1-1	3-3	2-2	16)			
U	1-1	1-1	1-1	3-3	12)	=	30	*Lasiurus ega, L. intermedius, Nycticeius*
L	3-3	1-1	2-2	3-3	18)			
U	1-1	1-1	2-2	3-3	14)	=	30	*Eumops, Tadarida femorosacca, T. molossa*
L	2-2	1-1	2-2	3-3	16)			
U	3-3	1-1	3-3	1-1	16)	=	30	*Felis*
L	3-3	1-1	2-2	1-1	14)			
U	3-3	1-1	1-1	3-3	16)	=	28	*Notiosorex*
L	1-1	1-1	1-1	3-3	12)			
U	1-1	1-1	1-1	3-3	12)	=	28	*Antrozous*
L	2-2	1-1	2-2	3-3	16)			
U	3-3	1-1	2-2	1-1	14)	=	28	*Lynx*
L	3-3	1-1	2-2	1-1	14)			

DENTAL FORMULAE (continued)

	Incisors	Canines	Premolars	Molars	U and L	Total	Land Mammals
U	2-2	0-0	3-3	3-3	16		
L	1-1	0-0	2-2	3-3	12	= 28	Lepus, Sylvilagus
U	0-0	0-0		{7-7}	14		
L	0-0	0-0		{7-7}	14	= 28	Dasypus
U	2-2	0-0	3-3	2-2	14		
L	1-1	0-0	2-2	3-3	12	= 26	Ochotona
U	2-2	1-1	1-1	2-2	12		
L	2-2	1-1	2-2	2-2	14	= 26	Diphylla
U	1-1	0-0	2-2	3-3	12		Ammospermophilus, Aplodontia, Citellus, Cynomys, Eutamias, Glaucomys, Marmota, Sciurus aberti, S. carolinensis, S. griseus, Tamiasciurus
L	1-1	0-0	1-1	3-3	10	= 22	
U	1-1	0-0	1-1	3-3	10		Castor, Pappogeomys, Dipodomys, Erethizon, Geomys, Liomys, Microdipodops, Myocastor, Perognathus, Sciurus apache, S. arizonensis, S. niger, Tamias, Tamiasciurus, Thomomys
L	1-1	0-0	1-1	3-3	10	= 20	
U	1-1	0-0	1-1	3-3	10		
L	1-1	0-0	0-0	3-3	8	= 18	Zapus
U	1-1	0-0	0-0	3-3	8		Baiomys, Clethrionomys, Dicrostonyx, Lagurus, Lemmus, Microtus, Mus, Napaeozapus, Neofiber, Neotoma, Ondatra, Onychomys, Oryzomys, Peromyscus, Phenacomys, Pitymys, Rattus, Reithrodontomys, Sigmodon, Synaptomys
L	1-1	0-0	0-0	3-3	8	= 16	

References

FOR THE STUDENT whose interest carries him beyond the limits of this book, there follows a short list of general references and the most recent accounts for the states and provinces. These lists are far from complete, but the bibliography within each publication listed will guide the reader to additional literature. Older publications, often not available except in the larger universities and colleges, have been purposely omitted.

General

Anderson, S., and J. K. Jones, eds. Recent mammals of the world. New York: Ronald Press, 1967.

Hall, E. R., and K. R. Kelson. The mammals of North America. New York: Ronald Press, 1959. 2 vols. A general reference with short descriptions, technical keys for identification, and distribution maps.

Hamilton, W. J. American mammals. New York: McGraw-Hill, 1939. Contains information on habits of many mammals.

Journal of Mammalogy. 1919 to present. A quarterly published by The American Society of Mammalogists; devoted to articles on mammals, chiefly of N. America.

Journal of Wildlife Management. 1937 to present. A quarterly published by The Wildlife Society; devoted to articles on management practices; contains many arcticles on mammals.

Miller, Gerrit S., and Remington Kellogg. List of North American Recent mammals. U.S. Natl. Mus. Bull. 205. 1955. A checklist; no aid to identification beyond giving names of species and subspecies, and approximate ranges.

North American Fauna. 1889 to present. No regular time of publication; a series published by U.S. Dept. of the Interior (formerly the Dept. of Agriculture); revisions of groups and state lists.

States and Provinces

Alabama
Howell, A. H. A biological survey of Alabama. North Amer. Fauna, 45:1-88. 1921.
Alaska
Bee, J. W., and E. R. Hall. Mammals of northern Alaska. Univ. Kans. Mus. Nat. Hist., Misc. Publ. no. 8.

Dufresne, Frank. Alaska's animals and fishes. New York: Barnes, 1946.

Manville, R. H., and S. P. Young. Distribution of Alaskan mammals. Washington, D.C.: Bur. Sport Fisheries and Wildlife, Circular 211. 1965.

Murie, O. J. Fauna of the Aleutian Islands and Alaska Peninsula. North Amer. Fauna, 61. 1959.

Alberta

Banfield, A. W. F. Mammals of Banff National Park, Alberta. Natl. Mus. of Canada, Bull. 159. 1958.

Rand, A. L. Mammals of the eastern Rockies and western plains of Canada. Natl. Mus. of Canada, Bull. 108. 1948.

Soper, J. D. Mammals of Wood Buffalo Park, northern Alberta and District of Mackenzie. Jour. Mamm., 23:119–45. 1942.

———. Mammal notes from the Grande Prairie–Peace River region, Alberta. Jour. Mamm., 29:49–64. 1948.

Arizona

Cockrum, E. L. The Recent mammals of Arizona. Tucson, Ariz.: Univ. Ariz. Press, 1960.

Arkansas

Sealander, J. A., Jr. A provisional check-list and key to the mammals of Arkansas (with annotations). Amer. Mid. Nat., 56:257–96. 1956.

British Columbia

Cowan, I. McT., and C. J. Guiguet. The mammals of British Columbia. B.C. Prov. Mus., Handbook no. 11. 1956.

California

Grinnell, J., J.S. Dixon, and J. M. Linsdale. Fur-bearing mammals of California, their natural history, systematic status, and relations to man. Berkeley, Calif.: Univ. Calif. Press, 1937. 2 vols.

Ingles, L. G. Mammals of California and its coastal waters. Stanford, Calif.: Stanford Univ. Press, 1954. 2nd ed.

Colorado

Armstrong, David M. Distribution of mammals in Colorado. Univ. Kans. Mus. Nat. Hist., Monograph no. 3, 1972.

Connecticut

Goodwin, G. G. The mammals of Connecticut. State of Conn., Geol. and Nat. Hist. Survey Bull., 53:1–221. 1935.

Delaware (see *New York*)

Florida (see also *New York*)

Sherman, H. B. A list of the Recent land mammals of Florida. Proc. Fla. Acad. Sci., 1:102–28. 1936.

Georgia

Golley, F. B. Mammals of Georgia. Athens, Ga.: Univ. Ga. Press, 1962.

Harper, Francis. The mammals of the Okefenokee Swamp region of Georgia. Proc. Boston Soc. Nat. Hist., 38 (7): 191–396. 1927.

———. Mammal notes from Randolph County, Georgia. Jour. Mamm., 10:84–85. 1929.

Idaho

Davis, W. B. The Recent mammals of Idaho. Caldwell, Idaho: Caxton Printers, 1939.

Illinois
Hoffmeister, D. F., and Carl O. Mohr. Fieldbook of Illinois mammals. Ill. Nat. Hist. Survey Div., Manual 3. 1957

Indiana
Mumford, Russell E. Distribution of the mammals of Indiana. Ind. Acad. Sci. 1969.

Iowa
Scott, T. G. Mammals of Iowa. Iowa State College, Jour. Sci., 12 (1):43–97. 1937.

Kansas
Cockrum, E. L. Mammals of Kansas. Univ. Kans. Publ., Mus. Nat. Hist., 7:1–303. 1952.
Hall, E. R. Handbook of mammals of Kansas. Univ. Kans. Mus. Nat. Hist., Misc. Publ. no. 7. 1955.

Keewatin District
Harper, Francis. The mammals of Keewatin. Univ. Kans. Mus. Nat. Hist., Misc. Publ. no. 12. 1956.
Sutton, G. M., and W. J. Hamilton, Jr. The mammals of Southampton Island. Mem. Carnegie Mus., vol. 12, pt. 2, sec. 1, pp. 9–111. 1932.

Kentucky (see also *New York*)
Bailey, Vernon. Cave life in Kentucky. Mainly in the Mammoth Cave region. Amer. Mid. Nat., 14 (5):385–635. 1933.
Hamilton, W. J., Jr. Notes on the mammals of Breathitt County, Kentucky. Jour. Mamm., 11:306–11. 1930.
Welter, W. A., and D. E. Sollberger. Notes on the mammals of Rowan and adjacent counties in eastern Kentucky. Jour. Mamm., 20:77–81. 1939.

Labrador (see *Ontario*)

Louisiana
Lowery, G. H., Jr. The mammals of Louisiana and adjacent waters. La. State Univ. Press. 1974.

Mackenzie District
Harper, Francis. Mammals of the Athabaska and Great Slave Lakes region. Jour. Mamm., 13:19–36. 1932.

Maine (see also *New York*)
Manville, R. H. Notes on the mammals of Mount Desert Island, Maine. Jour. Mamm., 23:391–98. 1942.
Norton, A. H. Mammals of Portland, Maine, and vicinity. Proc. Portland Soc. Nat. Hist., 4:1–151. 1930.

Manitoba
Breckenridge, W. J. Mammals collected in northern Manitoba. Jour. Mamm., 17:61–62. 1936.
Green, H. U. Mammals of the Riding Mountain National Park, Manitoba. Canad. Field-Nat., 46 (7):149–52. 1932.

Maryland (see also *New York*)
Gardner, M. C. A list of Maryland mammals. Pt. I, Marsupials and Insectivores, pt. II, Bats. Proc. Biol. Soc. Washington, 63:65–68, 111–14. 1950.
Goldman, E. A., and H. H. T. Jackson. Natural history of Plum-

mers Island, Maryland. IX, Mammals. Proc. Biol. Soc. Washington, 52:131–34. 1939.

Massachusetts (see also *New York*)

Parker, H. C. A preliminary list of the mammals of Worcester
County, Massachusetts. Proc. Boston Soc. Nat. Hist., 41:403–15.
1939.

Warfel, H. E. Notes on some mammals of western Massachusetts.
Jour. Mamm., 18:82–85. 1937.

Michigan

Burt, William H. Mammals of the Great Lakes Region. Ann Arbor,
Mich.: Univ. Mich. Press, 1957.

Minnesota

Gunderson, H. L., and J. R. Beer. The mammals of Minnesota.
Minn. Mus. Nat. Hist., Occ. Paper no. 6. 1953.

Mississippi (see also *New York*)

Kennedy, M. L., K. N. Randolph, and T. L. Best. A review of
Mississippi mammals. Nat. Sci. Res. Inst., Eastern N. Mex. Univ.,
Studies in Nat. Sci., 2:1–36. 1974.

Missouri

Schwartz, C. W., and E. R. Schwartz. The wild mammals of
Missouri. Columbia, Mo.: Univ. Mo. Press and Mo. Conserv.
Comm., 1959.

Montana

Lechleitner, R. R. Mammals of Glacier National Park. Glacier
Nat. Hist. Assoc., Bull. no. 6. 1955

Nebraska

Jones, J. K. Checklist of mammals of Nebraska. Trans. Kans.
Acad. Sci., 60:273–82. 1957.

Nevada

Hall, E. Raymond. Mammals of Nevada. Berkeley, Calif.: Univ.
Calif. Press, 1946.

New Brunswick (see *Ontario*)

Newfoundland (see *Ontario*)

New Hampshire (see also *New York*)

Jackson, C. F. Notes on New Hampshire mammals. Jour. Mamm.,
3:13–15. 1922.

New Jersey (see also *New York*)

Connor, P. F. Notes on the mammals of a New Jersey pine barrens
area. Jour. Mamm., 34:227–35. 1953.

New Mexico

Findley, J. S., A. H. Harris, D. E. Wilson, and C. Jones. Mammals
of New Mexico. Univ. N. Mex. Press. 1975.

New York

Hamilton, W. J., Jr. The mammals of Eastern United States.
Ithaca, N.Y.: Comstock, 1943.

North Carolina (see also *New York*)

Conaway, C. H., and J. C. Howell. Observations on the mammals
of Johnson and Carter Counties, Tennessee, and Avery County,
North Carolina. Jour. Tenn. Acad. Sci., 28:53–61. 1953.

Komarek, E. V., and Roy Komarek. Mammals of the Great Smoky
Mountains. Bull. Chicago Acad. Sci., 5:137–62. 1938.

Odum, E. P. Small mammals of the Highlands (North Carolina) Plateau. Jour. Mamm., 30:179–92. 1949.

North Dakota
Bailey, Vernon. A biological survey of North Dakota. I, Physiography and life zones. II, The mammals. North Amer. Fauna, 49:1–226. 1927.

Nova Scotia (see *Ontario*)
Ohio (see also *Michigan*)
Bole, B. P., Jr., and P. N. Moulthrop. The Ohio Recent mammal collection in the Cleveland Museum of Natural History. Cleveland Mus. Nat. Hist., Sci. Publs., 5 (6):83–181. 1942.

Oklahoma
Blair, W. F. Faunal relationships and geographic distribution of mammals in Oklahoma. Amer. Mid. Nat., 22:85–133. 1939.

Ontario
Peterson, Randolph L. The mammals of eastern Canada. Toronto: Oxford Univ. Press. 1966.

Oregon
Bailey, Vernon. The mammals and life zones of Oregon. North Amer. Fauna, 55:1–416. 1936.

Pennsylvania
Doutt, J. Kenneth, Caroline A. Heppenstall, and John E. Guilday. Mammals of Pennsylvania. Penna. Game Comm. 1967.

Prince Edward Island (see *Ontario*)
Quebec (see *Ontario*)
Rhode Island (see *New York*)
Saskatchewan
Beck, W. H. A guide to Saskatchewan mammals. Sask. Nat. Hist. Soc., Spec. Publ. no. 1. 1958.

South Carolina (see also *New York*)
Penney, J. T. Distribution and bibliography of the mammals of South Carolina. Jour. Mamm., 31:81–89. 1950.

South Dakota
Over, William H., and Edward P. Churchill. Mammals of South Dakota. Univ. South Dakota Mus. and Dept. Zool. 1941. Mimeo.
Turner, R. W. Mammals of the Black Hills of South Dakota and Wyoming. Univ. Kans., Misc. Publ. No. 60. 1974.

Tennessee (see also *New York*)
Kellogg, Remington. Annotated list of Tennessee mammals. Proc. U.S. Natl. Mus., 86 (3051): 245–303. 1939.

Texas
Davis, W. B. The mammals of Texas. Texas Game and Fish Comm. Bull., 41:1–252. 1960.

Utah
Durrant, S. D. Mammals of Utah. Univ. Kans. Publ., Mus. Nat. Hist., 6:1–549. 1952.

Vermont (see *New York*)
Osgood, F. L., Jr. The mammals of Vermont. Jour. Mamm., 19:435–41. 1938.

Virginia
Handley, C. O., Jr., and C. P. Patton. Wild mammals of Virginia. Richmond, Va.: Comm. Game and Inland Fisheries, 1947.

Washington

Dalquest, W. W. Mammals of Washington. Univ. Kans. Publ., Mus. Nat. Hist., 2:1–444. 1948.

West Virginia (see also *New York*)

Kellogg, Remington. Annotated list of West Virginia mammals. Proc. U.S. Natl. Mus., 84 (3022):443–79. 1937.

Wilson, L. W., and J. E. Friedel. A list of mammals collected in West Virginia. Proc. West Va. Acad. Sci. for 1941, vol. 15 (West Va. Univ. Bull. ser. 42, nos. 8–11), pp. 85–92. 1942.

Wisconsin

Jackson, H. H. T. Mammals of Wisconsin. Madison, Wisc.: Univ. Wisc. Press, 1961.

Wyoming (see also *South Dakota*)

Bailey, Vernon. Animal life of Yellowstone Park. Sierra Club Bull., 12 (4):333–45. 1927.

Negus, N. C., and J. S. Findley. Mammals of Jackson Hole, Wyoming. Jour. Mamm., 40:371–81. 1959.

Index

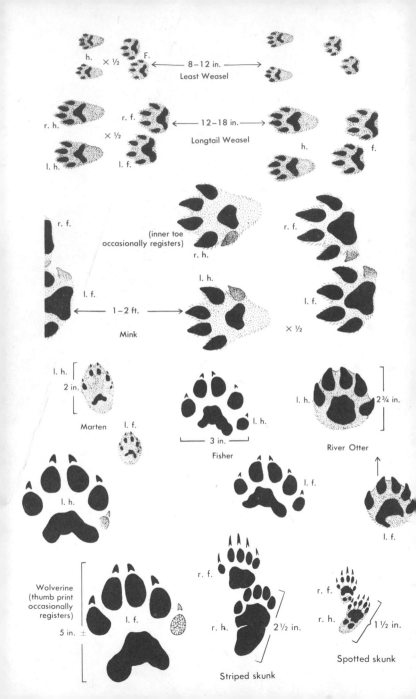

h. × ½ F. ←— 8–12 in. —→ Least Weasel

r. h. r. f. ←— 12–18 in. —→ h. f.
l. h. l. f. × ½ Longtail Weasel

r. f. (inner toe occasionally registers) r. h. r. f.
l. h.
l. f. ←— 1–2 ft. —→ l. f. × ½ Mink

l. h. 2 in. l. f. Marten
l. h. 3 in. l. h. Fisher
l. h. 2¾ in. River Otter
l. f.

l. h. l. f.
Wolverine (thumb print occasionally registers) l. f. 5 in. ±
r. f. r. h. 2½ in. Striped skunk
r. f. r. h. 1½ in. Spotted skunk

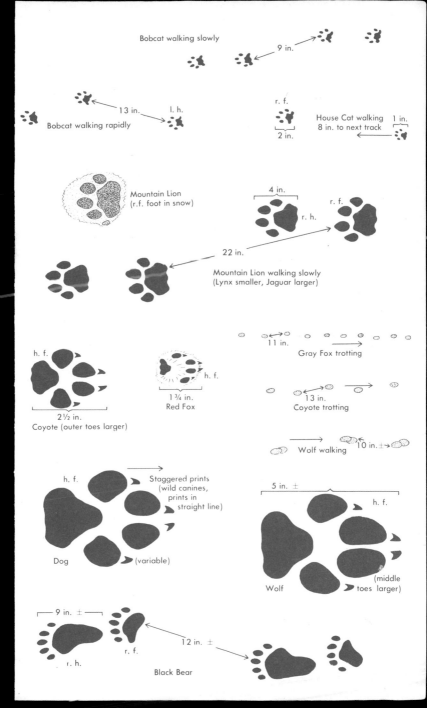

Bobcat walking slowly

9 in.

Bobcat walking rapidly

13 in.   l. h.

r. f.

House Cat walking
8 in. to next track   1 in.

2 in.

Mountain Lion
(r.f. foot in snow)

4 in.

r. h.   r. f.

22 in.

Mountain Lion walking slowly
(Lynx smaller, Jaguar larger)

h. f.

h. f.

1 ¾ in.
Red Fox

2 ½ in.
Coyote (outer toes larger)

Gray Fox trotting

11 in.

Coyote trotting

13 in.

Wolf walking   10 in. ± →

h. f.

Staggered prints
(wild canines,
prints in
straight line)

Dog

(variable)

5 in. ±

h. f.

Wolf

(middle
toes larger)

9 in. ±

r. f.

12 in. ±

r. h.

Black Bear